TRINITY SEVEN 11

STORY: KENJI SAITO
ART: AKINARI NAO

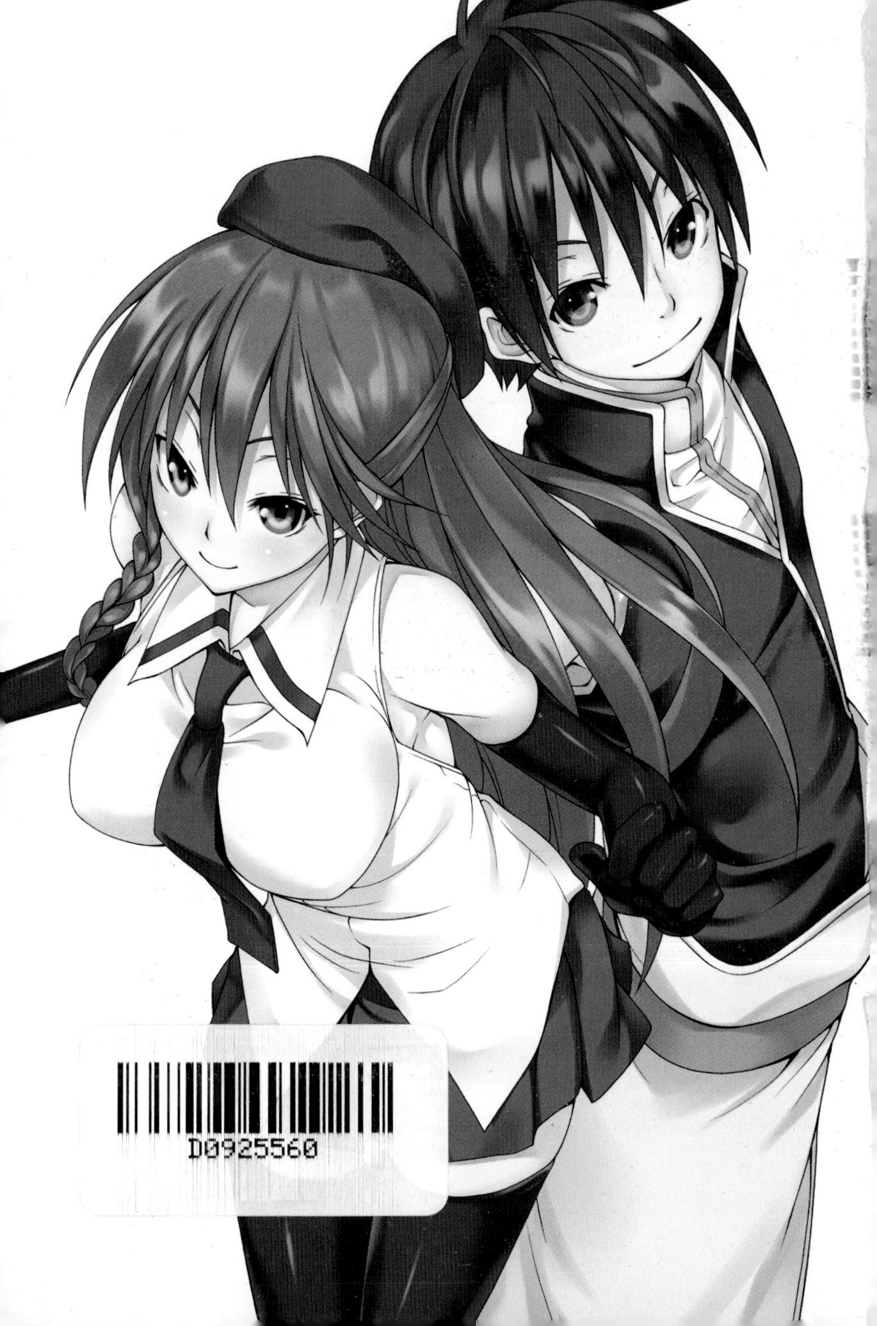

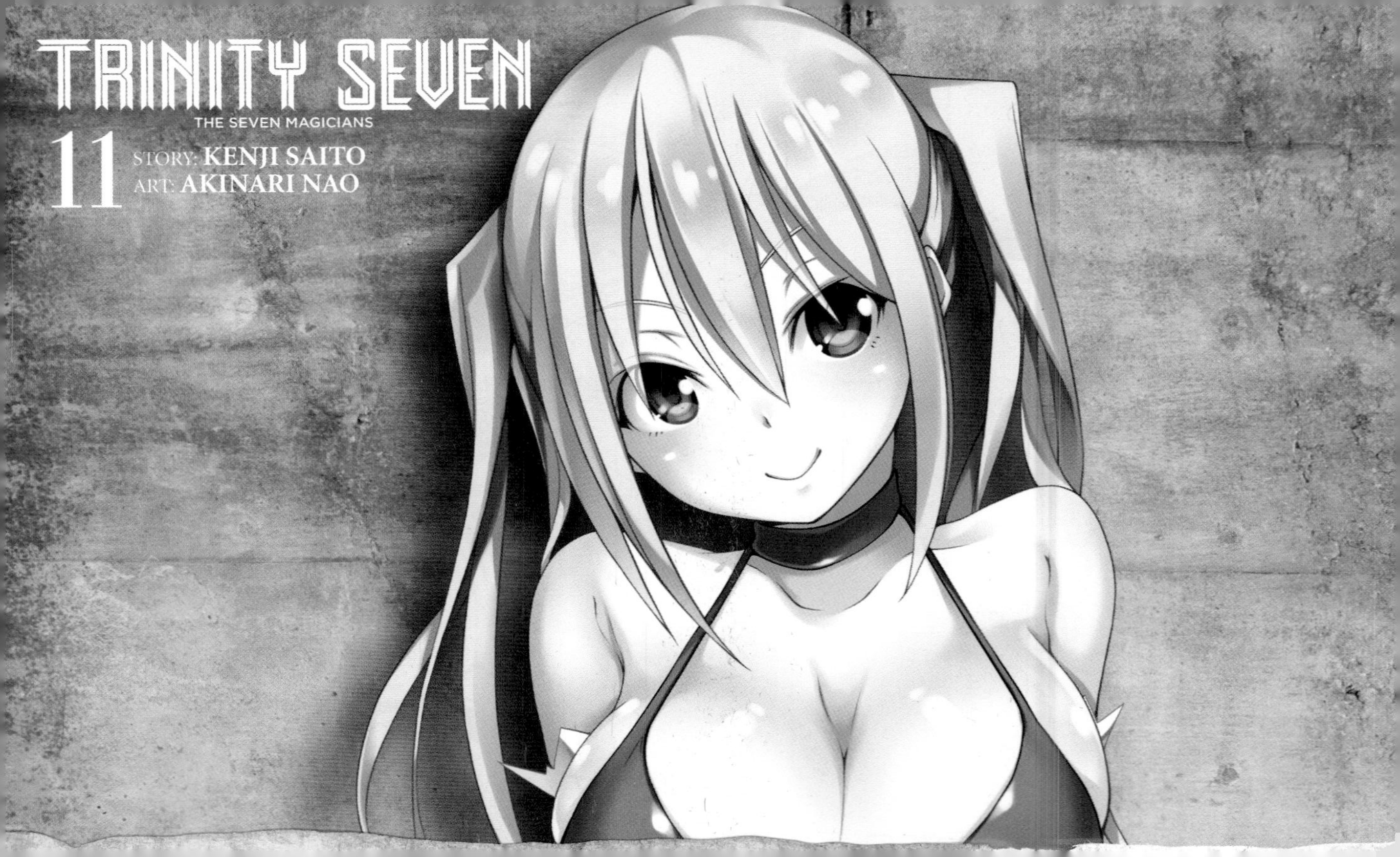
TRINITY SEVEN
THE SEVEN MAGICIANS
11
STORY: KENJI SAITO
ART: AKINARI NAO

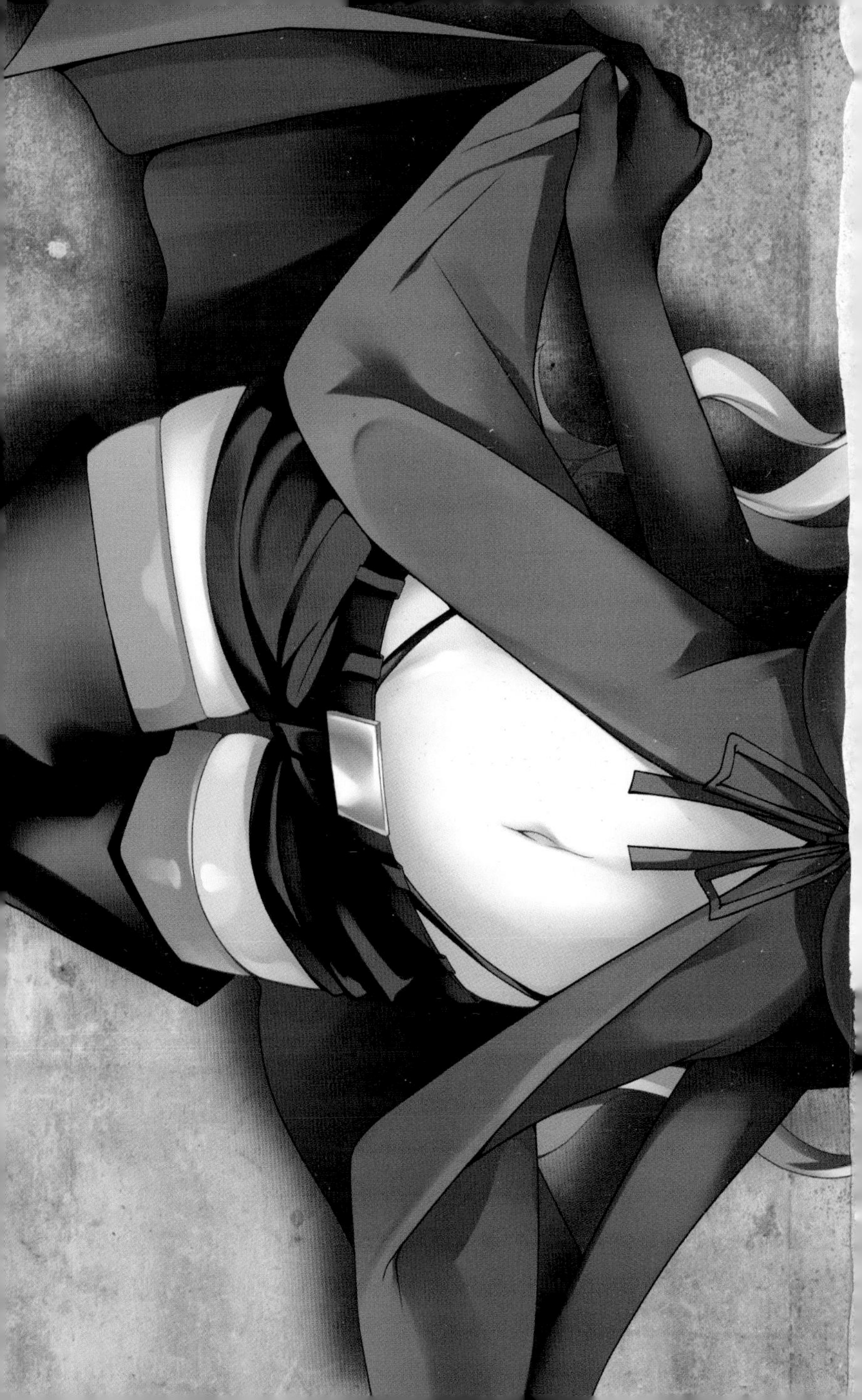

CONTENTS

44. Offense Type & Pure Breed

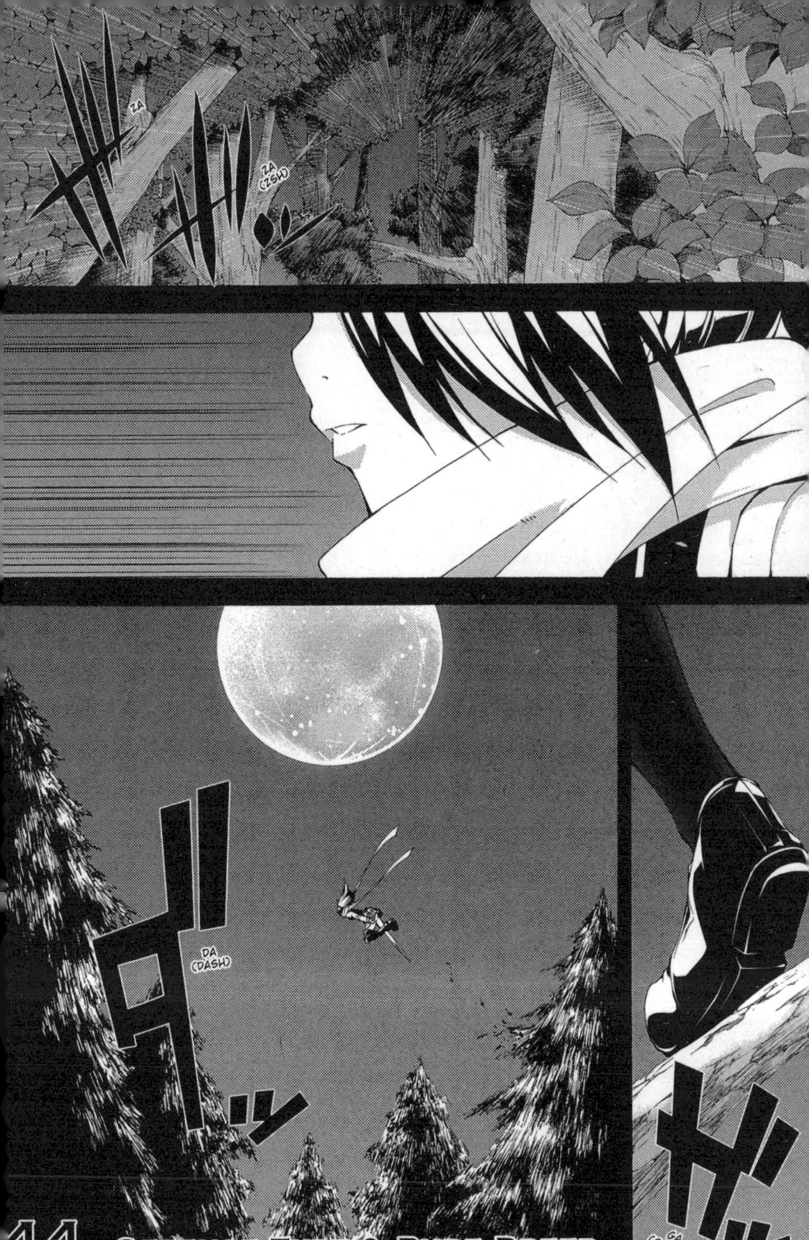
ZA
ZA (ZSH)
GA (STOMP)
DA (DASH)

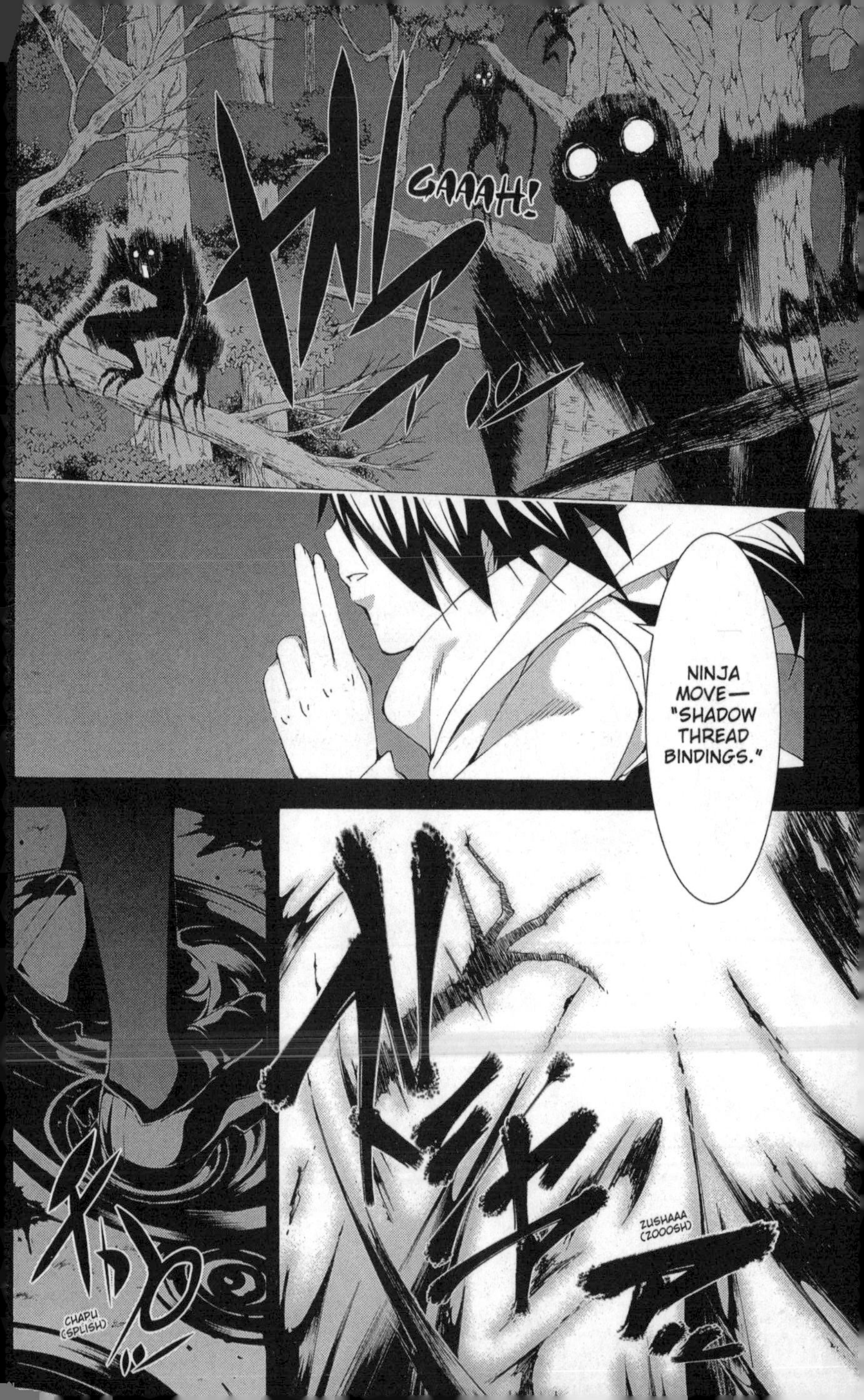
GAAAH!
NINJA MOVE— "SHADOW THREAD BINDINGS."
ZUSHAAA (ZOOOSH)
CHAPU (SPLISH)

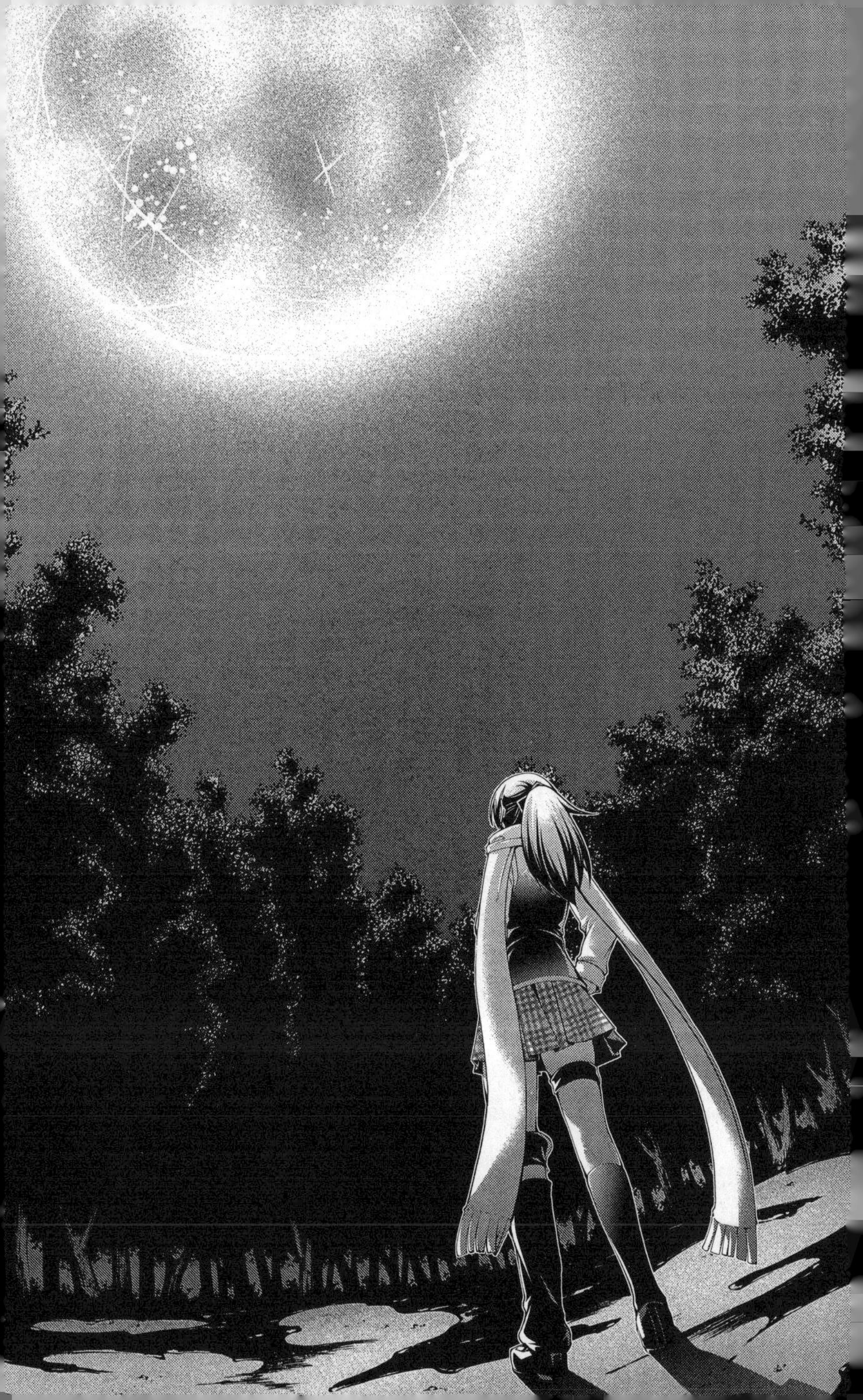

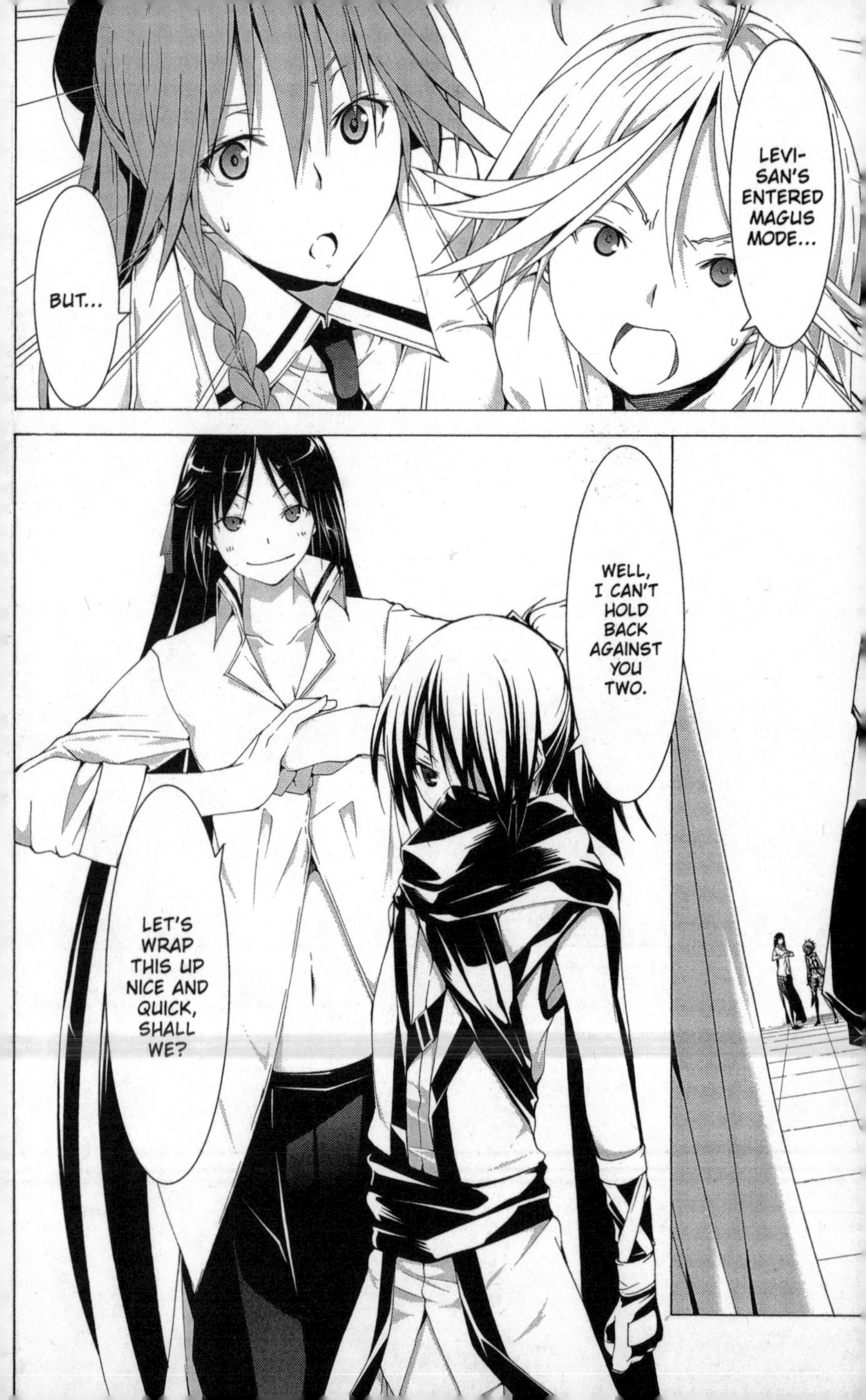
LEVI-SAN'S ENTERED MAGUS MODE...
BUT...
WELL, I CAN'T HOLD BACK AGAINST YOU TWO.
LET'S WRAP THIS UP NICE AND QUICK, SHALL WE?

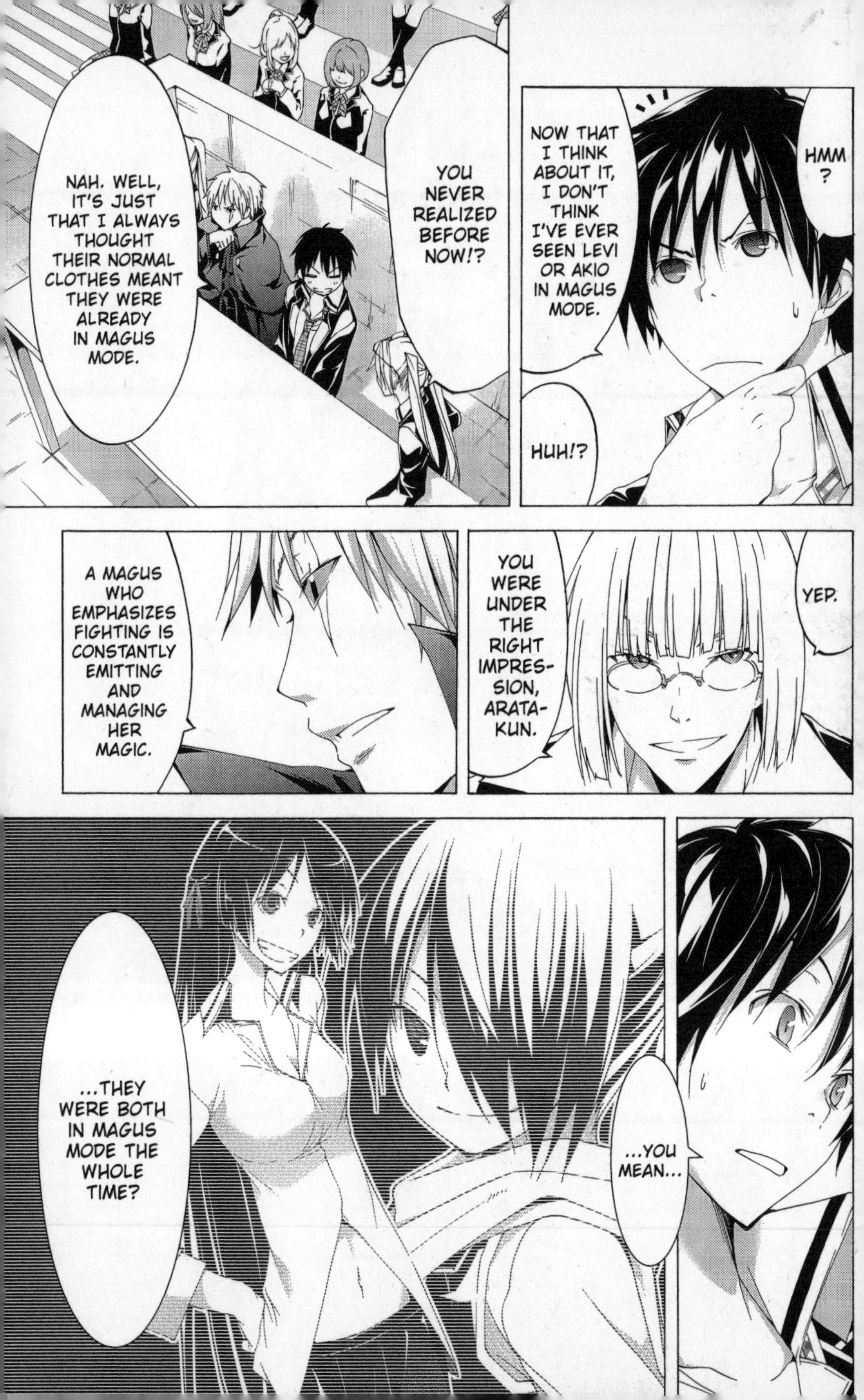
HMM?
NOW THAT I THINK ABOUT IT, I DON'T THINK I'VE EVER SEEN LEVI OR AKIO IN MAGUS MODE.
HUH!?
YOU NEVER REALIZED BEFORE NOW!?
NAH. WELL, IT'S JUST THAT I ALWAYS THOUGHT THEIR NORMAL CLOTHES MEANT THEY WERE ALREADY IN MAGUS MODE.
YEP.
YOU WERE UNDER THE RIGHT IMPRESSION, ARATA-KUN.
A MAGUS WHO EMPHASIZES FIGHTING IS CONSTANTLY EMITTING AND MANAGING HER MAGIC.
...YOU MEAN...
...THEY WERE BOTH IN MAGUS MODE THE WHOLE TIME?

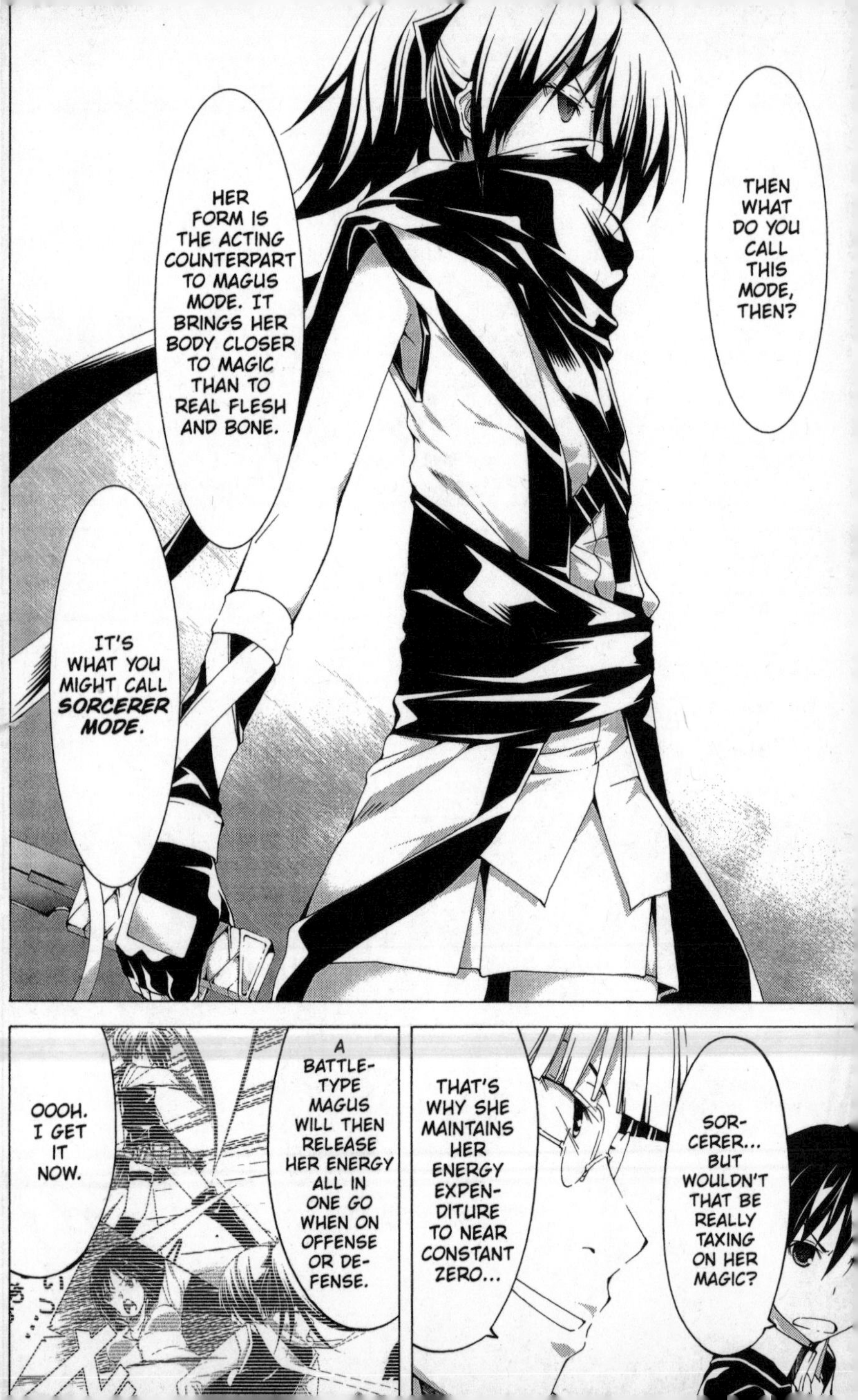
THEN WHAT DO YOU CALL THIS MODE, THEN?
HER FORM IS THE ACTING COUNTERPART TO MAGUS MODE. IT BRINGS HER BODY CLOSER TO MAGIC THAN TO REAL FLESH AND BONE.
IT'S WHAT YOU MIGHT CALL ***SORCERER MODE.***
SOR-CERER... BUT WOULDN'T THAT BE REALLY TAXING ON HER MAGIC?
THAT'S WHY SHE MAINTAINS HER ENERGY EXPEN-DITURE TO NEAR CONSTANT ZERO...
A BATTLE-TYPE MAGUS WILL THEN RELEASE HER ENERGY ALL IN ONE GO WHEN ON OFFENSE OR DE-FENSE.
OOOH. I GET IT NOW.

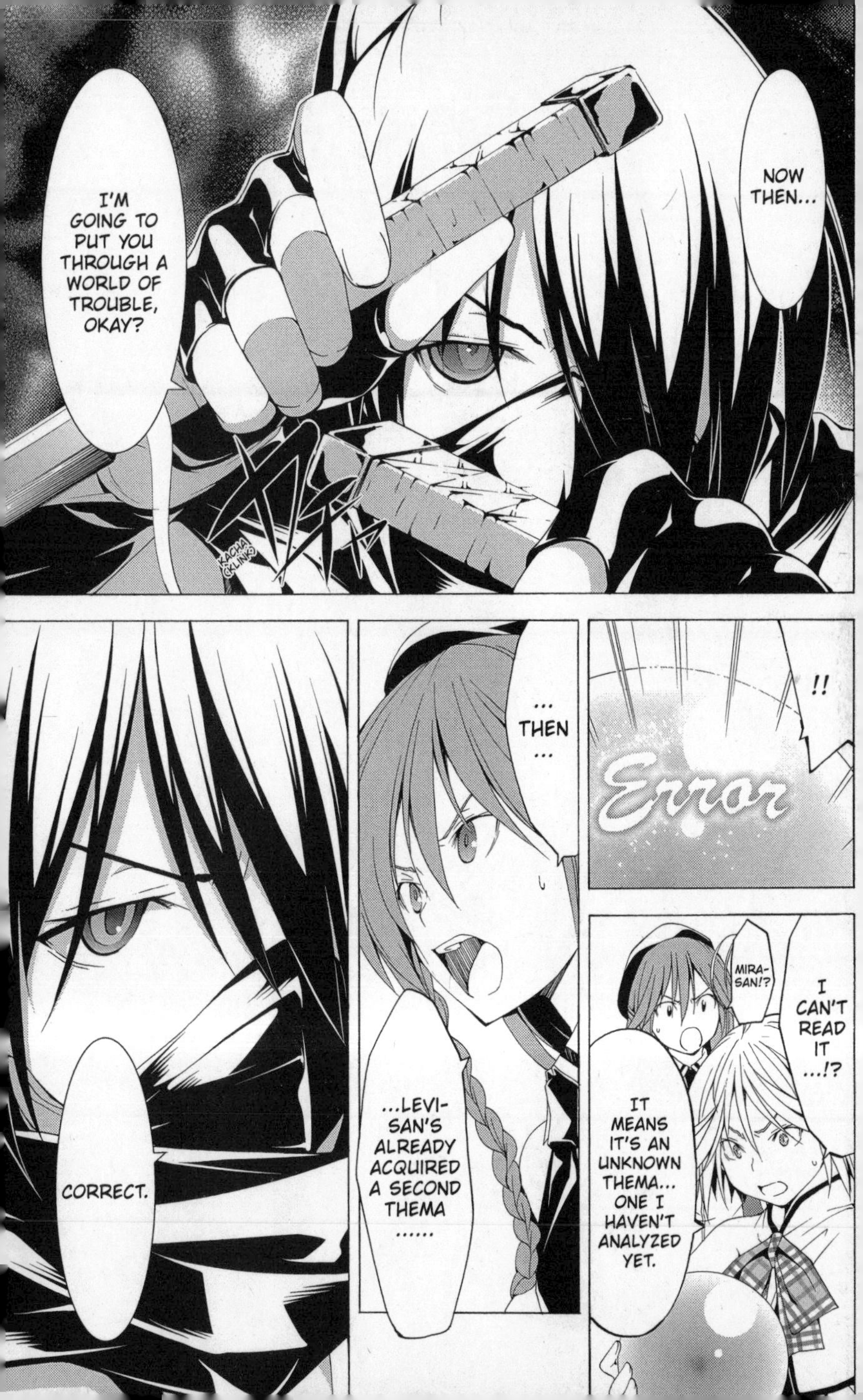
NOW THEN...
I'M GOING TO PUT YOU THROUGH A WORLD OF TROUBLE, OKAY?
KACHA (KLINK)
!!
Error
I CAN'T READ IT ...!?
MIRA-SAN!?
IT MEANS IT'S AN UNKNOWN THEMA... ONE I HAVEN'T ANALYZED YET.
...THEN...
...LEVI-SAN'S ALREADY ACQUIRED A SECOND THEMA ......
CORRECT.

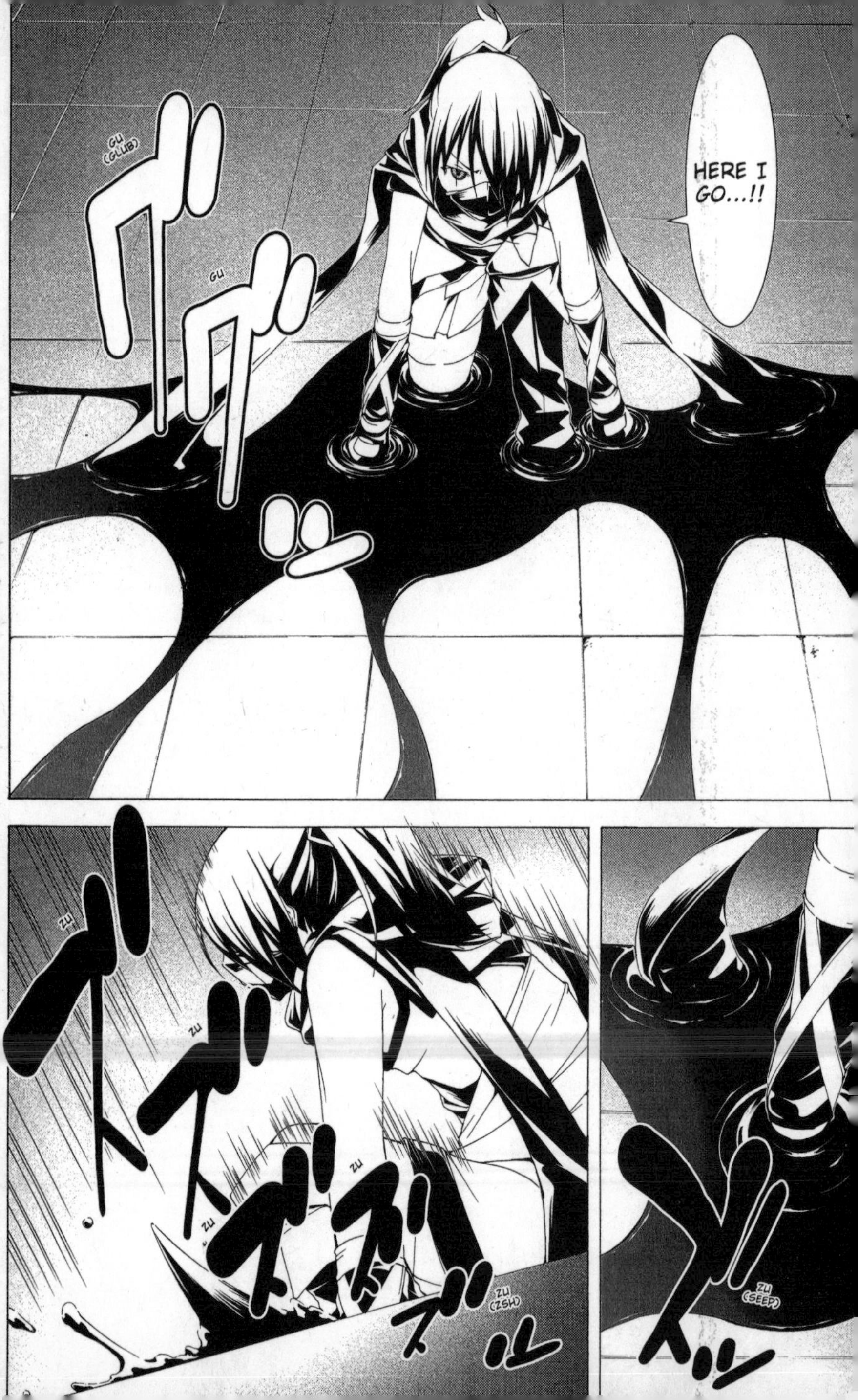
HERE I GO...!!
GU (GLUB)
GU
ZU (SEEP)
ZU
ZU
ZU
ZU
ZU (ZSH)

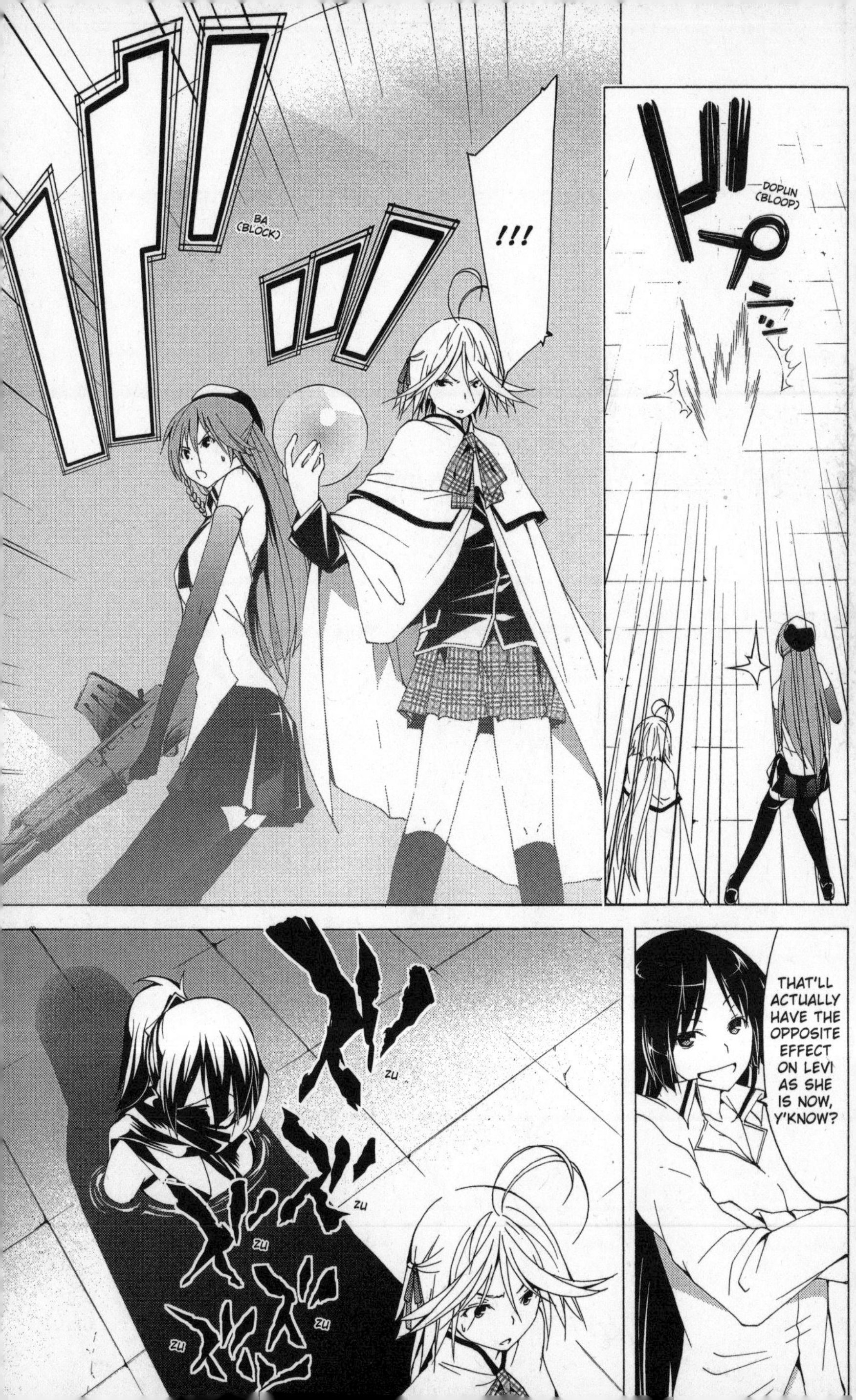
DOPUN (BLOOP)
BA (BLOCK)
!!!
THAT'LL ACTUALLY HAVE THE OPPOSITE EFFECT ON LEVI AS SHE IS NOW, Y'KNOW?
ZU
ZU
ZU
ZU
ZU

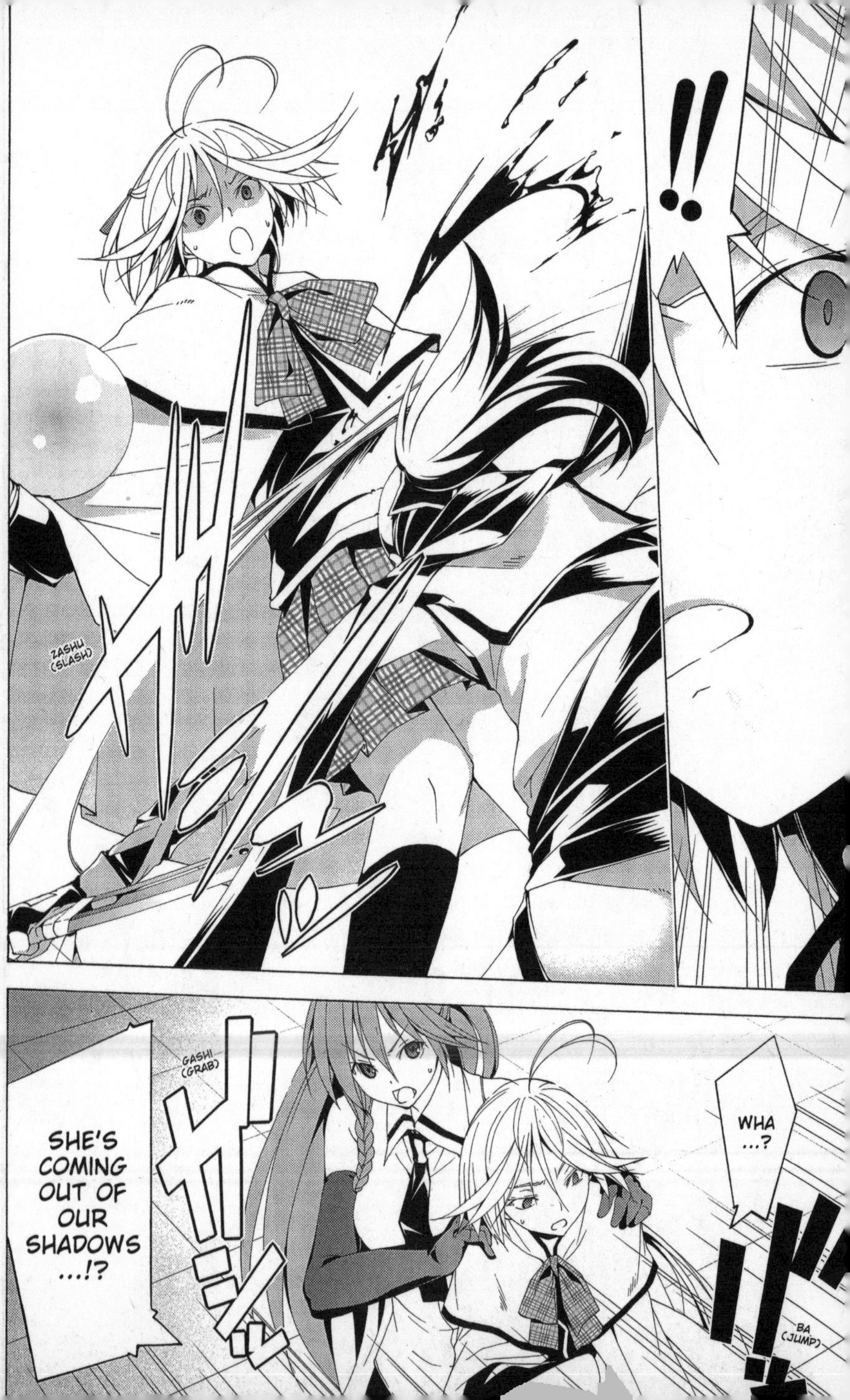
ZASHU (SLASH)
WHA ...?
GASHI (GRAB)
SHE'S COMING OUT OF OUR SHADOWS ...!?
BA (JUMP)

ZUZU
(CREEP)

MY "SHADOW-LESS SLASH" IS A NON-PHYSICAL BLADE.

IT SUPERSEDES ALL PHYSICAL LAW AND CUTS WITH A NONEXISTENT BLADE.

OUR FORCE FIELD AND BARRIER WON'T WORK...

...IS WHAT SHE'S SAYING.

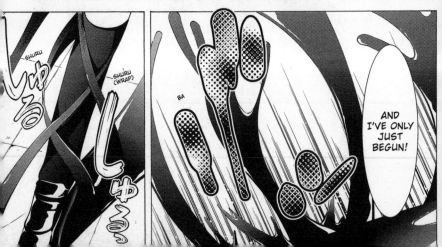

SHURU

SHURU
(WRAP)

BA

AND I'VE ONLY JUST BEGUN!

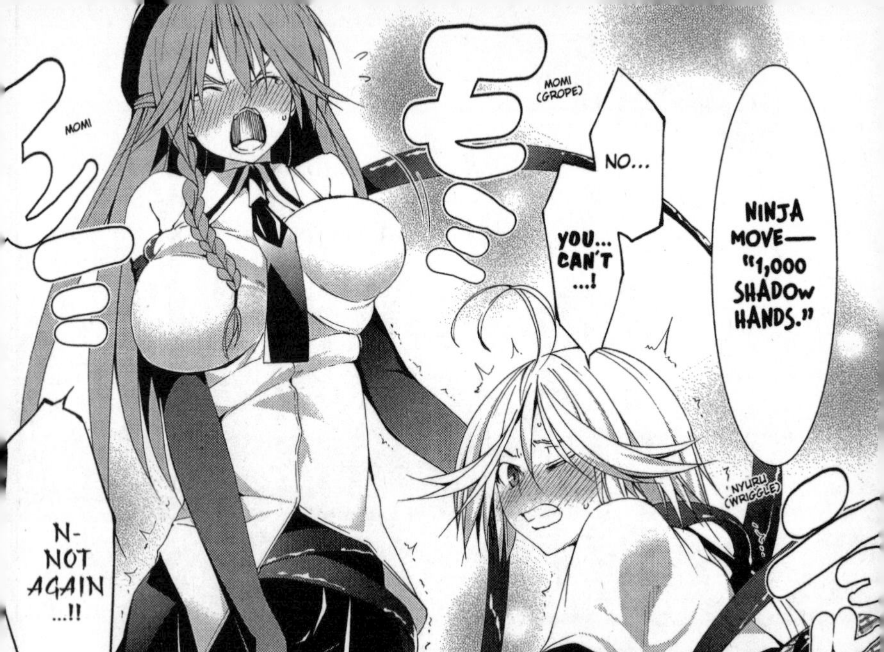
NINJA MOVE— "1,000 SHADOW HANDS."
NO...
YOU... CAN'T ...!
MOMI (GROPE)
MOMI
NYURU (WRIGGLE)
N-NOT AGAIN ...!!
NYURU
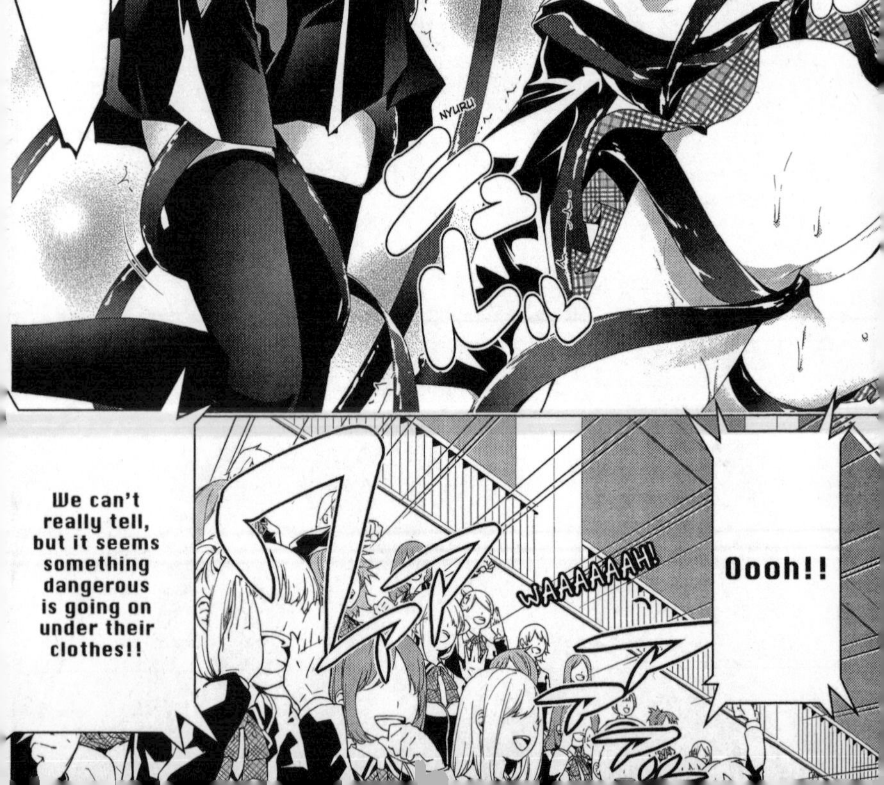
Oooh!!
WAAAAAAAH!
We can't really tell, but it seems something dangerous is going on under their clothes!!

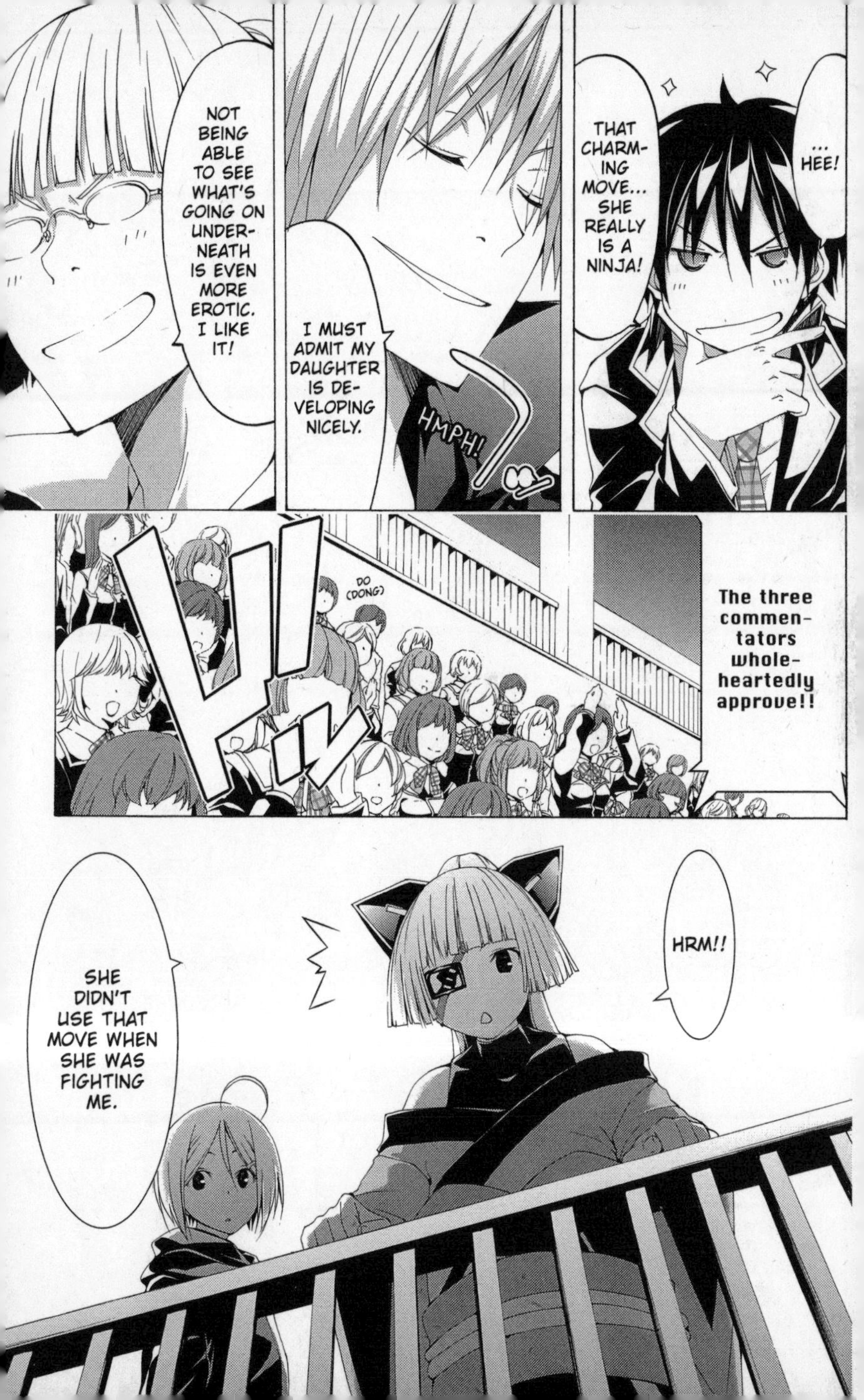

...HEE!
THAT CHARMING MOVE... SHE REALLY IS A NINJA!
I MUST ADMIT MY DAUGHTER IS DEVELOPING NICELY.
HMPH!
NOT BEING ABLE TO SEE WHAT'S GOING ON UNDERNEATH IS EVEN MORE EROTIC. I LIKE IT!
The three commentators wholeheartedly approve!!
DO (DONG)
HRM!!
SHE DIDN'T USE THAT MOVE WHEN SHE WAS FIGHTING ME.

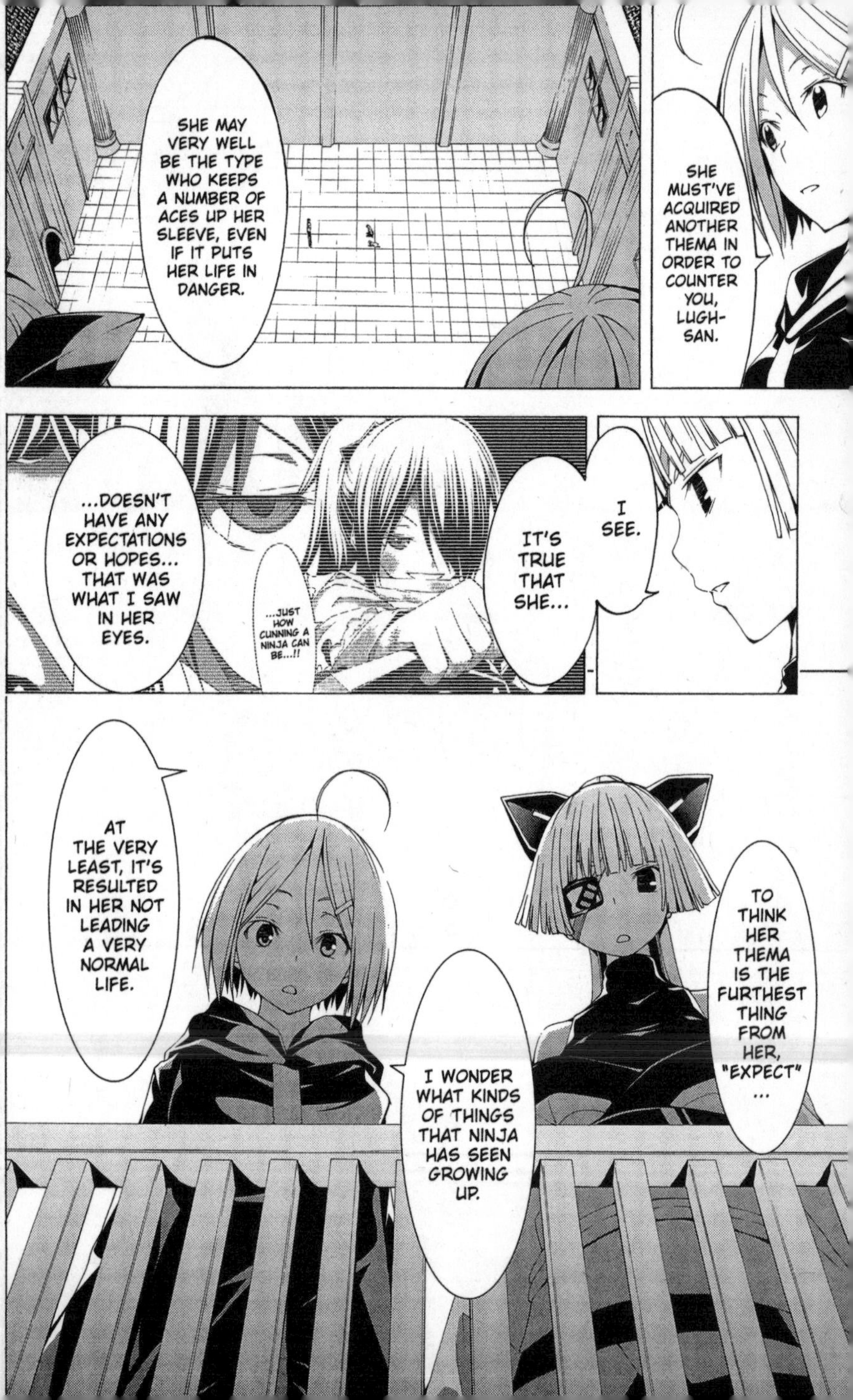
SHE MUST'VE ACQUIRED ANOTHER THEMA IN ORDER TO COUNTER YOU, LUGH-SAN.
SHE MAY VERY WELL BE THE TYPE WHO KEEPS A NUMBER OF ACES UP HER SLEEVE, EVEN IF IT PUTS HER LIFE IN DANGER.
I SEE.
IT'S TRUE THAT SHE...
...DOESN'T HAVE ANY EXPECTATIONS OR HOPES... THAT WAS WHAT I SAW IN HER EYES.
...JUST HOW CUNNING A NINJA CAN BE...!!
TO THINK HER THEMA IS THE FURTHEST THING FROM HER, "EXPECT"...
AT THE VERY LEAST, IT'S RESULTED IN HER NOT LEADING A VERY NORMAL LIFE.
I WONDER WHAT KINDS OF THINGS THAT NINJA HAS SEEN GROWING UP.

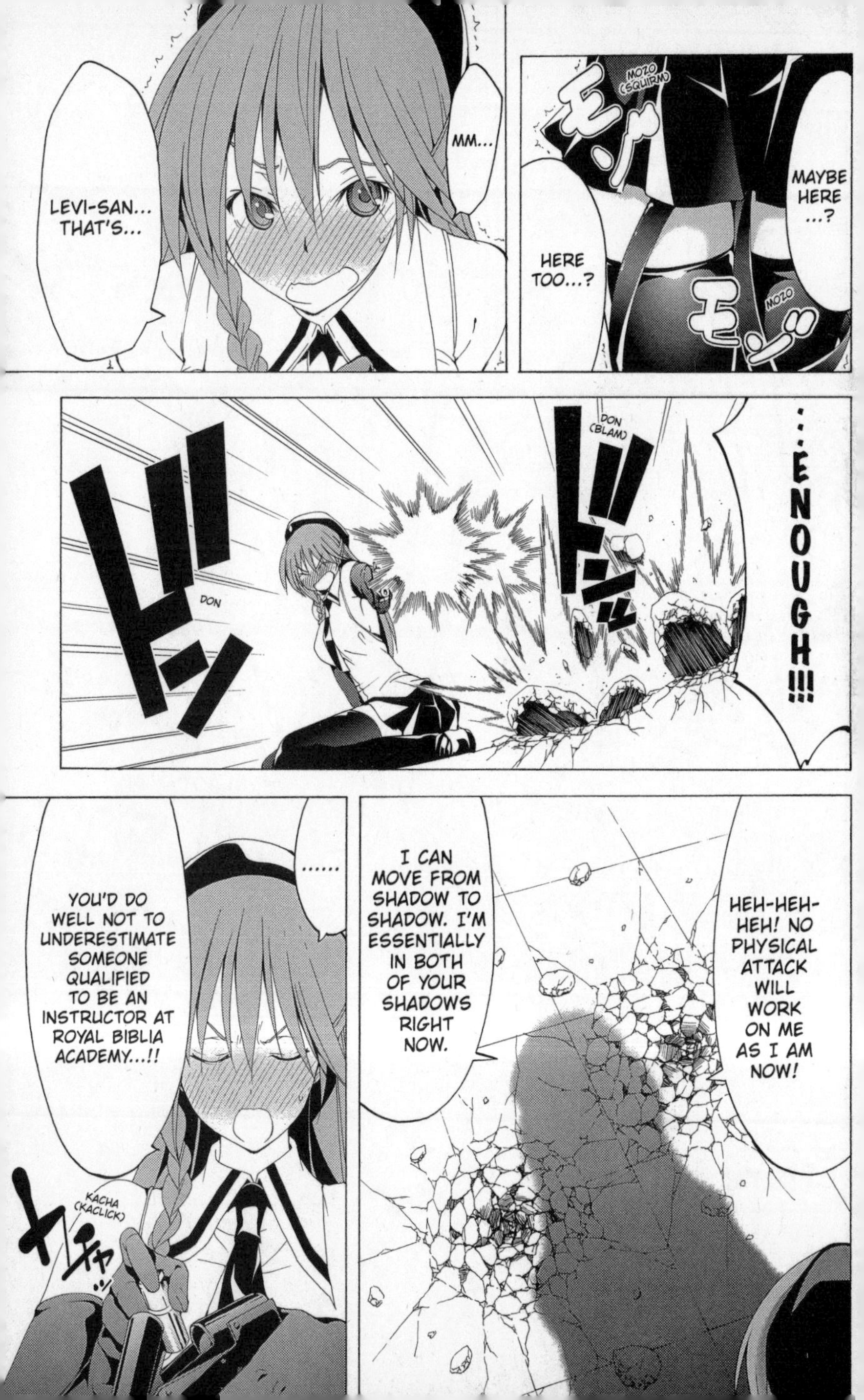
MOZO (SQUIRM)
MAYBE HERE ...?
HERE TOO...?
MOZO
MM...
LEVI-SAN... THAT'S...
...ENOUGH!!!
DON (BLAM)
DON
HEH-HEH-HEH! NO PHYSICAL ATTACK WILL WORK ON ME AS I AM NOW!
I CAN MOVE FROM SHADOW TO SHADOW. I'M ESSENTIALLY IN BOTH OF YOUR SHADOWS RIGHT NOW.
......
YOU'D DO WELL NOT TO UNDERESTIMATE SOMEONE QUALIFIED TO BE AN INSTRUCTOR AT ROYAL BIBLIA ACADEMY...!!
KACHA (KACLICK)

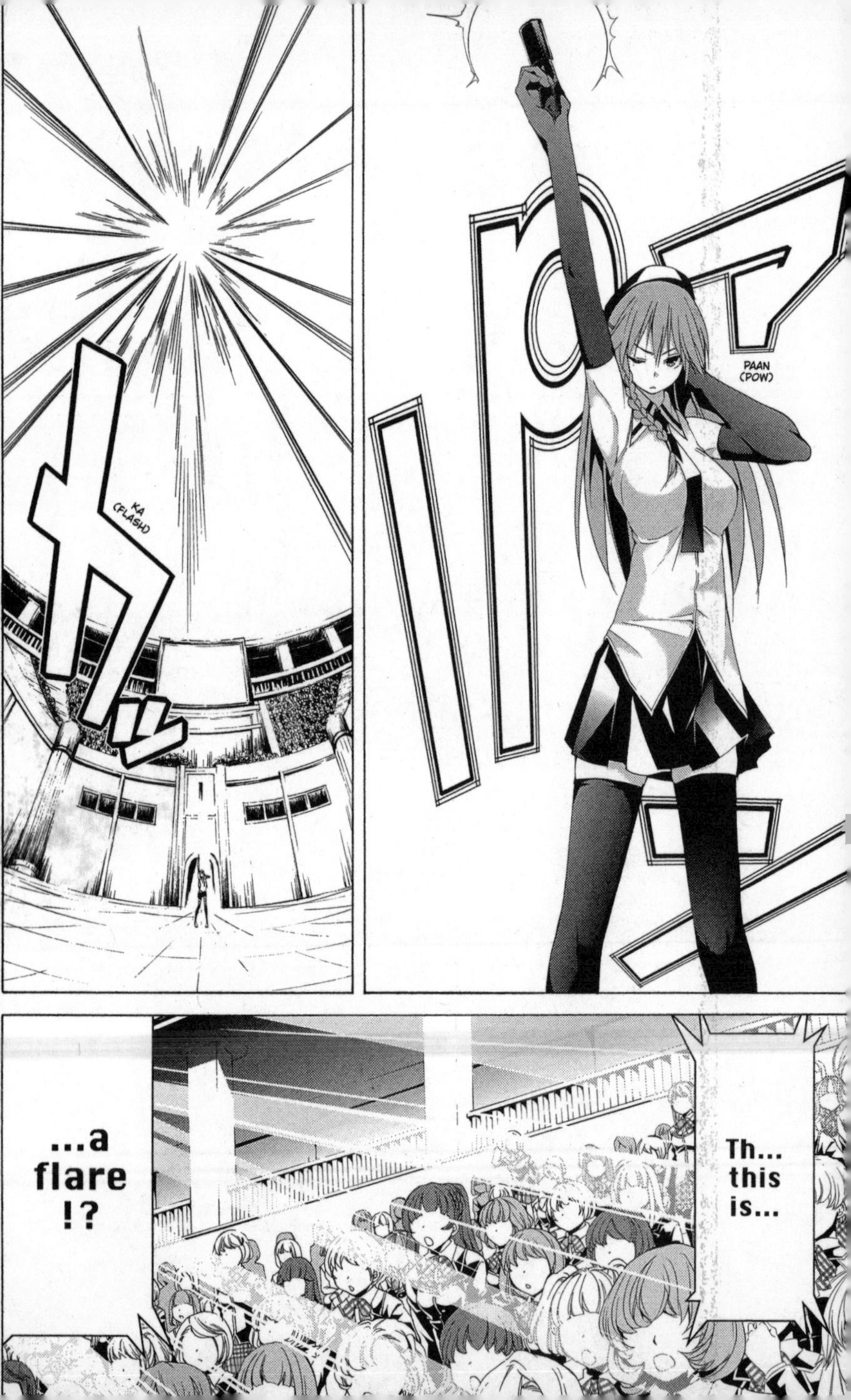
PAAN (POW)
KA (FLASH)
Th... this is...
...a flare !?

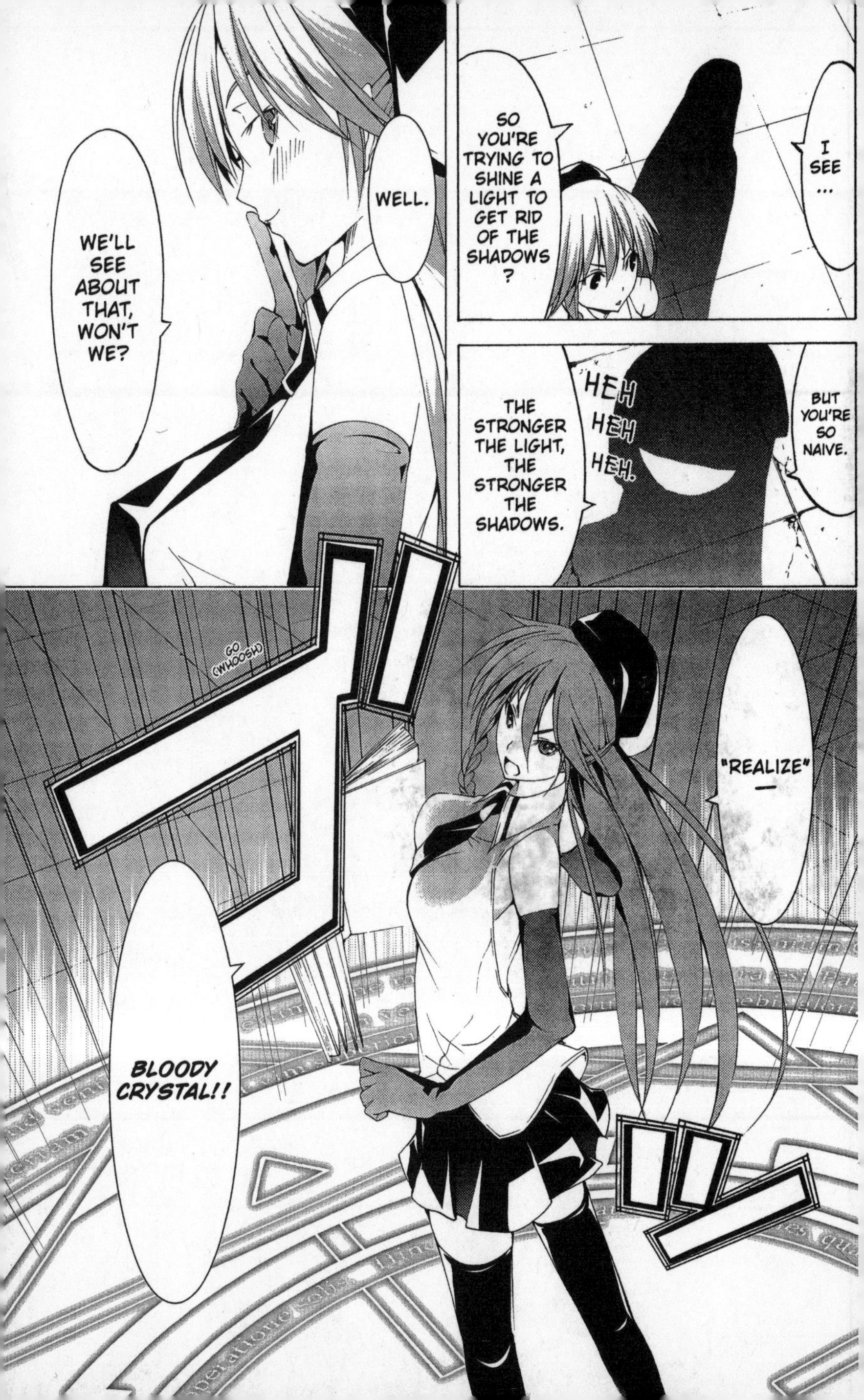
I SEE …
SO YOU'RE TRYING TO SHINE A LIGHT TO GET RID OF THE SHADOWS ?
BUT YOU'RE SO NAIVE.
HEH HEH HEH.
THE STRONGER THE LIGHT, THE STRONGER THE SHADOWS.
WELL.
WE'LL SEE ABOUT THAT, WON'T WE?
"REALIZE" —
GO (WHOOSH)
BLOODY CRYSTAL!!

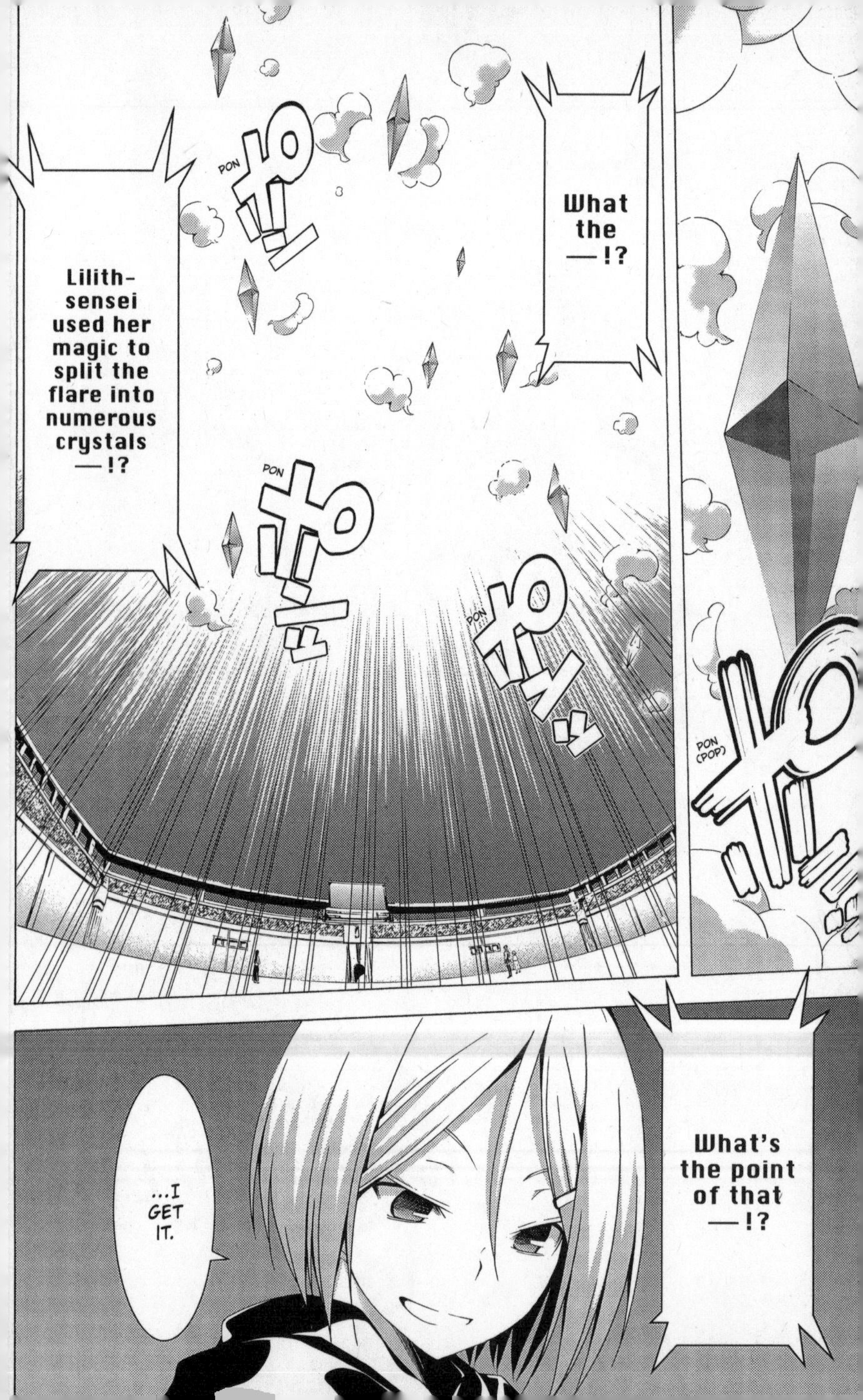
PON (POP)
What the —!?
PON
PON
PON
Lilith-sensei used her magic to split the flare into numerous crystals —!?
What's the point of that —!?
...I GET IT.

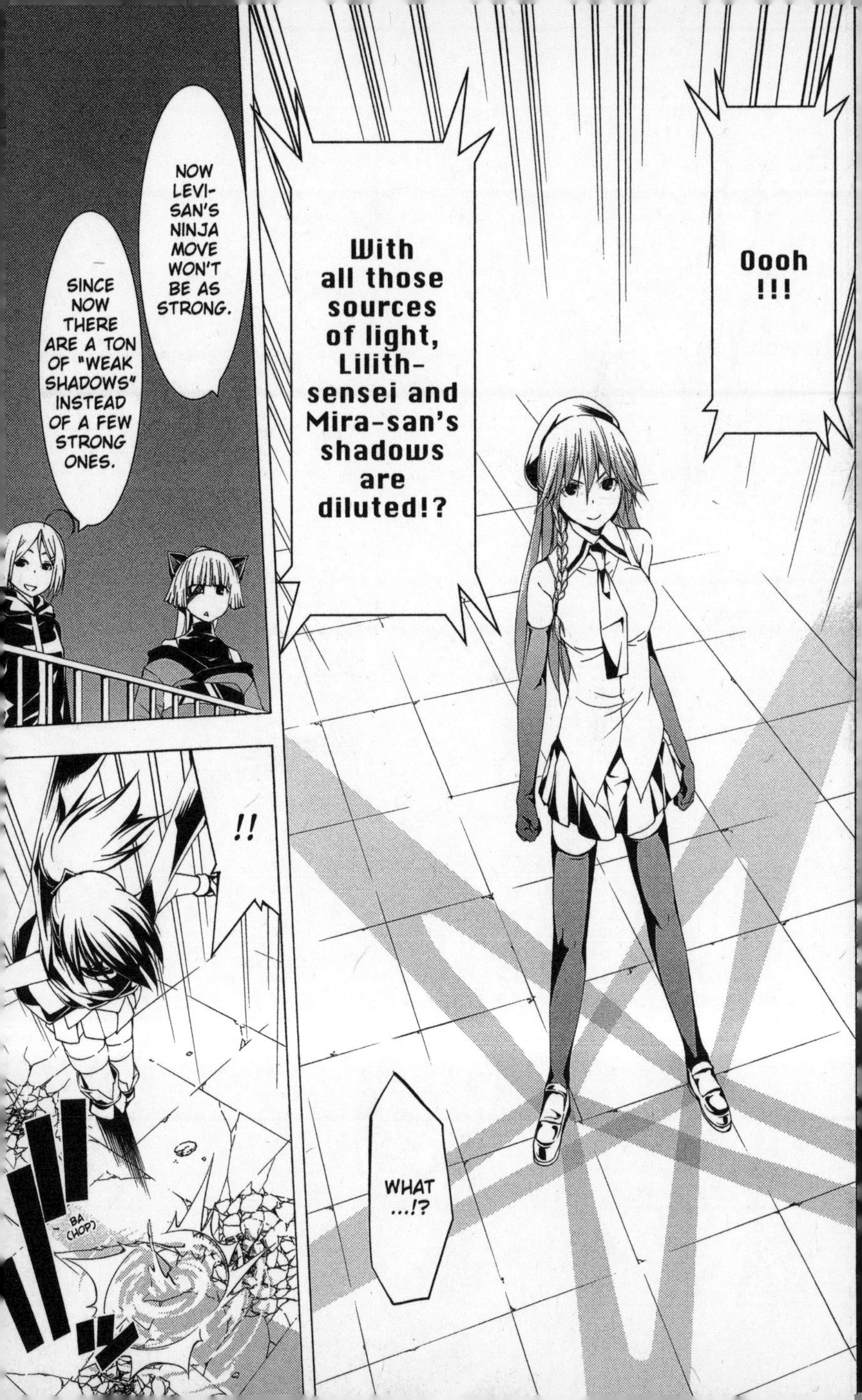
Oooh!!!
With all those sources of light, Lilith-sensei and Mira-san's shadows are diluted!?
WHAT...!?
NOW LEVI-SAN'S NINJA MOVE WON'T BE AS STRONG.
SINCE NOW THERE ARE A TON OF "WEAK SHADOWS" INSTEAD OF A FEW STRONG ONES.
!!
BA (HOP)

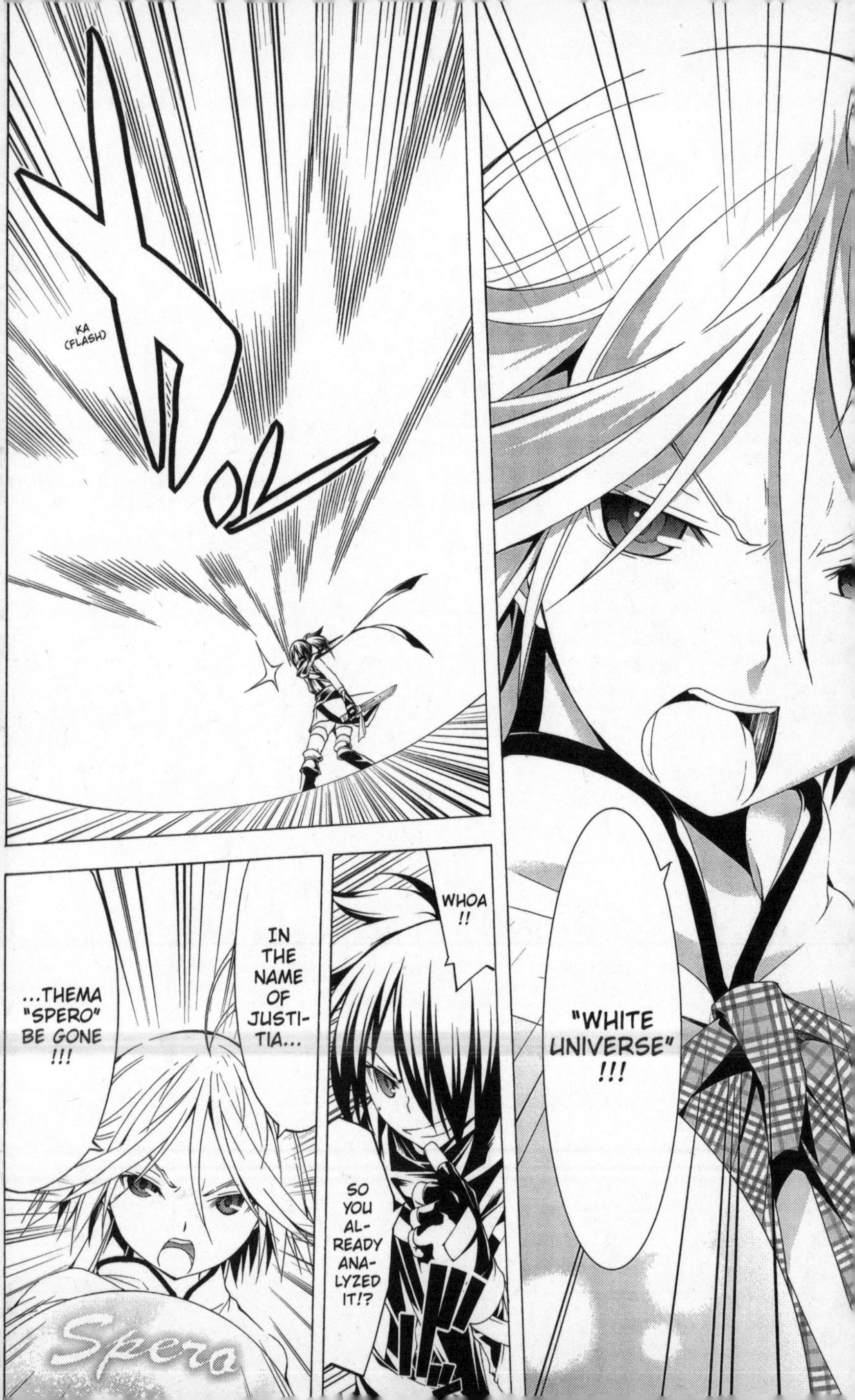
"WHITE UNIVERSE" !!!
KA (FLASH)
WHOA !!
SO YOU AL-READY ANA-LYZED IT!?
IN THE NAME OF JUSTI-TIA...
...THEMA "SPERO" BE GONE !!!
Spero

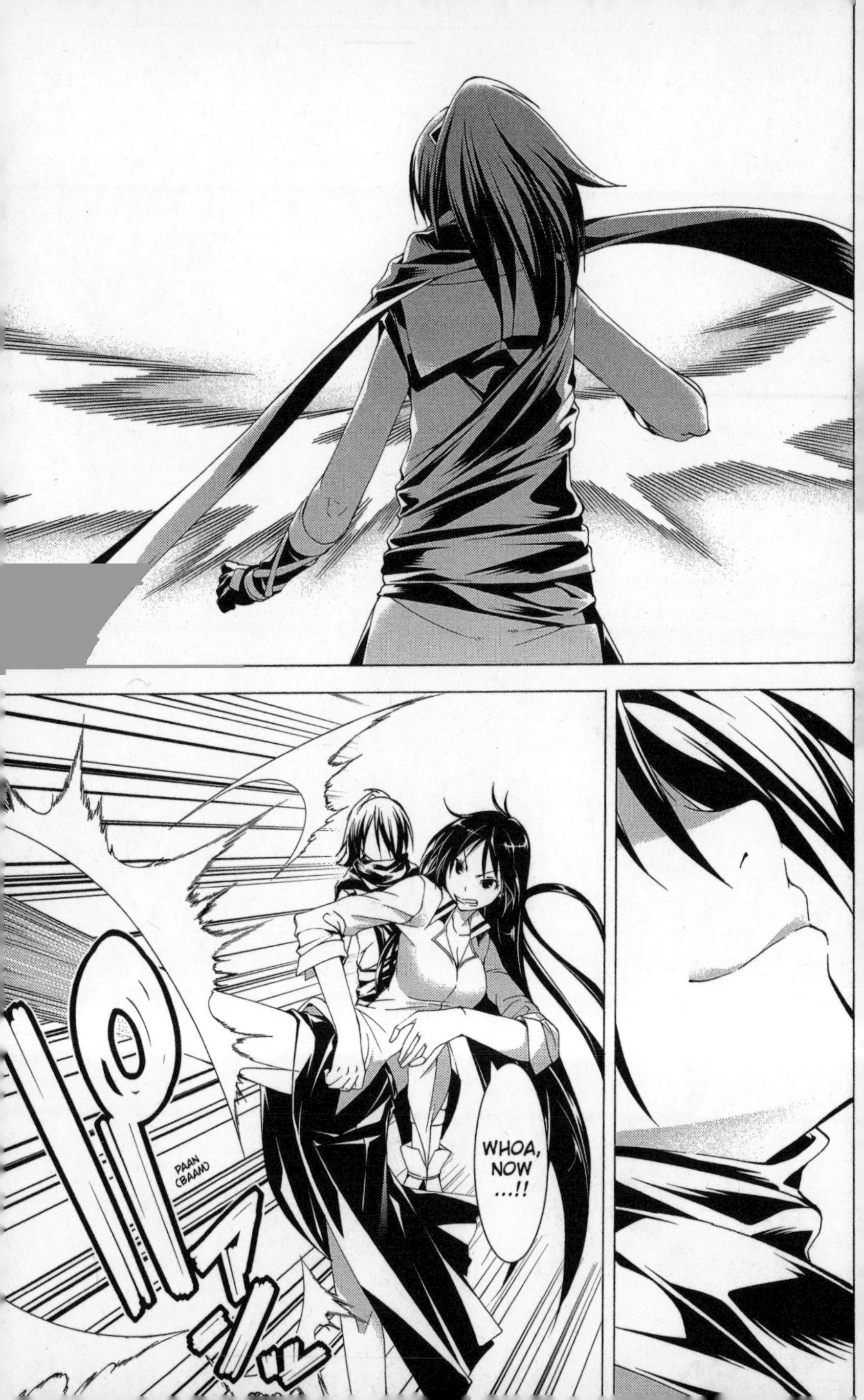
WHOA, NOW ...!!
PAAN (BAAM)

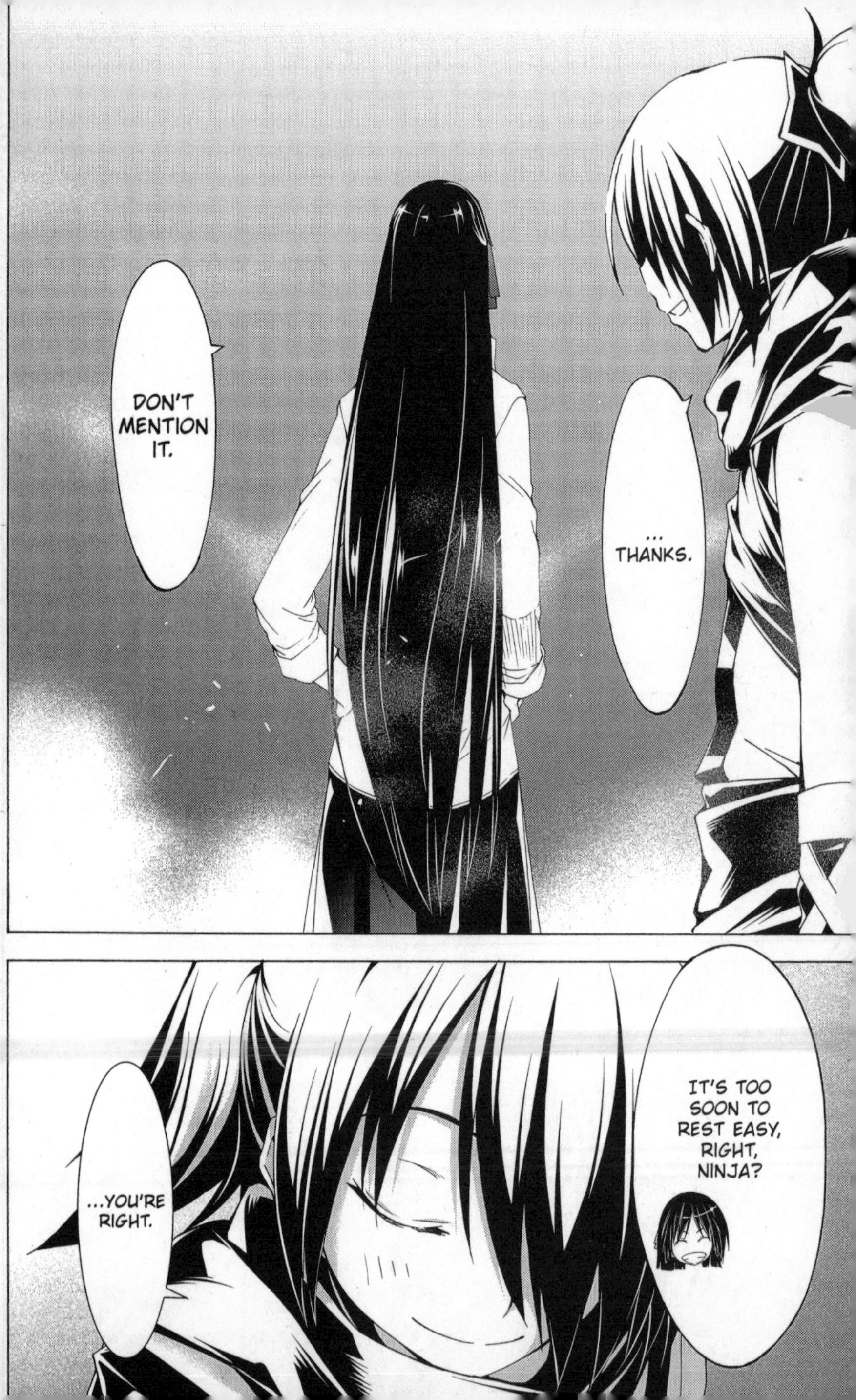
...THANKS.
DON'T MENTION IT.
IT'S TOO SOON TO REST EASY, RIGHT, NINJA?
...YOU'RE RIGHT.

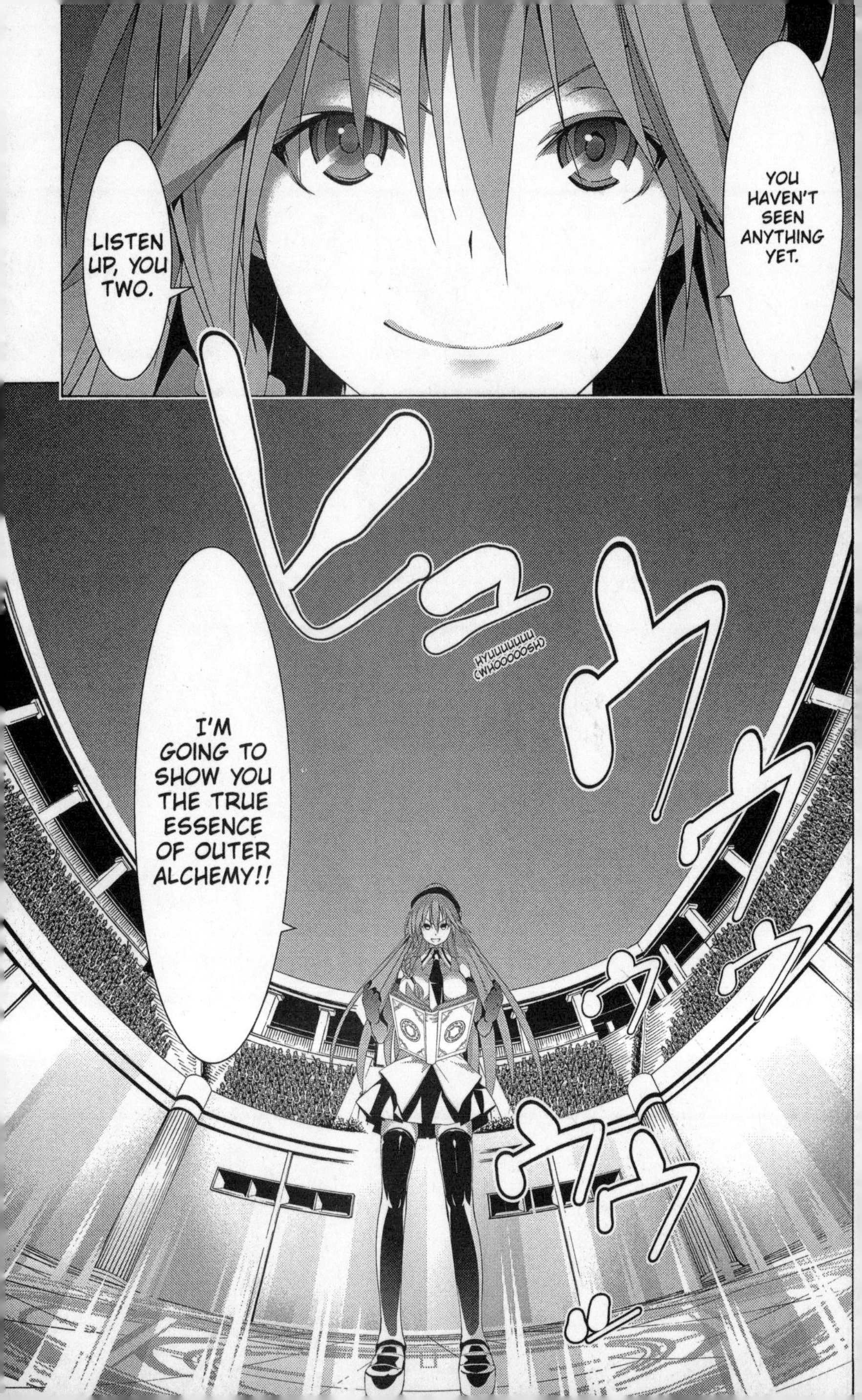
YOU HAVEN'T SEEN ANYTHING YET.
LISTEN UP, YOU TWO.
HYUUUUUUU (WHOOOOOOSH)
I'M GOING TO SHOW YOU THE TRUE ESSENCE OF OUTER ALCHEMY!!

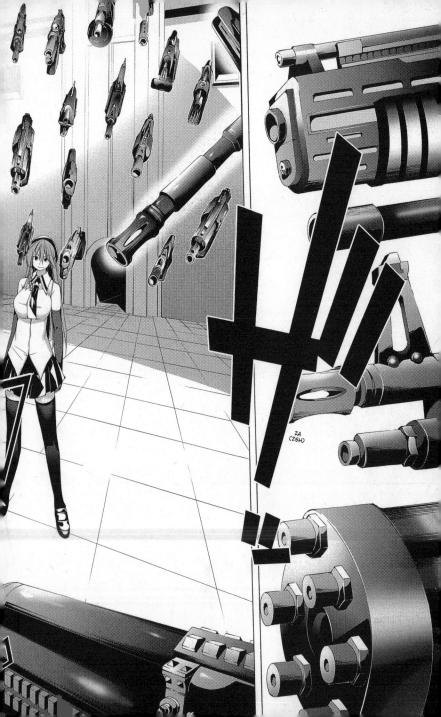

ZA
(ZSH)

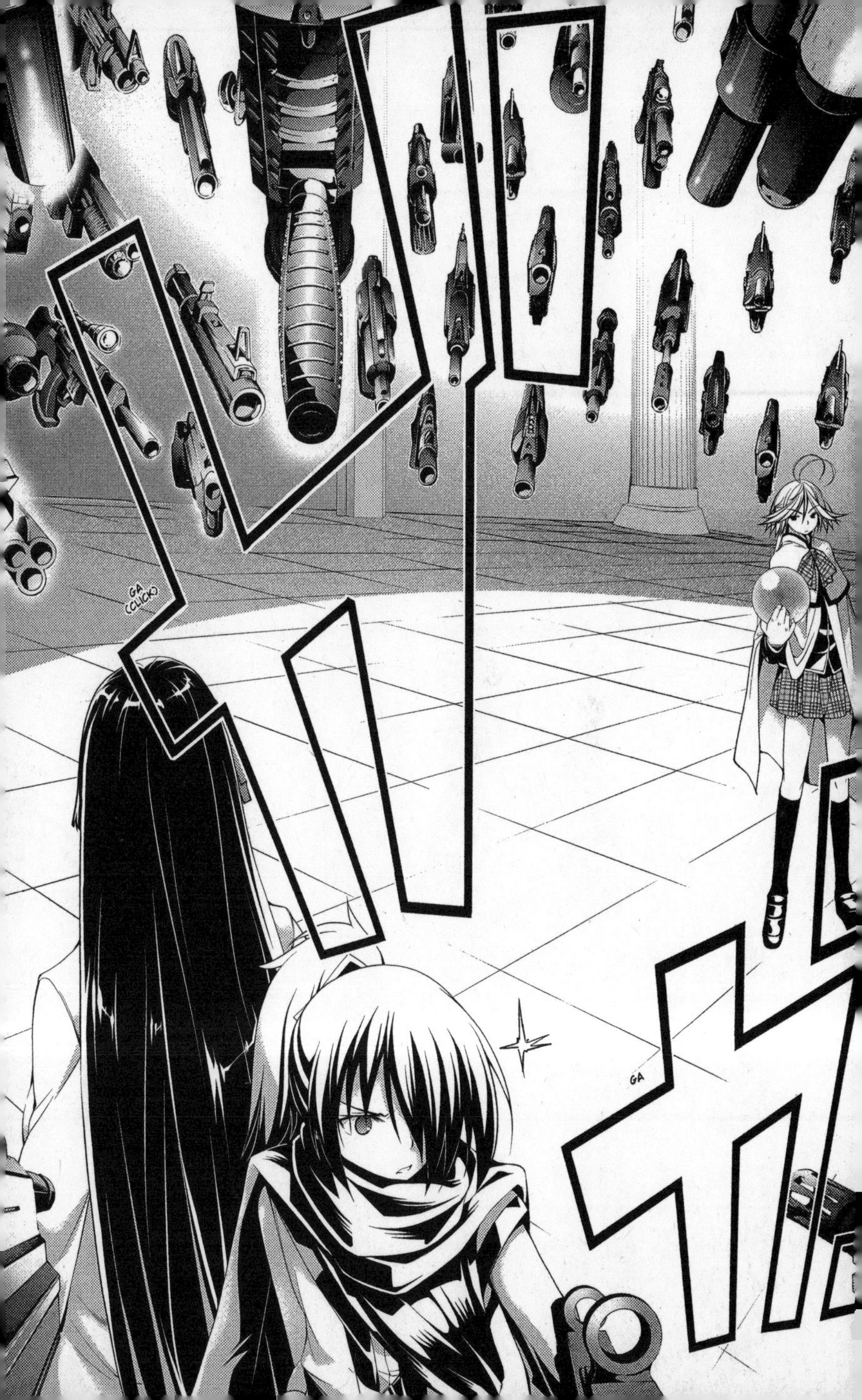
GA
GA (CLICK)

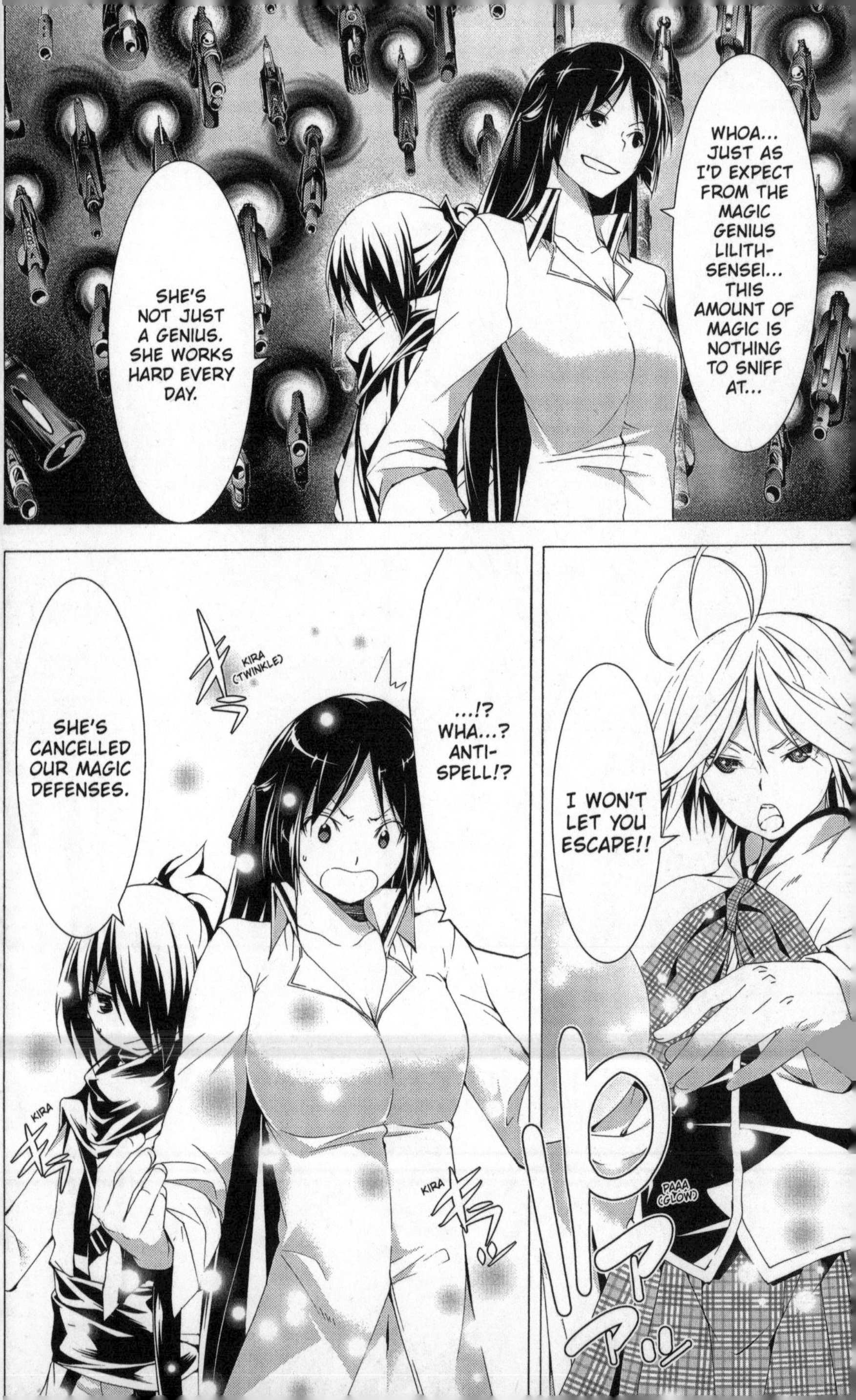
WHOA... JUST AS I'D EXPECT FROM THE MAGIC GENIUS LILITH-SENSEI... THIS AMOUNT OF MAGIC IS NOTHING TO SNIFF AT...
SHE'S NOT JUST A GENIUS. SHE WORKS HARD EVERY DAY.
I WON'T LET YOU ESCAPE!!
PAAA (GLOW)
...!? WHA...? ANTI-SPELL!?
KIRA (TWINKLE)
SHE'S CANCELLED OUR MAGIC DEFENSES.
KIRA
KIRA

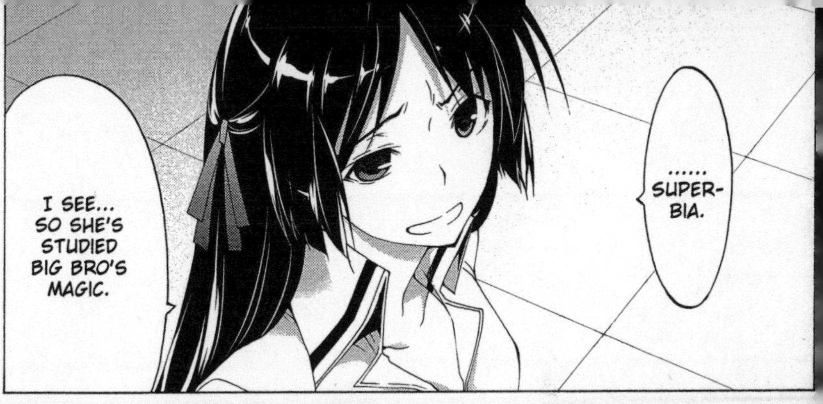
......SUPER-BIA.
I SEE... SO SHE'S STUDIED BIG BRO'S MAGIC.
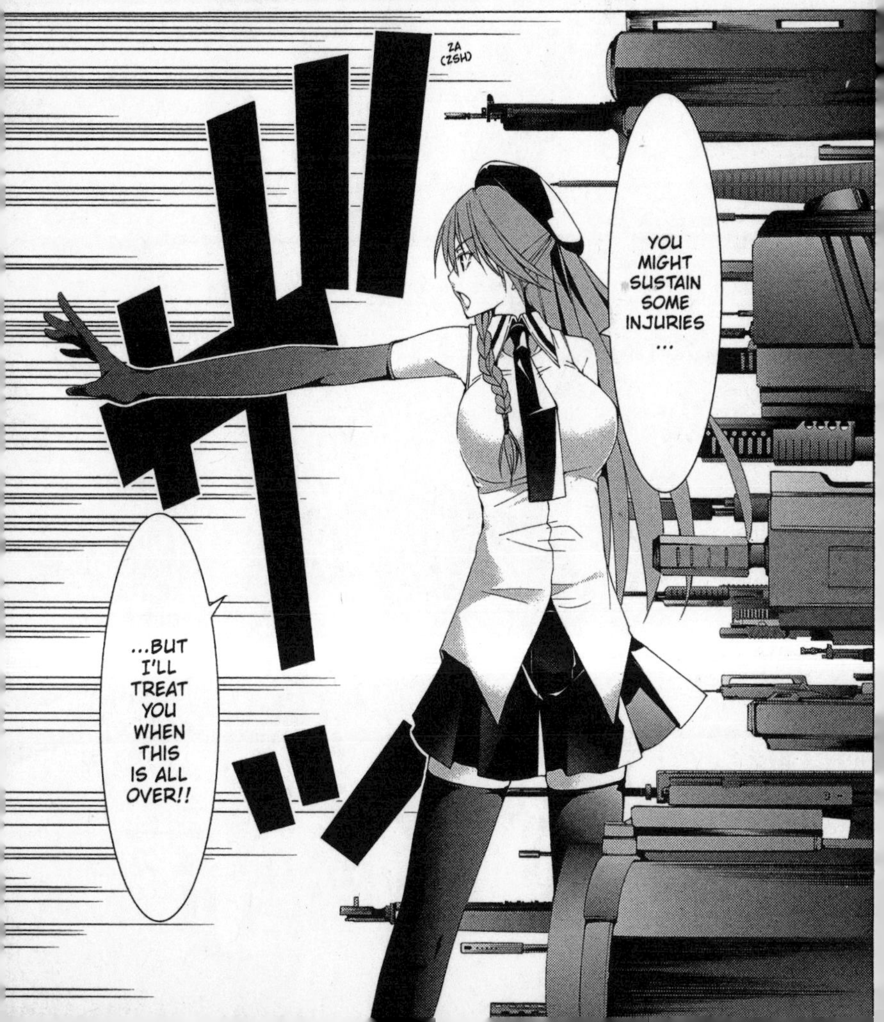
ZA (ZSH)
YOU MIGHT SUSTAIN SOME INJURIES ...
...BUT I'LL TREAT YOU WHEN THIS IS ALL OVER!!

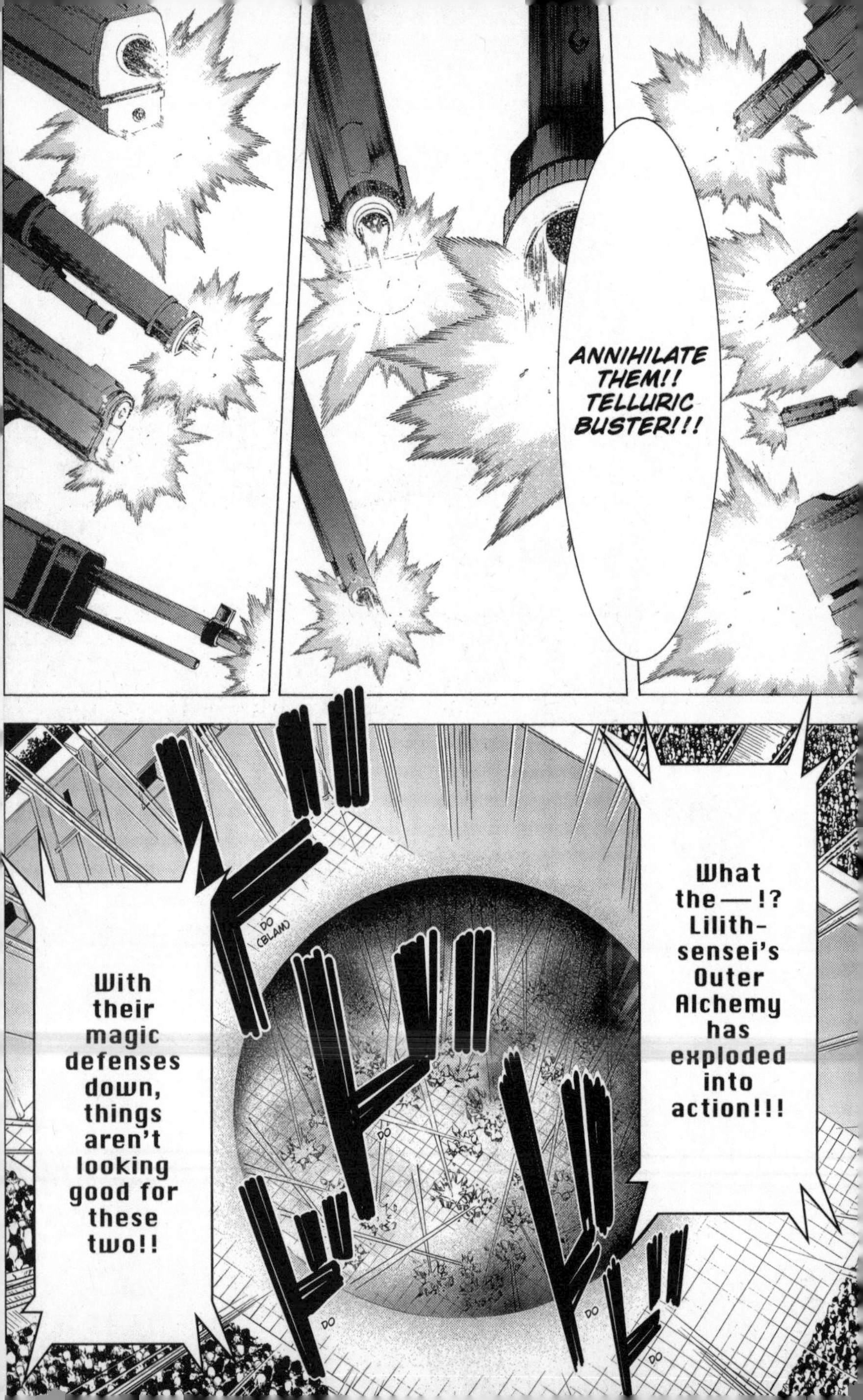
ANNIHILATE THEM!! TELLURIC BUSTER!!!
What the—!? Lilith-sensei's Outer Alchemy has exploded into action!!!
DO (BLAM)
DO
With their magic defenses down, things aren't looking good for these two!!
DO
DO
DO

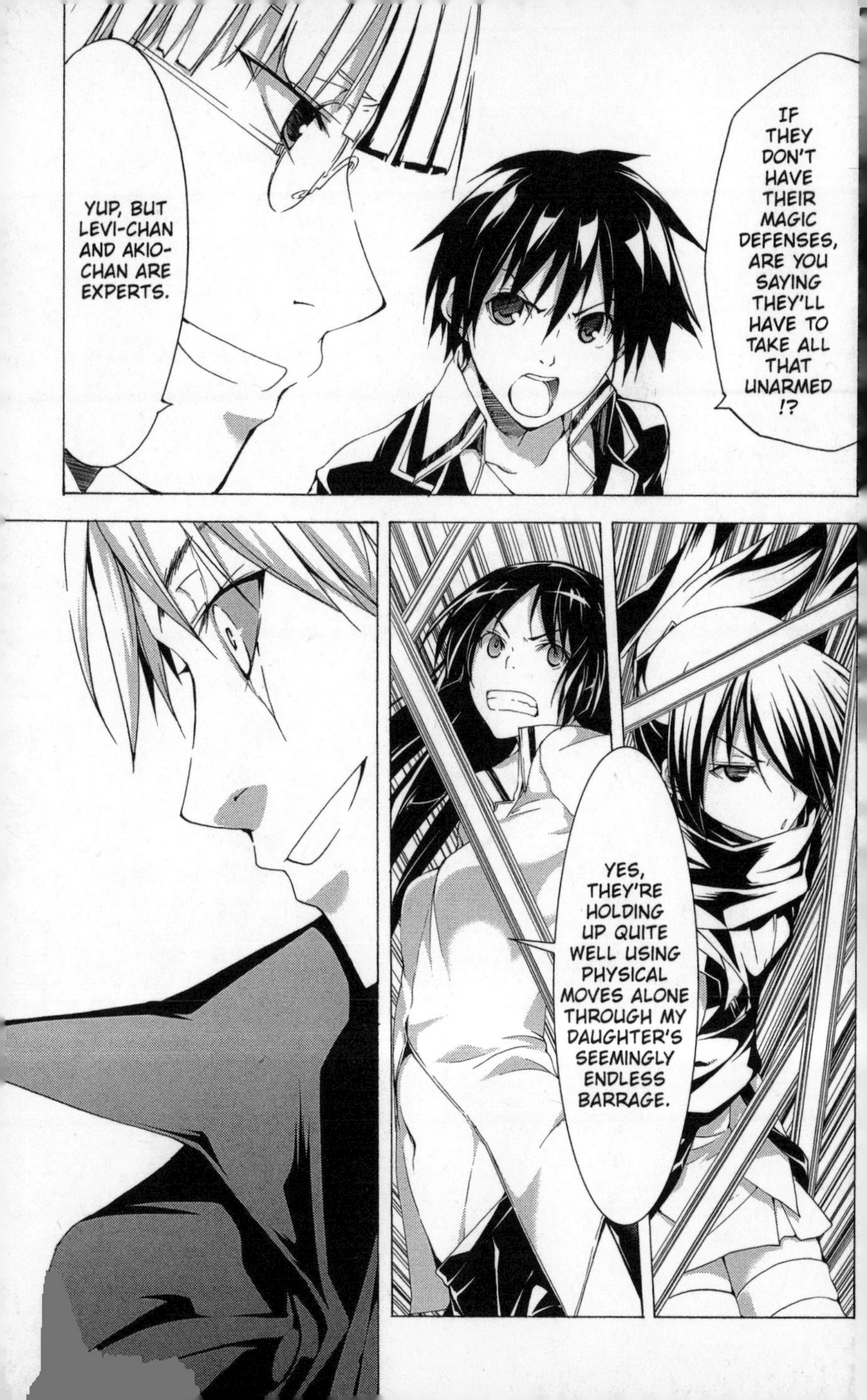
IF THEY DON'T HAVE THEIR MAGIC DEFENSES, ARE YOU SAYING THEY'LL HAVE TO TAKE ALL THAT UNARMED!?
YUP, BUT LEVI-CHAN AND AKIO-CHAN ARE EXPERTS.
YES, THEY'RE HOLDING UP QUITE WELL USING PHYSICAL MOVES ALONE THROUGH MY DAUGHTER'S SEEMINGLY ENDLESS BARRAGE.

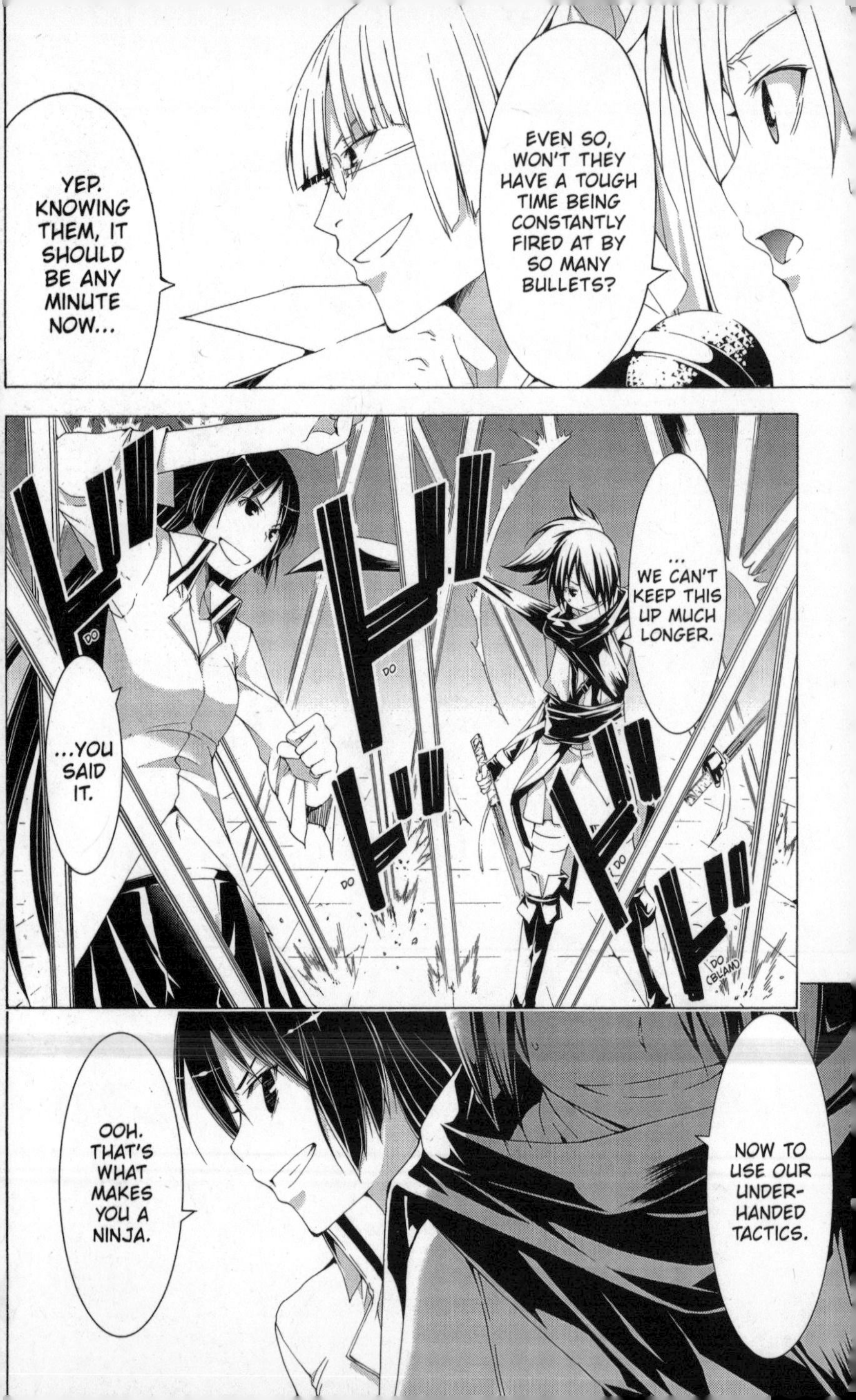
EVEN SO, WON'T THEY HAVE A TOUGH TIME BEING CONSTANTLY FIRED AT BY SO MANY BULLETS?
YEP. KNOWING THEM, IT SHOULD BE ANY MINUTE NOW...
... WE CAN'T KEEP THIS UP MUCH LONGER.
...YOU SAID IT.
DO
DO
DO
DO
DO (BLAM)
NOW TO USE OUR UNDER-HANDED TACTICS.
OOH. THAT'S WHAT MAKES YOU A NINJA.

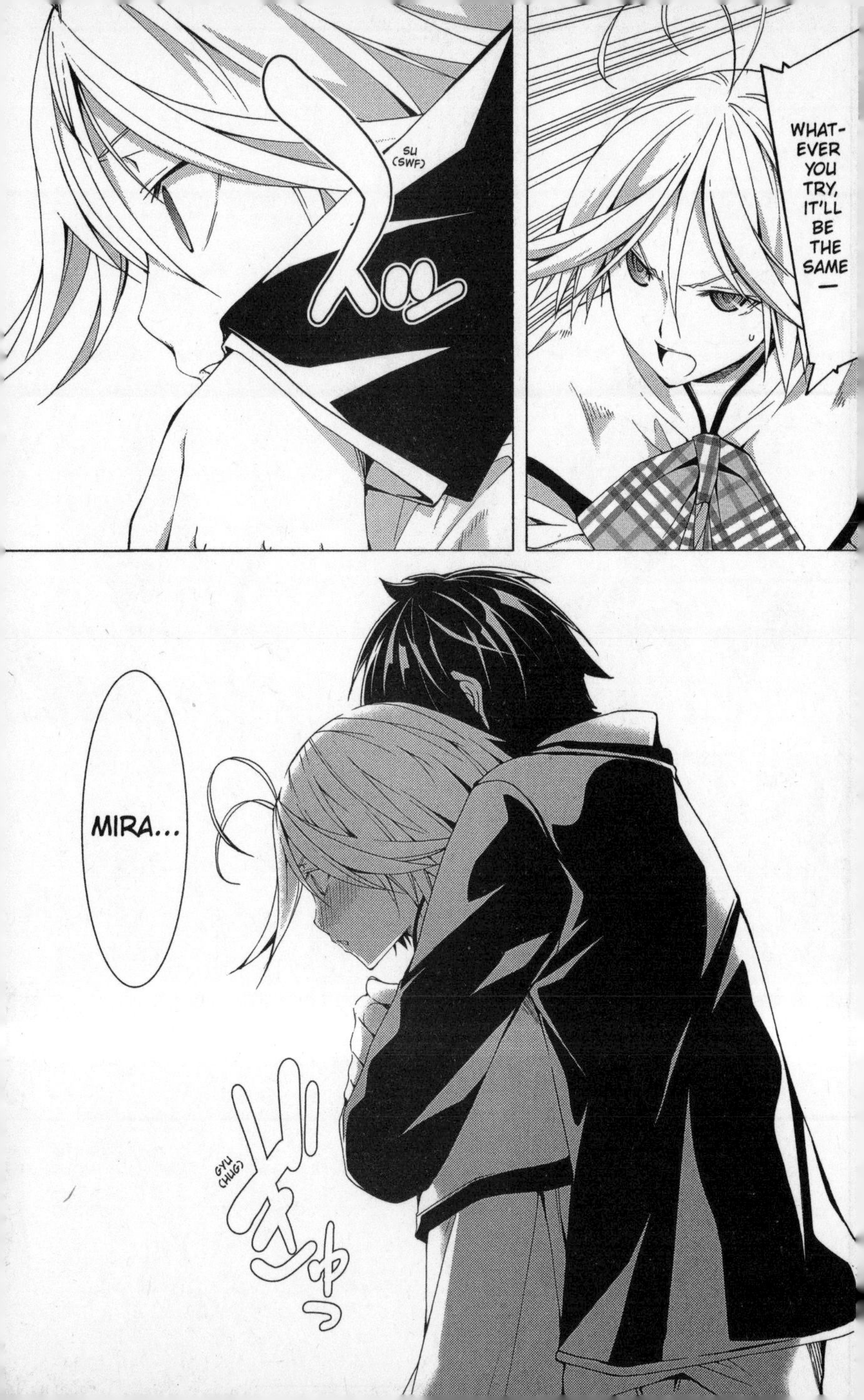

WHAT-EVER YOU TRY, IT'LL BE THE SAME —
スッ
SU (SWF)
MIRA...
ぎゅっ
GYU (HUG)

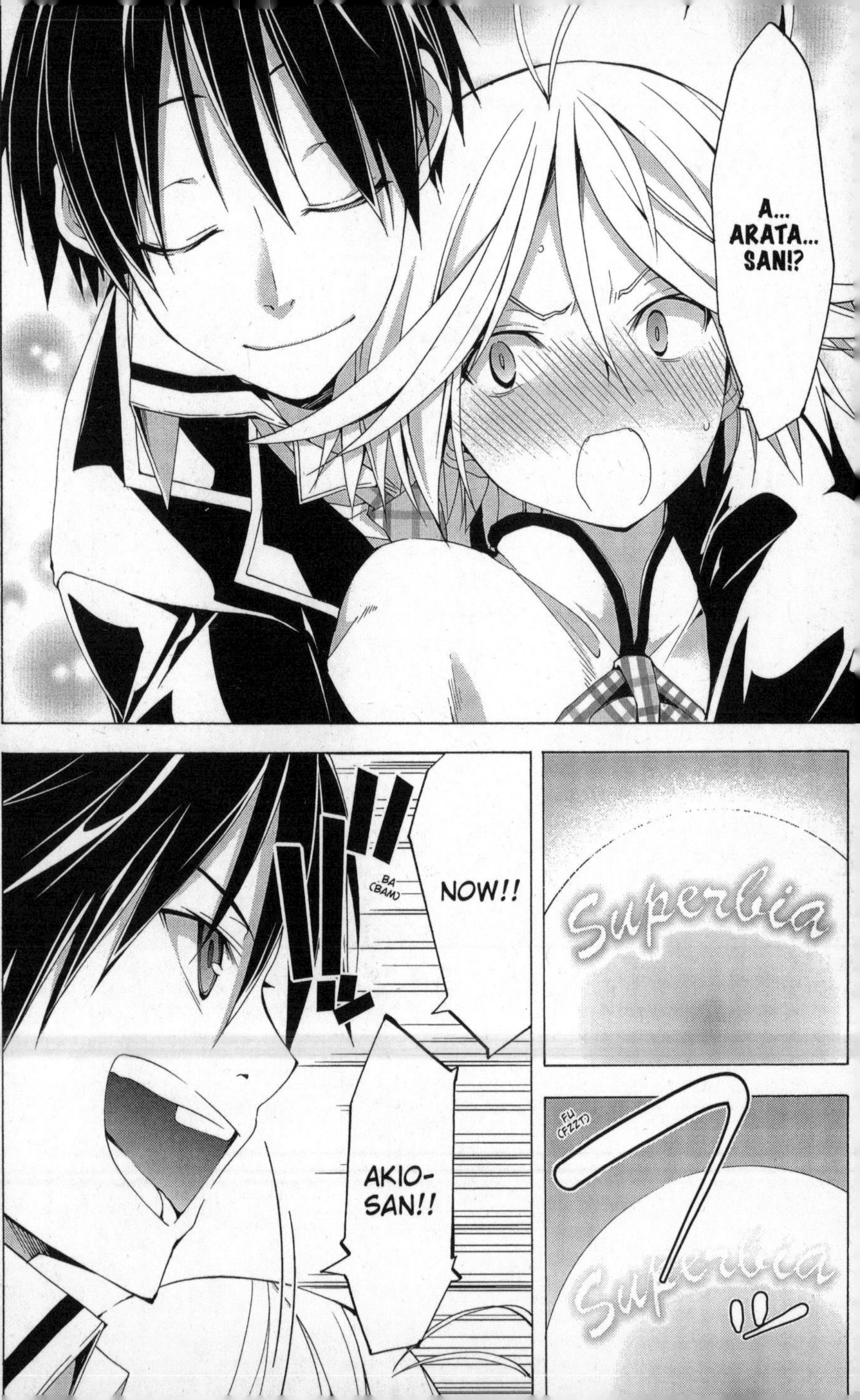
A... ARATA... SAN!?
Superbia
FU (FZZT)
Superbia
NOW!!
BA (BAM)
AKIO-SAN!!

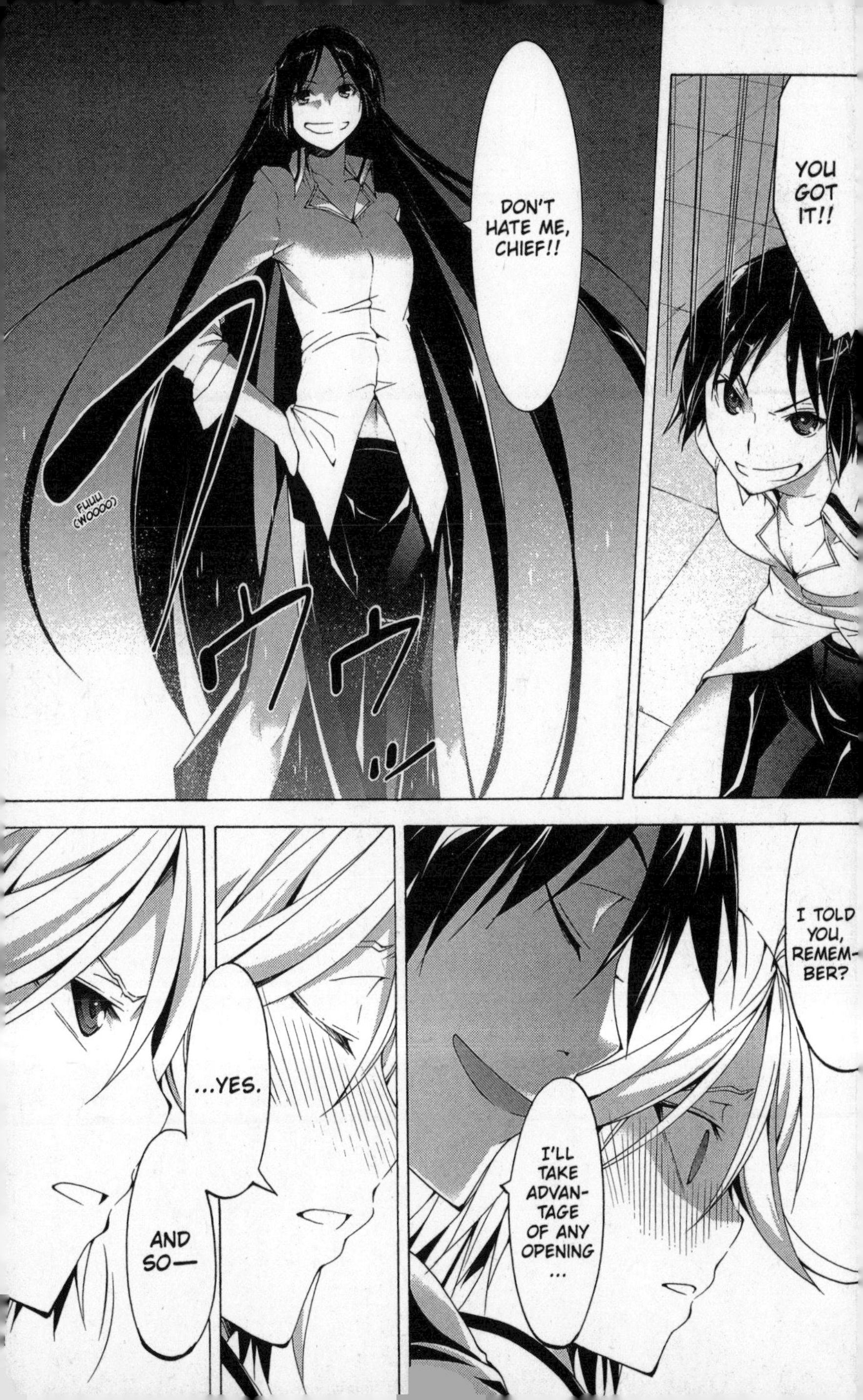
YOU GOT IT!!
DON'T HATE ME, CHIEF!!
FUUU (WOOOO)
I TOLD YOU, REMEMBER?
I'LL TAKE ADVANTAGE OF ANY OPENING...
...YES.
AND SO—

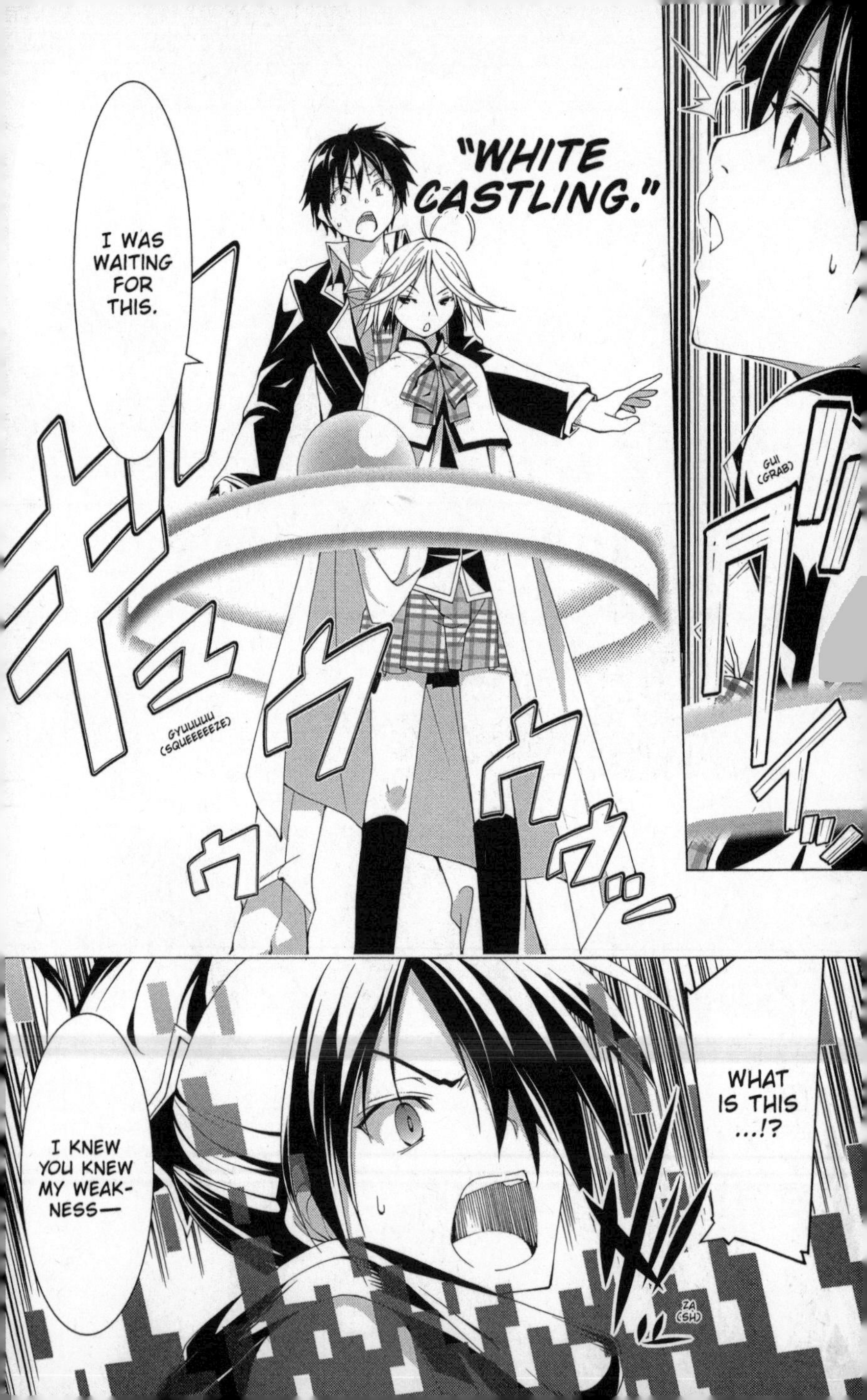
GUI
(GRAB)
"WHITE CASTLING."
I WAS WAITING FOR THIS.
GYUUUUUU
(SQUEEEEEEZE)
WHAT IS THIS ...!?
ZA
(SH)
I KNEW YOU KNEW MY WEAK-NESS—

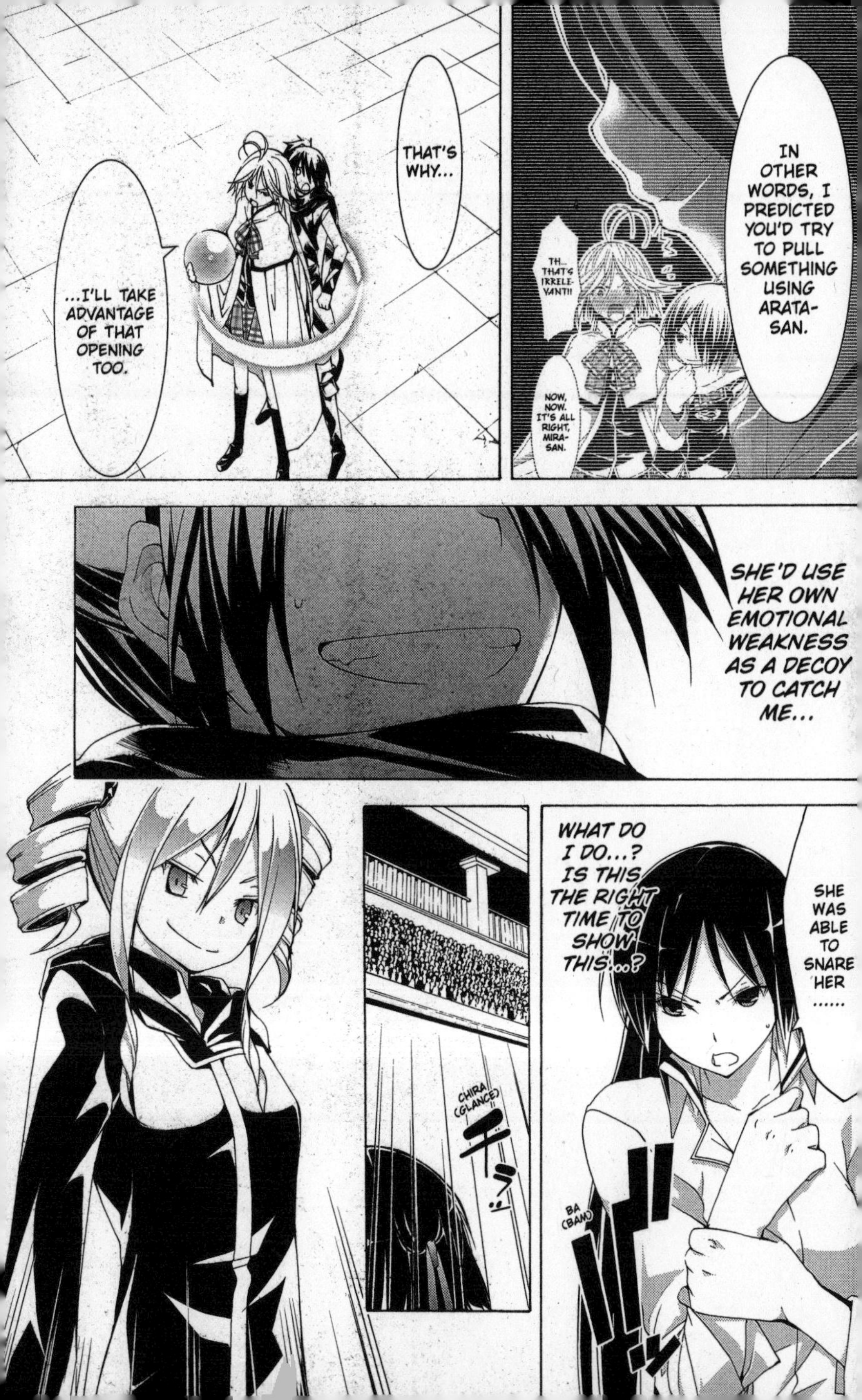
IN OTHER WORDS, I PREDICTED YOU'D TRY TO PULL SOMETHING USING ARATA-SAN.
TH... THAT'S IRRELEVANT!!
NOW, NOW. IT'S ALL RIGHT, MIRA-SAN.
THAT'S WHY...
...I'LL TAKE ADVANTAGE OF THAT OPENING TOO.
SHE'D USE HER OWN EMOTIONAL WEAKNESS AS A DECOY TO CATCH ME...
SHE WAS ABLE TO SNARE HER ......
WHAT DO I DO...? IS THIS THE RIGHT TIME TO SHOW THIS...?
BA (BAM)
CHIRA (GLANCE)

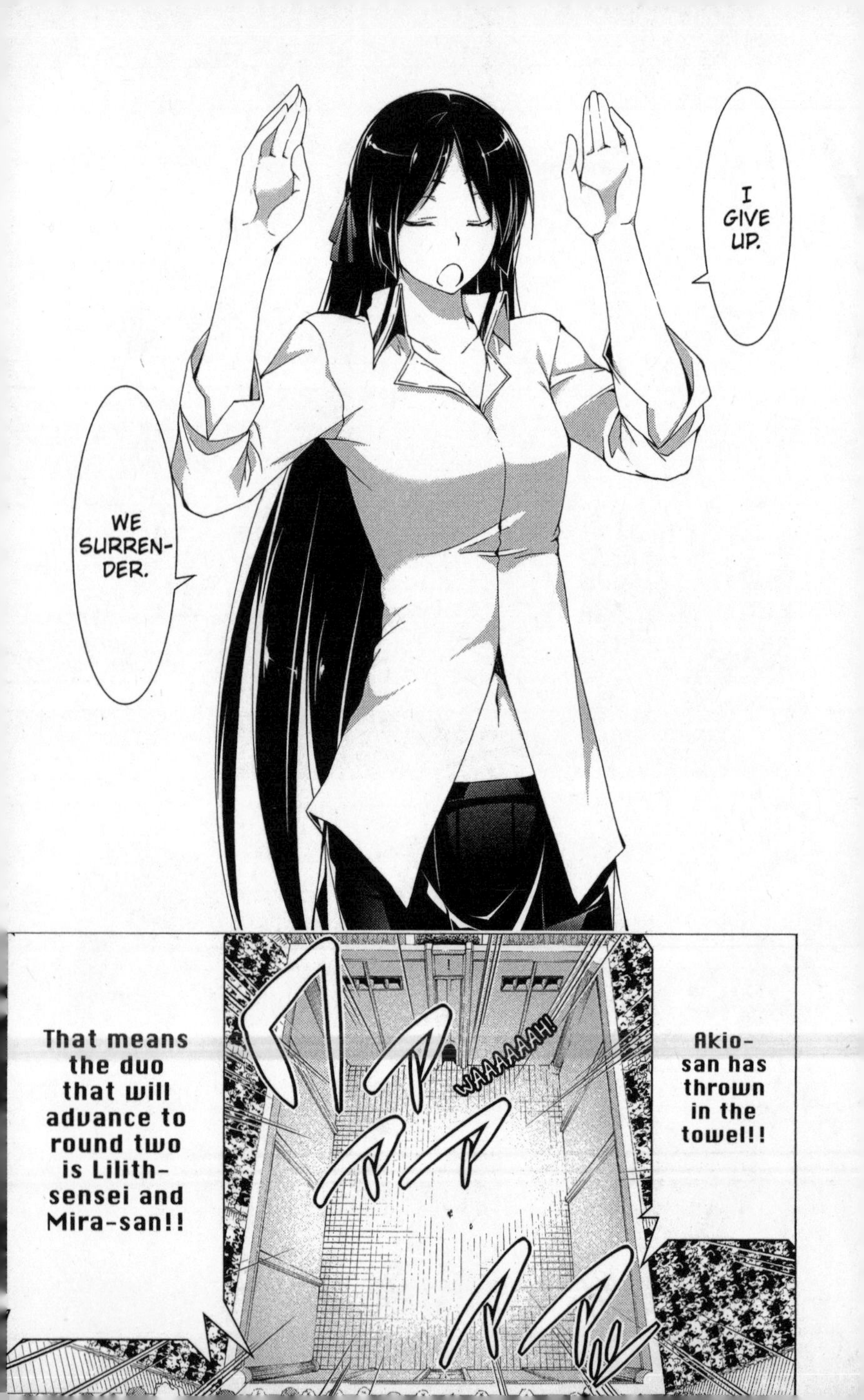

I GIVE UP.
WE SURREN-DER.
Akio-san has thrown in the towel!!
WAAAAAAH!
That means the duo that will advance to round two is Lilith-sensei and Mira-san!!

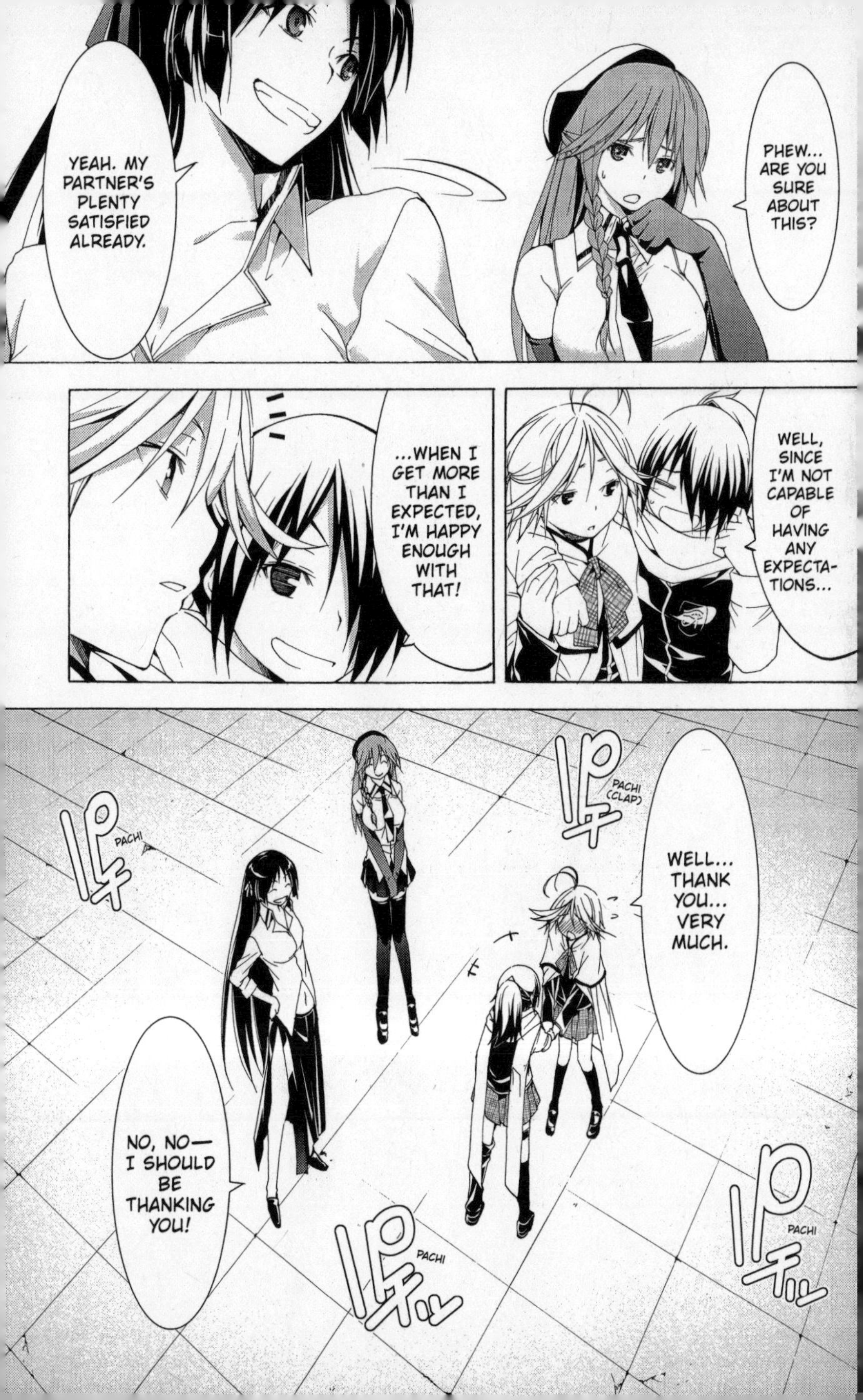
PHEW... ARE YOU SURE ABOUT THIS?
YEAH. MY PARTNER'S PLENTY SATISFIED ALREADY.
WELL, SINCE I'M NOT CAPABLE OF HAVING ANY EXPECTATIONS...
...WHEN I GET MORE THAN I EXPECTED, I'M HAPPY ENOUGH WITH THAT!
PACHI (CLAP)
WELL... THANK YOU... VERY MUCH.
PACHI
PACHI
NO, NO— I SHOULD BE THANKING YOU!
PACHI

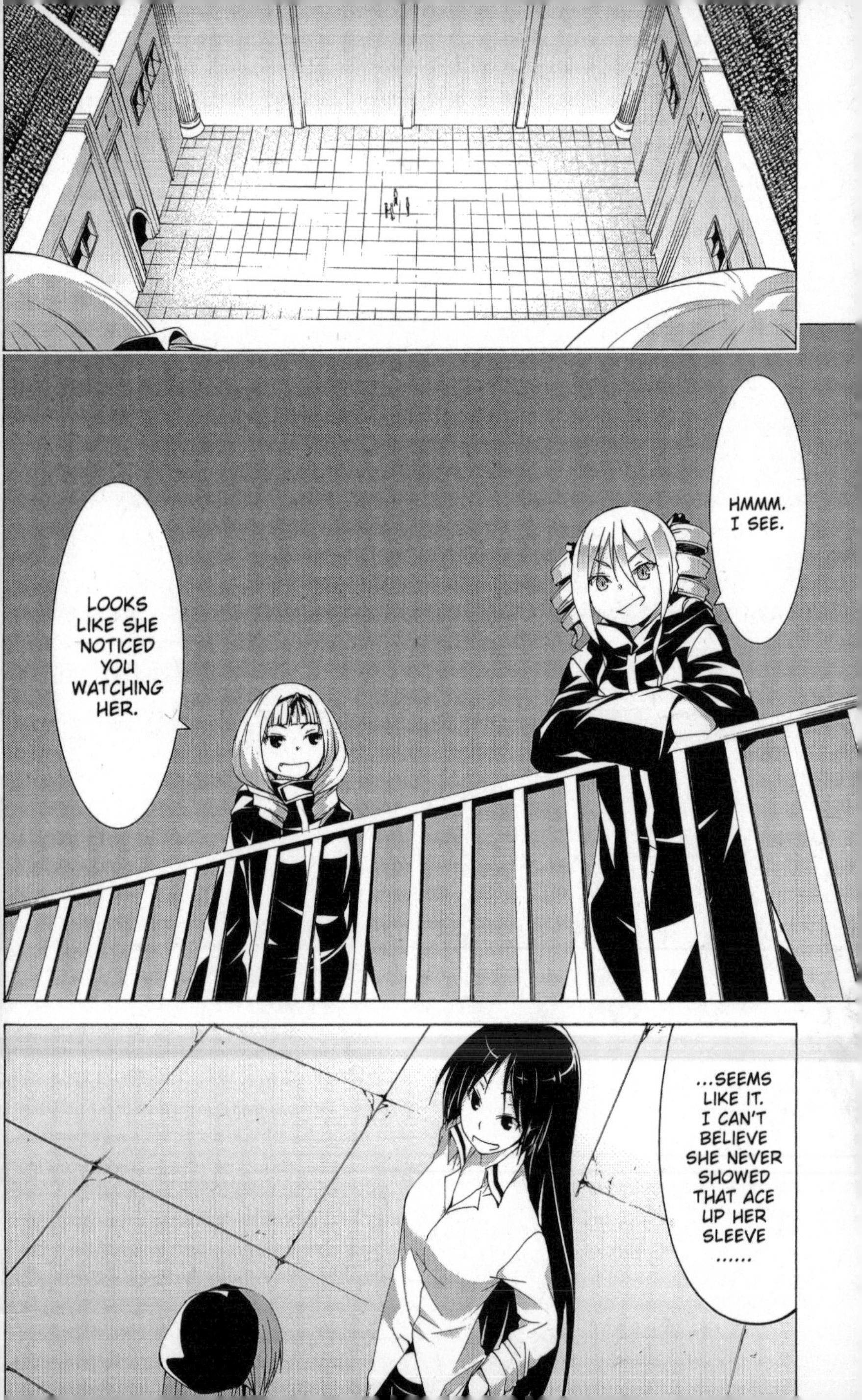
HMMM. I SEE.
LOOKS LIKE SHE NOTICED YOU WATCHING HER.
...SEEMS LIKE IT. I CAN'T BELIEVE SHE NEVER SHOWED THAT ACE UP HER SLEEVE ......

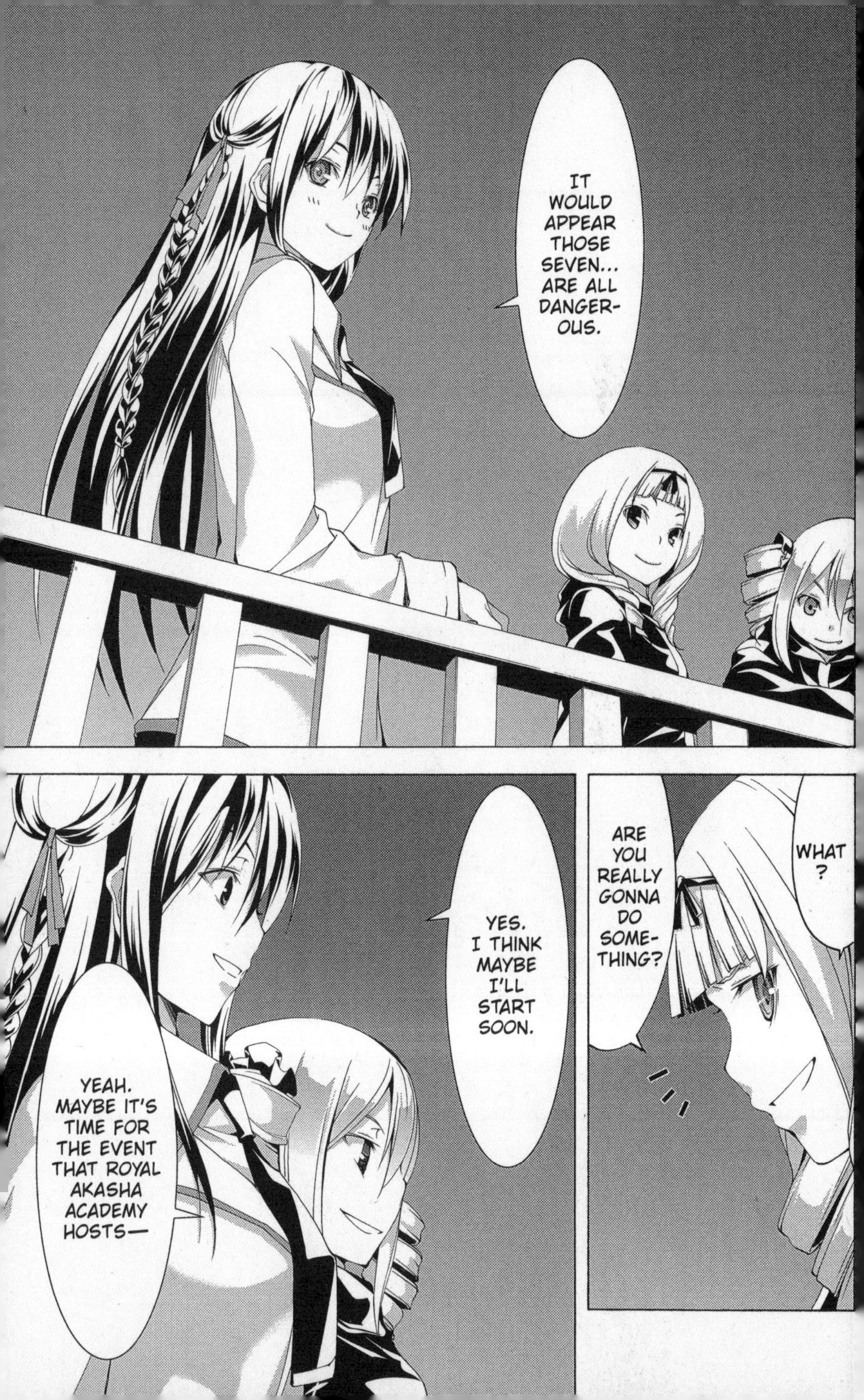
IT WOULD APPEAR THOSE SEVEN... ARE ALL DANGER-OUS.
WHAT?
ARE YOU REALLY GONNA DO SOME-THING?
YES. I THINK MAYBE I'LL START SOON.
YEAH. MAYBE IT'S TIME FOR THE EVENT THAT ROYAL AKASHA ACADEMY HOSTS—

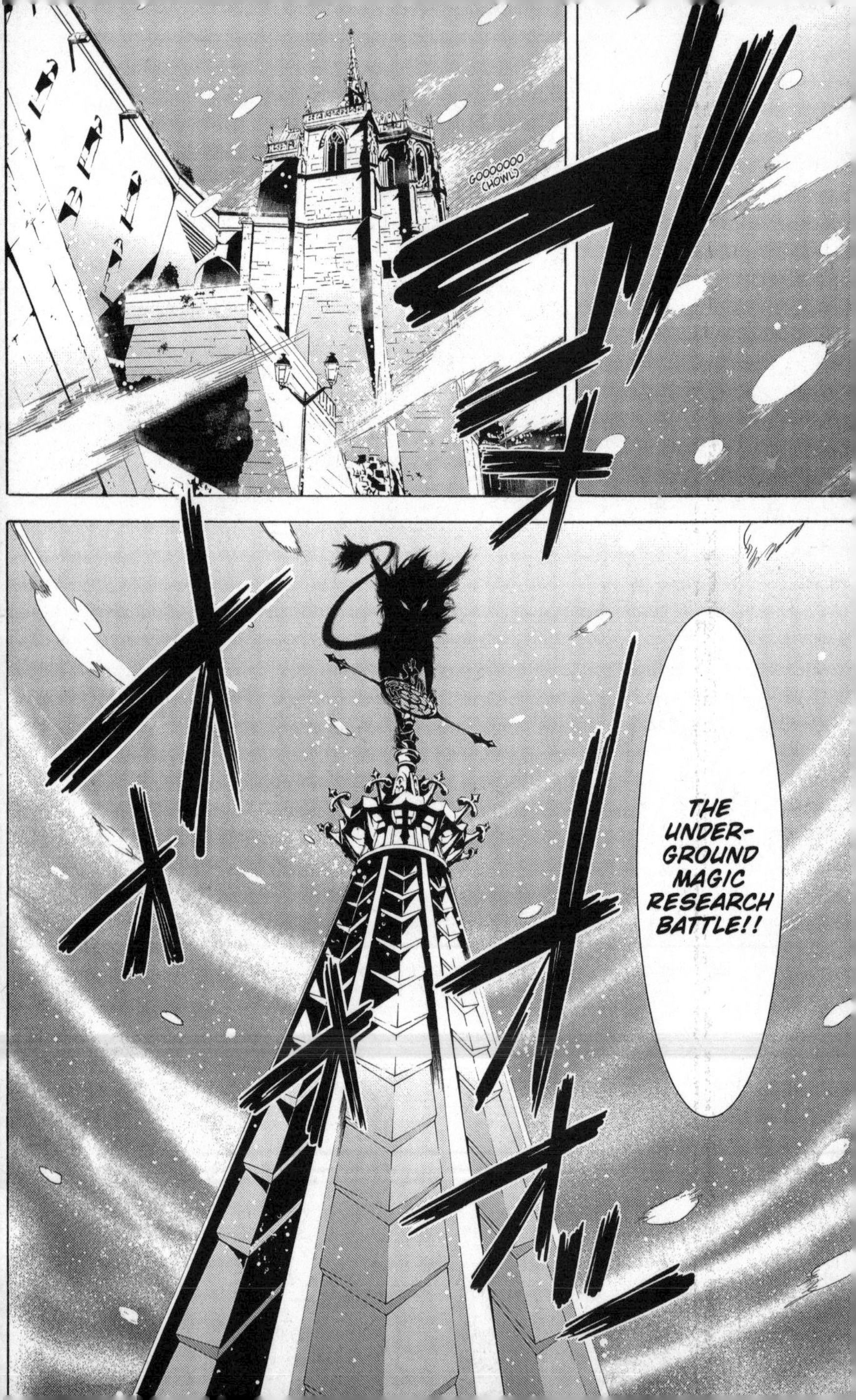
GOOOOOOO (HOWL)
THE UNDER-GROUND MAGIC RESEARCH BATTLE!!

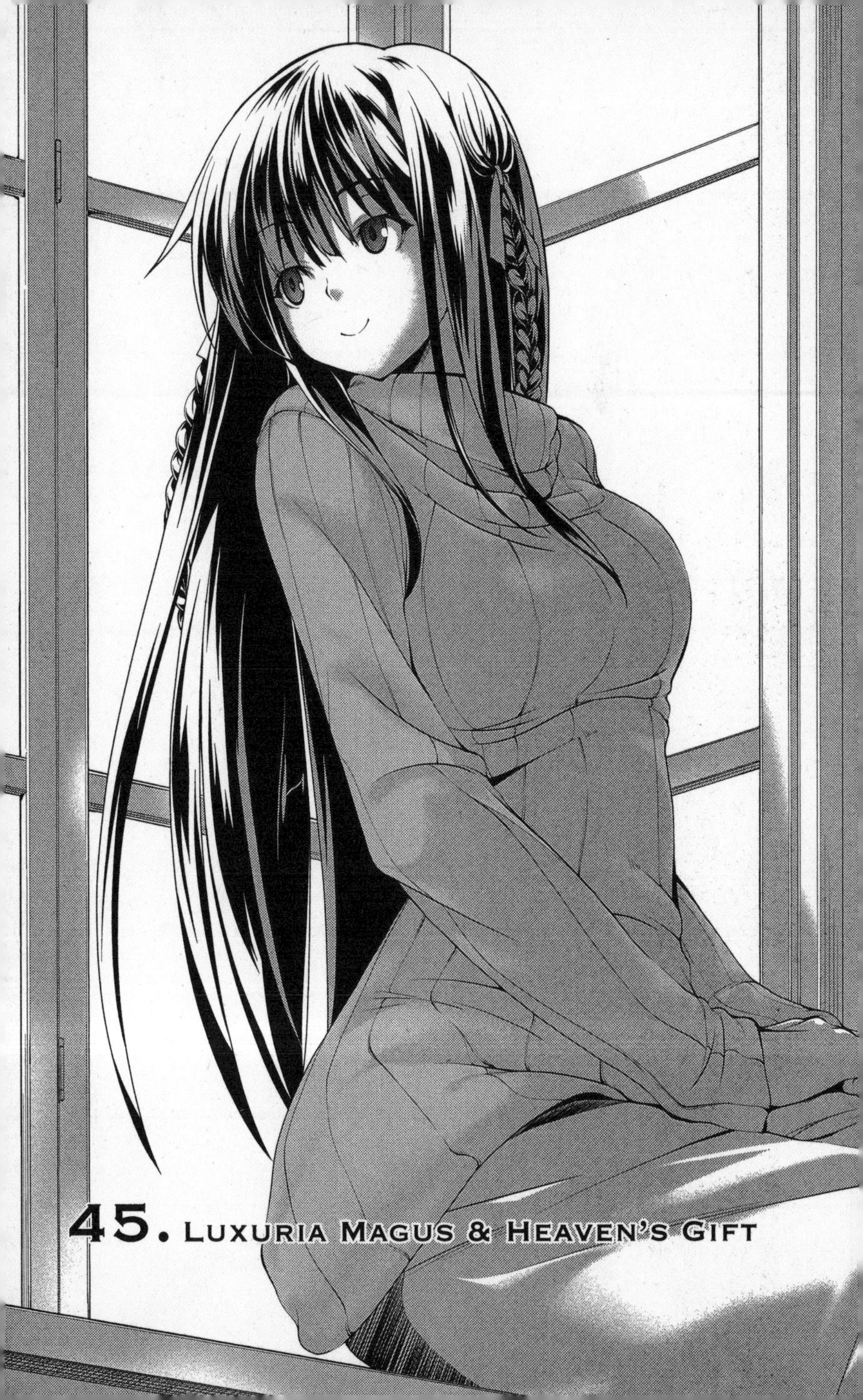

45. Luxuria Magus & Heaven's Gift

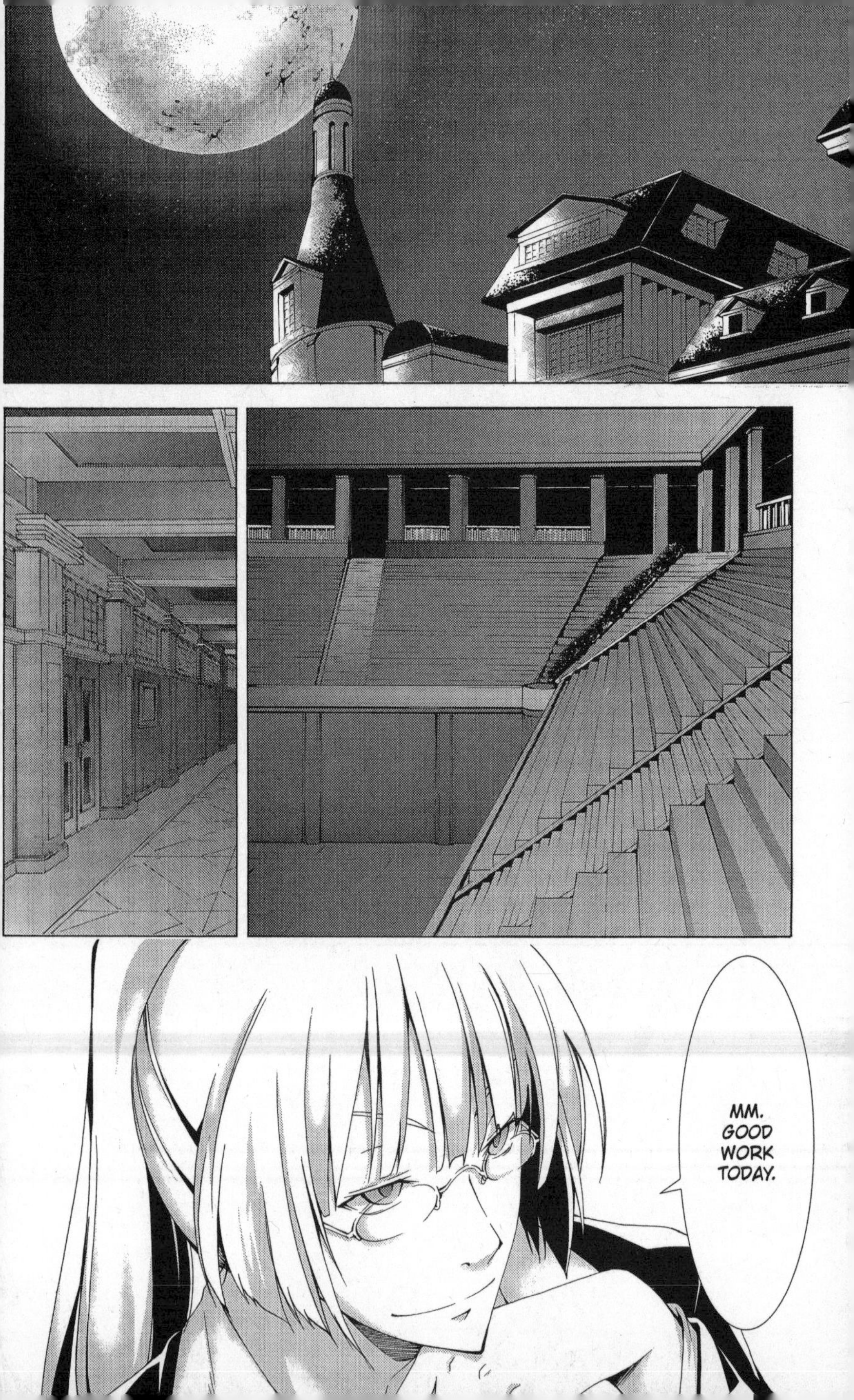
MM. GOOD WORK TODAY.

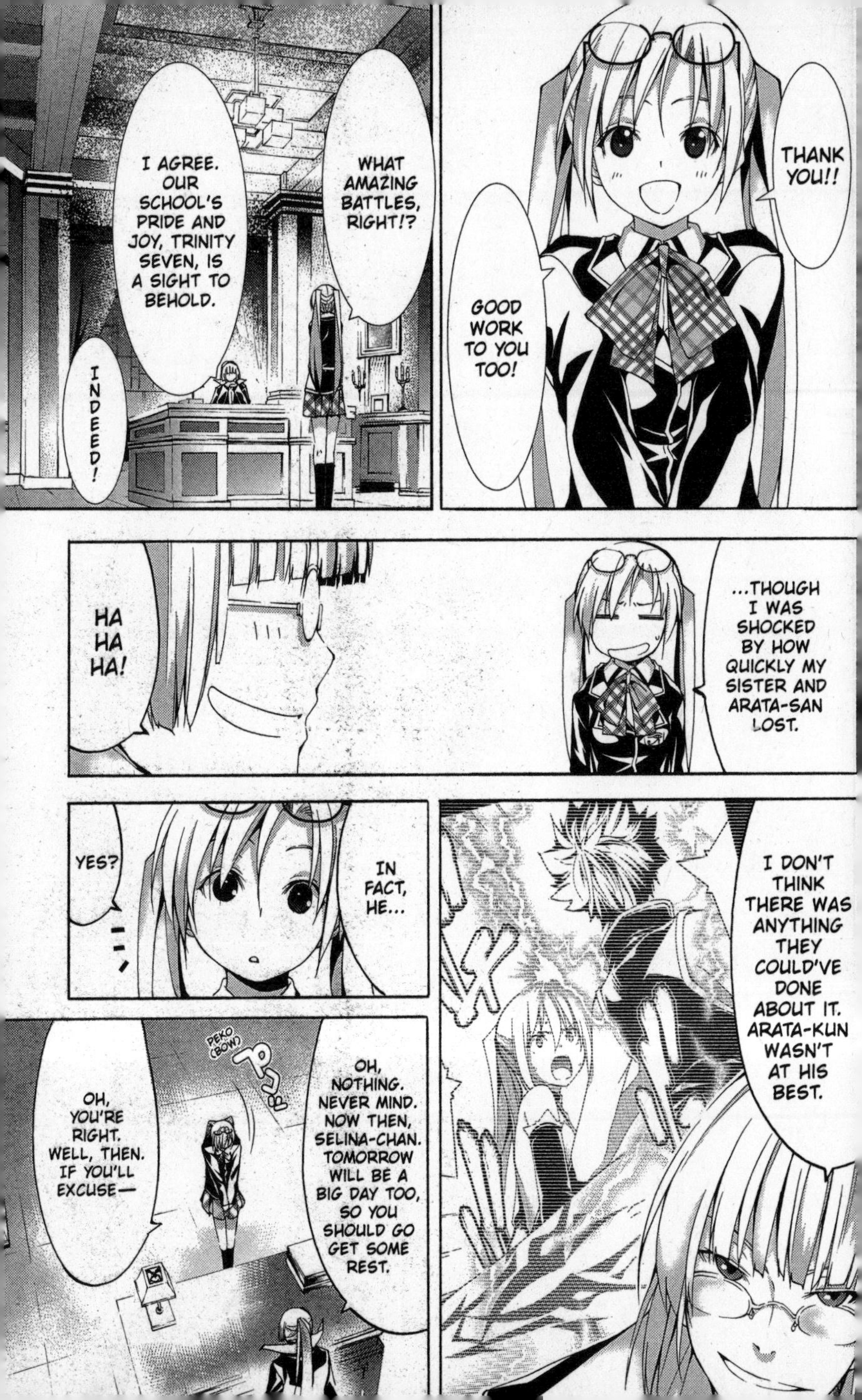
THANK YOU!!
GOOD WORK TO YOU TOO!
WHAT AMAZING BATTLES, RIGHT!?
I AGREE. OUR SCHOOL'S PRIDE AND JOY, TRINITY SEVEN, IS A SIGHT TO BEHOLD.
INDEED!
...THOUGH I WAS SHOCKED BY HOW QUICKLY MY SISTER AND ARATA-SAN LOST.
HA HA HA!
I DON'T THINK THERE WAS ANYTHING THEY COULD'VE DONE ABOUT IT. ARATA-KUN WASN'T AT HIS BEST.
IN FACT, HE...
YES?
OH, NOTHING. NEVER MIND. NOW THEN, SELINA-CHAN. TOMORROW WILL BE A BIG DAY TOO, SO YOU SHOULD GO GET SOME REST.
PEKO (BOW)
OH, YOU'RE RIGHT. WELL, THEN. IF YOU'LL EXCUSE—

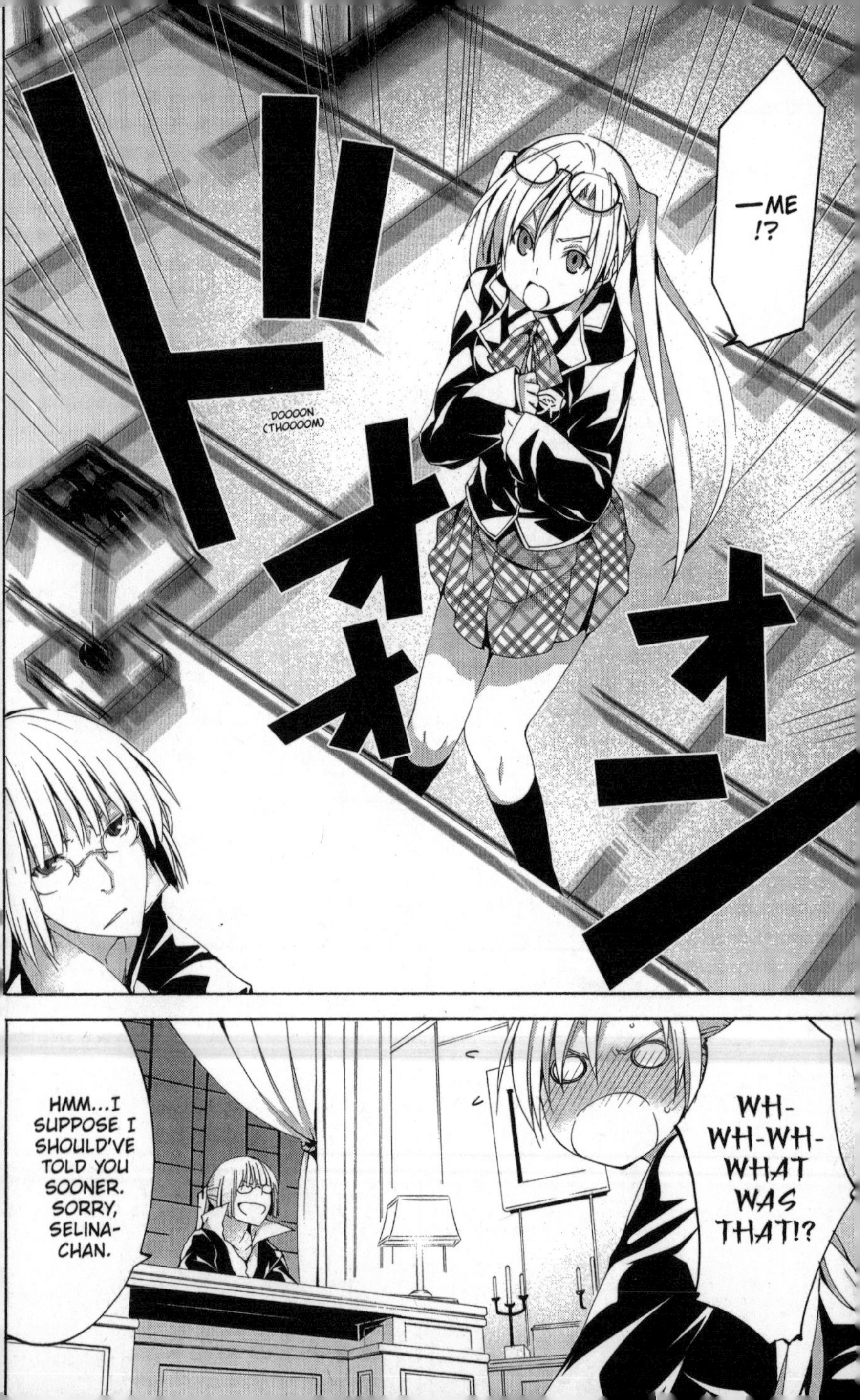
—ME !?
DOOOON (THOOOOM)
WH-WH-WH-WHAT WAS THAT!?
HMM...I SUPPOSE I SHOULD'VE TOLD YOU SOONER. SORRY, SELINA-CHAN.

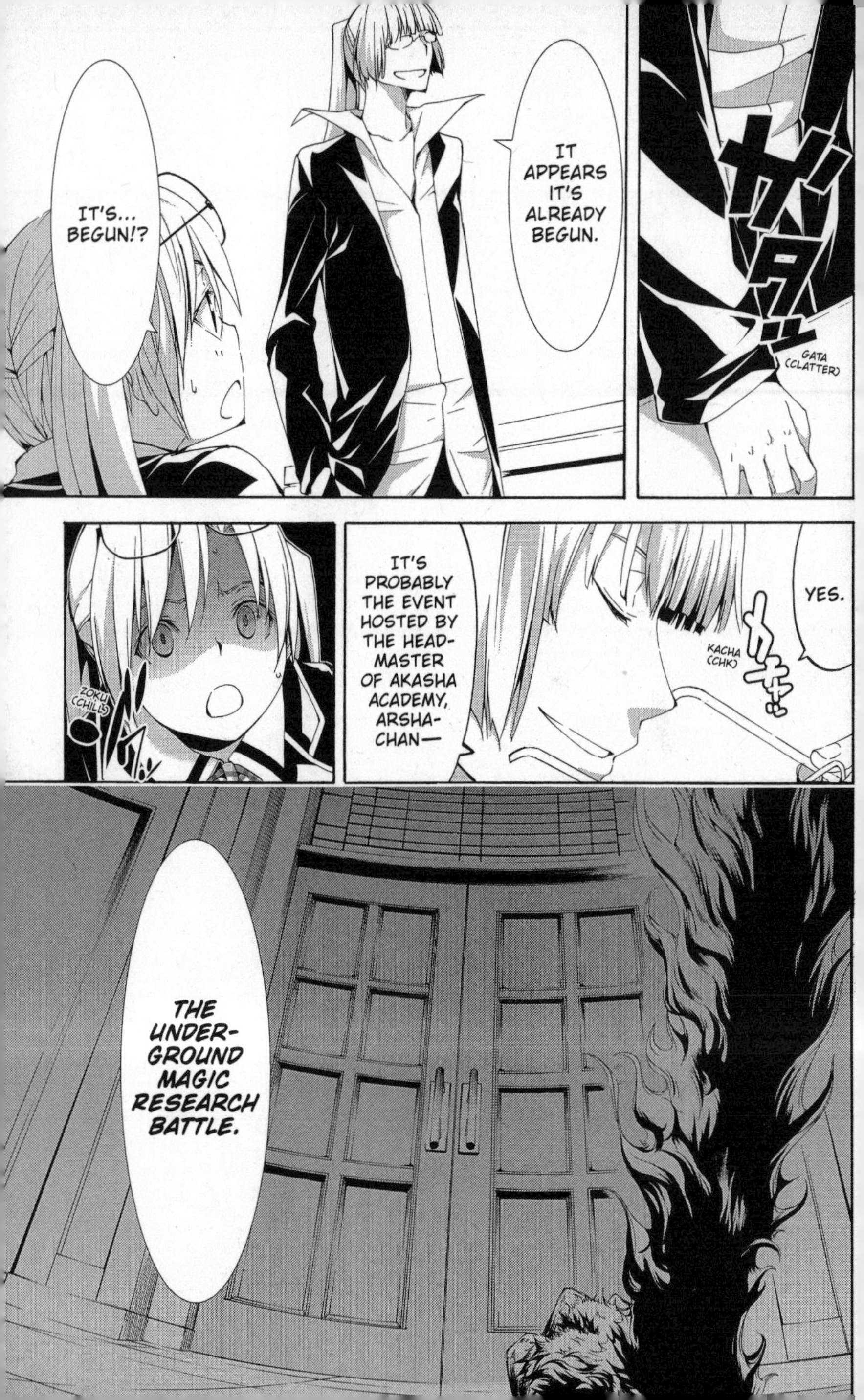
GATA (CLATTER)
IT APPEARS IT'S ALREADY BEGUN.
IT'S... BEGUN!?
YES.
KACHA (CHK)
IT'S PROBABLY THE EVENT HOSTED BY THE HEAD-MASTER OF AKASHA ACADEMY, ARSHA-CHAN—
ZOKU (CHILL)
THE UNDER-GROUND MAGIC RESEARCH BATTLE.

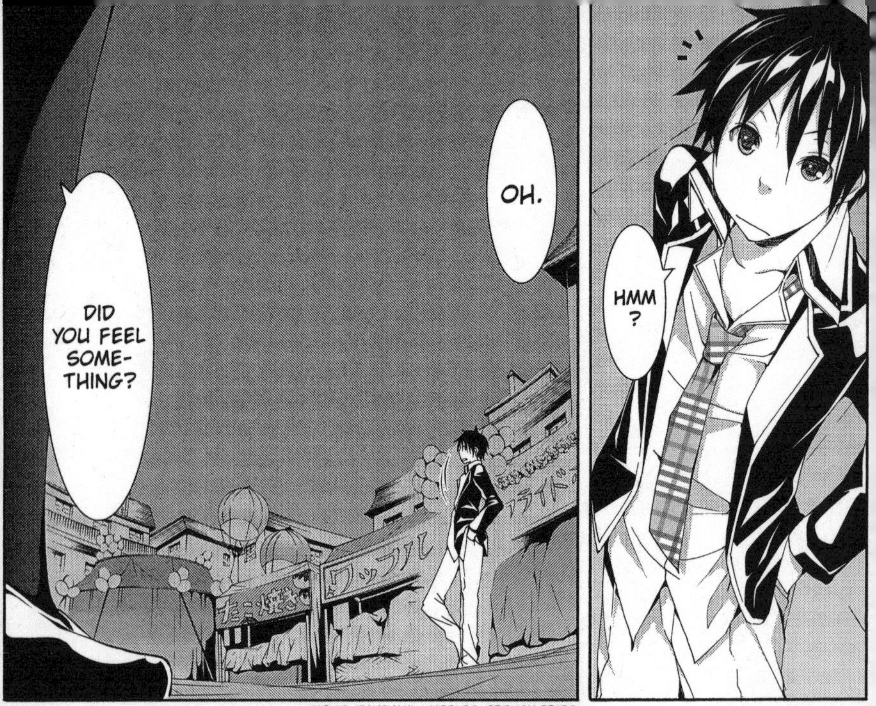
HMM ?
OH.
DID YOU FEEL SOMETHING?
SIGNS: TAKOYAKI, WAFFLES, FRENCH FRIES

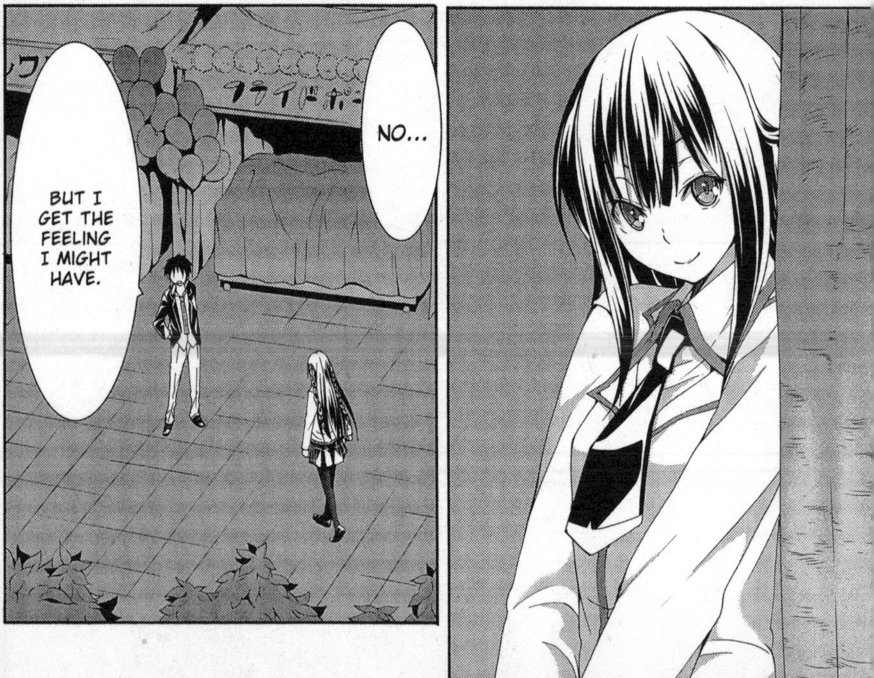
NO...
BUT I GET THE FEELING I MIGHT HAVE.

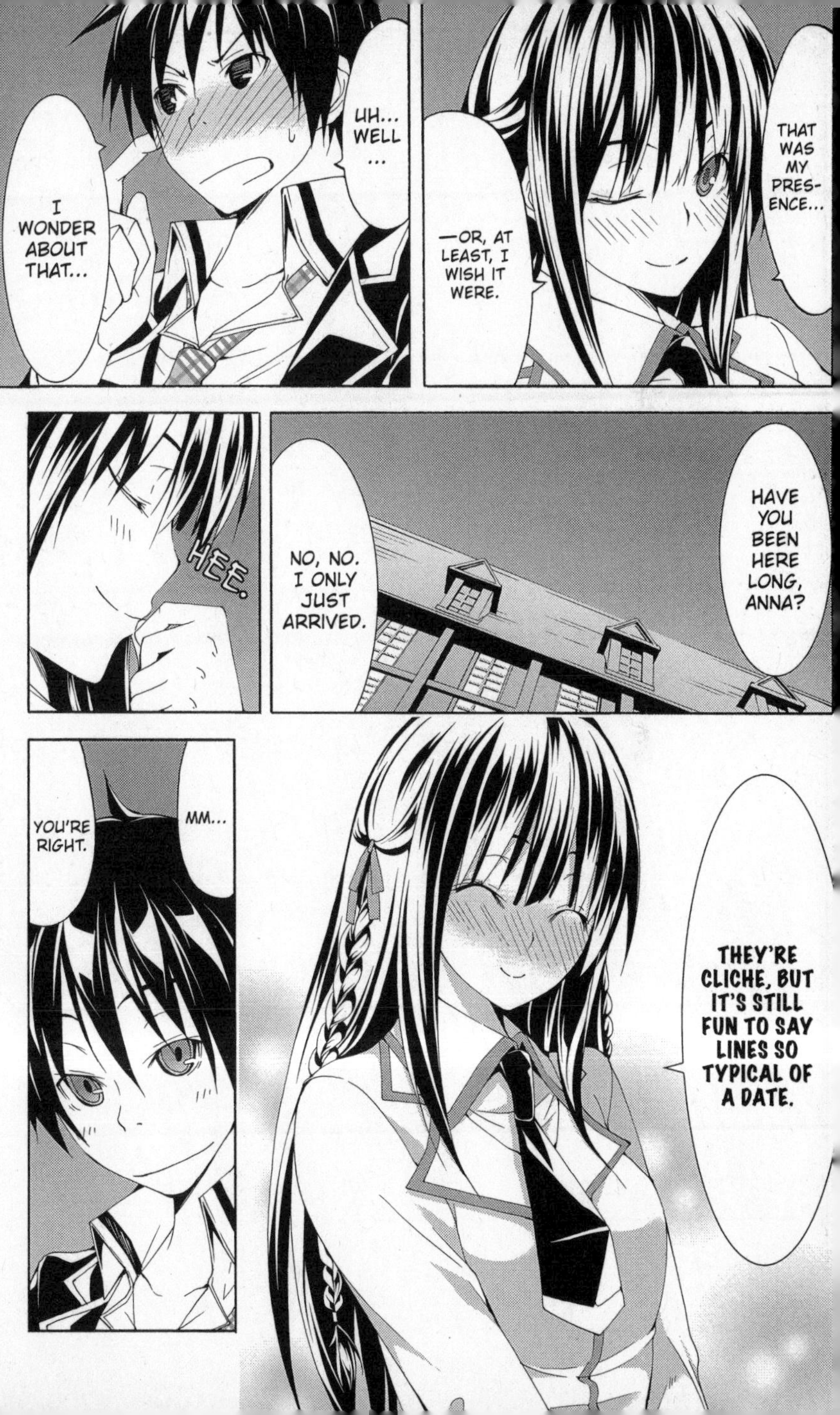

THAT WAS MY PRESENCE...
—OR, AT LEAST, I WISH IT WERE.
UH... WELL ...
I WONDER ABOUT THAT...
HAVE YOU BEEN HERE LONG, ANNA?
NO, NO. I ONLY JUST ARRIVED.
HEE.
THEY'RE CLICHE, BUT IT'S STILL FUN TO SAY LINES SO TYPICAL OF A DATE.
MM...
YOU'RE RIGHT.

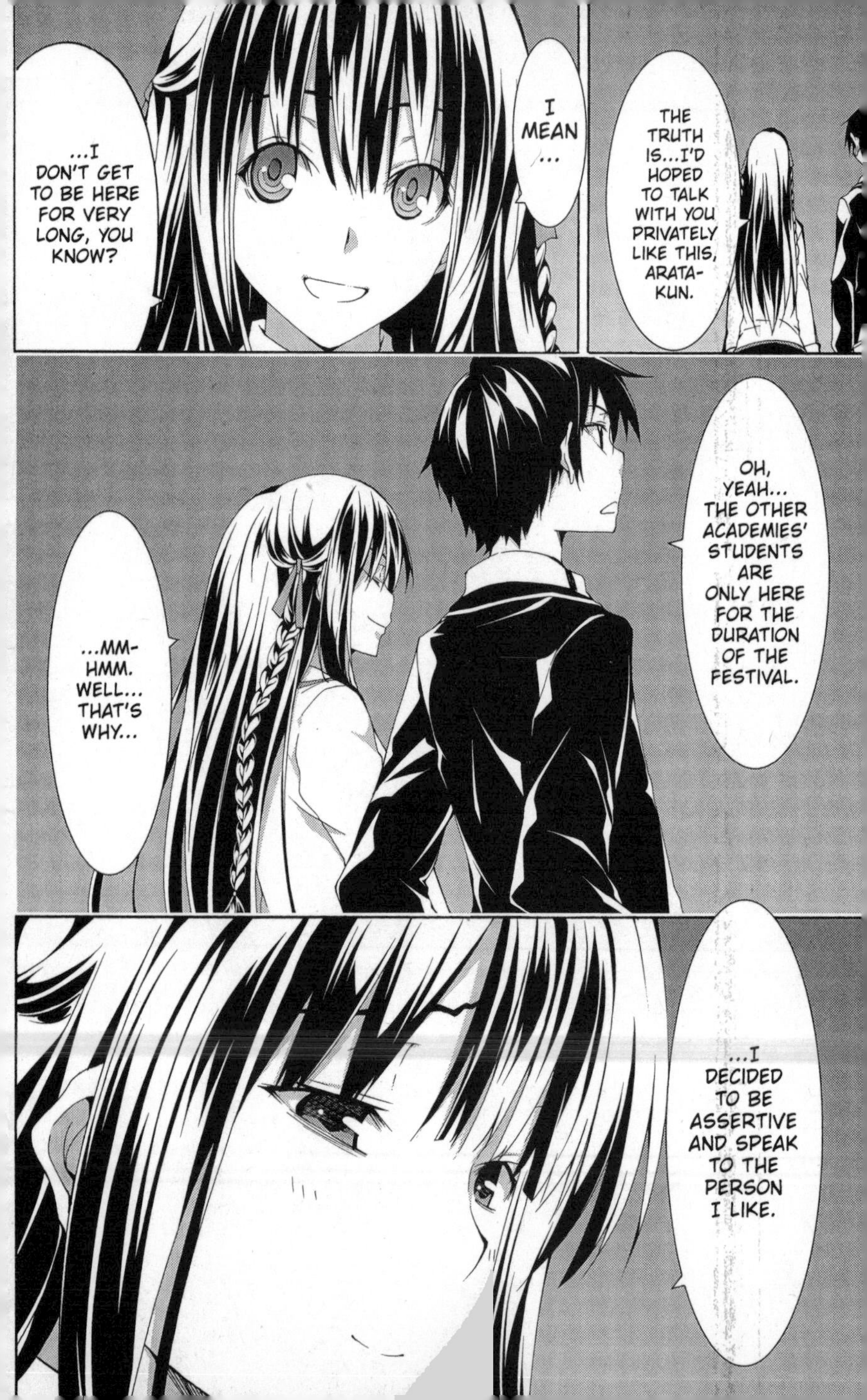
THE TRUTH IS...I'D HOPED TO TALK WITH YOU PRIVATELY LIKE THIS, ARATA-KUN.
I MEAN...
...I DON'T GET TO BE HERE FOR VERY LONG, YOU KNOW?
OH, YEAH... THE OTHER ACADEMIES' STUDENTS ARE ONLY HERE FOR THE DURATION OF THE FESTIVAL.
...MM-HMM. WELL... THAT'S WHY...
...I DECIDED TO BE ASSERTIVE AND SPEAK TO THE PERSON I LIKE.

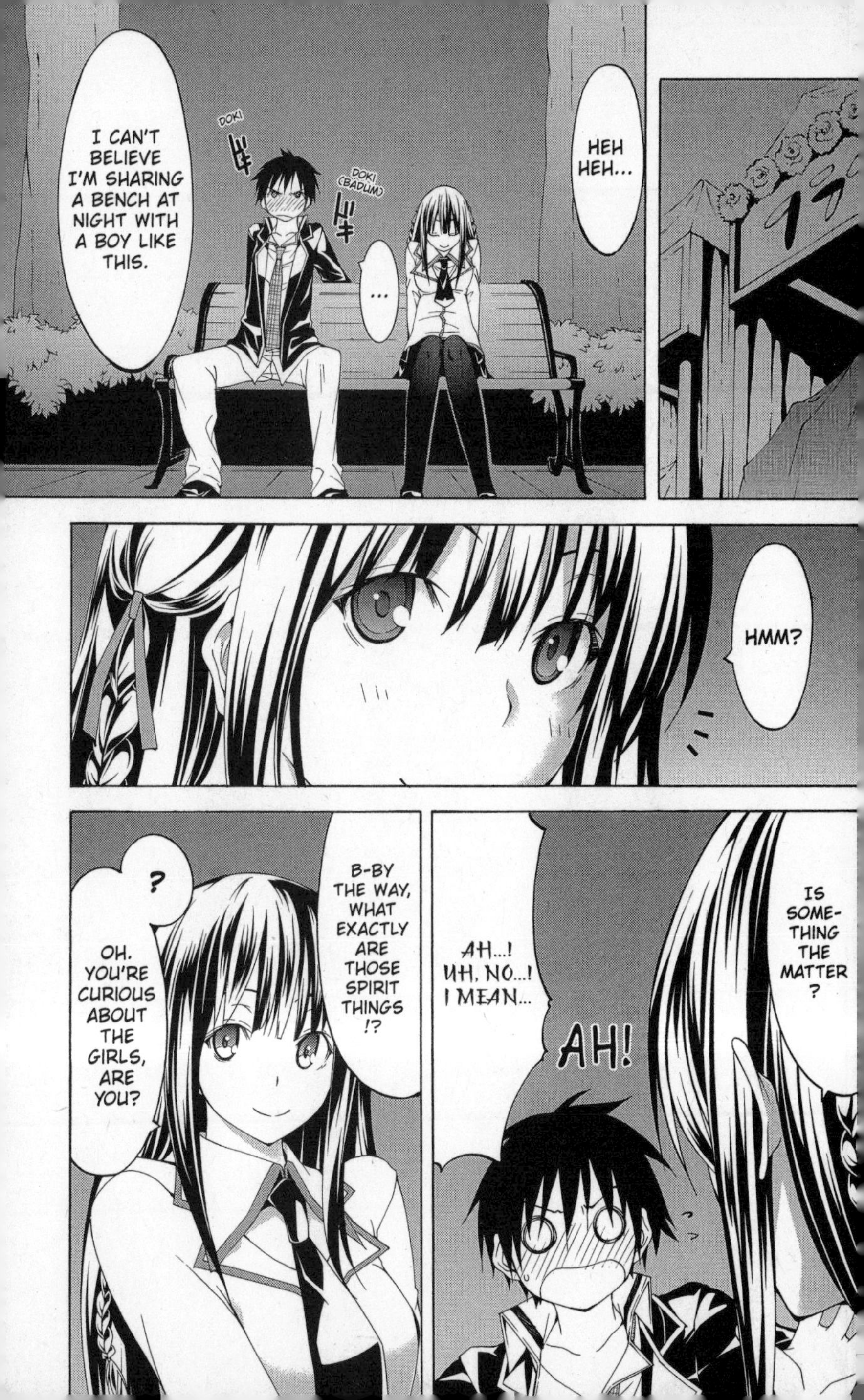
HEH HEH...
DOKI (BADUM)
...
DOKI
I CAN'T BELIEVE I'M SHARING A BENCH AT NIGHT WITH A BOY LIKE THIS.
HMM?
IS SOMETHING THE MATTER?
AH!
AH...! UH, NO...! I MEAN...
B-BY THE WAY, WHAT EXACTLY ARE THOSE SPIRIT THINGS!?
?
OH. YOU'RE CURIOUS ABOUT THE GIRLS, ARE YOU?

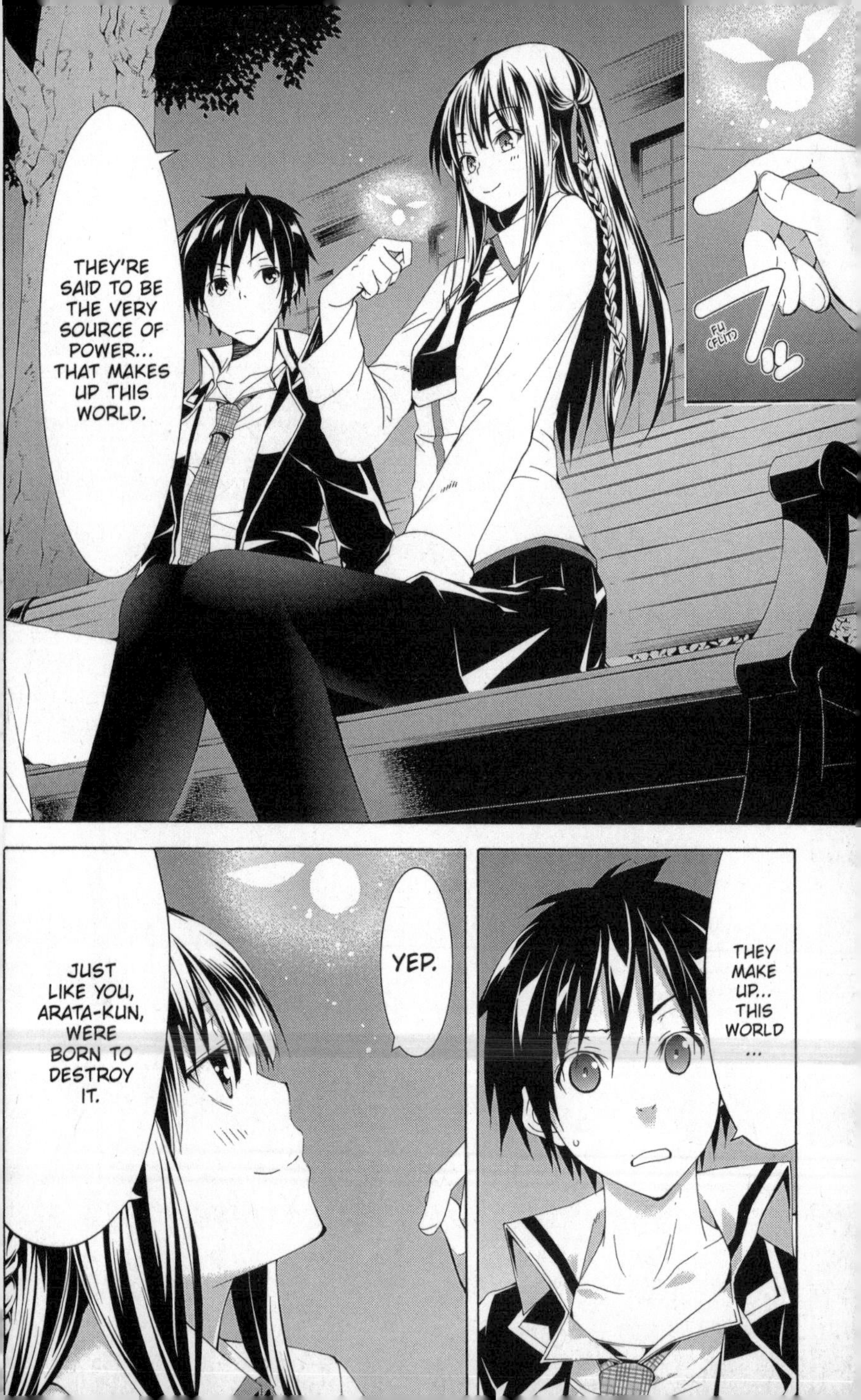
FU (FLIT)
THEY'RE SAID TO BE THE VERY SOURCE OF POWER... THAT MAKES UP THIS WORLD.
THEY MAKE UP... THIS WORLD ...
YEP.
JUST LIKE YOU, ARATA-KUN, WERE BORN TO DESTROY IT.

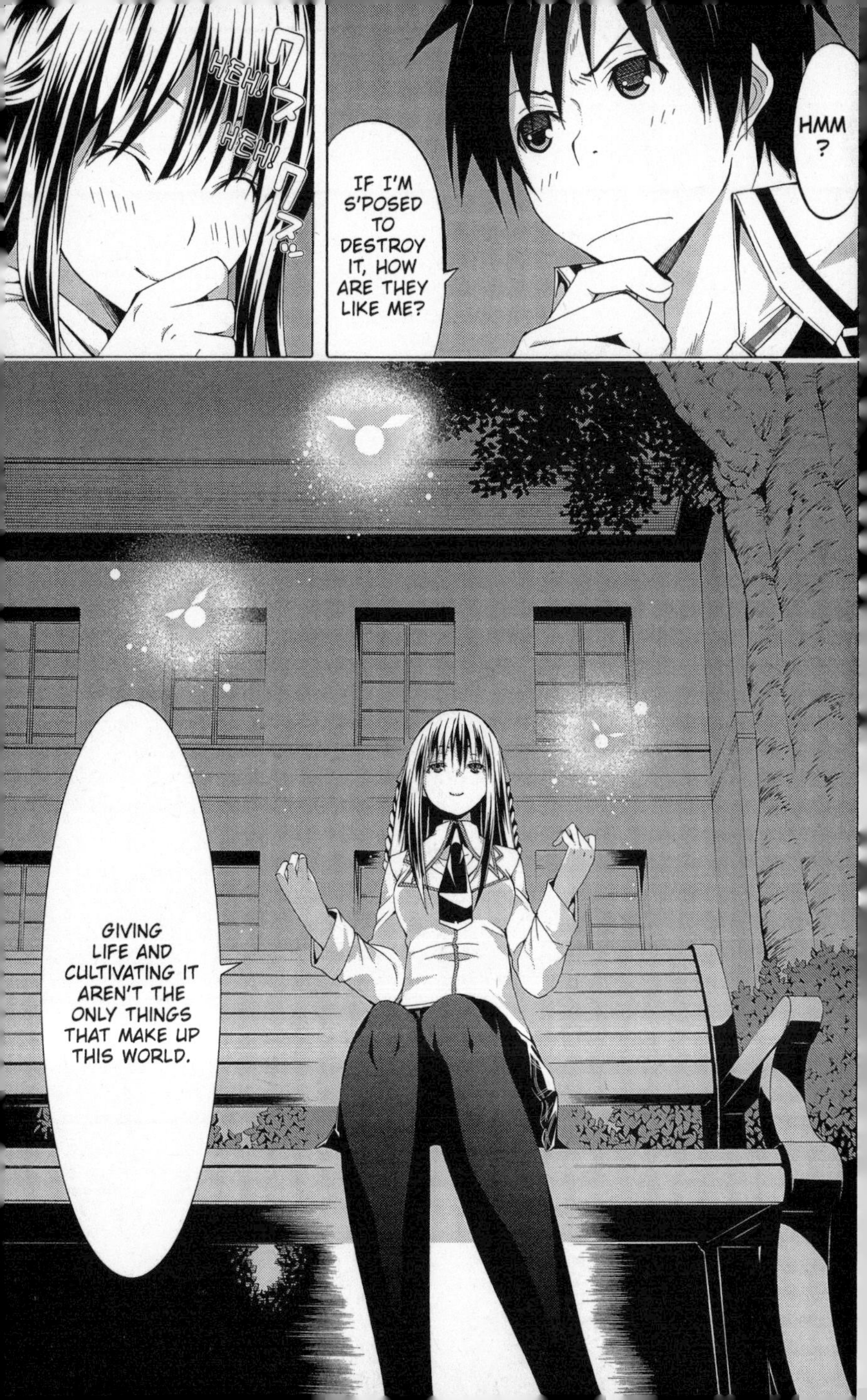
HMM ?
IF I'M S'POSED TO DESTROY IT, HOW ARE THEY LIKE ME?
HEH! HEH!
GIVING LIFE AND CULTIVATING IT AREN'T THE ONLY THINGS THAT MAKE UP THIS WORLD.

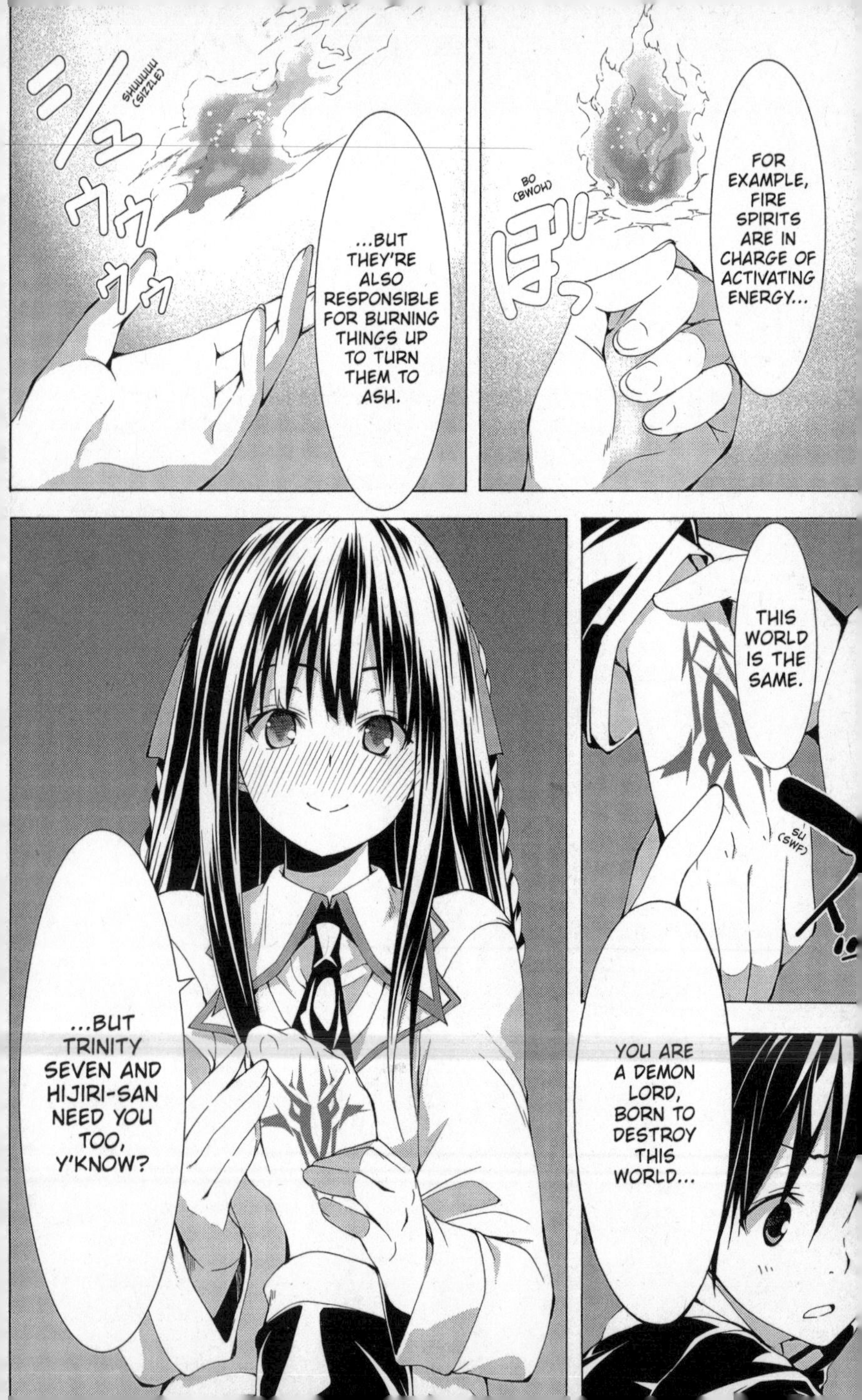
FOR EXAMPLE, FIRE SPIRITS ARE IN CHARGE OF ACTIVATING ENERGY...
BO (BWOH)
ぼっ
...BUT THEY'RE ALSO RESPONSIBLE FOR BURNING THINGS UP TO TURN THEM TO ASH.
SHUUUUU (SIZZLE)
シュウウウ
THIS WORLD IS THE SAME.
SU (SWF)
YOU ARE A DEMON LORD, BORN TO DESTROY THIS WORLD...
...BUT TRINITY SEVEN AND HIJIRI-SAN NEED YOU TOO, Y'KNOW?

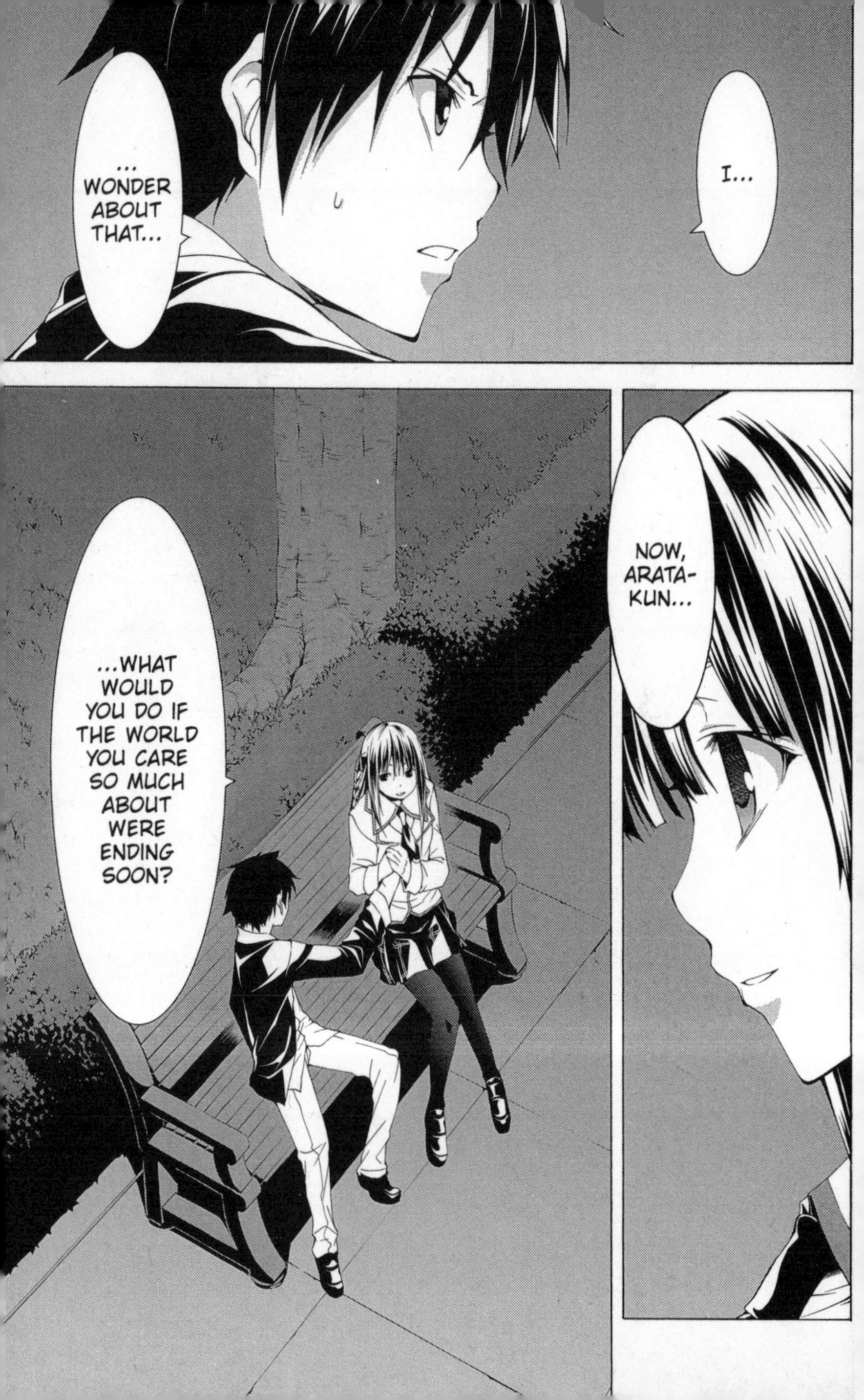
I...
...WONDER ABOUT THAT...
NOW, ARATA-KUN...
...WHAT WOULD YOU DO IF THE WORLD YOU CARE SO MUCH ABOUT WERE ENDING SOON?

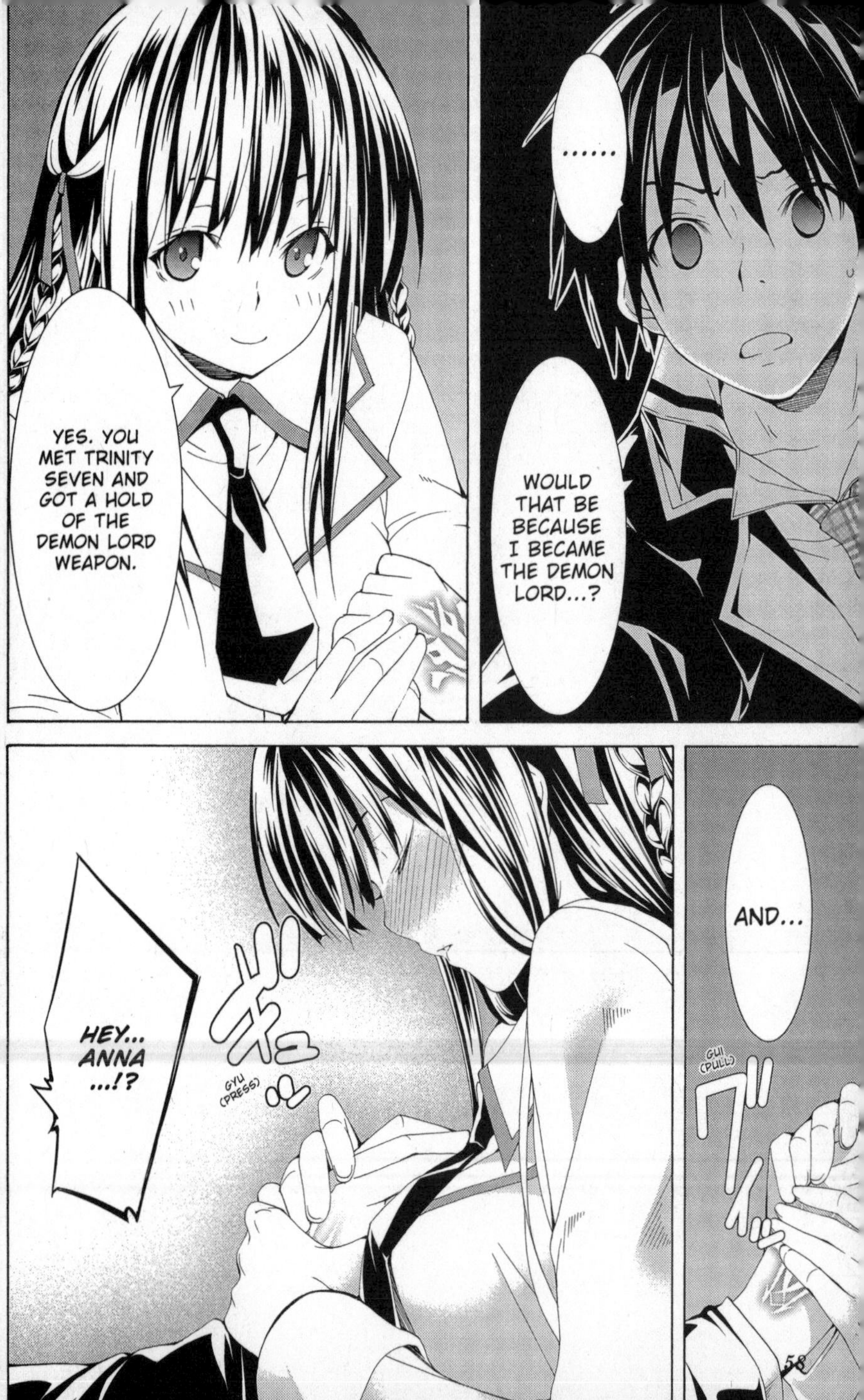
......
WOULD THAT BE BECAUSE I BECAME THE DEMON LORD...?
YES. YOU MET TRINITY SEVEN AND GOT A HOLD OF THE DEMON LORD WEAPON.
AND...
GUI (PULL)
GYU (PRESS)
HEY... ANNA ...!?

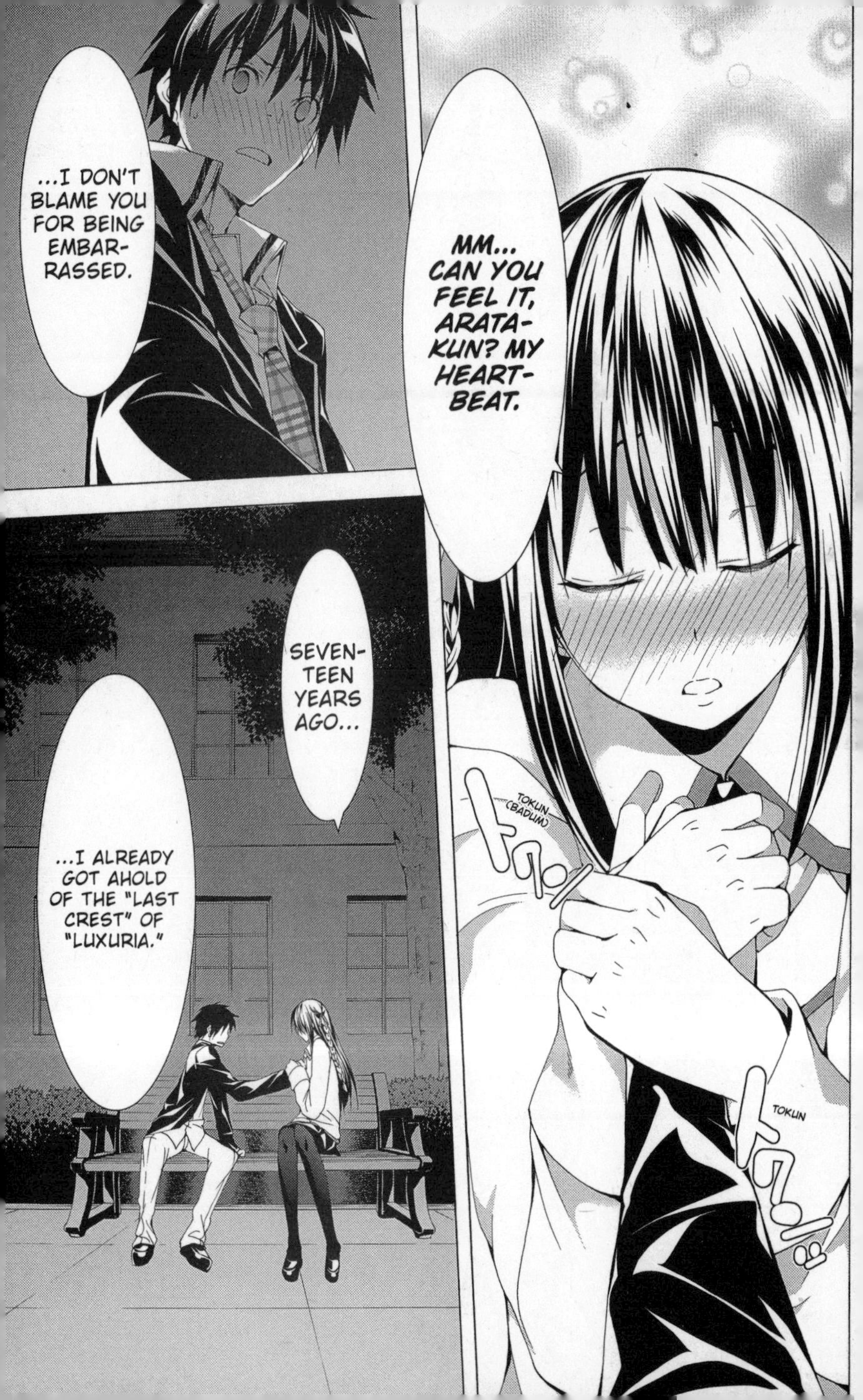
MM... CAN YOU FEEL IT, ARATA-KUN? MY HEART-BEAT.
TOKUN (BADUM)
TOKUN
...I DON'T BLAME YOU FOR BEING EMBAR-RASSED.
SEVEN-TEEN YEARS AGO...
...I ALREADY GOT AHOLD OF THE "LAST CREST" OF "LUXURIA."

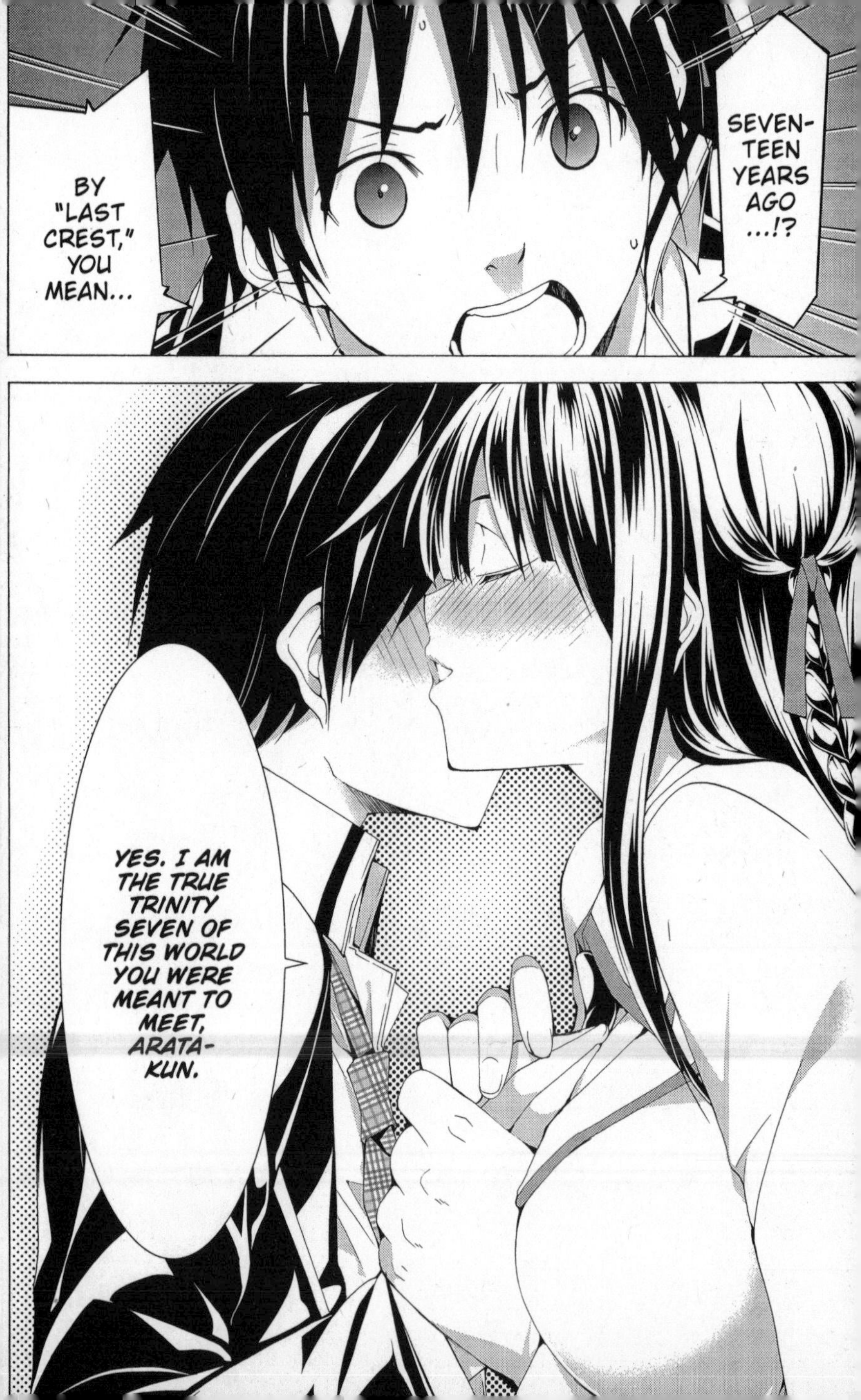
SEVEN-TEEN YEARS AGO ...!?
BY "LAST CREST," YOU MEAN...
YES. I AM THE TRUE TRINITY SEVEN OF THIS WORLD YOU WERE MEANT TO MEET, ARATA-KUN.

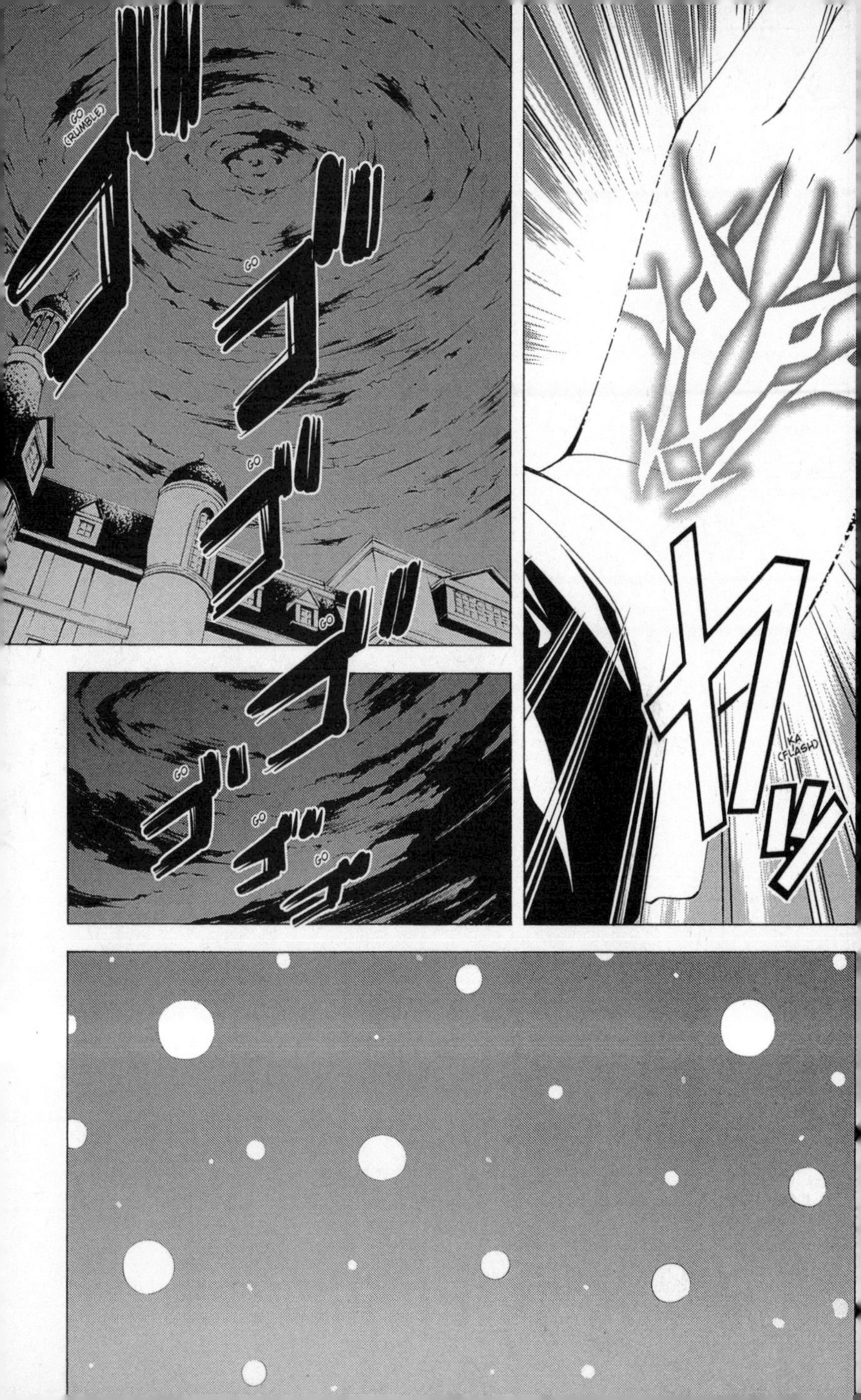
KA (FLASH)
GO (RUMBLE)
GO
GO
GO
GO
GO
GO

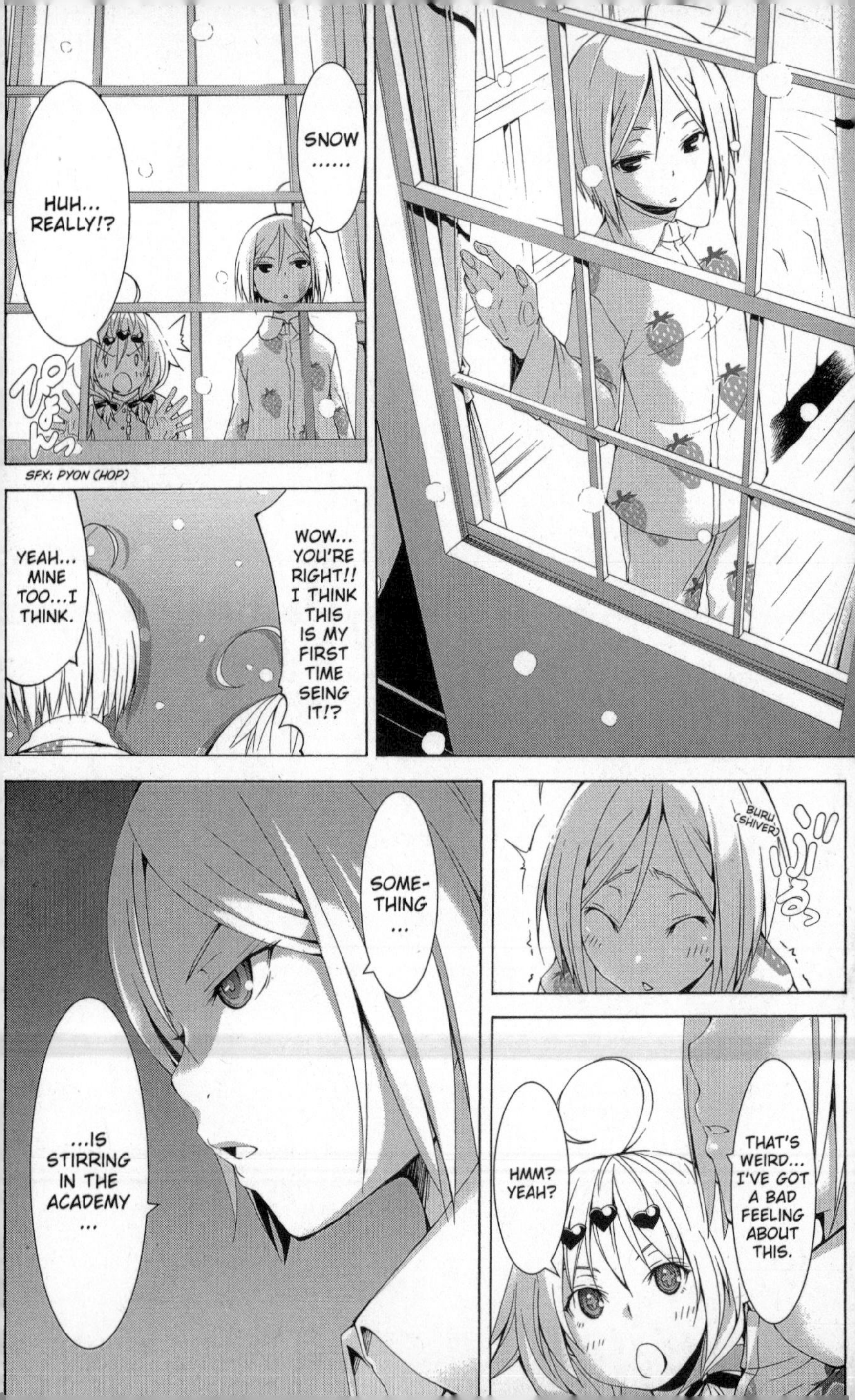
SNOW ......
HUH... REALLY!?
SFX: PYON (HOP)
WOW... YOU'RE RIGHT!! I THINK THIS IS MY FIRST TIME SEING IT!?
YEAH... MINE TOO...I THINK.
BURU (SHIVER)
THAT'S WEIRD... I'VE GOT A BAD FEELING ABOUT THIS.
HMM? YEAH?
SOME-THING ...
...IS STIRRING IN THE ACADEMY ...

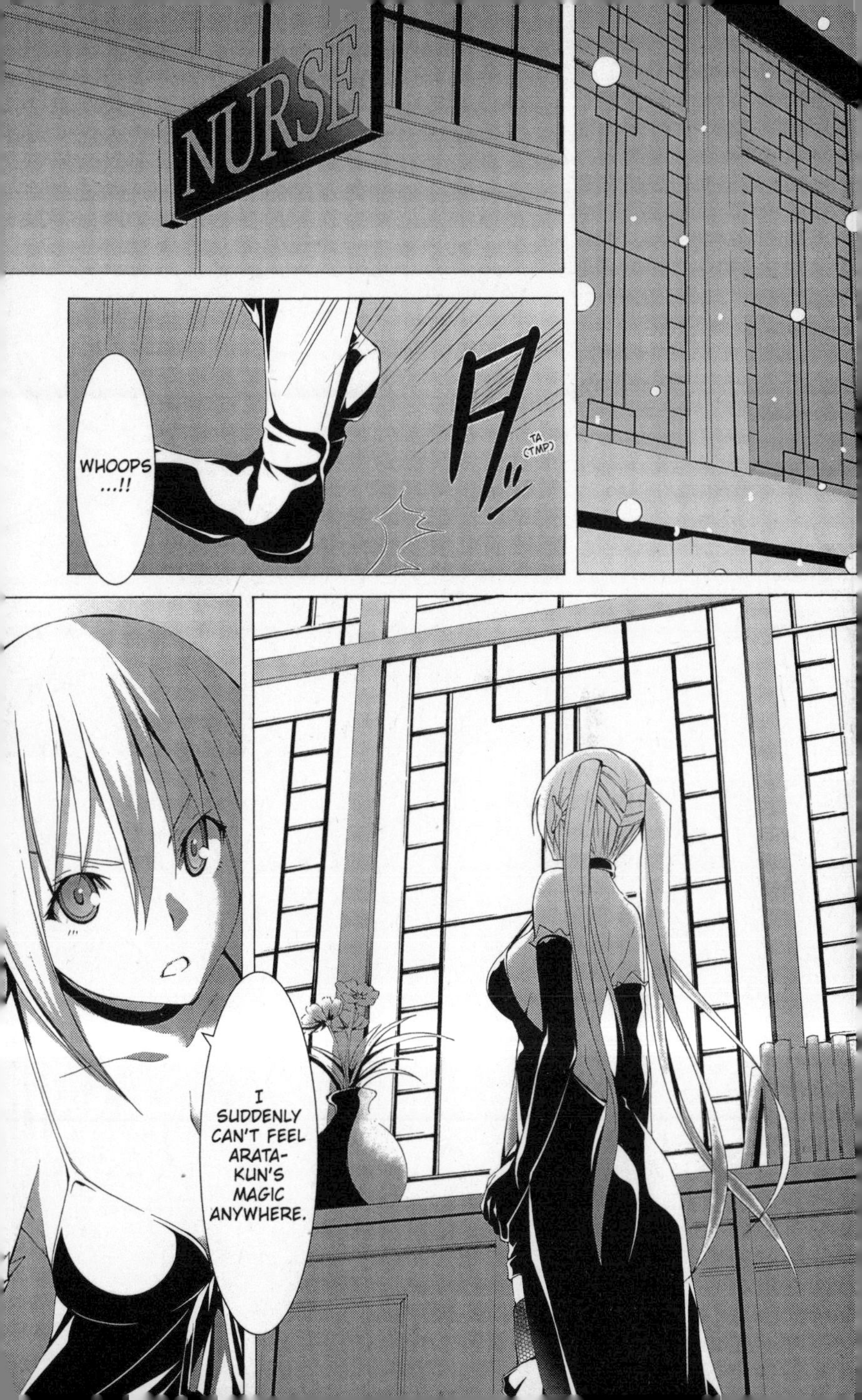
NURSE
TA (TMP)
WHOOPS ...!!
I SUDDENLY CAN'T FEEL ARATA-KUN'S MAGIC ANYWHERE.

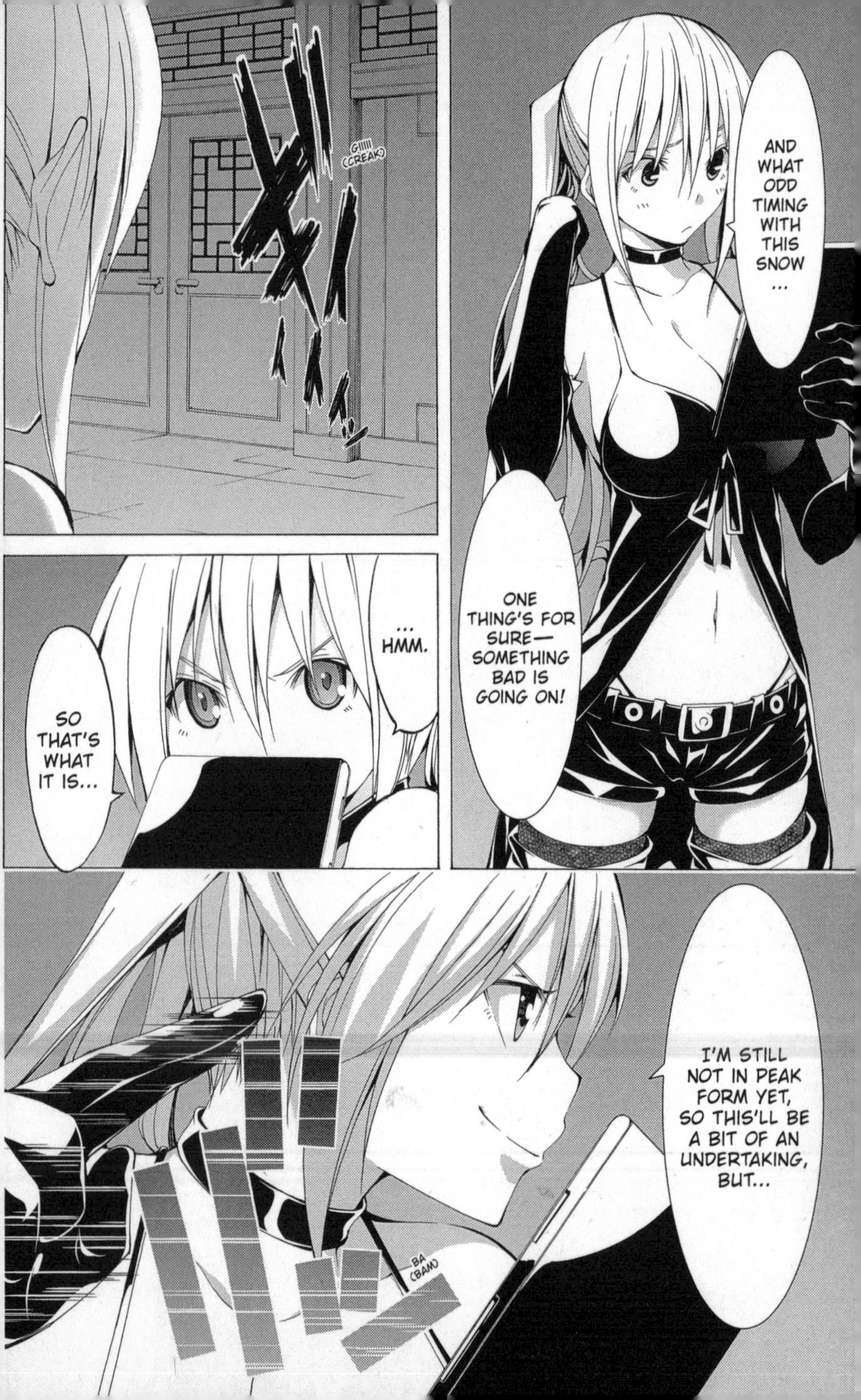
AND WHAT ODD TIMING WITH THIS SNOW...
ONE THING'S FOR SURE—SOMETHING BAD IS GOING ON!
GIIII (CREAK)
...HMM.
SO THAT'S WHAT IT IS...
I'M STILL NOT IN PEAK FORM YET, SO THIS'LL BE A BIT OF AN UNDERTAKING, BUT...
BA (BAM)

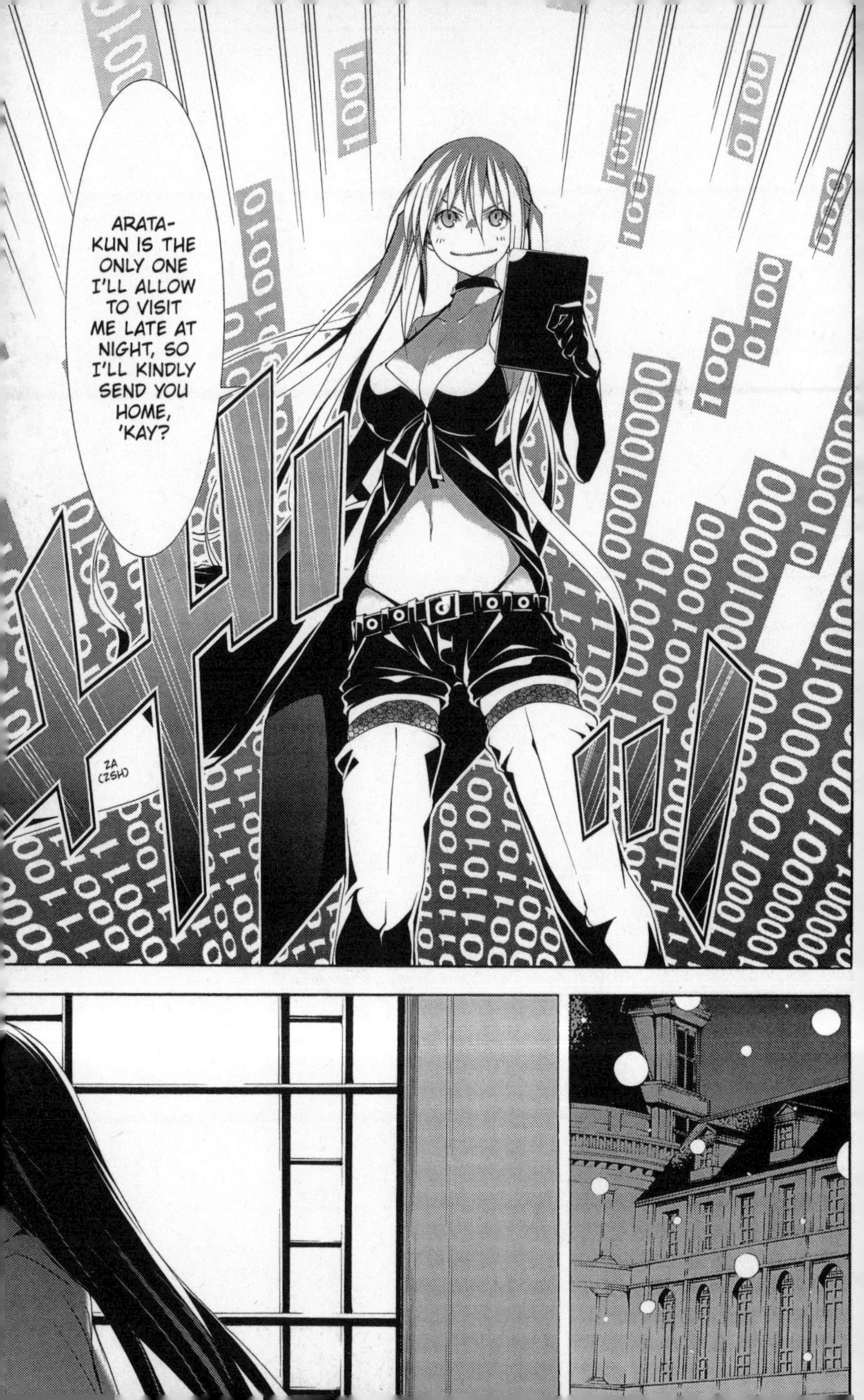
ARATA-KUN IS THE ONLY ONE I'LL ALLOW TO VISIT ME LATE AT NIGHT, SO I'LL KINDLY SEND YOU HOME, 'KAY?
ZA (ZSH)

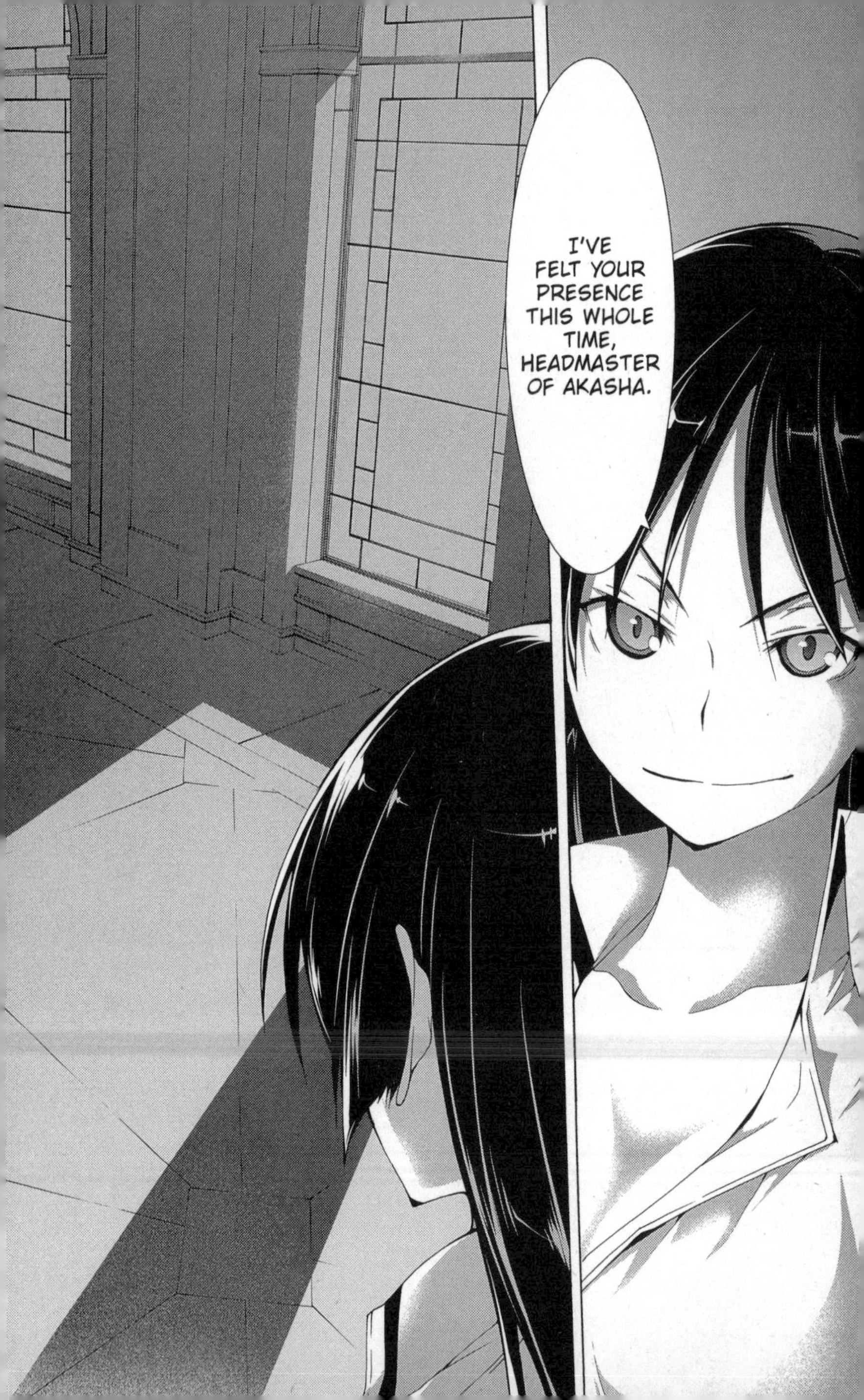
I'VE FELT YOUR PRESENCE THIS WHOLE TIME, HEADMASTER OF AKASHA.

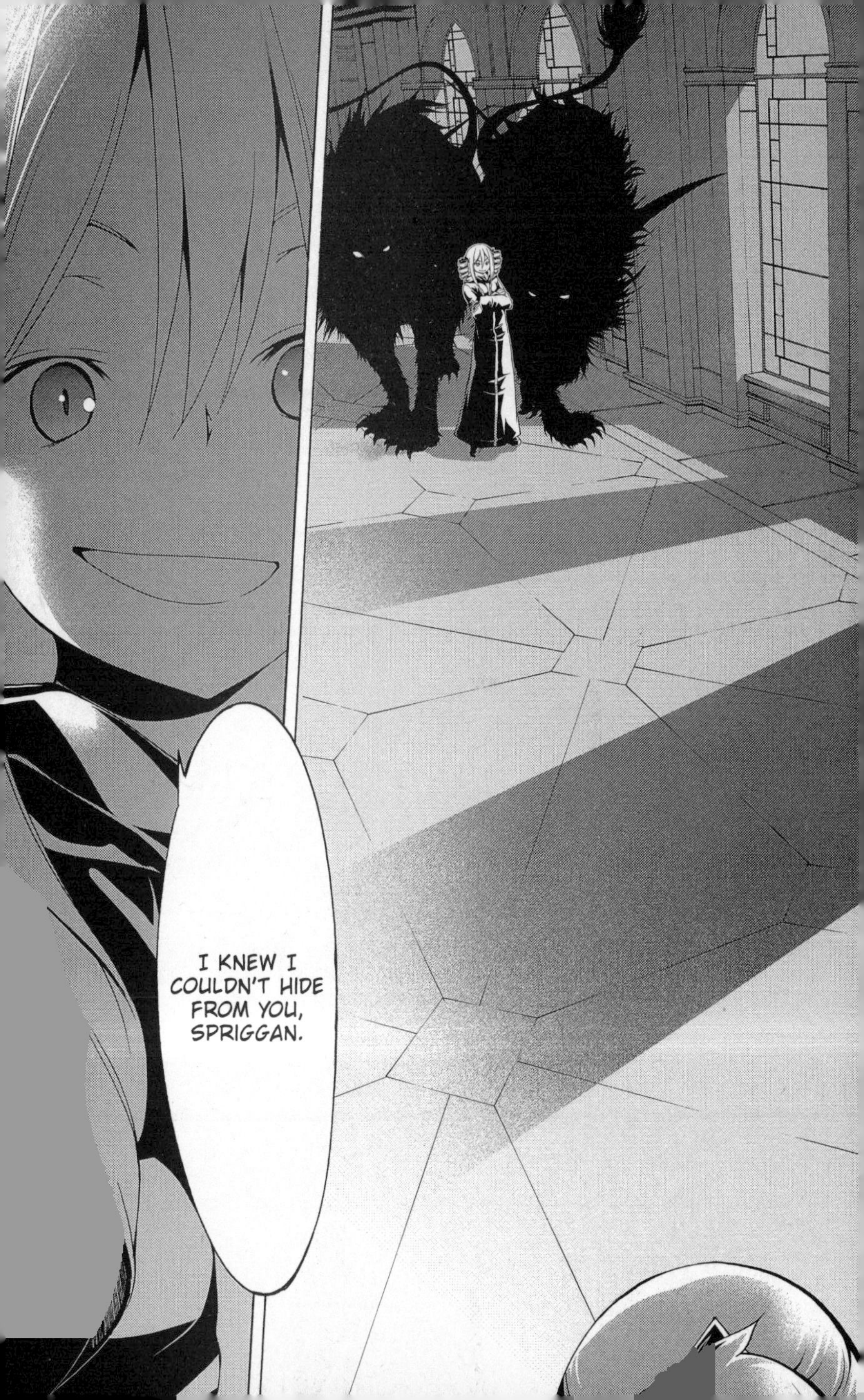
I KNEW I COULDN'T HIDE FROM YOU, SPRIGGAN.

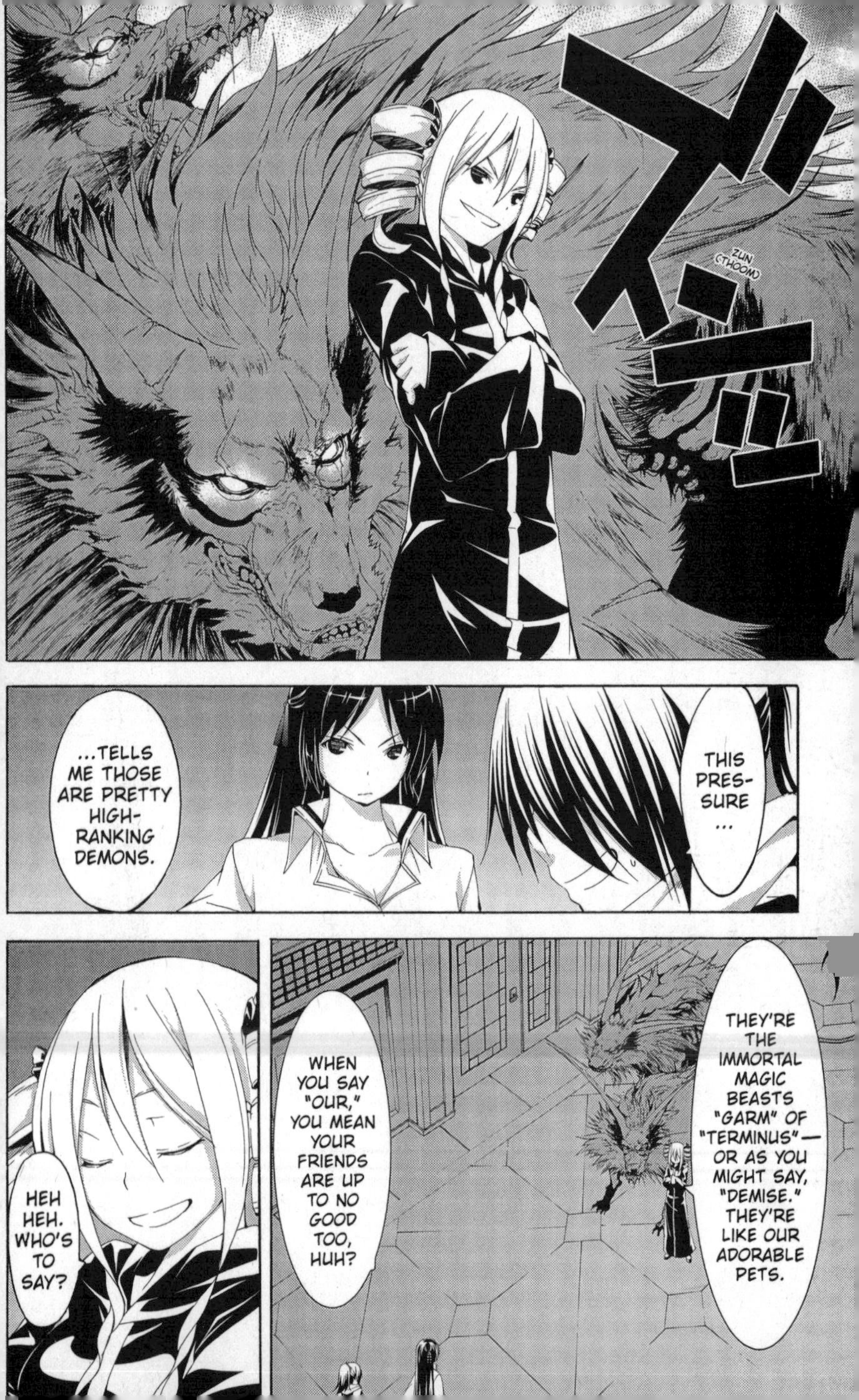
ZUN (THOOM)
THIS PRES-SURE ...
...TELLS ME THOSE ARE PRETTY HIGH-RANKING DEMONS.
THEY'RE THE IMMORTAL MAGIC BEASTS "GARM" OF "TERMINUS"— OR AS YOU MIGHT SAY, "DEMISE." THEY'RE LIKE OUR ADORABLE PETS.
WHEN YOU SAY "OUR," YOU MEAN YOUR FRIENDS ARE UP TO NO GOOD TOO, HUH?
HEH HEH. WHO'S TO SAY?

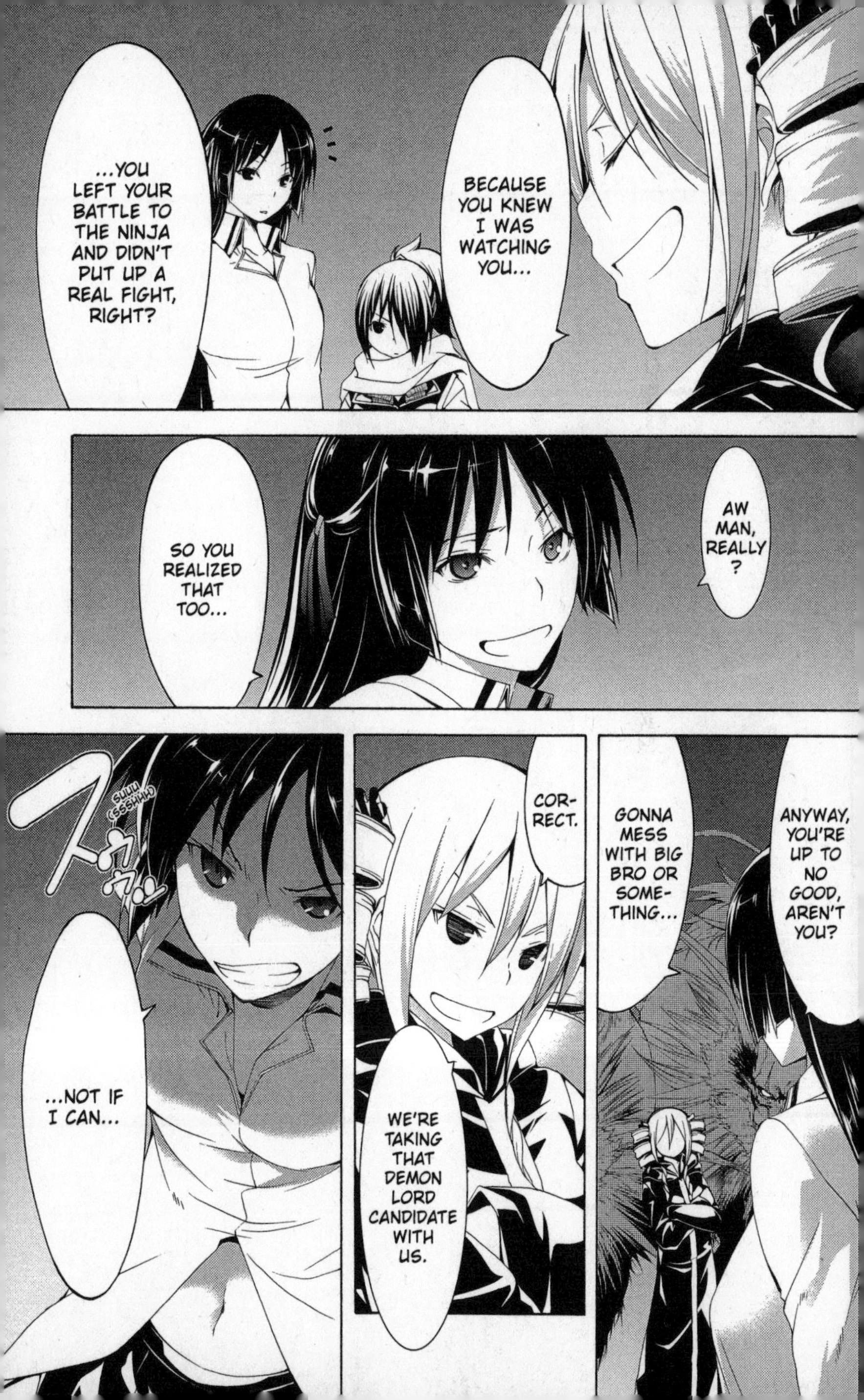
BECAUSE YOU KNEW I WAS WATCHING YOU...
...YOU LEFT YOUR BATTLE TO THE NINJA AND DIDN'T PUT UP A REAL FIGHT, RIGHT?
AW MAN, REALLY?
SO YOU REALIZED THAT TOO...
ANYWAY, YOU'RE UP TO NO GOOD, AREN'T YOU?
GONNA MESS WITH BIG BRO OR SOMETHING...
COR-RECT.
WE'RE TAKING THAT DEMON LORD CANDIDATE WITH US.
SUUU (SSSHHH)
...NOT IF I CAN...

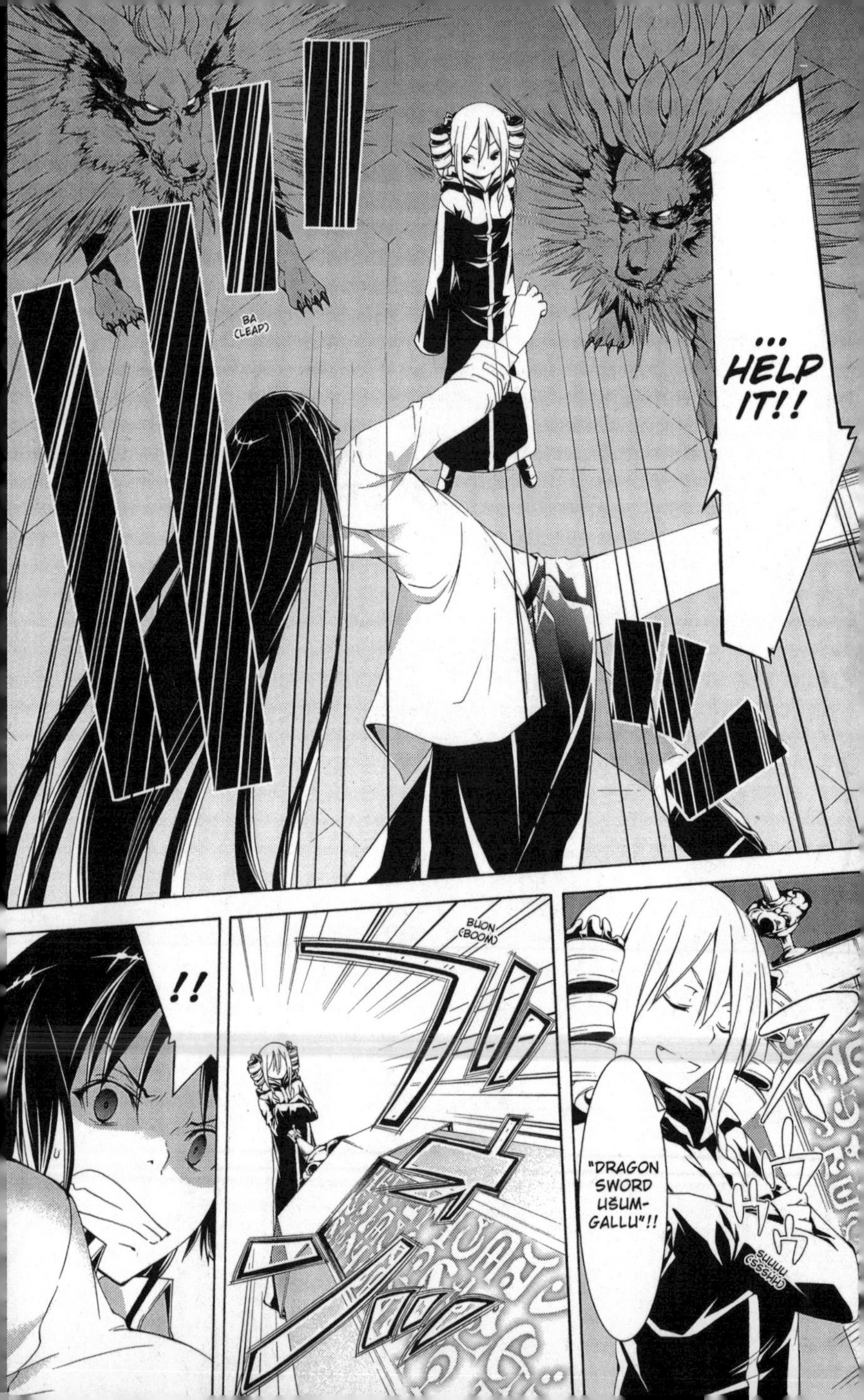
...HELP IT!!
BA (LEAP)
"DRAGON SWORD UŠUM-GALLU"!!
SUUUU (SSSSH)
BUON (BOOM)
!!

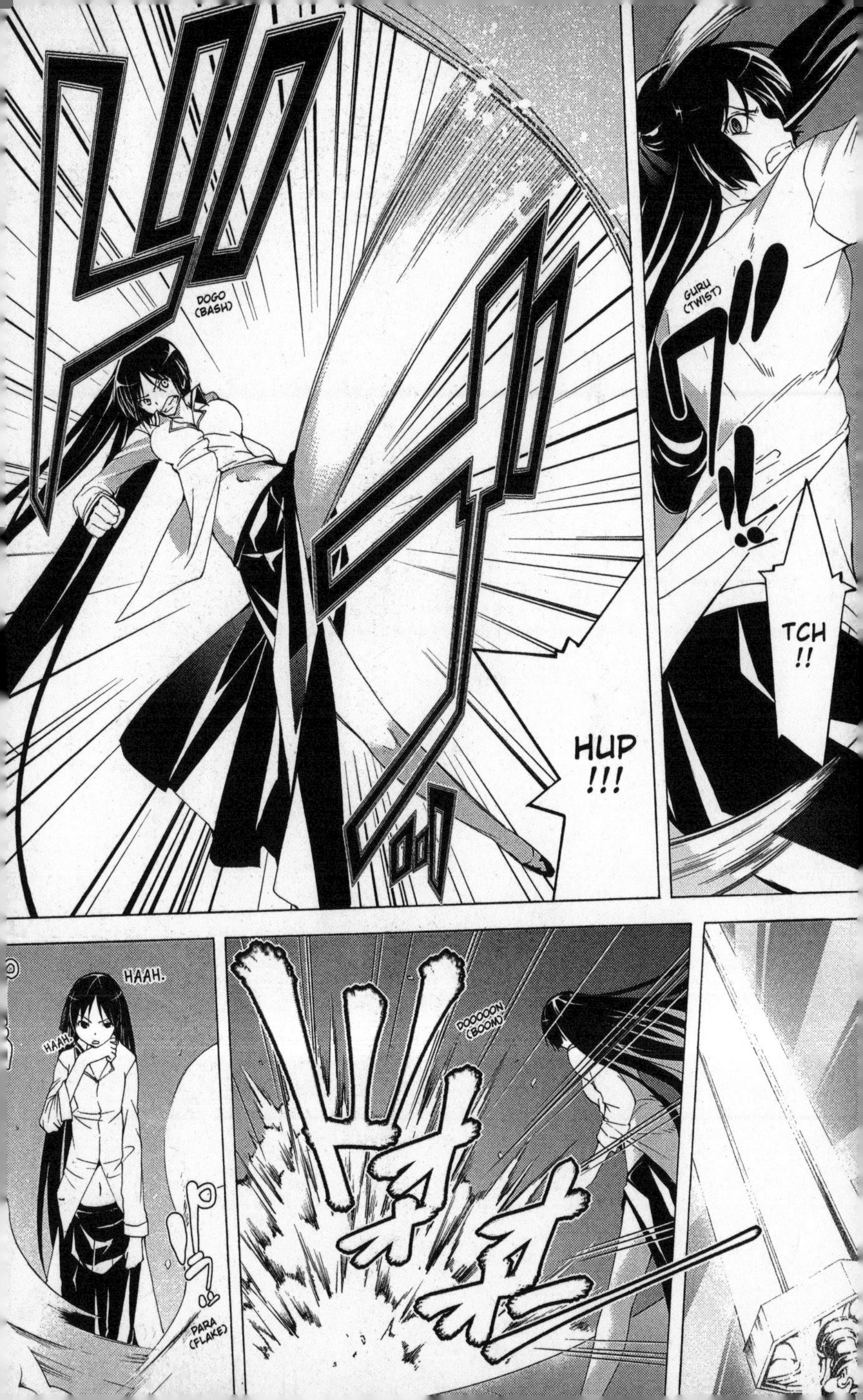
GURU (TWIST)
TCH !!
DOGO (BASH)
HUP !!!
DOOOOON (BOOM)
HAAH.
HAAH.
PARA (FLAKE)

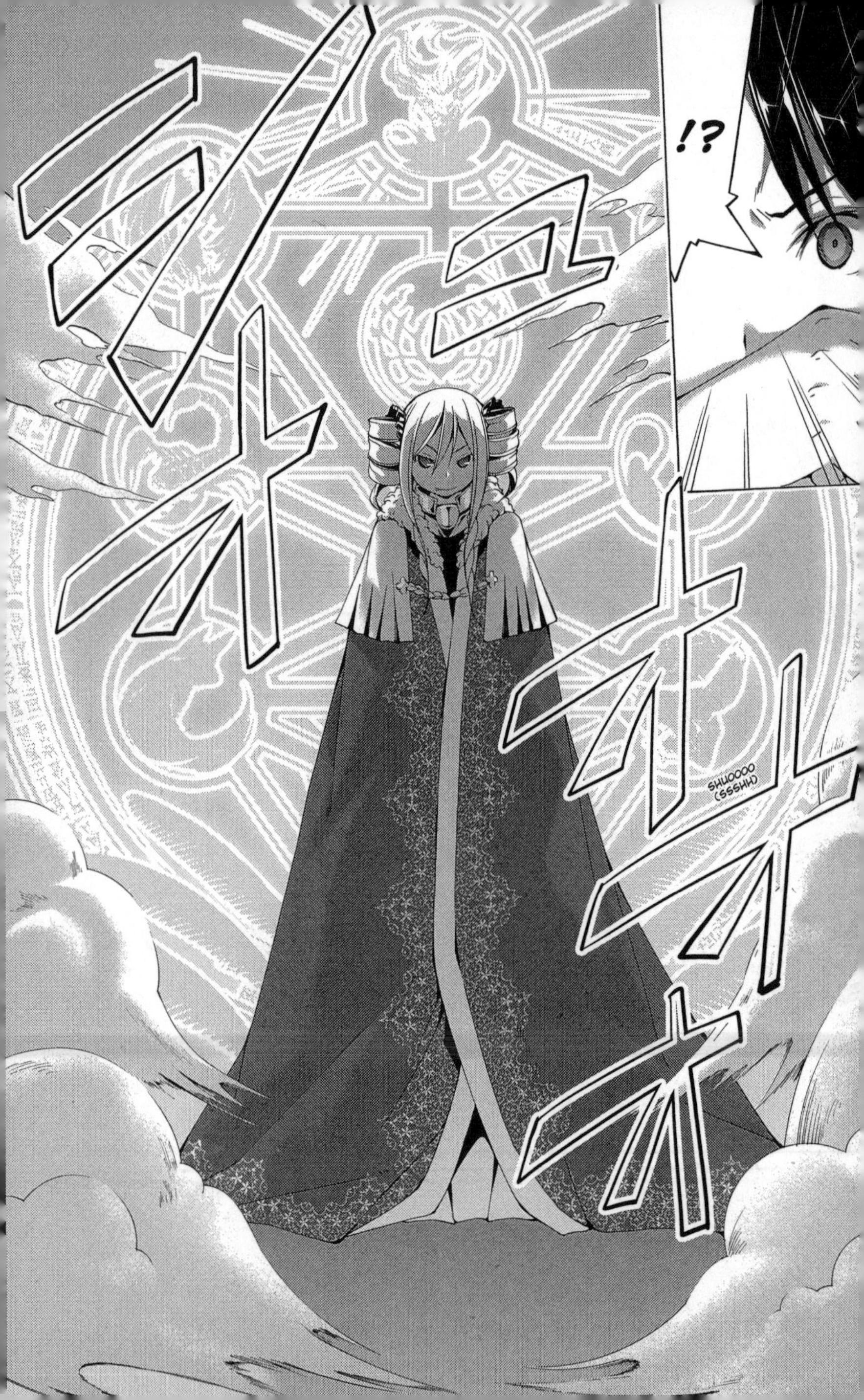
!?
SHUOOOO
(SSSHH)

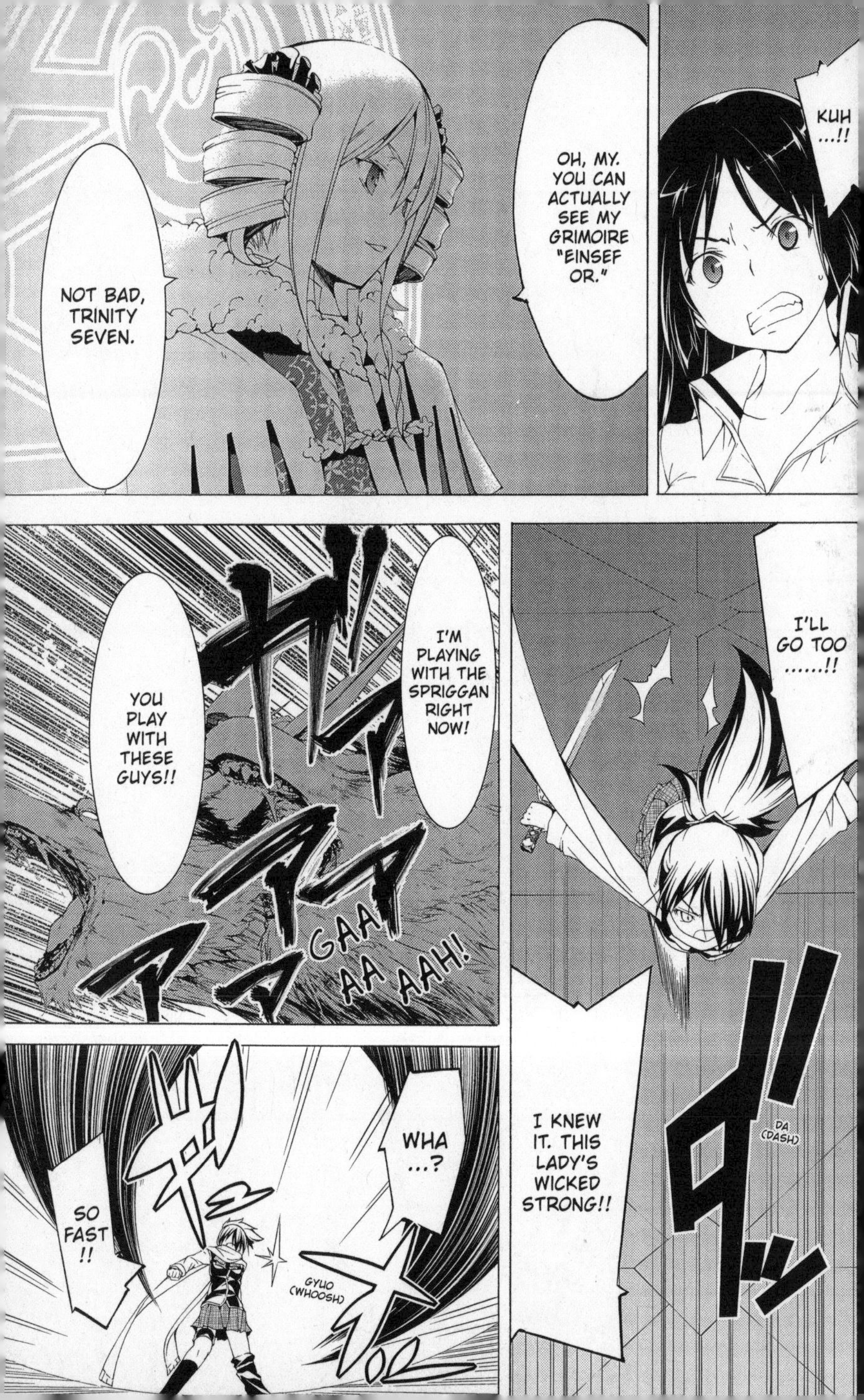
KUH ...!!
OH, MY. YOU CAN ACTUALLY SEE MY GRIMOIRE "EINSEF OR."
NOT BAD, TRINITY SEVEN.
I'LL GO TOO ......!!
I KNEW IT. THIS LADY'S WICKED STRONG!!
DA (DASH)
I'M PLAYING WITH THE SPRIGGAN RIGHT NOW!
YOU PLAY WITH THESE GUYS!!
GAAAA AAAH!
WHA ...?
GYUO (WHOOSH)
SO FAST !!

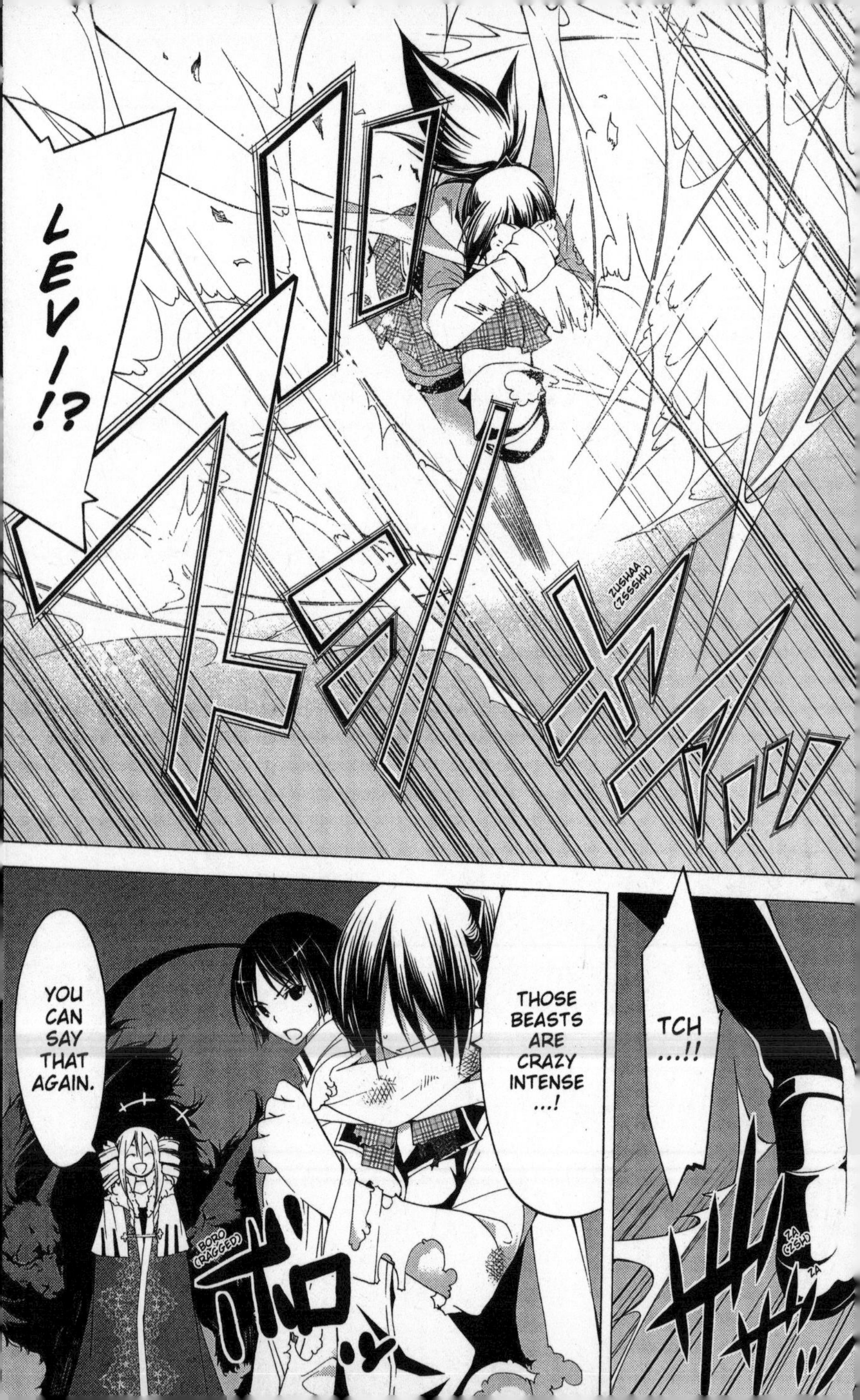

LEVI!?
ZUSHAA (ZSSSHH)
TCH ...!!
ZA (ZSH) ZA
THOSE BEASTS ARE CRAZY INTENSE ...!
YOU CAN SAY THAT AGAIN.
BORO (RAGGED)

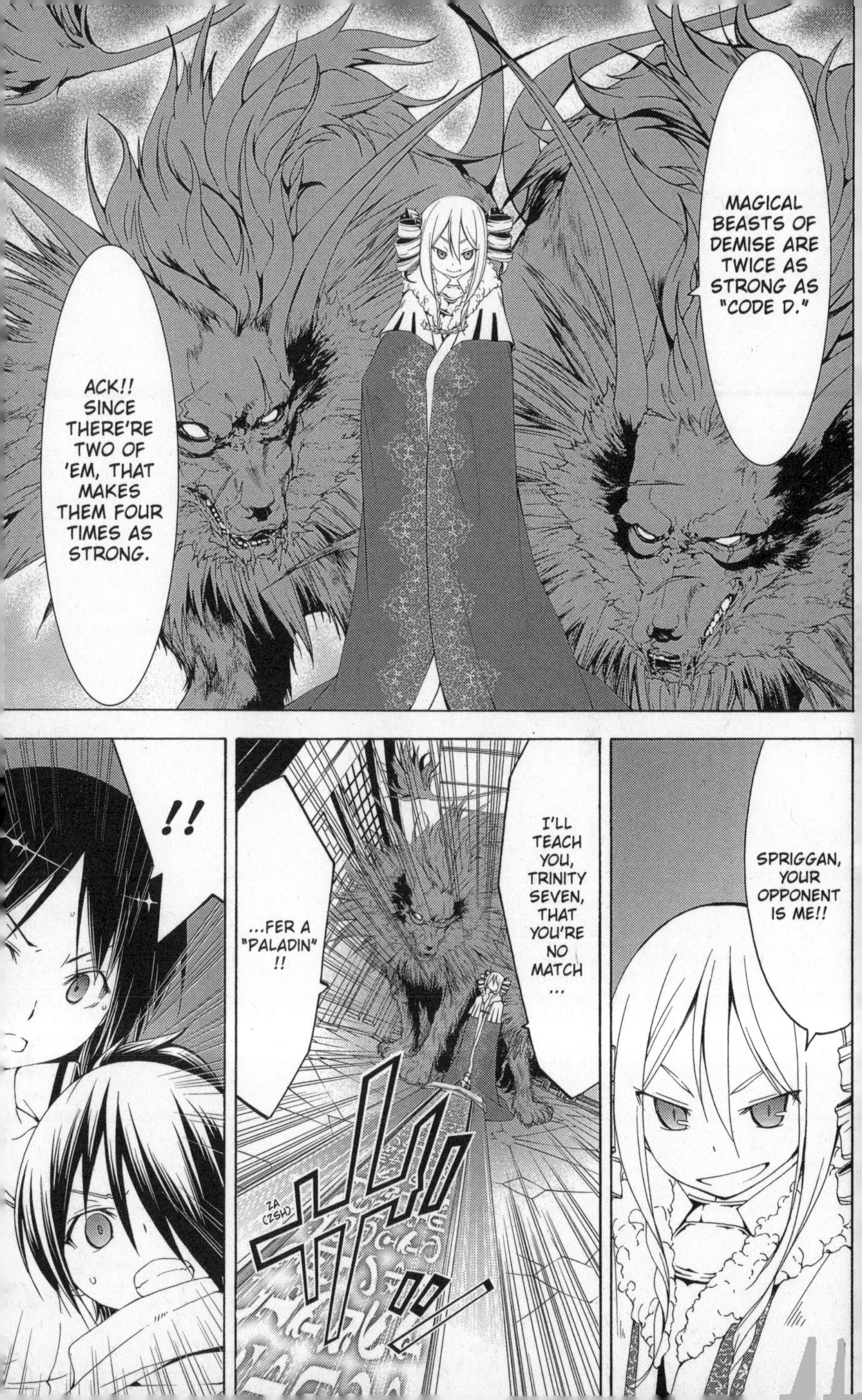
MAGICAL BEASTS OF DEMISE ARE TWICE AS STRONG AS "CODE D."
ACK!! SINCE THERE'RE TWO OF 'EM, THAT MAKES THEM FOUR TIMES AS STRONG.
SPRIGGAN, YOUR OPPONENT IS ME!!
I'LL TEACH YOU, TRINITY SEVEN, THAT YOU'RE NO MATCH ...
...FER A "PALADIN" !!
ZA (ZSH)
!!

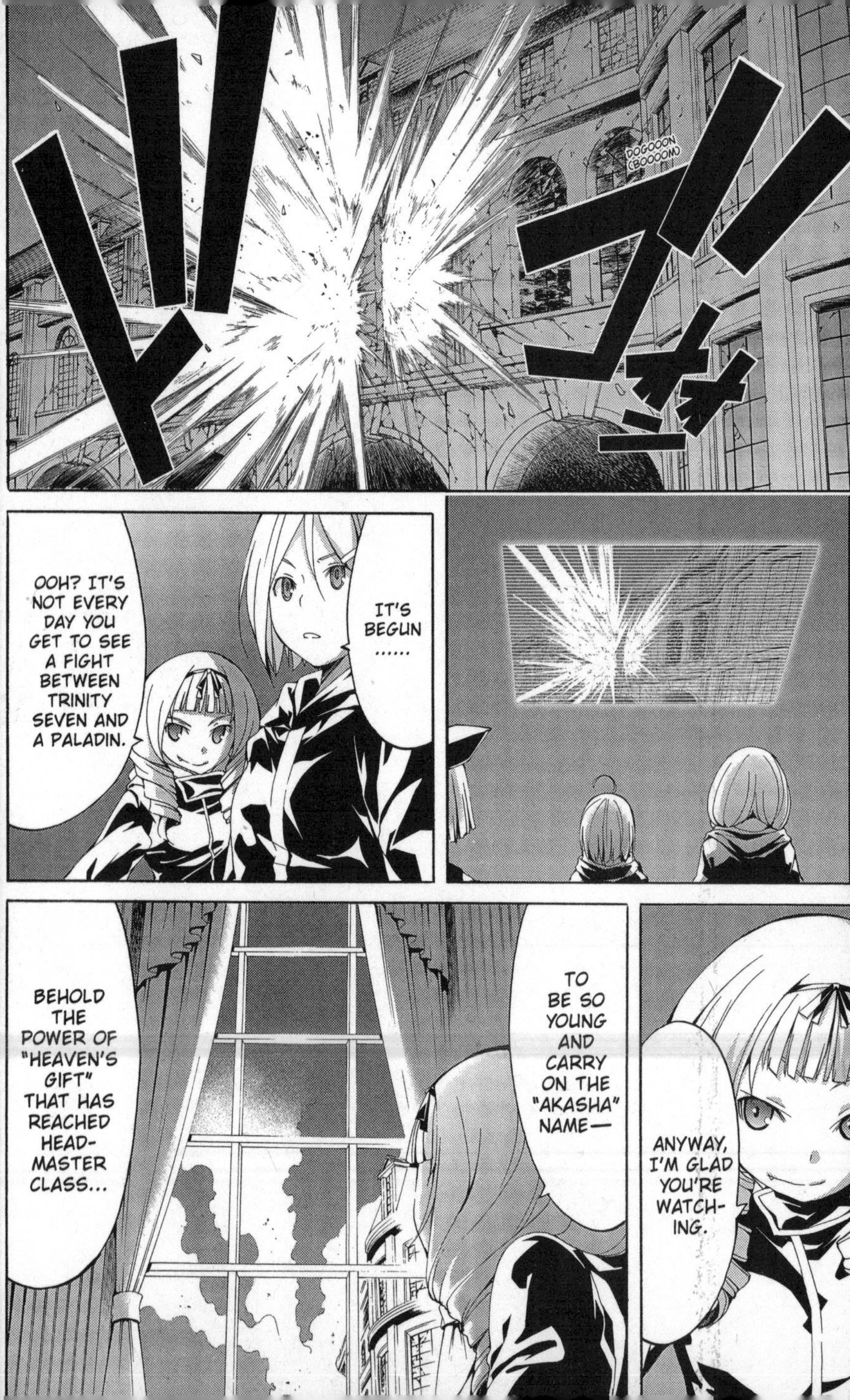
DOGOOON (BOOOOM)
IT'S BEGUN ......
OOH? IT'S NOT EVERY DAY YOU GET TO SEE A FIGHT BETWEEN TRINITY SEVEN AND A PALADIN.
ANYWAY, I'M GLAD YOU'RE WATCH-ING.
TO BE SO YOUNG AND CARRY ON THE "AKASHA" NAME—
BEHOLD THE POWER OF "HEAVEN'S GIFT" THAT HAS REACHED HEAD-MASTER CLASS...

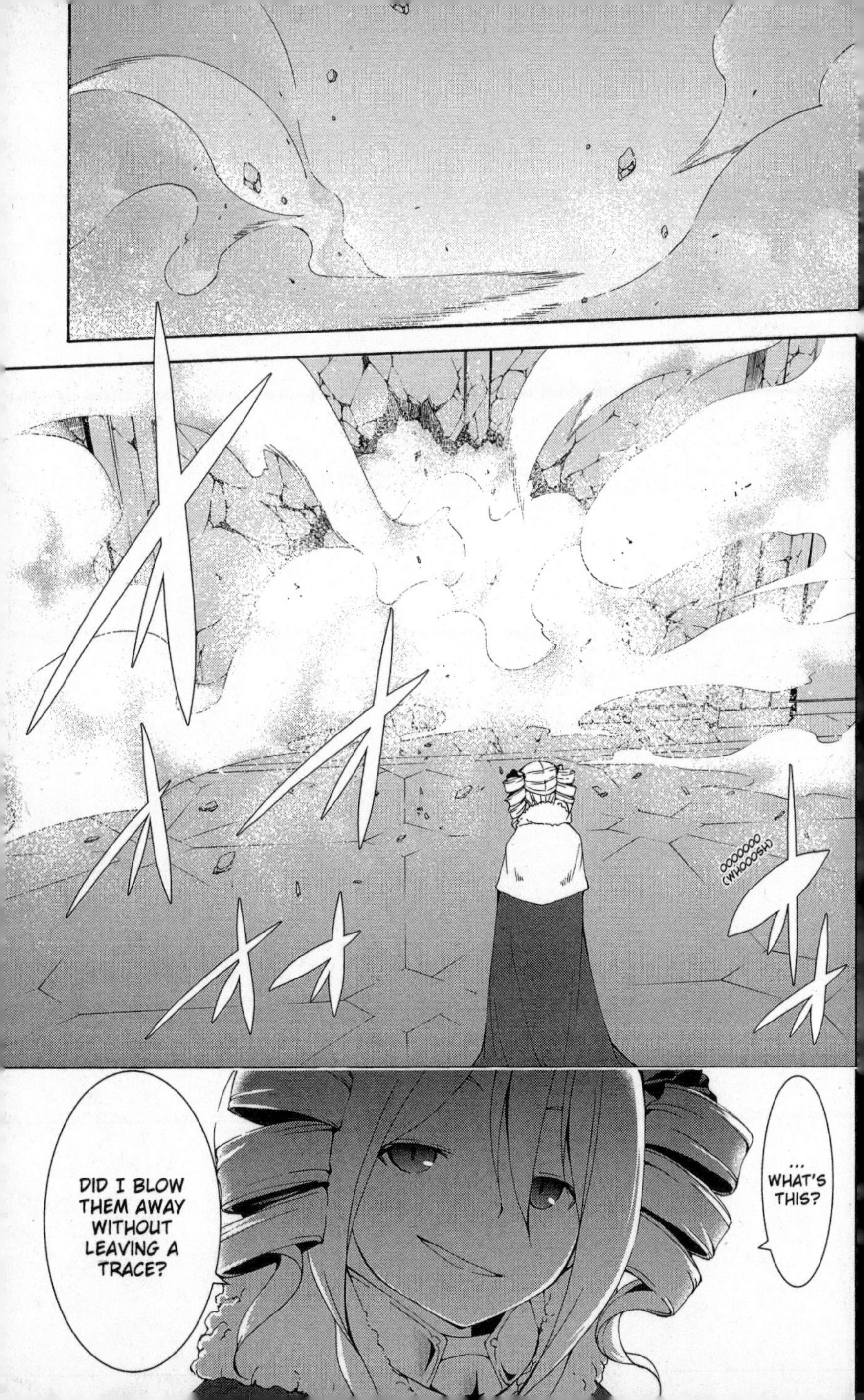
OOOOOOO
(WHOOOSH)
...WHAT'S THIS?
DID I BLOW THEM AWAY WITHOUT LEAVING A TRACE?

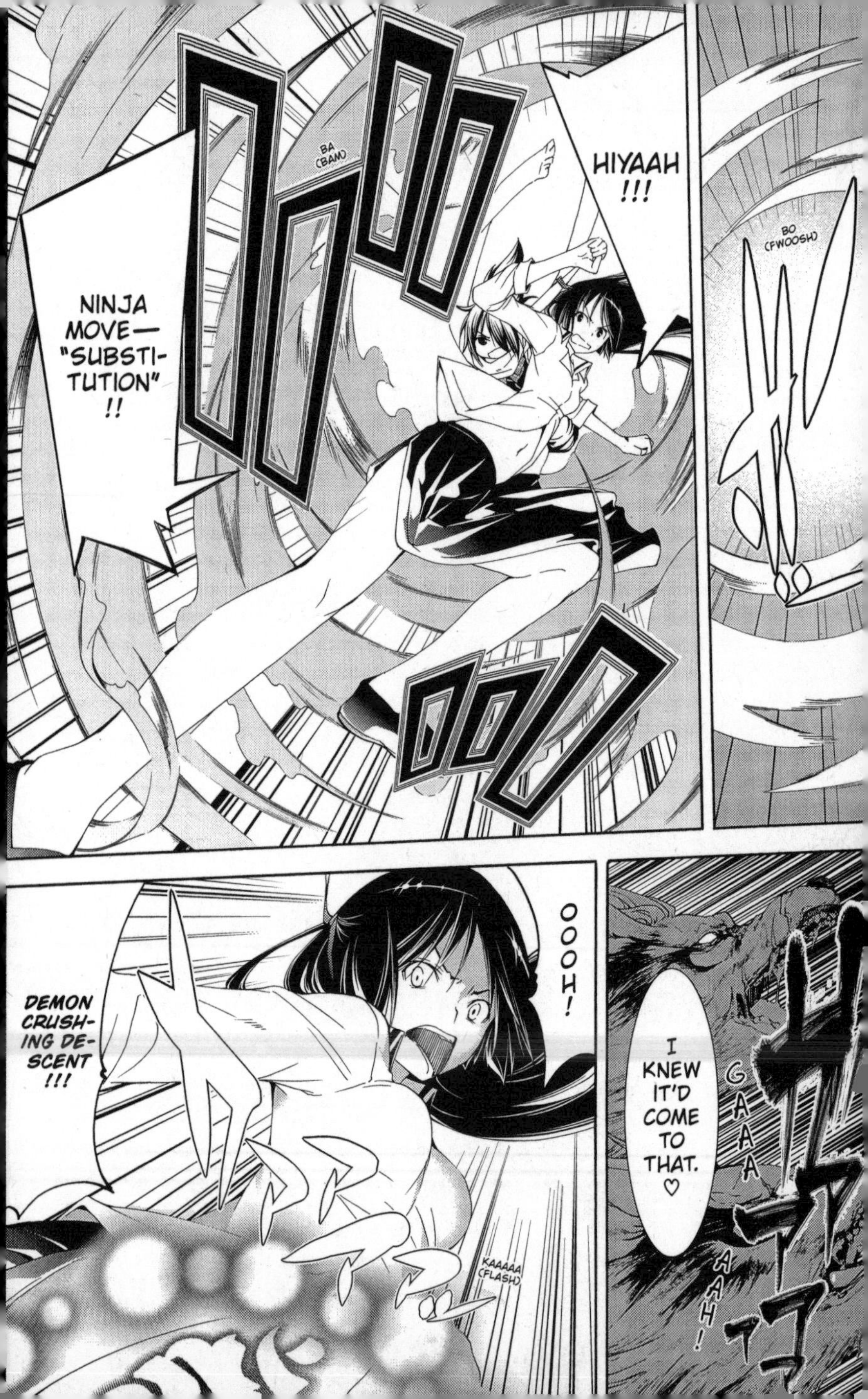
BO (FWOOSH)
HIYAAH!!!
BA (BAM)
NINJA MOVE—"SUBSTI-TUTION"!!
GAAAAAH!
I KNEW IT'D COME TO THAT. ♡
OOOOH!
DEMON CRUSHING DESCENT!!!
KAAAAA (FLASH)

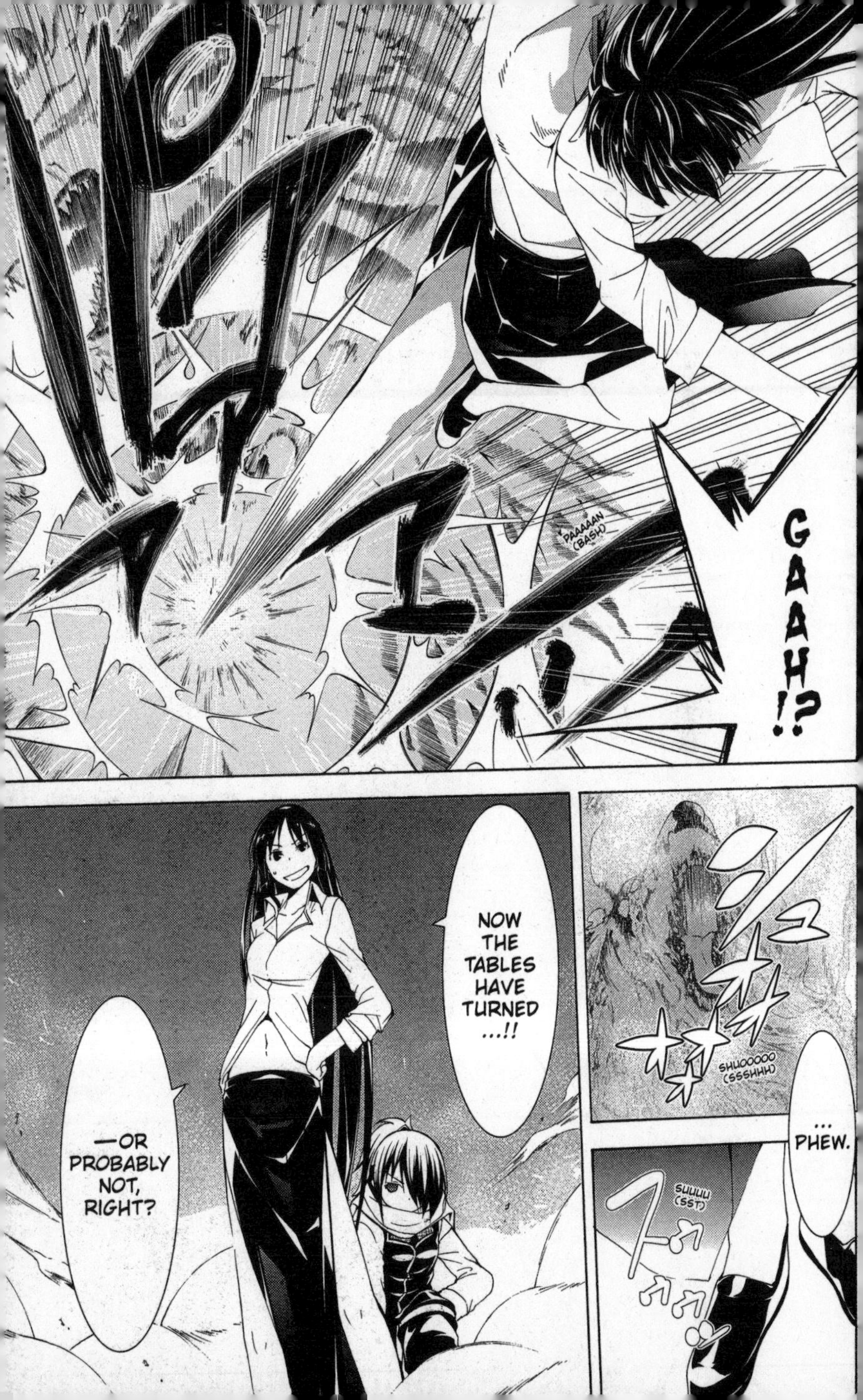
GAAH!?
PAAAAAN (BASH)
SHUOOOOO (SSSHHH)
...PHEW.
SUUUU (SST)
NOW THE TABLES HAVE TURNED ...!!
—OR PROBABLY NOT, RIGHT?

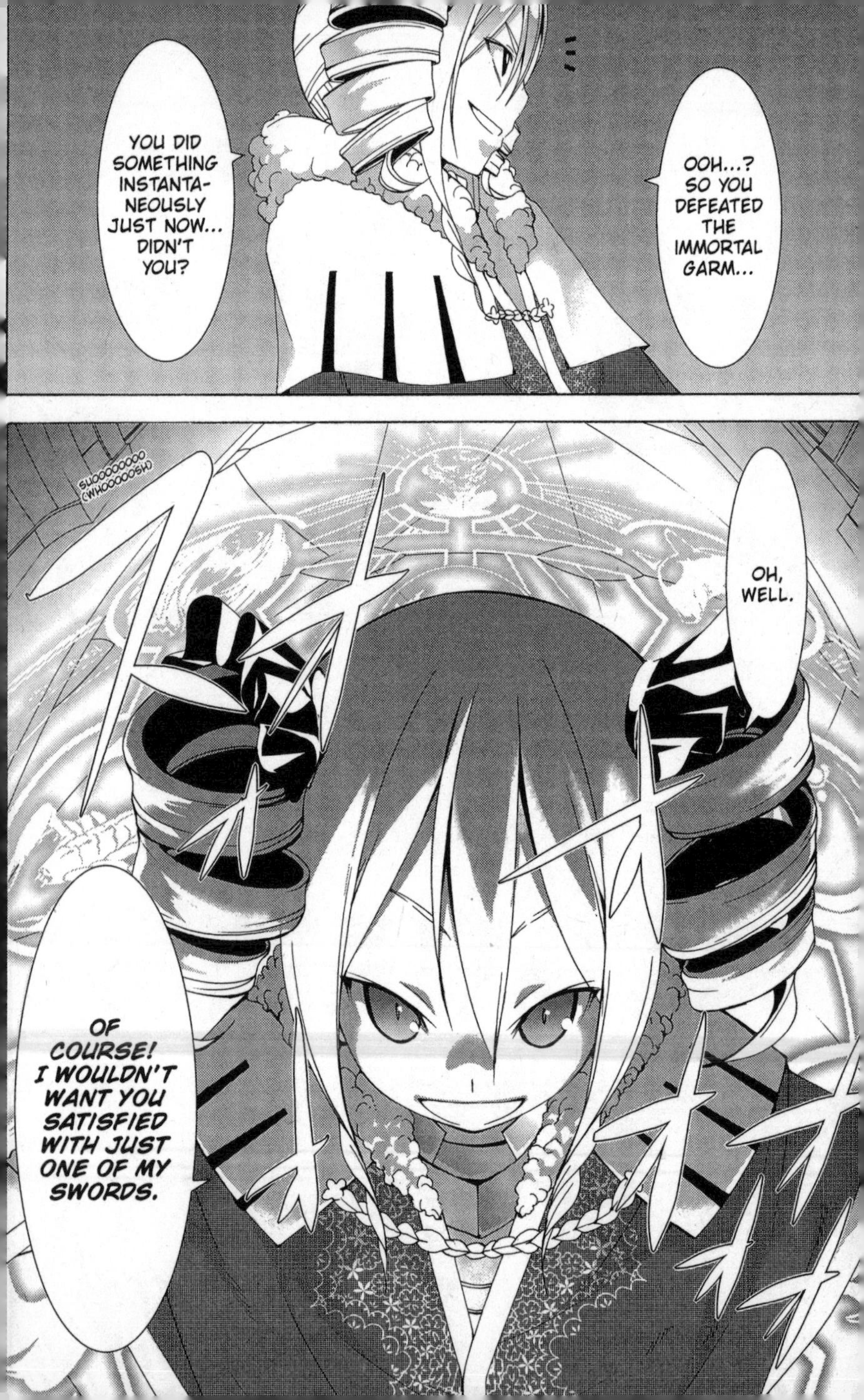
OOH...? SO YOU DEFEATED THE IMMORTAL GARM...
YOU DID SOMETHING INSTANTA-NEOUSLY JUST NOW... DIDN'T YOU?
SUOOOOOOOOO (WHOOOOOOSH)
OH, WELL.
OF COURSE! I WOULDN'T WANT YOU SATISFIED WITH JUST ONE OF MY SWORDS.

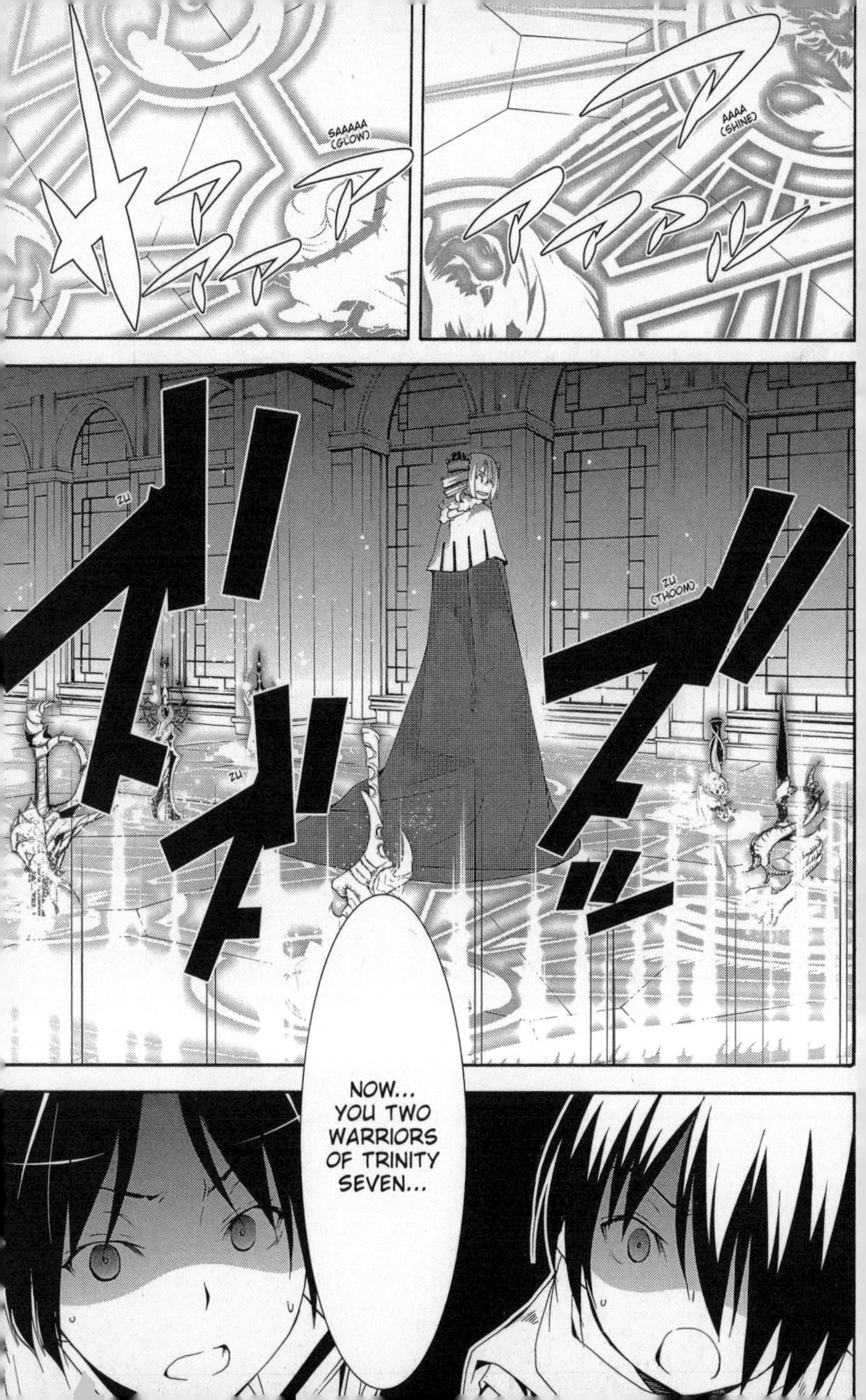
AAAA
(SHINE)
SAAAAA
(GLOW)
ZU
(THOOM)
ZU
ZU
NOW... YOU TWO WARRIORS OF TRINITY SEVEN...

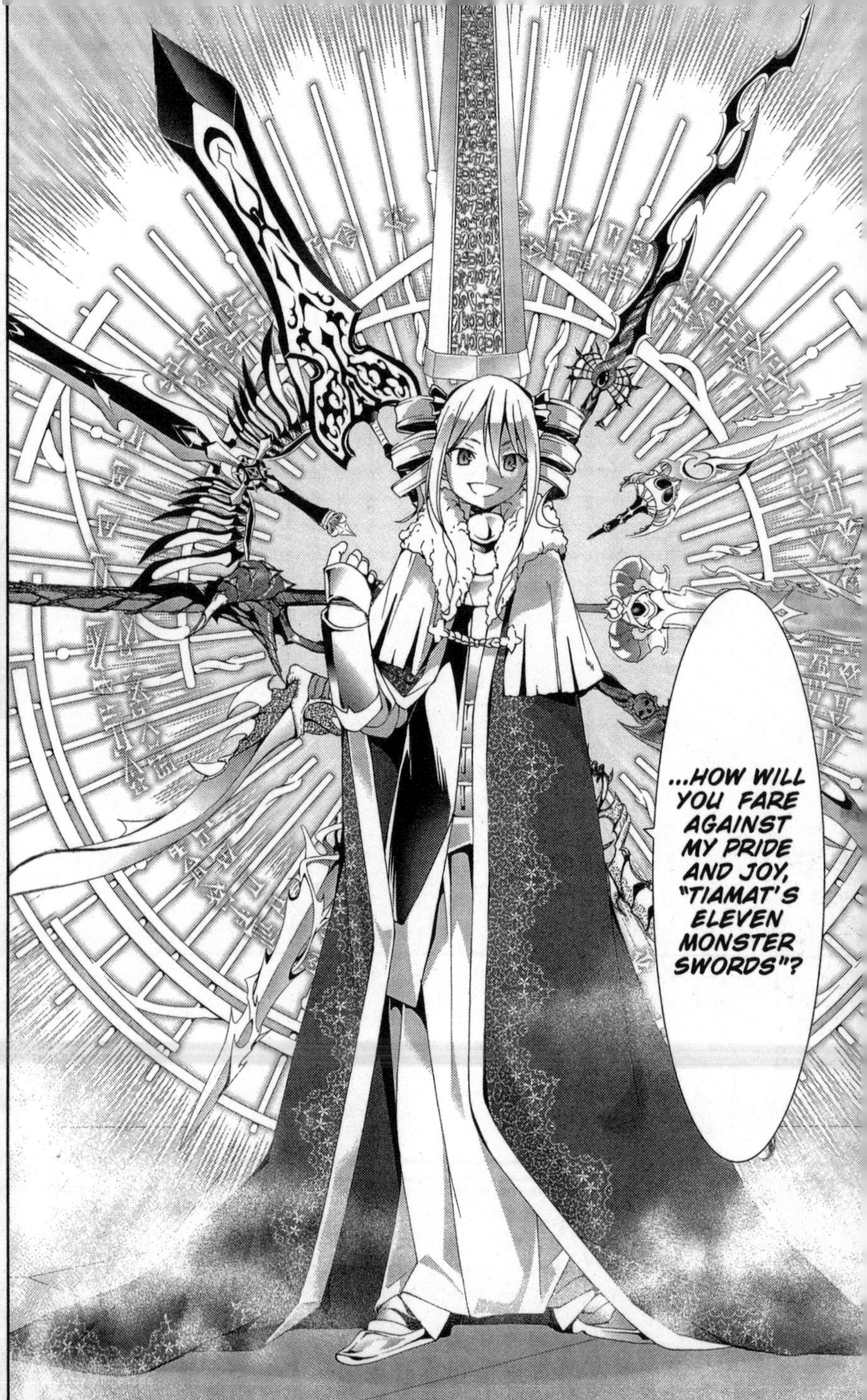
...HOW WILL YOU FARE AGAINST MY PRIDE AND JOY, "TIAMAT'S ELEVEN MONSTER SWORDS"?

46. Backstage & Chrono Gemini

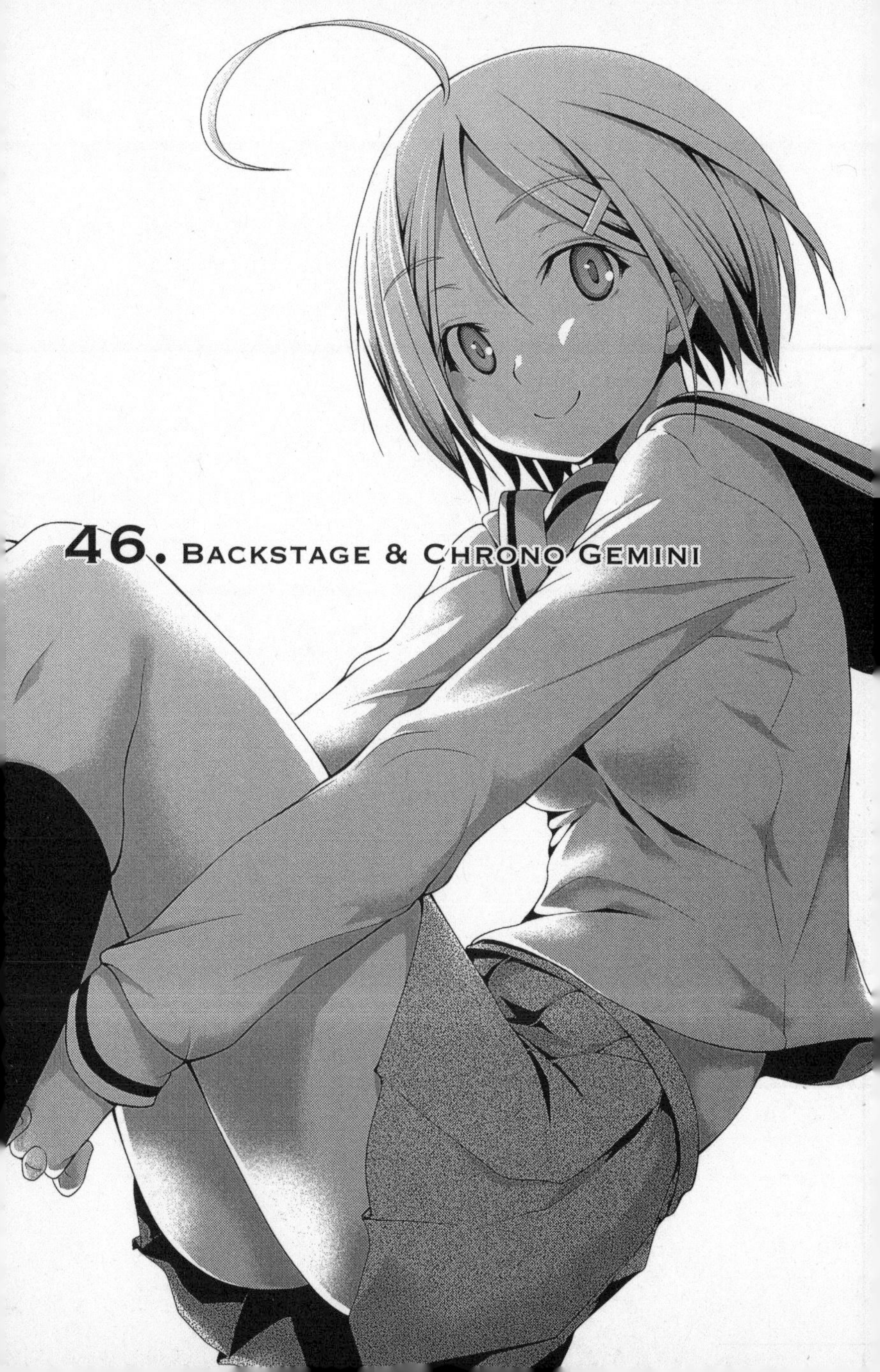

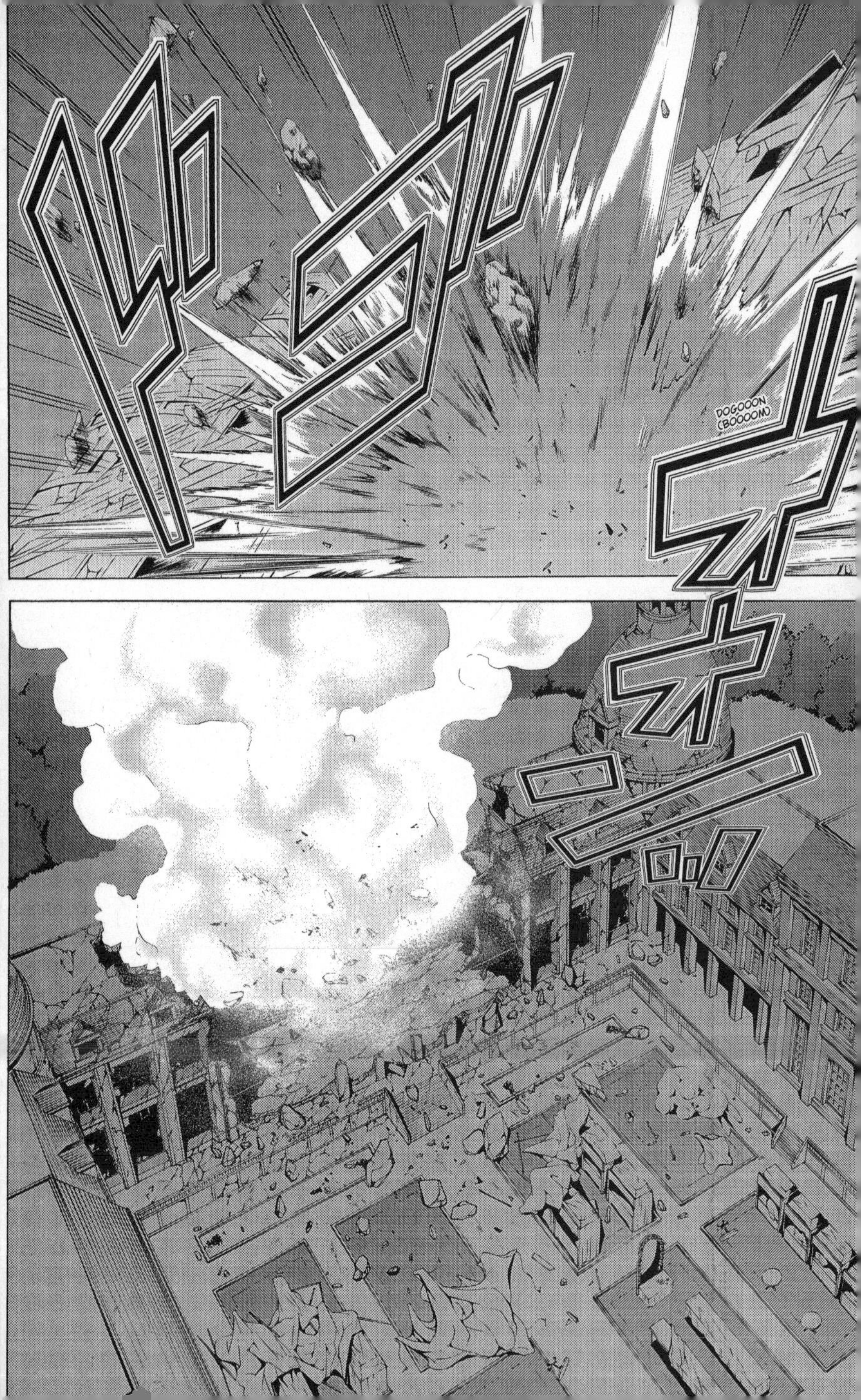
DOGOOON
(BOOOOM)

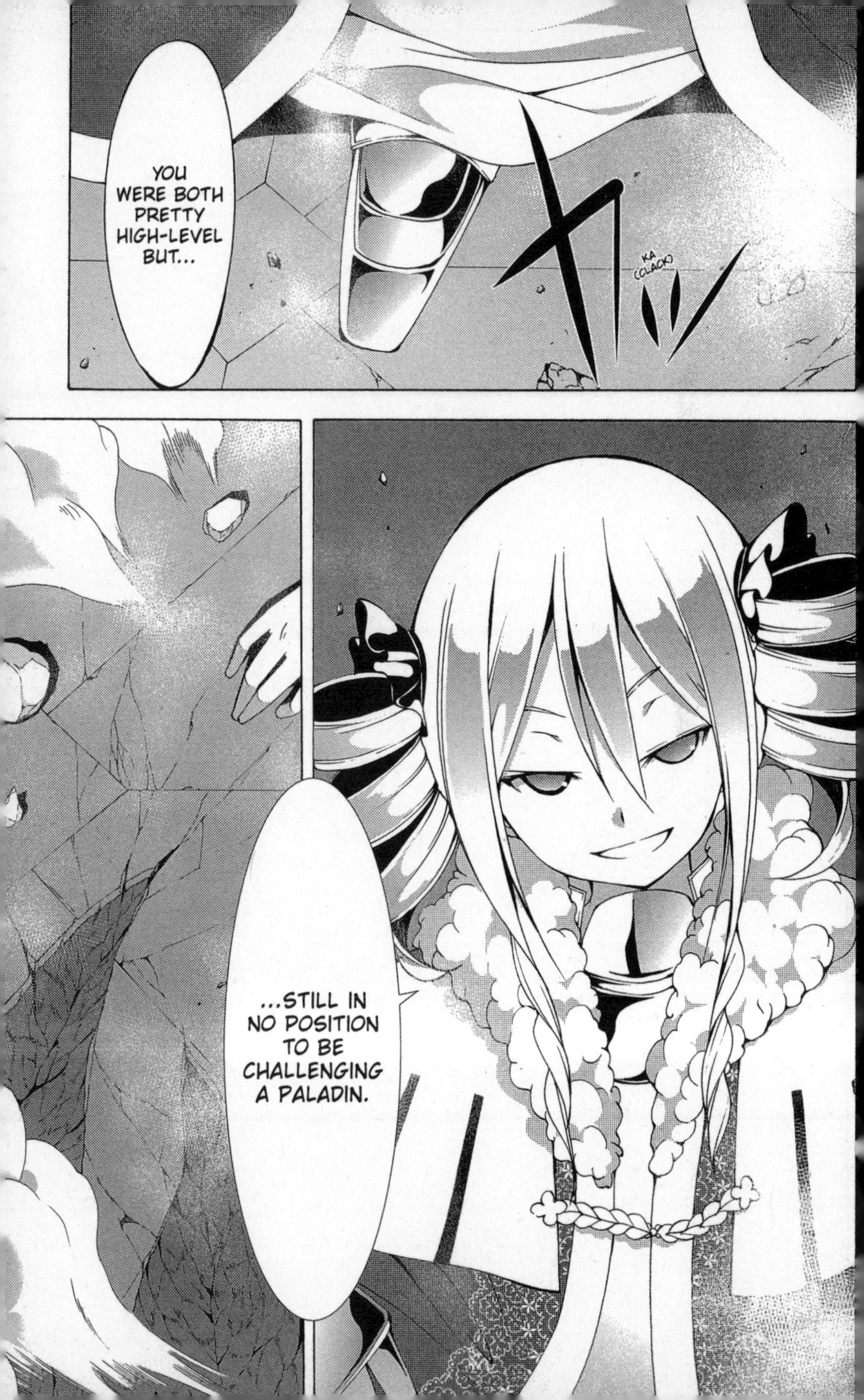
YOU WERE BOTH PRETTY HIGH-LEVEL BUT...
カッ
KA (CLACK)
...STILL IN NO POSITION TO BE CHALLENGING A PALADIN.

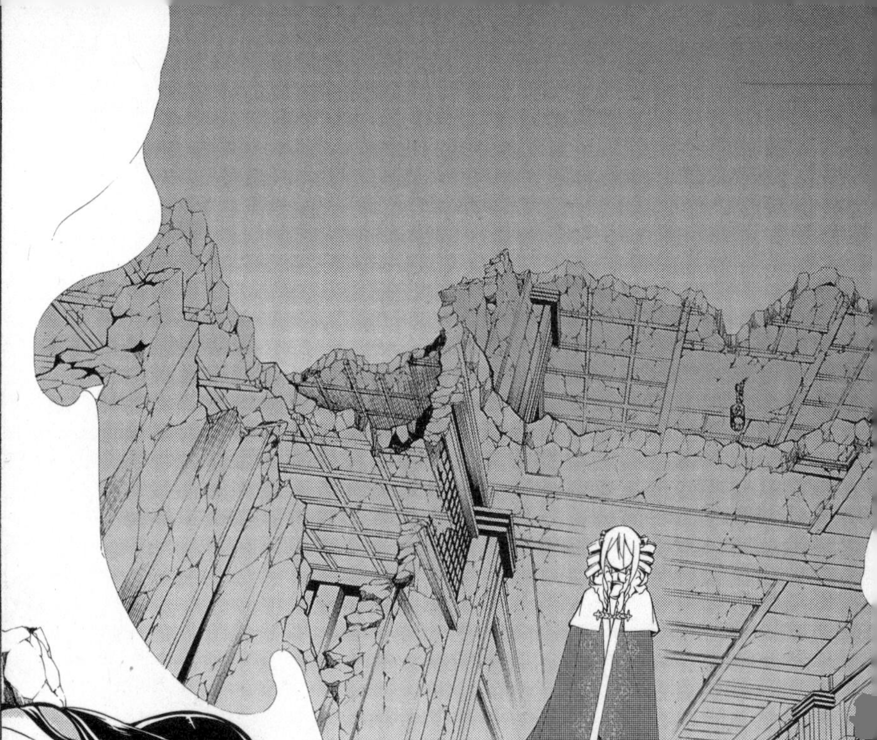
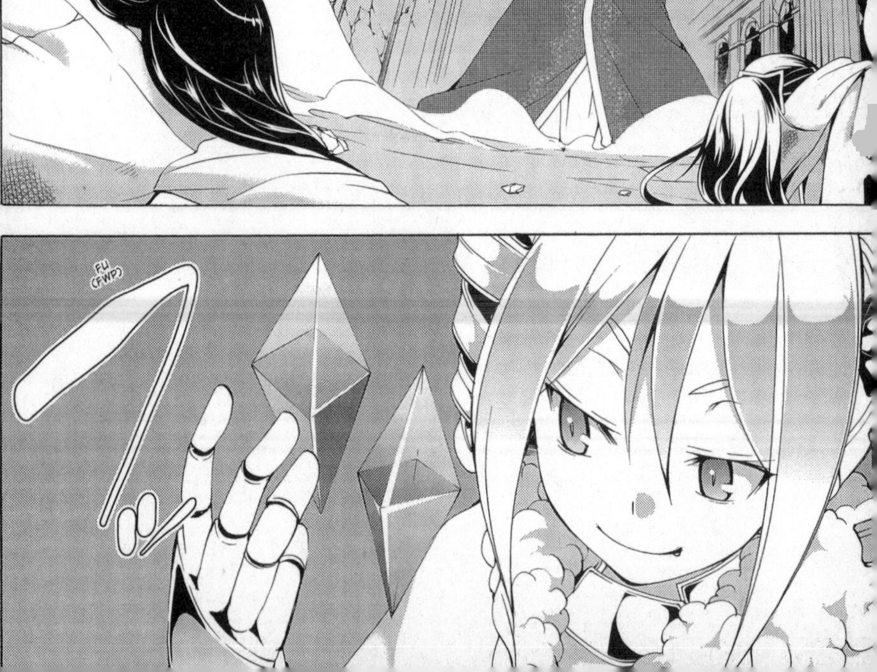
FU
(FWP)

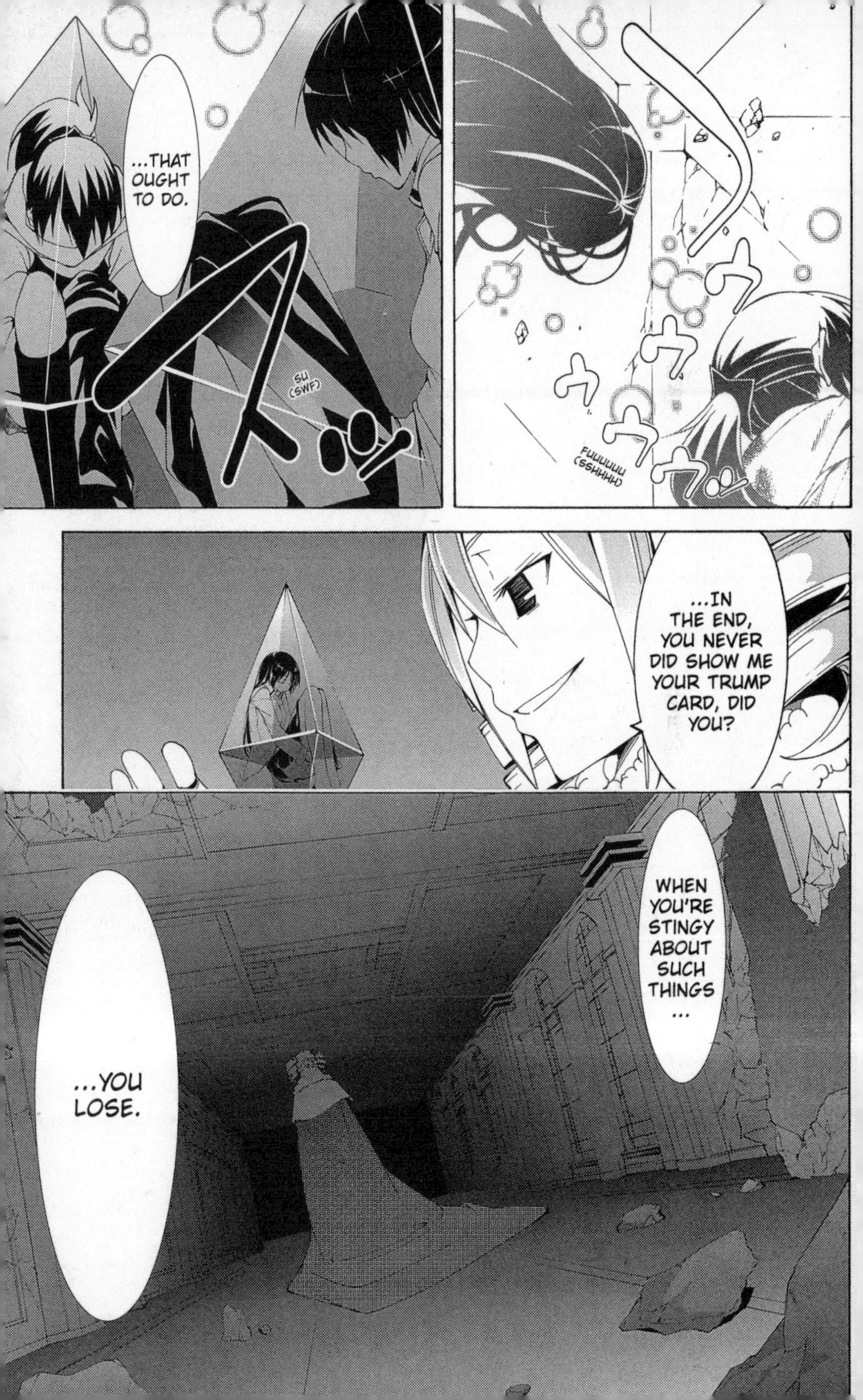
FUUUUUU (SSHHHH)
...THAT OUGHT TO DO.
SU (SWF)
...IN THE END, YOU NEVER DID SHOW ME YOUR TRUMP CARD, DID YOU?
WHEN YOU'RE STINGY ABOUT SUCH THINGS ...
...YOU LOSE.

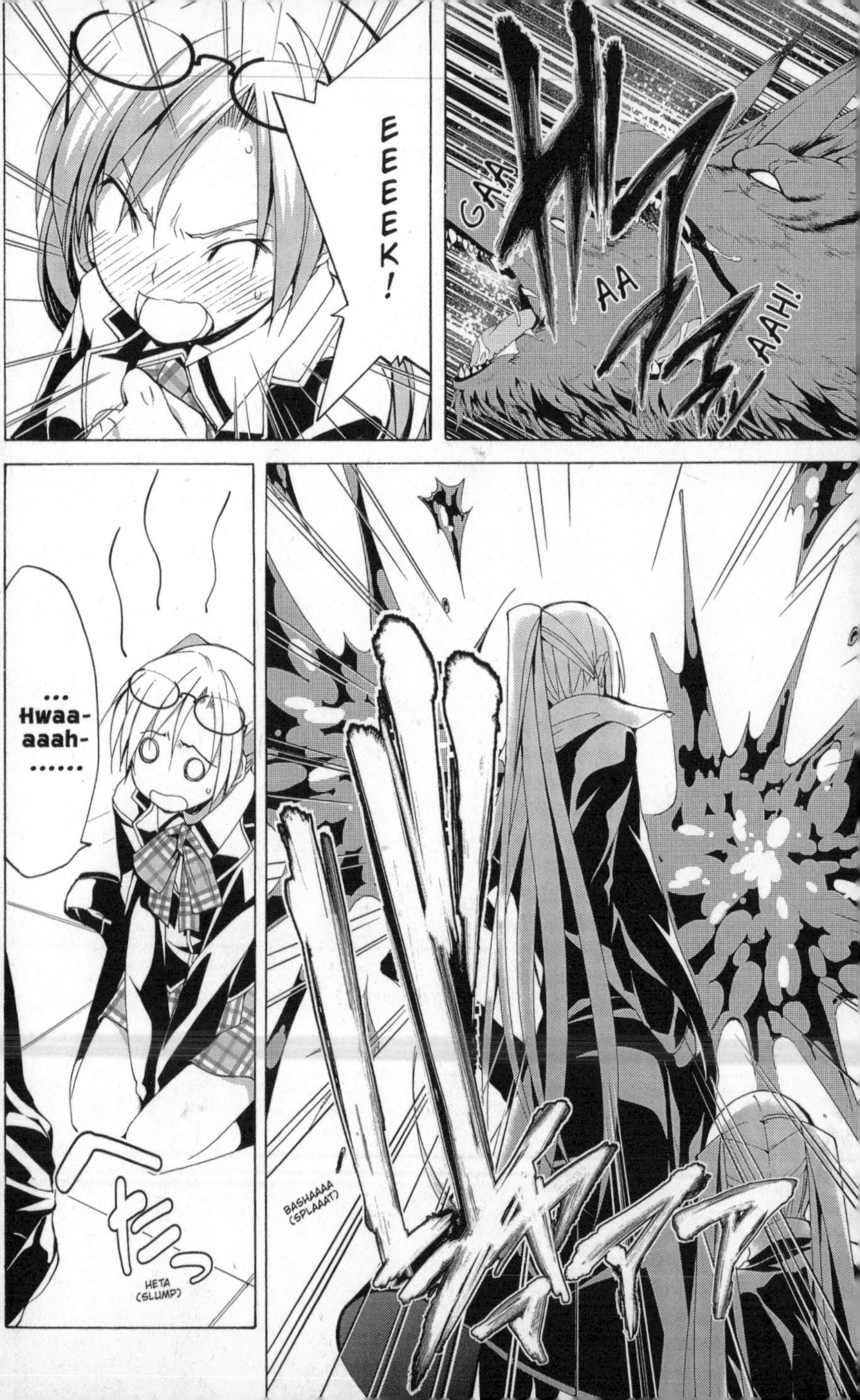
GAAAAAH!
EEEEEK!
BASHAAA (SPLAAAT)
... Hwaa-aaah-......
HETA (SLUMP)

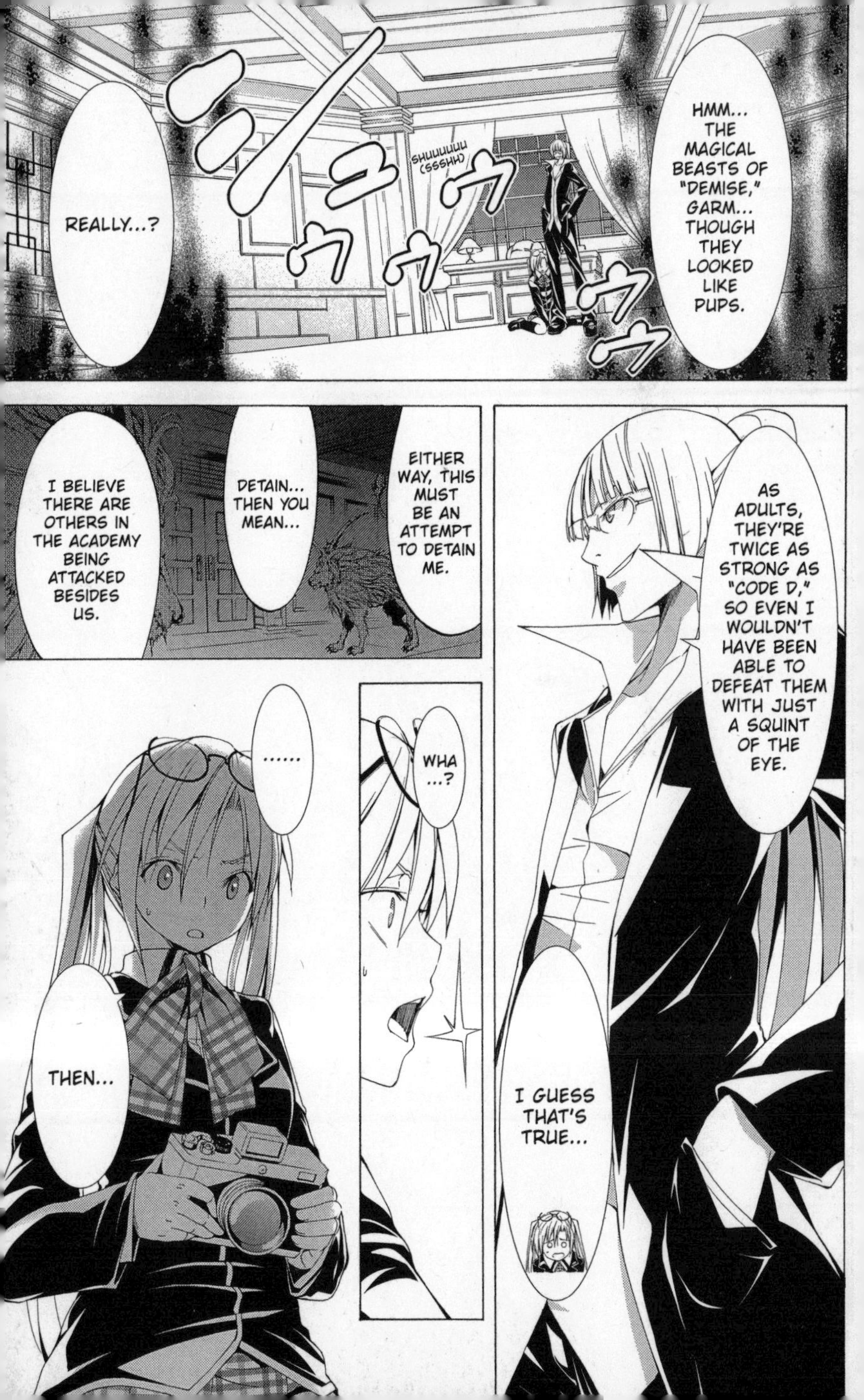
HMM... THE MAGICAL BEASTS OF "DEMISE," GARM... THOUGH THEY LOOKED LIKE PUPS.
SHUUUUUUU (SSSHH)
REALLY...?
AS ADULTS, THEY'RE TWICE AS STRONG AS "CODE D," SO EVEN I WOULDN'T HAVE BEEN ABLE TO DEFEAT THEM WITH JUST A SQUINT OF THE EYE.
I GUESS THAT'S TRUE...
EITHER WAY, THIS MUST BE AN ATTEMPT TO DETAIN ME.
DETAIN... THEN YOU MEAN...
I BELIEVE THERE ARE OTHERS IN THE ACADEMY BEING ATTACKED BESIDES US.
WHA ...?
......
THEN...

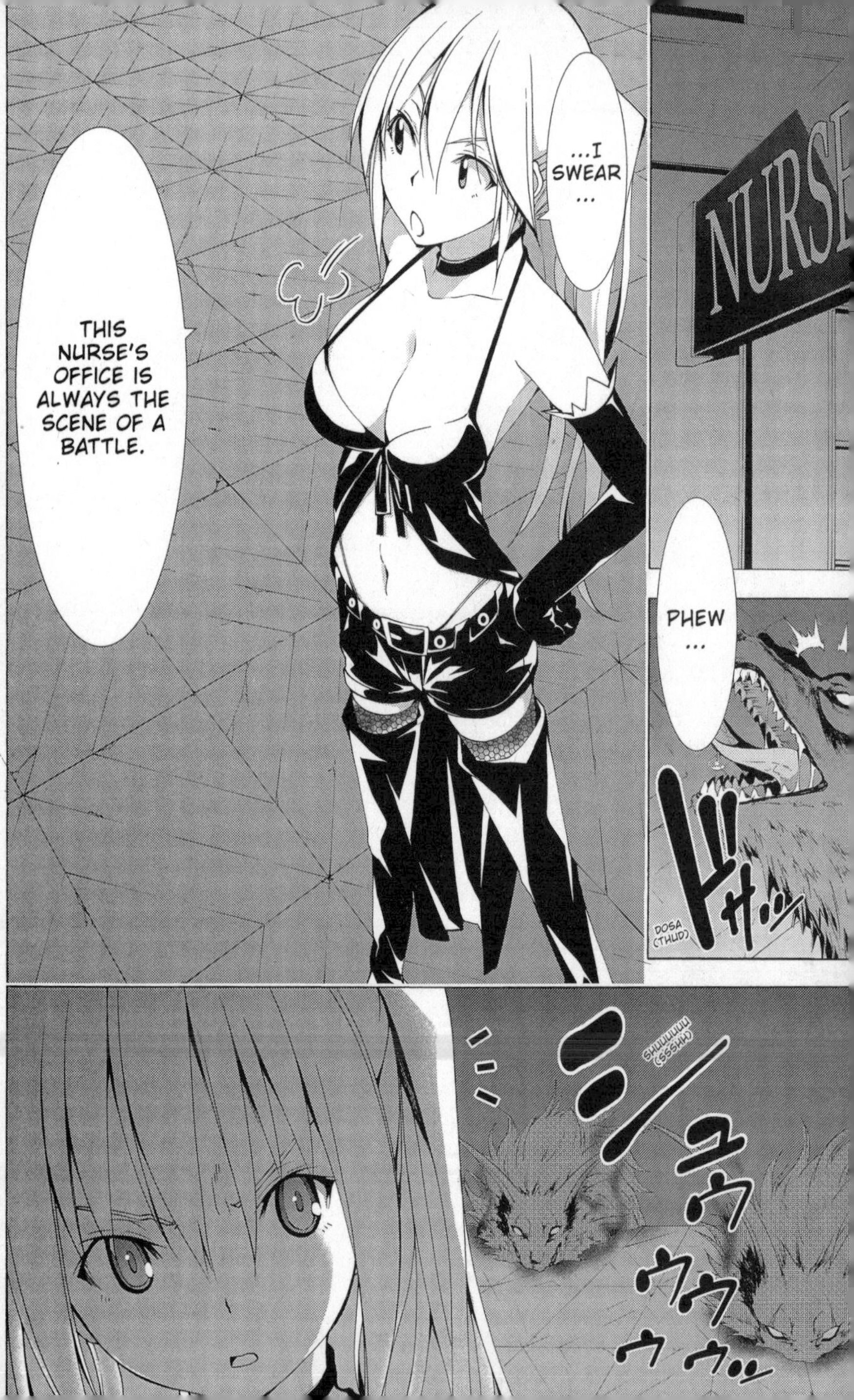
NURSE
PHEW ...
DOSA (THUD)
...I SWEAR ...
THIS NURSE'S OFFICE IS ALWAYS THE SCENE OF A BATTLE.
SHUUUUUU (SSSHH)

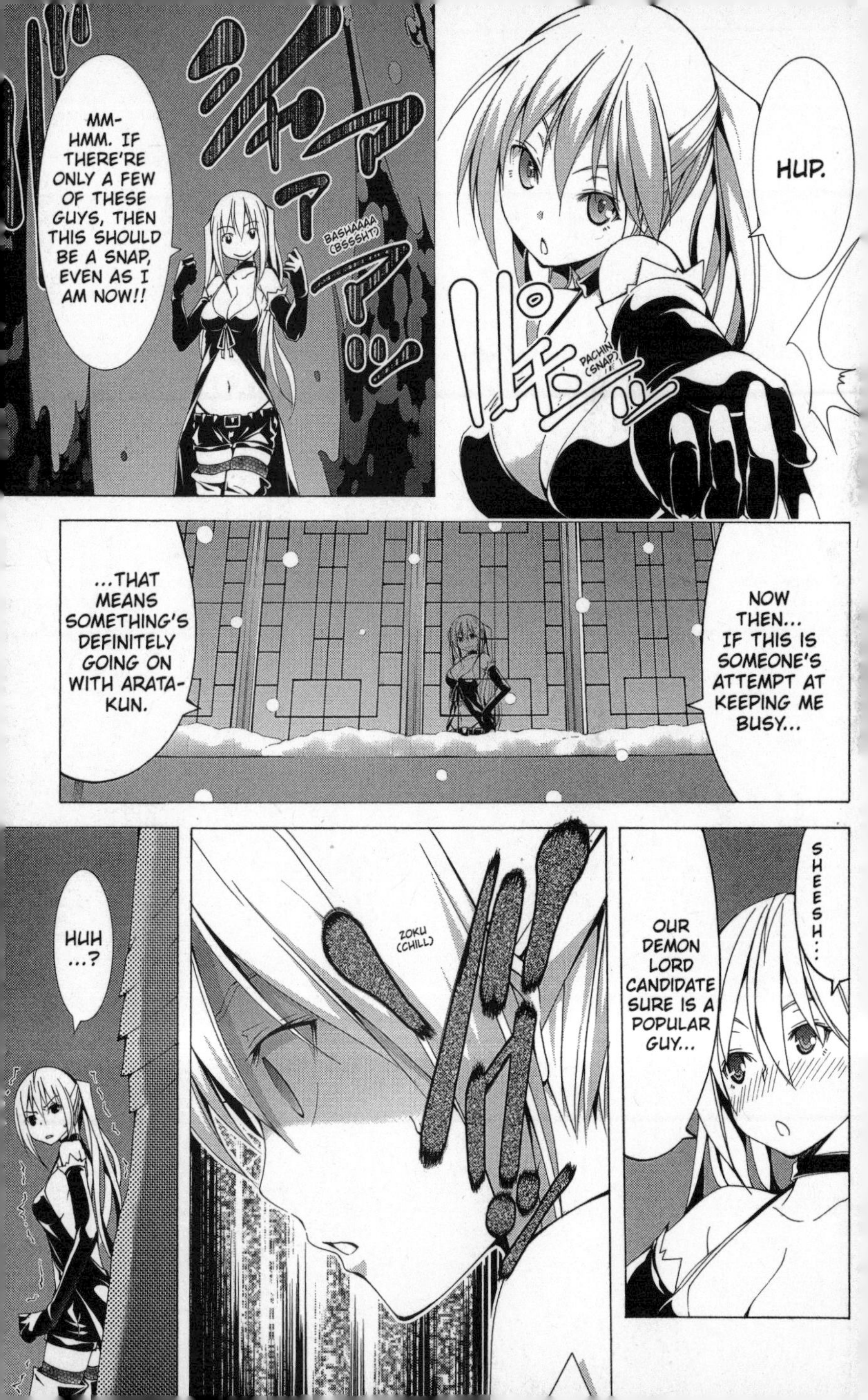
HUP.
PACHIN (SNAP)
BASHAAAA (BSSSHT)
MM-HMM. IF THERE'RE ONLY A FEW OF THESE GUYS, THEN THIS SHOULD BE A SNAP, EVEN AS I AM NOW!!
NOW THEN... IF THIS IS SOMEONE'S ATTEMPT AT KEEPING ME BUSY...
...THAT MEANS SOMETHING'S DEFINITELY GOING ON WITH ARATA-KUN.
SHEESH...
OUR DEMON LORD CANDIDATE SURE IS A POPULAR GUY...
ZOKU (CHILL)
HUH ...?

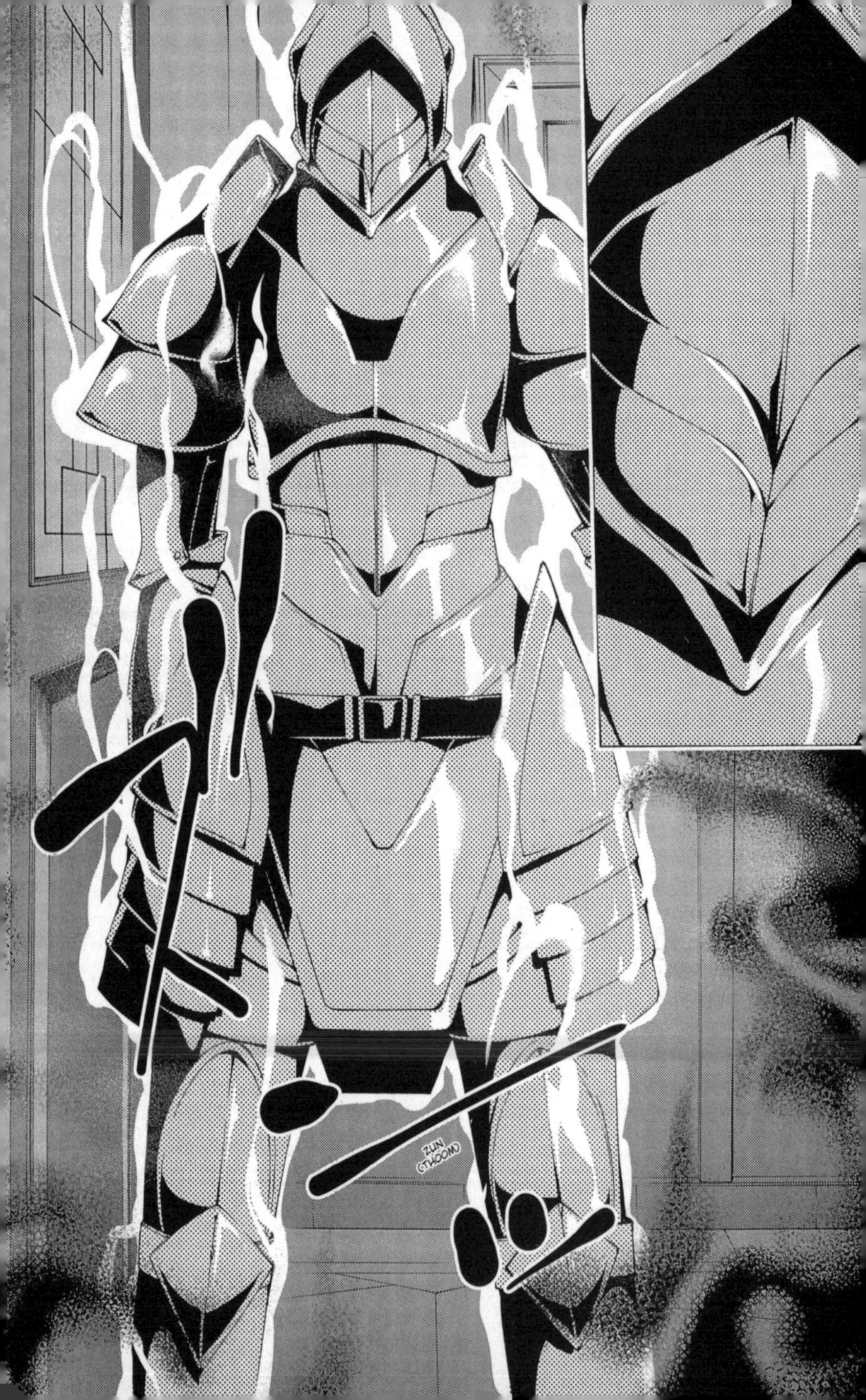
ZUN
(THOOM)

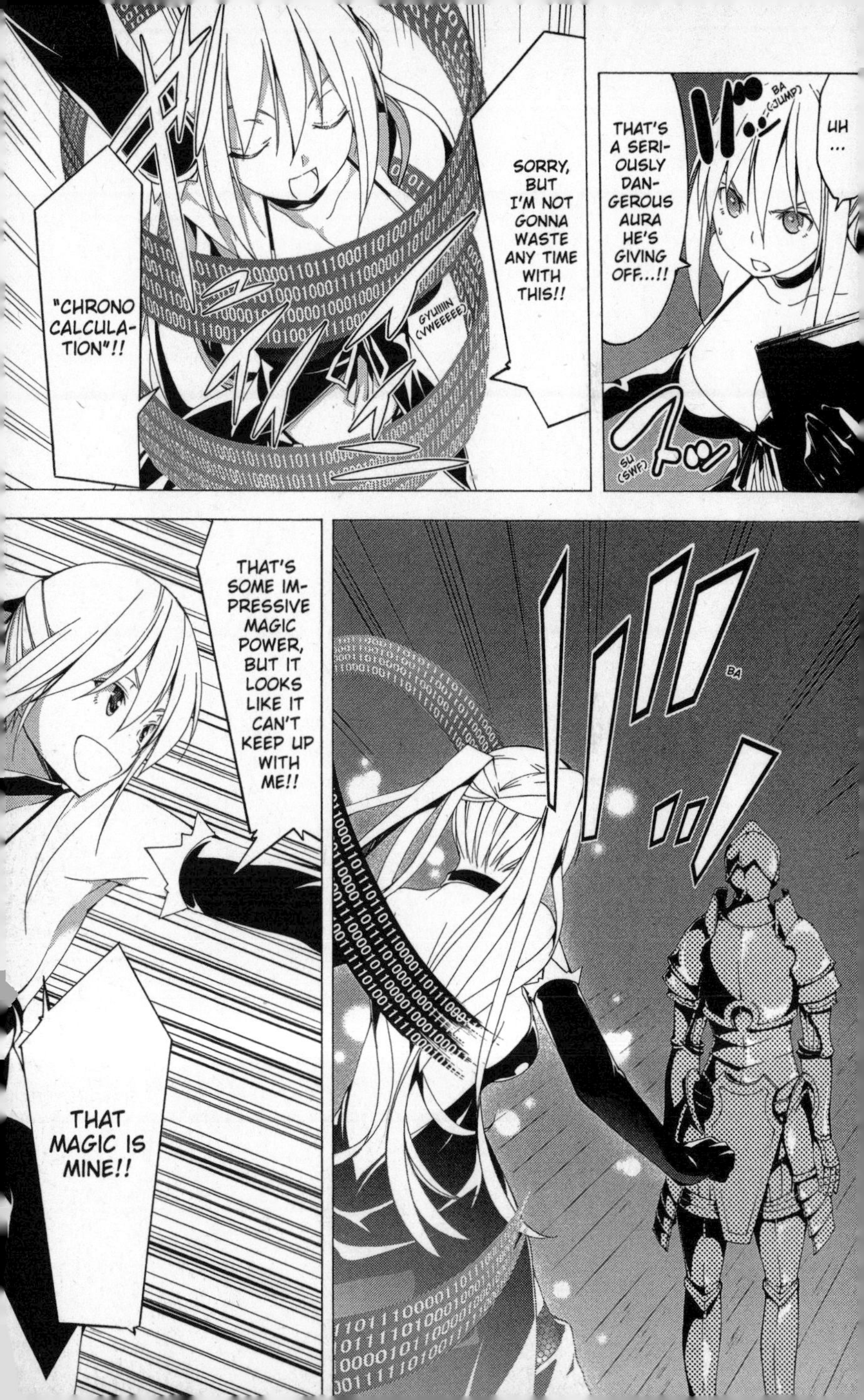
UH...
BA (JUMP)
THAT'S A SERIOUSLY DANGEROUS AURA HE'S GIVING OFF...!!
SU (SWF)
SORRY, BUT I'M NOT GONNA WASTE ANY TIME WITH THIS!!
GYUIIIIN (VWEEEEE)
"CHRONO CALCULATION"!!
BA
THAT'S SOME IMPRESSIVE MAGIC POWER, BUT IT LOOKS LIKE IT CAN'T KEEP UP WITH ME!!
THAT MAGIC IS MINE!!

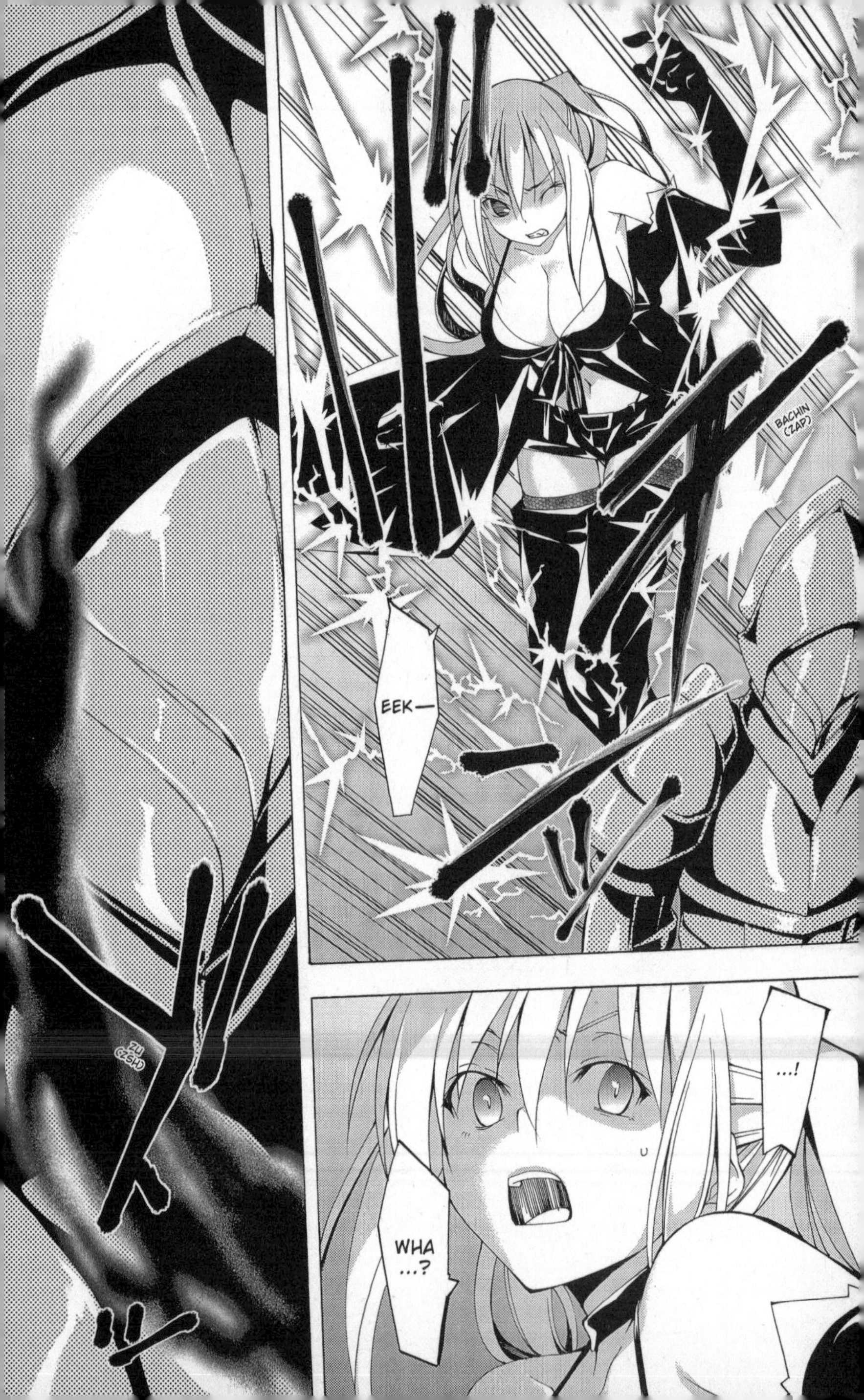
BACHIN (ZAP)
EEK—
...!
WHA ...?
ZU (ZSH)

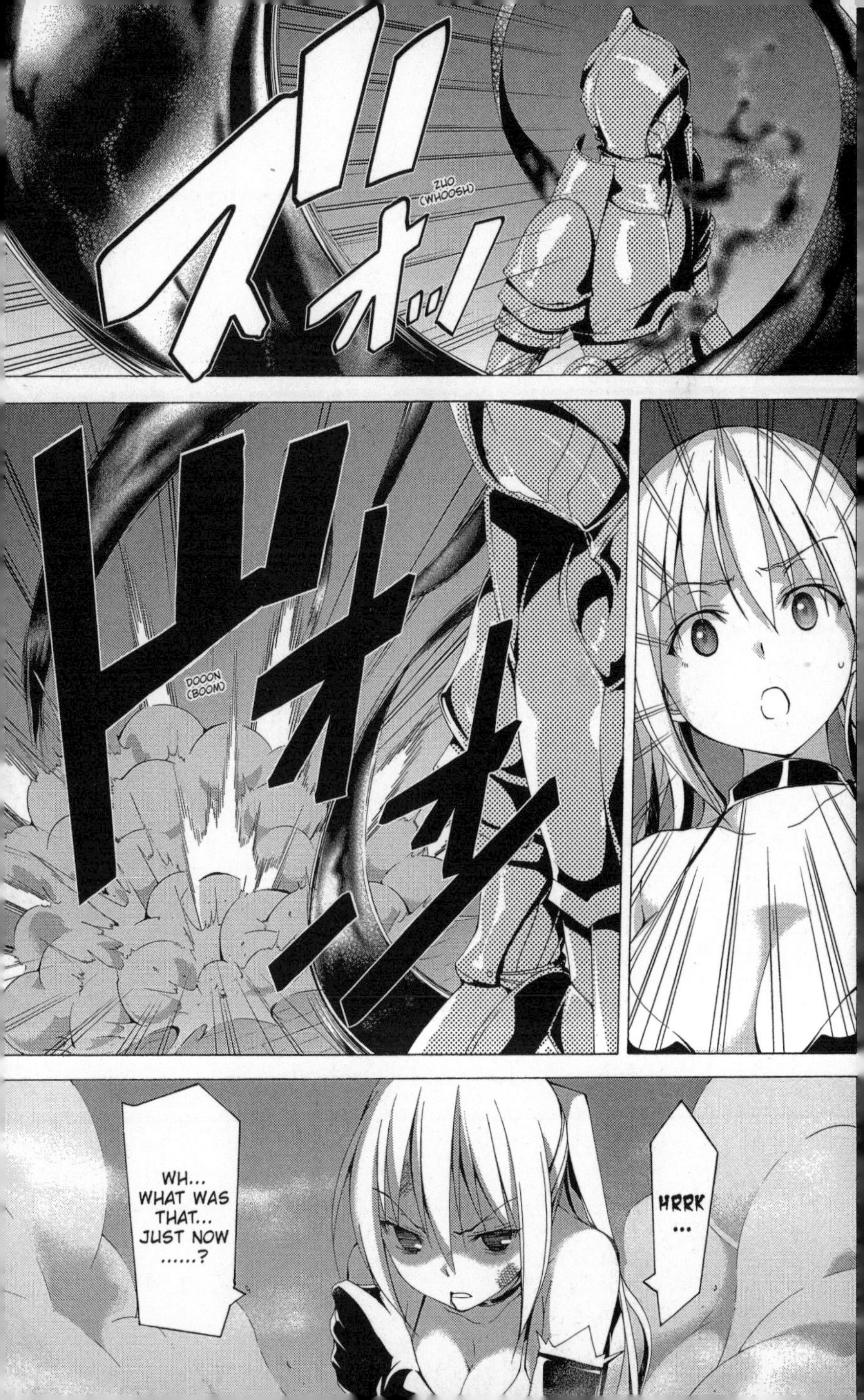
ZUO (WHOOSH)
DOOON (BOOM)
HRRK ...
WH... WHAT WAS THAT... JUST NOW ......?

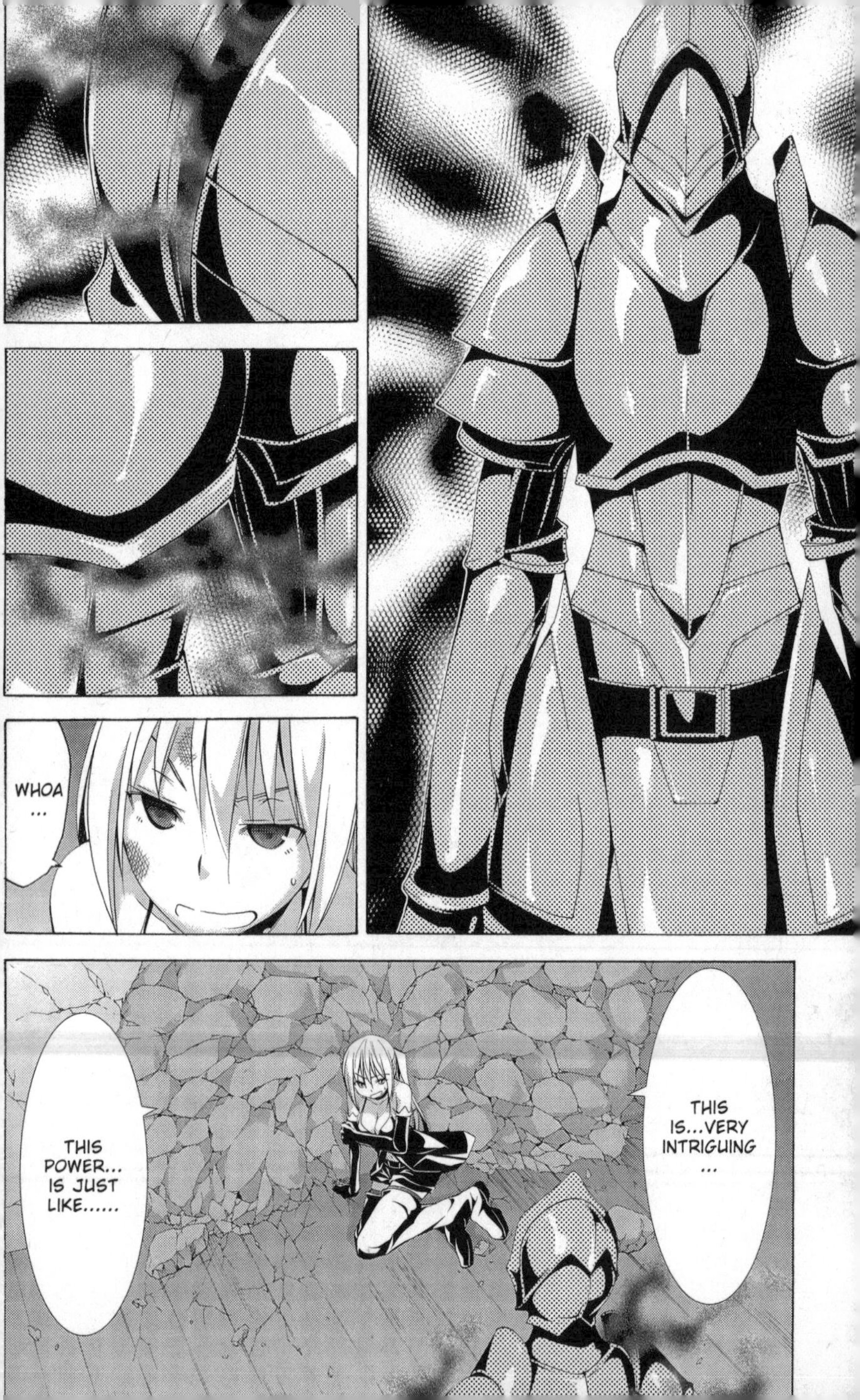
WHOA ...
THIS IS...VERY INTRIGUING ...
THIS POWER... IS JUST LIKE......

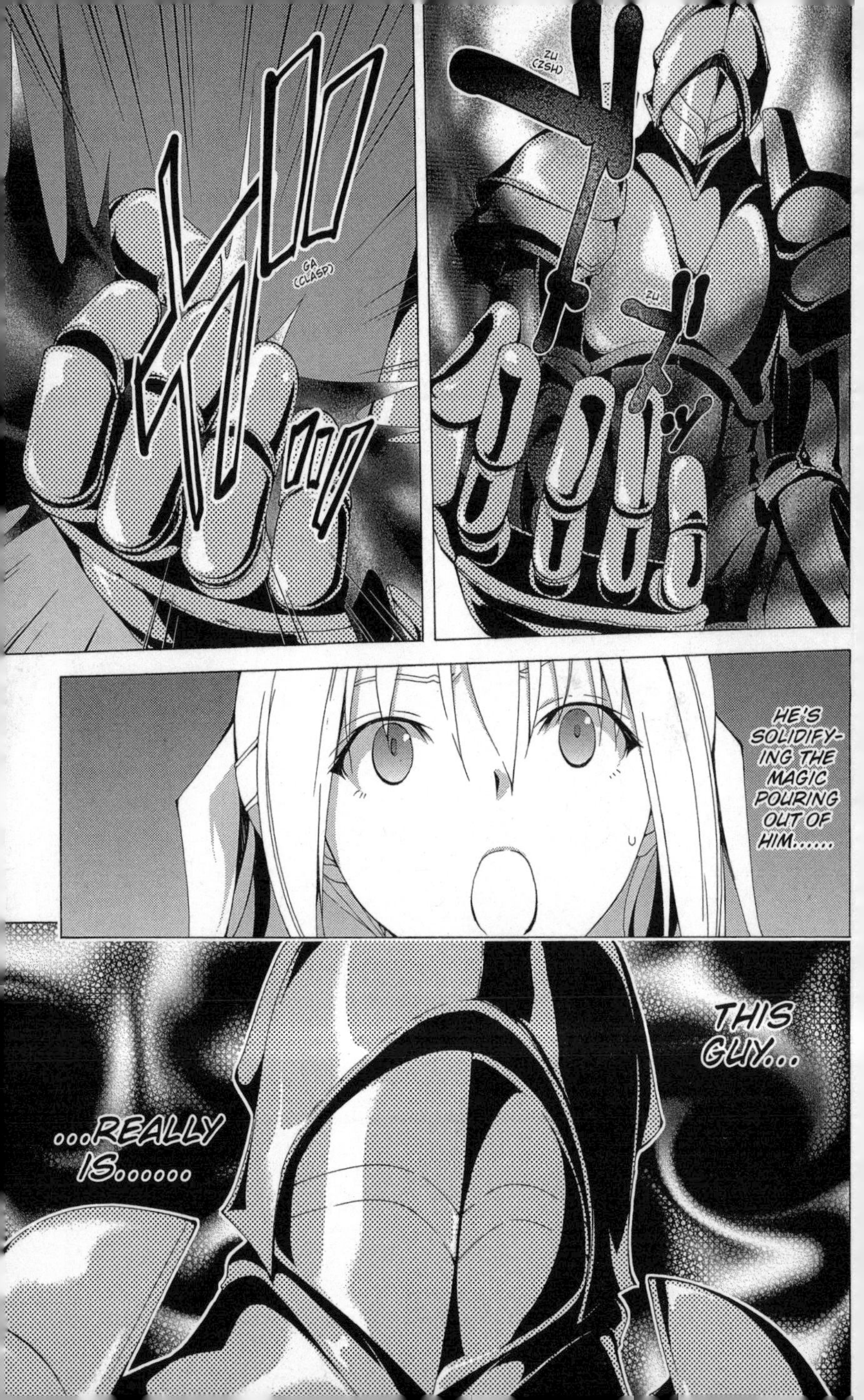
ZU (ZSH)
ZU
GA (CLASP)
HE'S SOLIDIFYING THE MAGIC POURING OUT OF HIM......
THIS GUY...
...REALLY IS.......

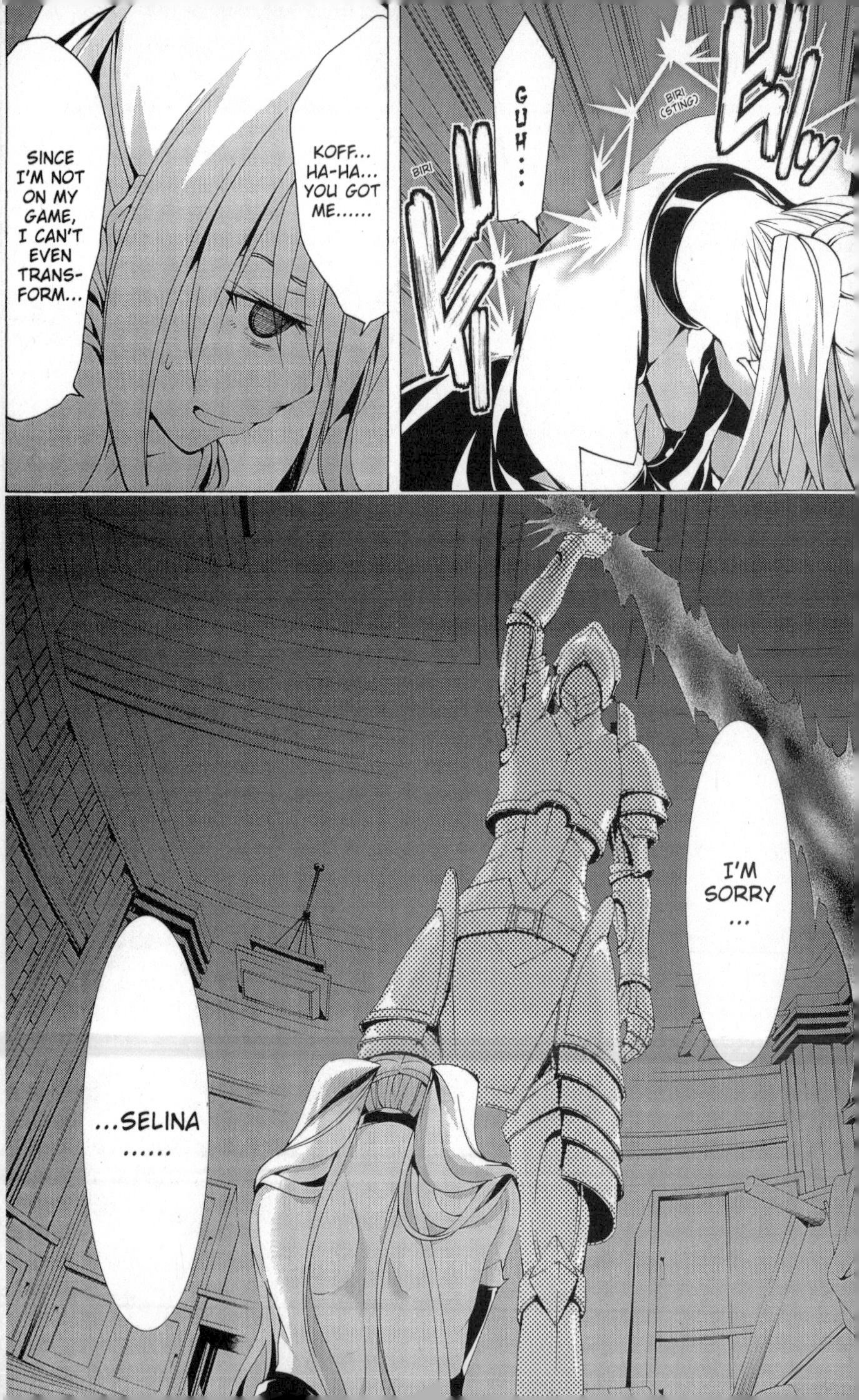
BIRI (STING)
GUH...
BIRI
KOFF... HA-HA... YOU GOT ME......
SINCE I'M NOT ON MY GAME, I CAN'T EVEN TRANS-FORM...
I'M SORRY ...
...SELINA ......

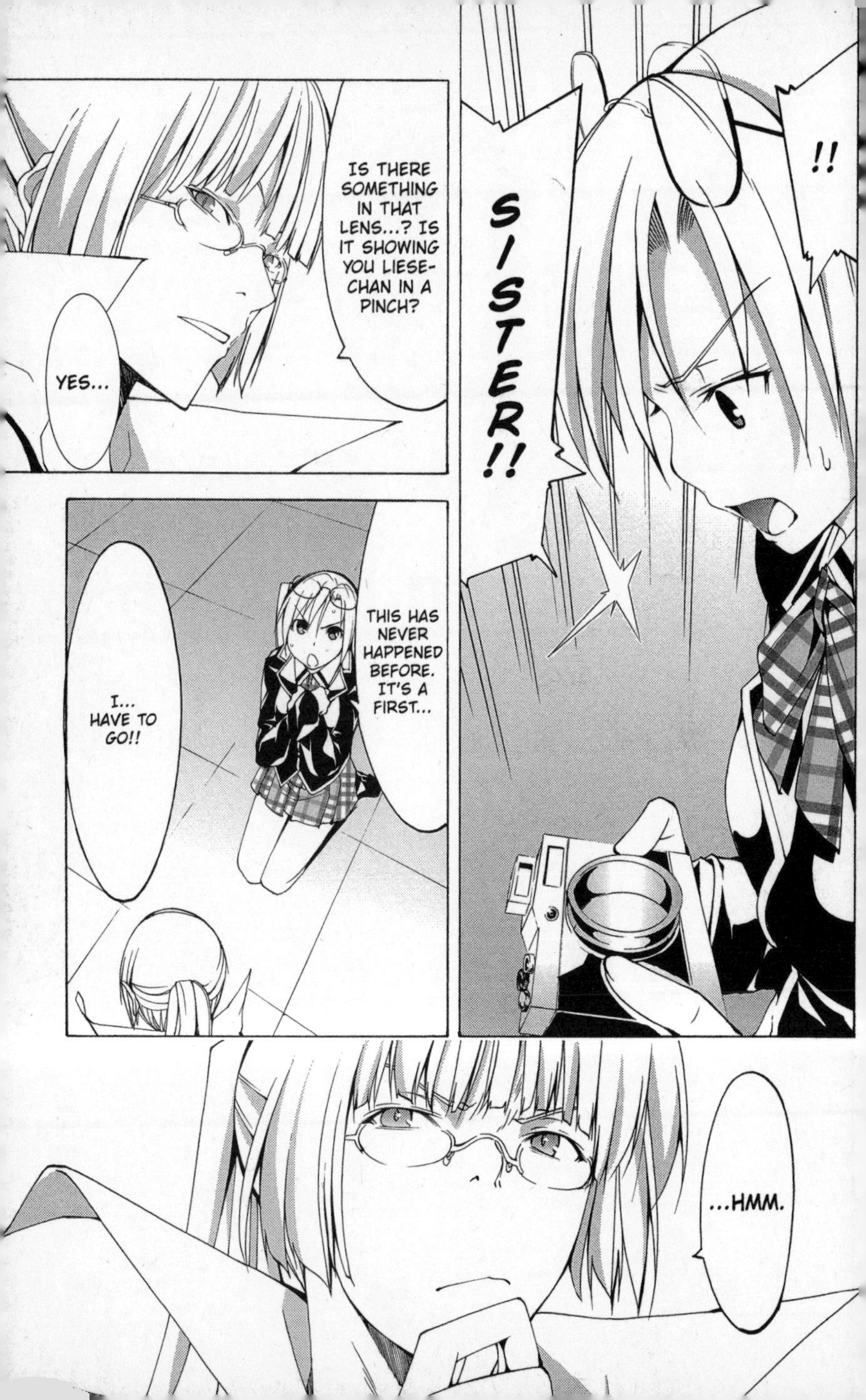
!!
SISTER!!
IS THERE SOMETHING IN THAT LENS...? IS IT SHOWING YOU LIESE-CHAN IN A PINCH?
YES...
THIS HAS NEVER HAPPENED BEFORE. IT'S A FIRST...
I... HAVE TO GO!!
...HMM.

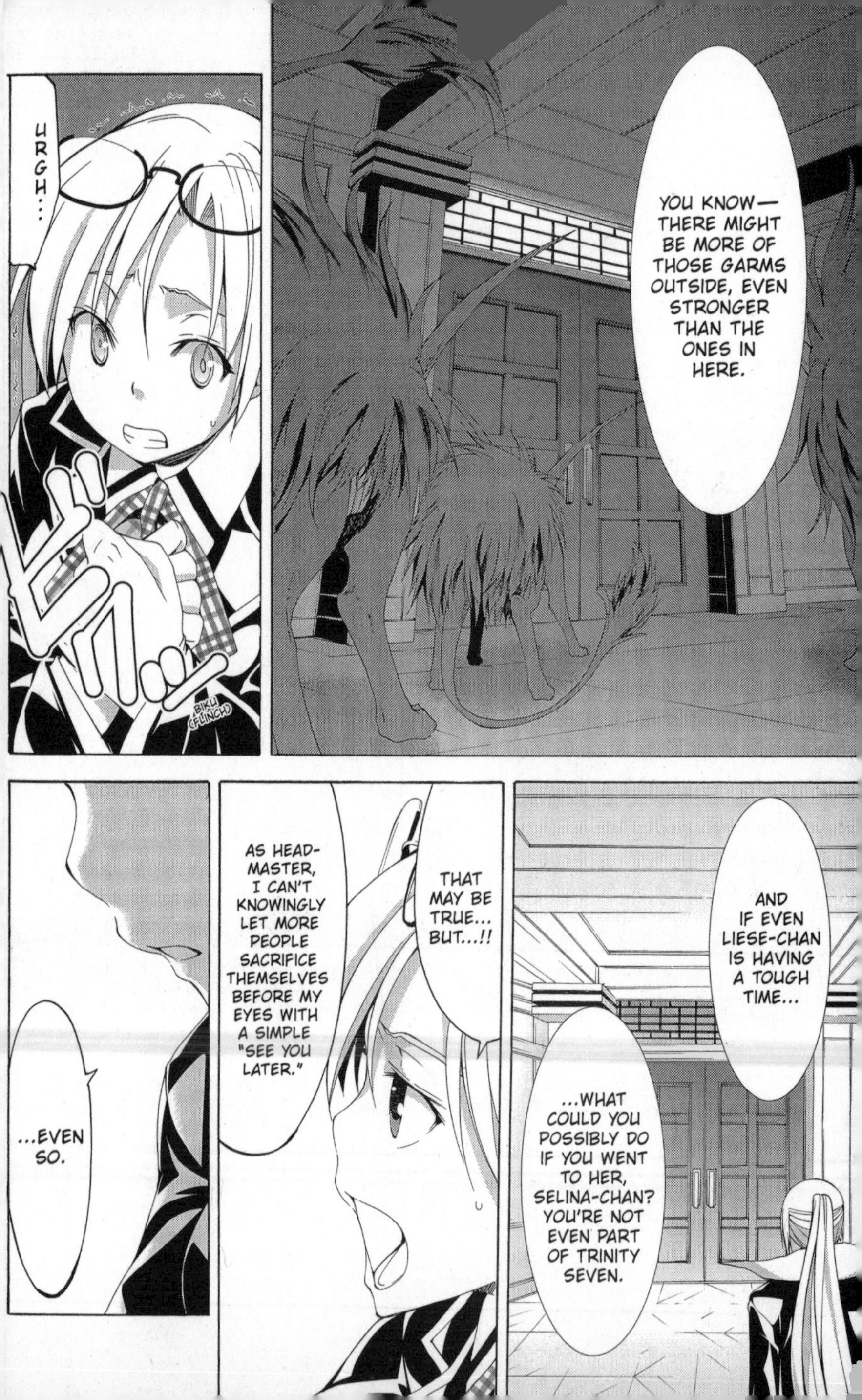
YOU KNOW— THERE MIGHT BE MORE OF THOSE GARMS OUTSIDE, EVEN STRONGER THAN THE ONES IN HERE.
URGH...
BIKU (FLINCH)
AND IF EVEN LIESE-CHAN IS HAVING A TOUGH TIME...
...WHAT COULD YOU POSSIBLY DO IF YOU WENT TO HER, SELINA-CHAN? YOU'RE NOT EVEN PART OF TRINITY SEVEN.
THAT MAY BE TRUE... BUT...!!
AS HEAD-MASTER, I CAN'T KNOWINGLY LET MORE PEOPLE SACRIFICE THEMSELVES BEFORE MY EYES WITH A SIMPLE "SEE YOU LATER."
...EVEN SO.

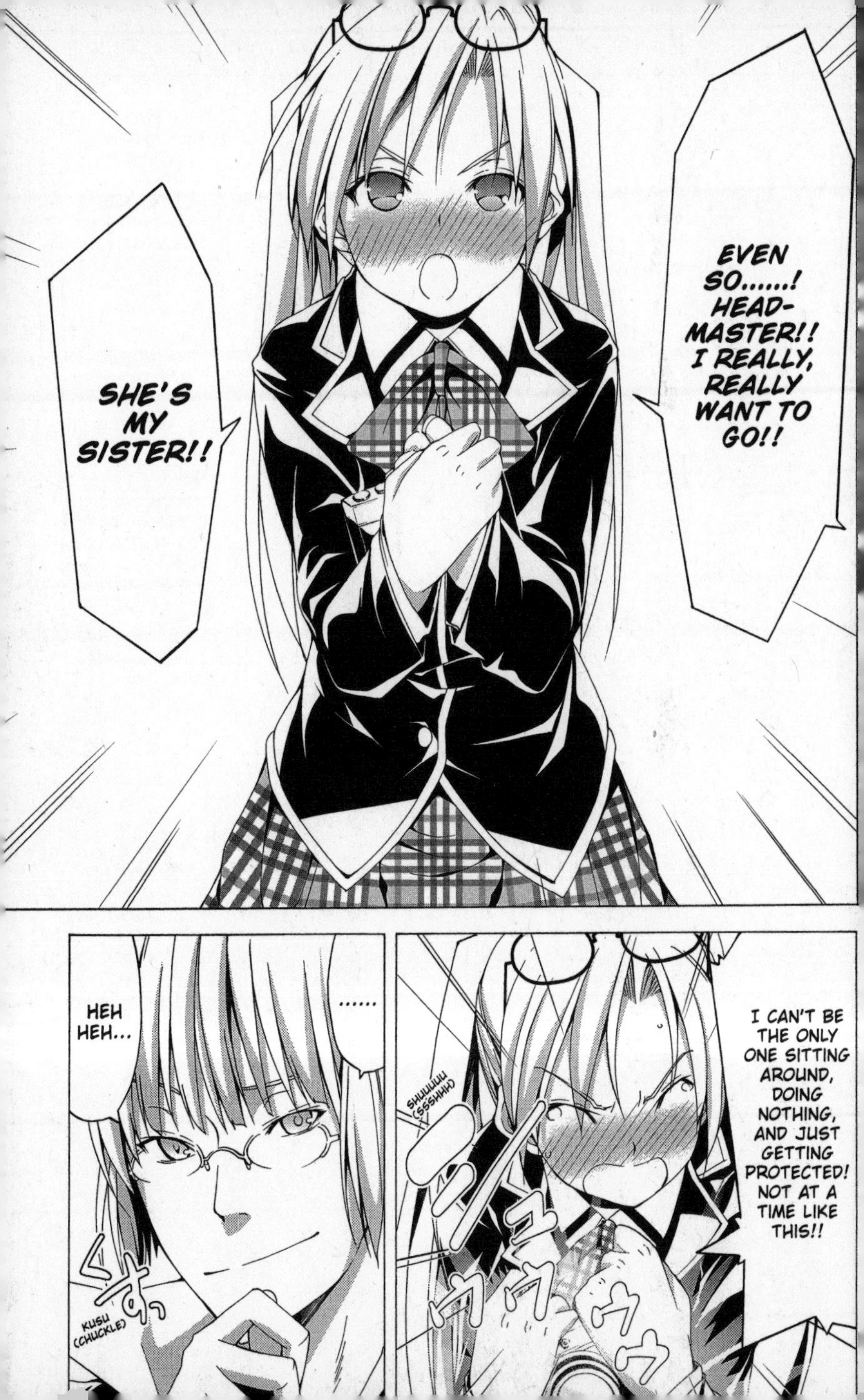
EVEN SO......! HEAD-MASTER!! I REALLY, REALLY WANT TO GO!!
SHE'S MY SISTER!!
I CAN'T BE THE ONLY ONE SITTING AROUND, DOING NOTHING, AND JUST GETTING PROTECTED! NOT AT A TIME LIKE THIS!!
SHUUUUU (SSSHHH)
......
HEH HEH...
KUSU (CHUCKLE)

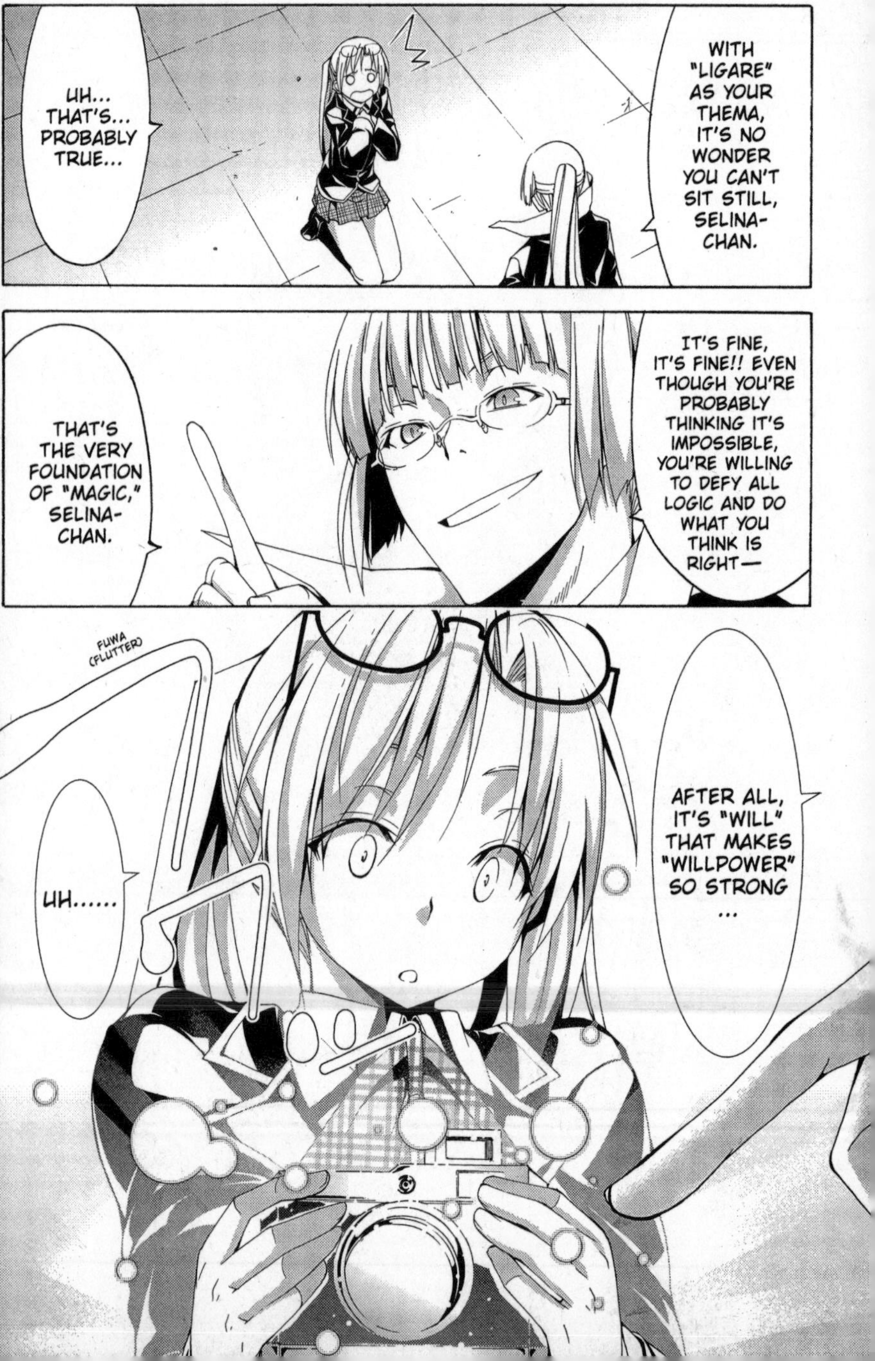
WITH "LIGARE" AS YOUR THEMA, IT'S NO WONDER YOU CAN'T SIT STILL, SELINA-CHAN.
UH... THAT'S... PROBABLY TRUE...
IT'S FINE, IT'S FINE!! EVEN THOUGH YOU'RE PROBABLY THINKING IT'S IMPOSSIBLE, YOU'RE WILLING TO DEFY ALL LOGIC AND DO WHAT YOU THINK IS RIGHT—
THAT'S THE VERY FOUNDATION OF "MAGIC," SELINA-CHAN.
AFTER ALL, IT'S "WILL" THAT MAKES "WILLPOWER" SO STRONG ...
FUWA (FLUTTER)
UH......

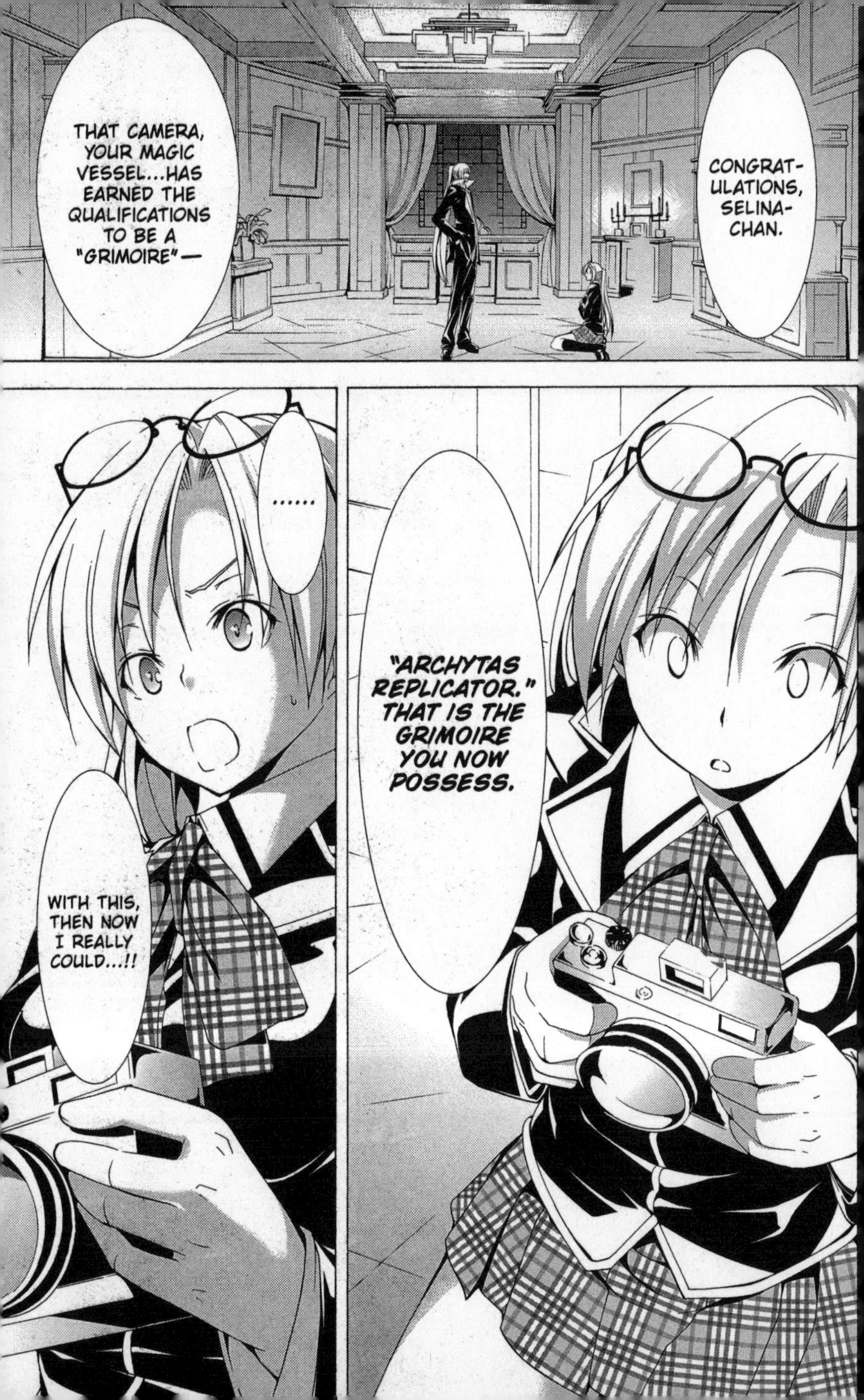
CONGRAT-ULATIONS, SELINA-CHAN.
THAT CAMERA, YOUR MAGIC VESSEL...HAS EARNED THE QUALIFICATIONS TO BE A "GRIMOIRE"—
"ARCHYTAS REPLICATOR." THAT IS THE GRIMOIRE YOU NOW POSSESS.
......
WITH THIS, THEN NOW I REALLY COULD...!!

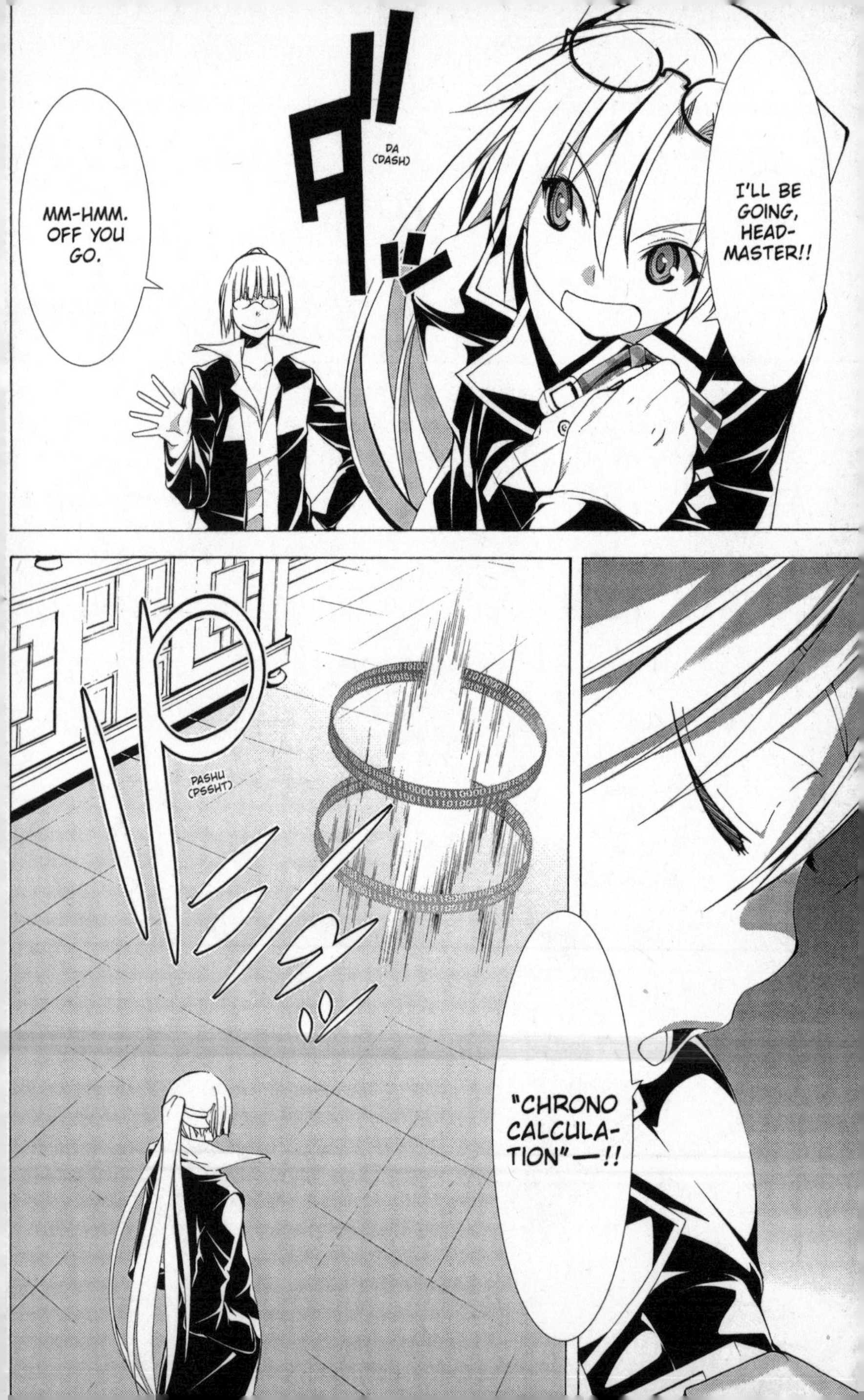
I'LL BE GOING, HEAD-MASTER!!
DA (DASH)
MM-HMM. OFF YOU GO.
"CHRONO CALCULA-TION"—!!
PASHU (PSSHT)

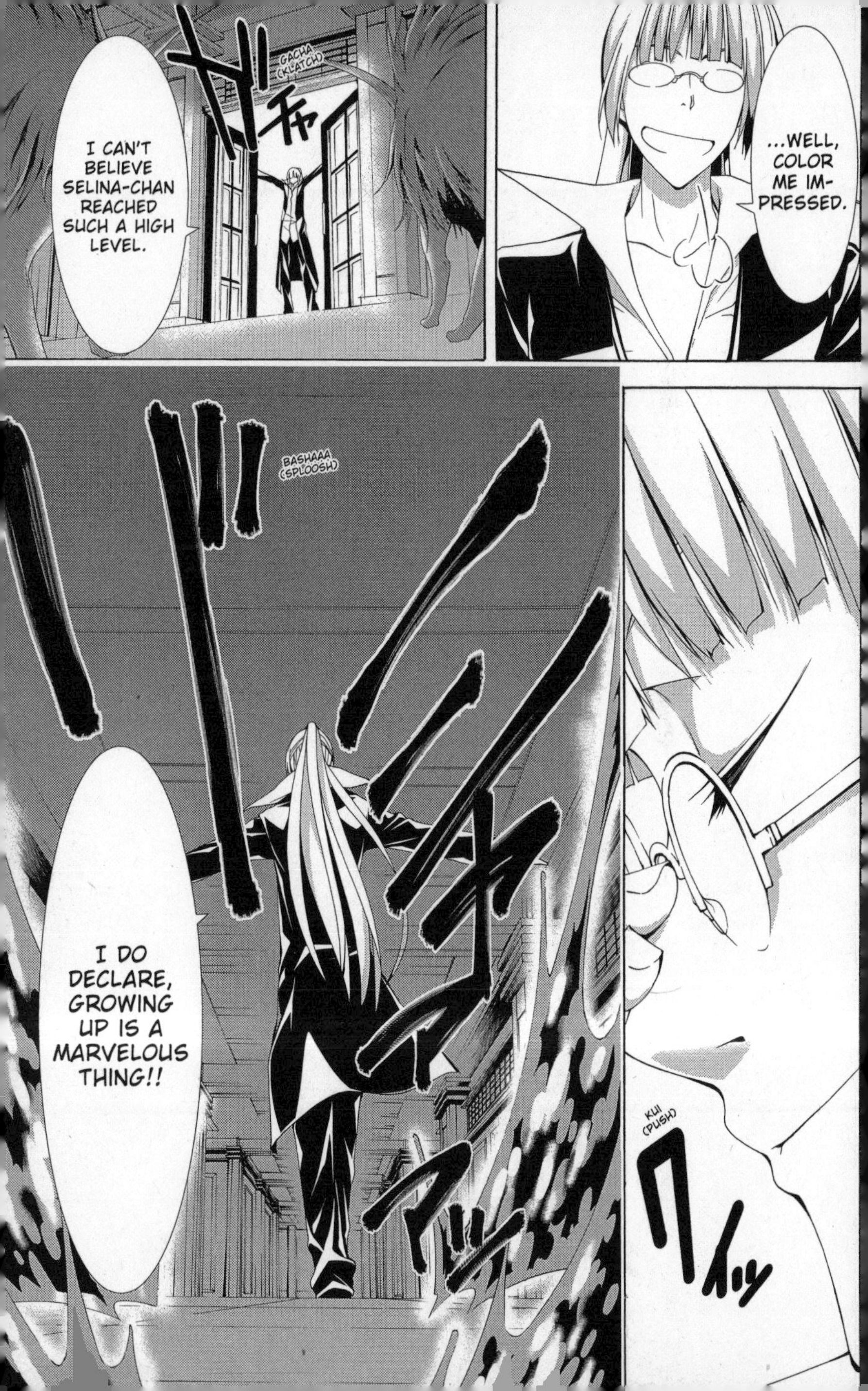
...WELL, COLOR ME IM-PRESSED.
GACHA (KLATCH)
I CAN'T BELIEVE SELINA-CHAN REACHED SUCH A HIGH LEVEL.
KUI (PUSH)
BASHAAA (SPLOOSH)
I DO DECLARE, GROWING UP IS A MARVELOUS THING!!

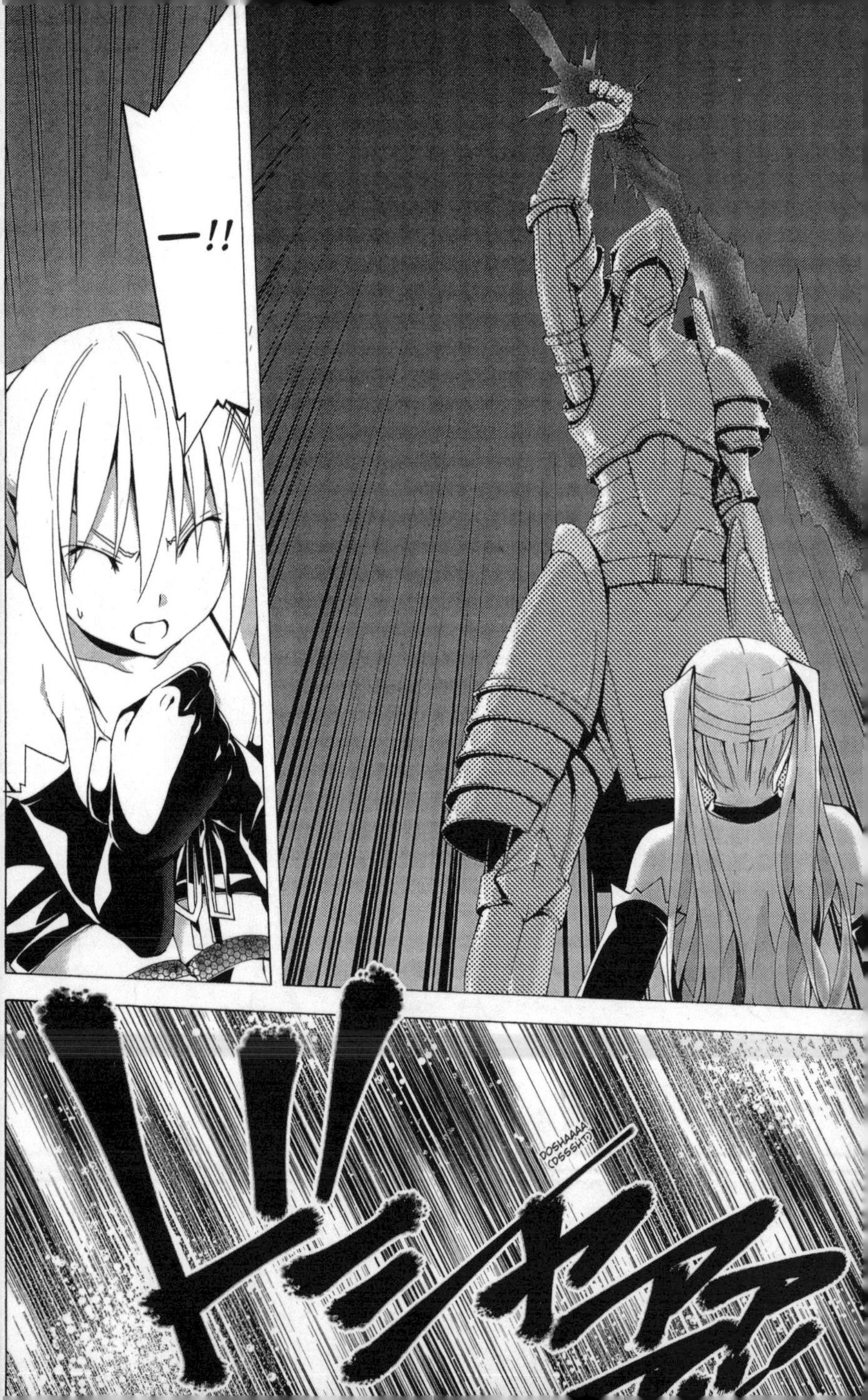
—!!
DOSHAAAA
(DSSSHT)

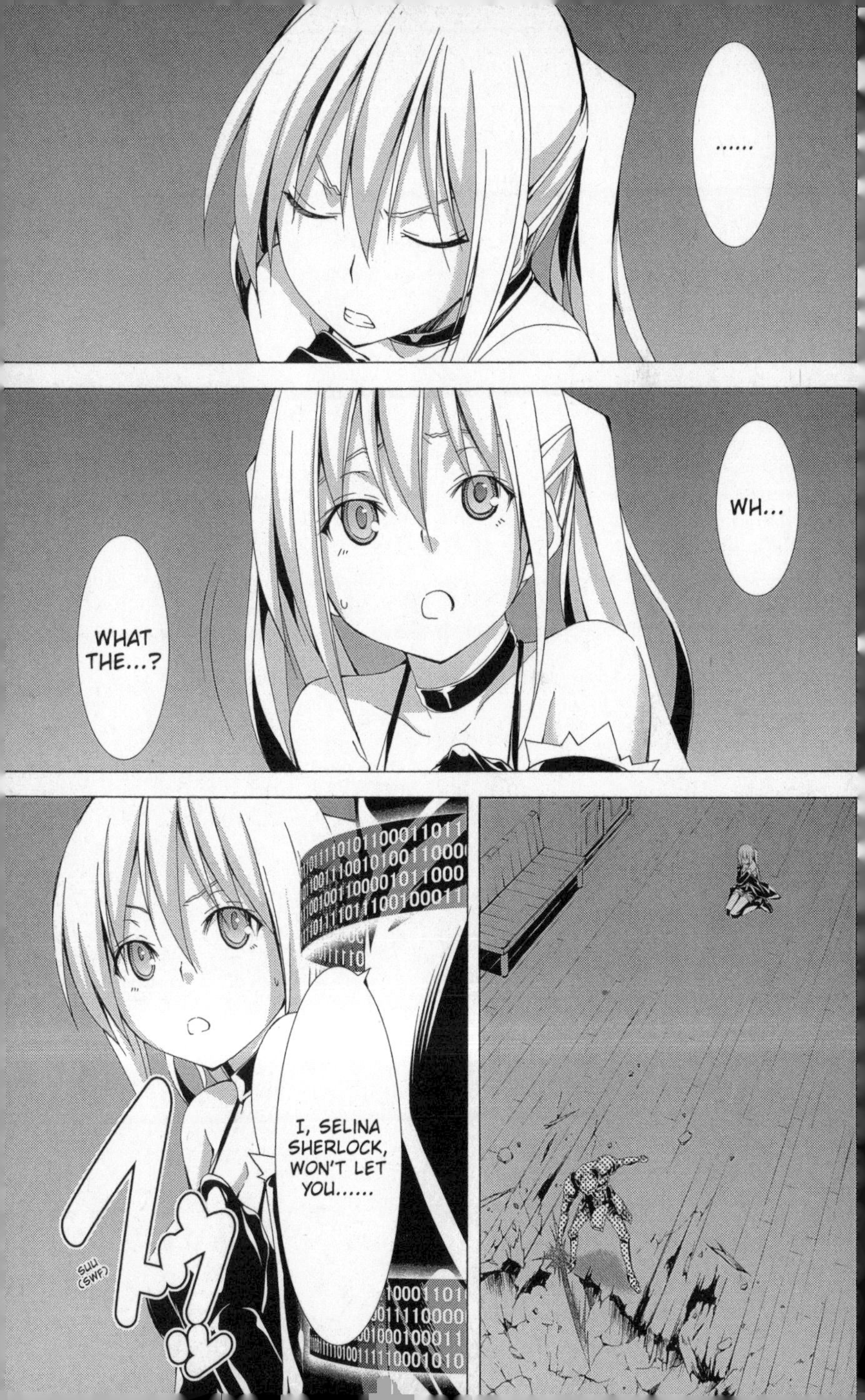
......
WH...
WHAT THE...?
I, SELINA SHERLOCK, WON'T LET YOU......
SUU (SWF)

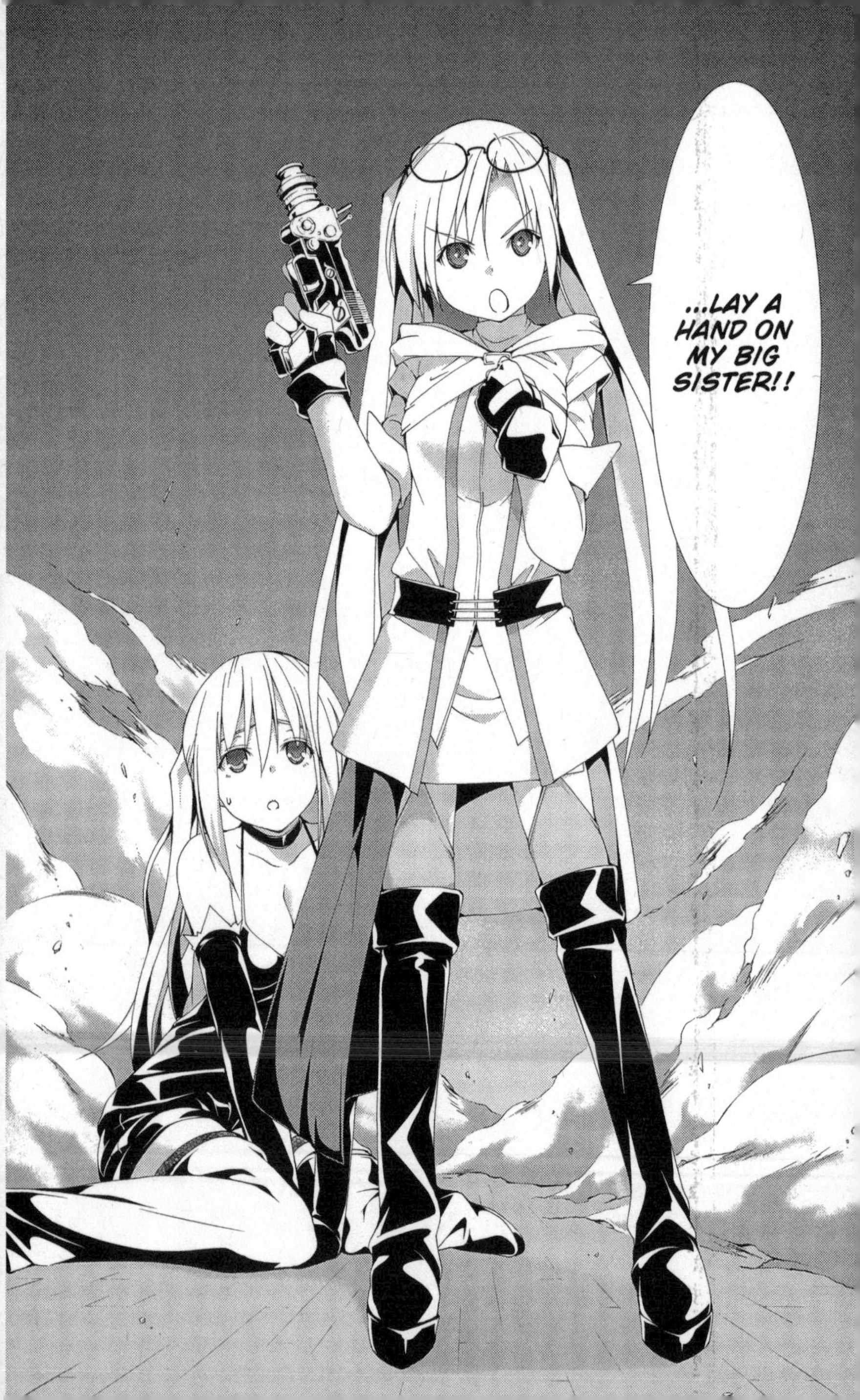
...LAY A HAND ON MY BIG SISTER!!

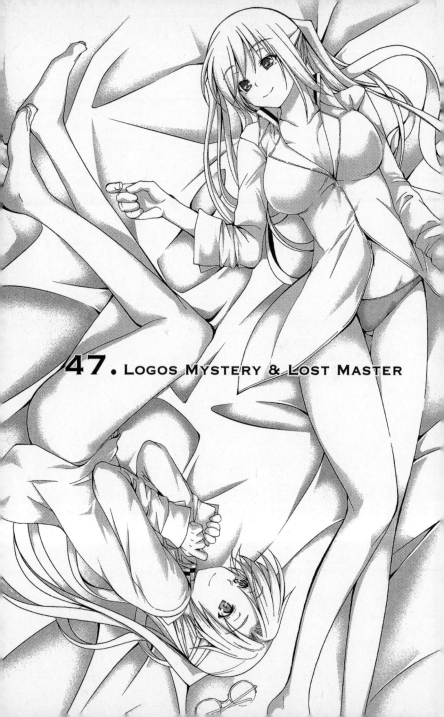

47. Logos Mystery & Lost Master

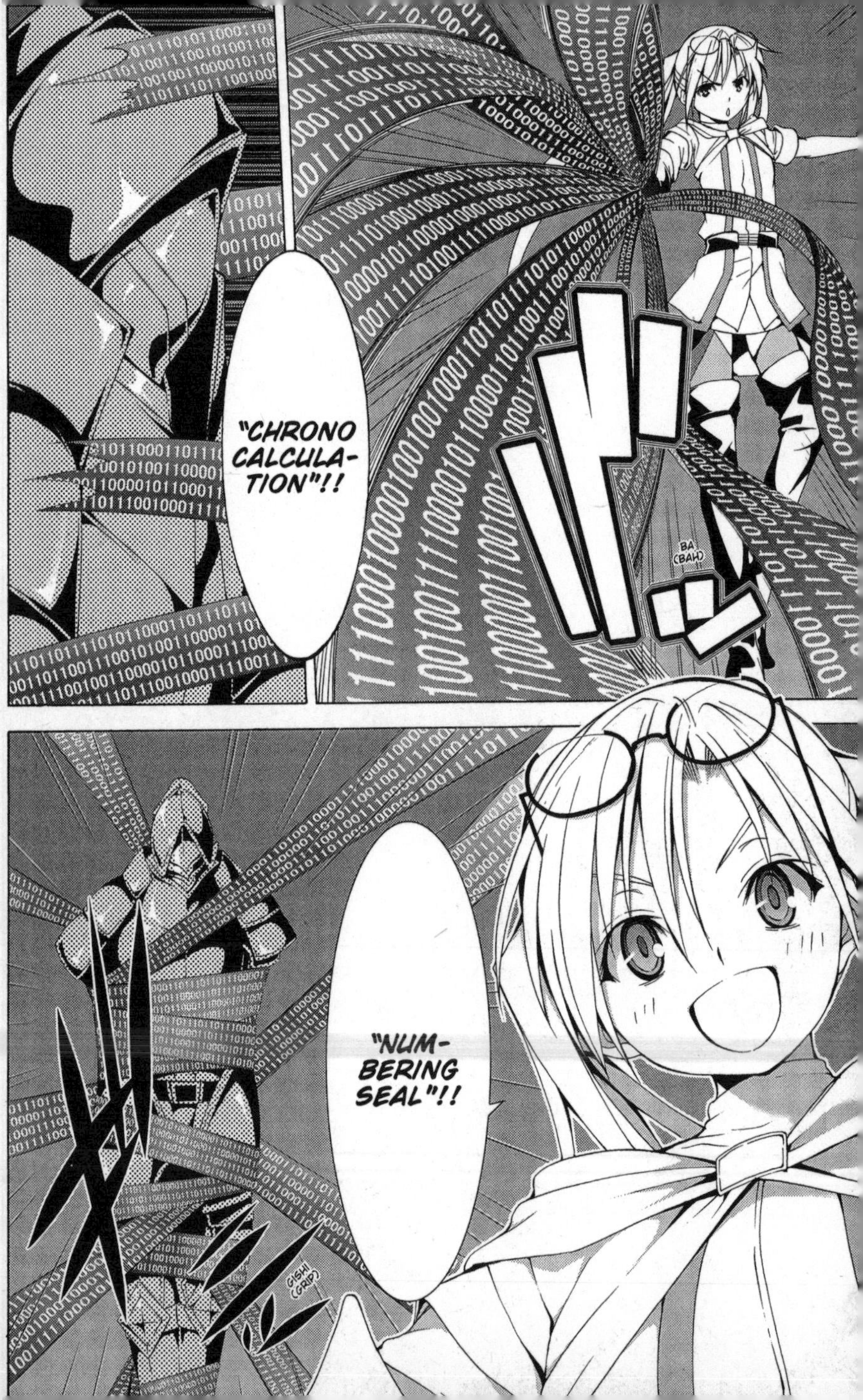
BA (BAH)
"CHRONO CALCULATION"!!
"NUMBERING SEAL"!!
GISHI (GRIP)

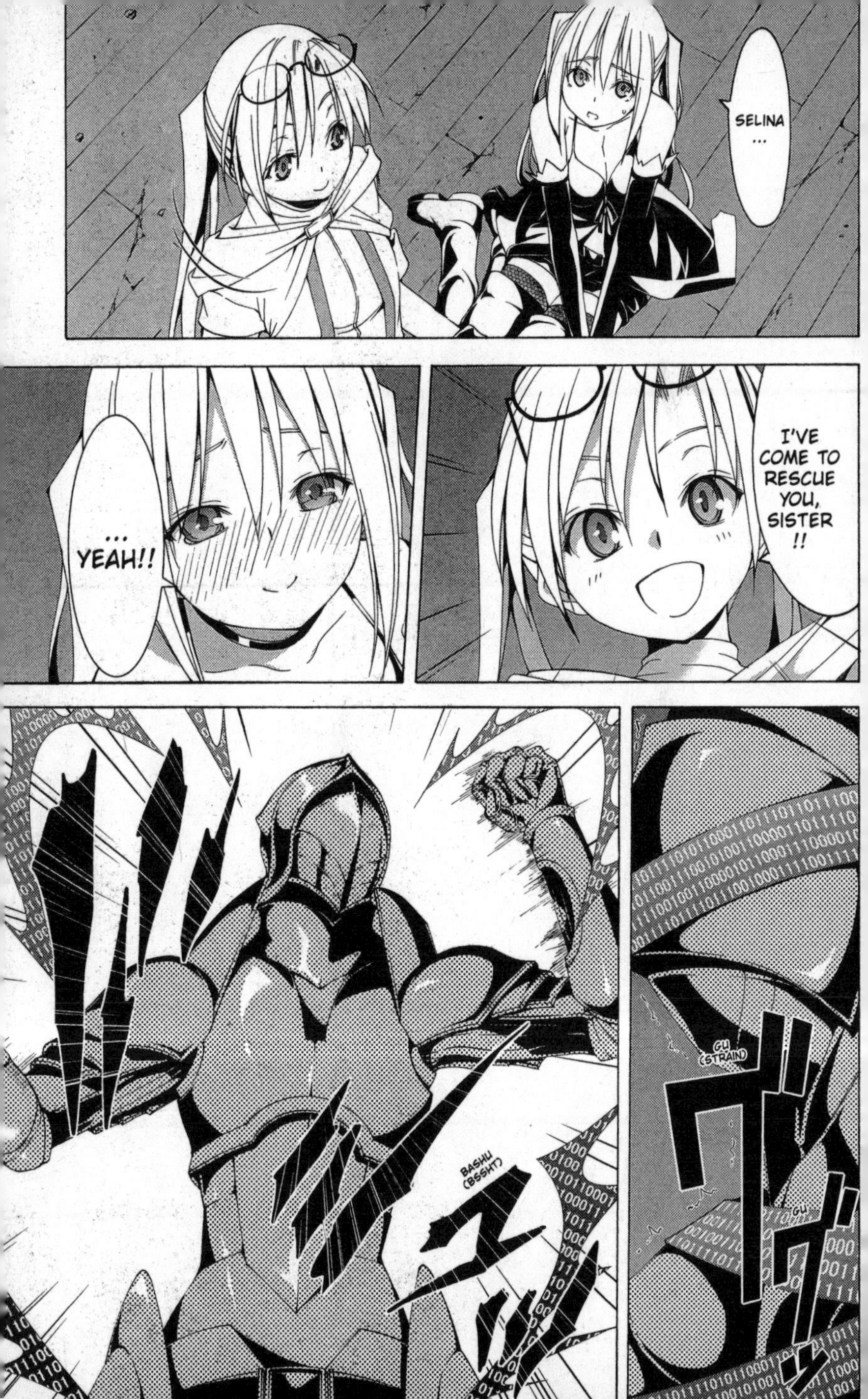
SELINA ...
I'VE COME TO RESCUE YOU, SISTER!!
... YEAH!!
GU (STRAIN)
GU
BASHU (BSSHT)

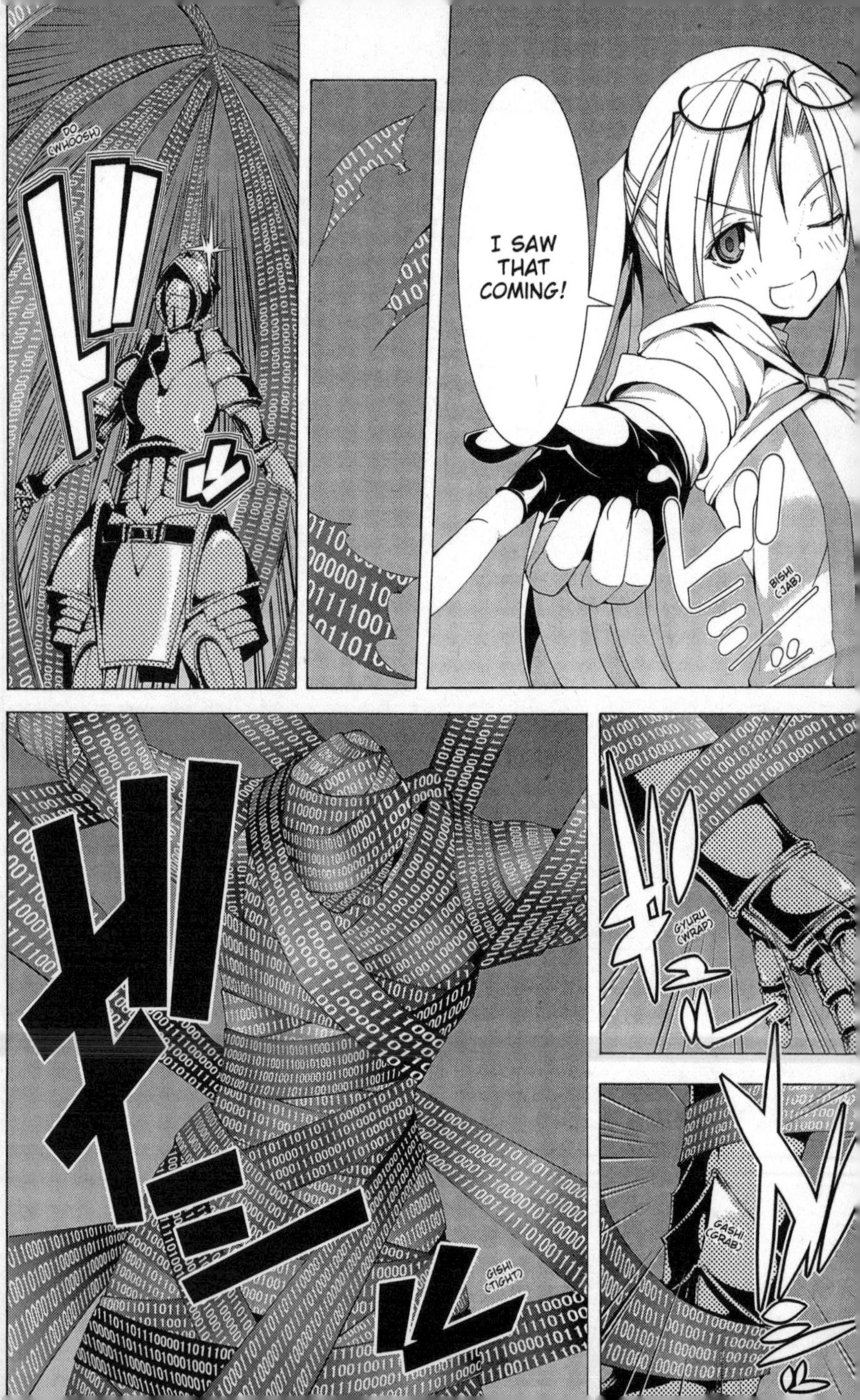
I SAW THAT COMING!
BISHI (JAB)
DO (WHOOSH)
GYURU (WRAP)
GASHI (GRAB)
GISHI (TIGHT)

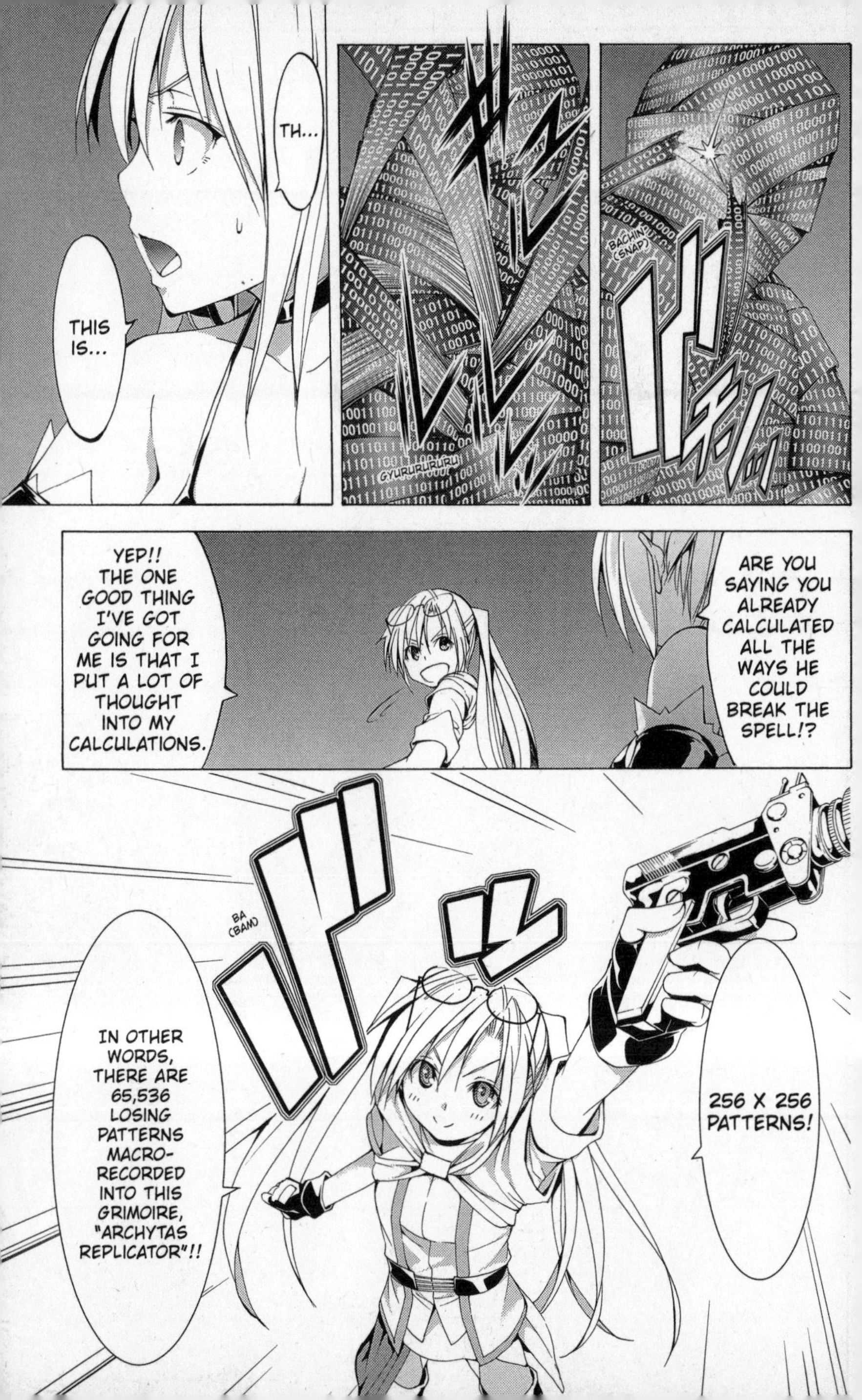
BACHIN (SNAP)
GYURURURURU
TH...
THIS IS...
ARE YOU SAYING YOU ALREADY CALCULATED ALL THE WAYS HE COULD BREAK THE SPELL!?
YEP!! THE ONE GOOD THING I'VE GOT GOING FOR ME IS THAT I PUT A LOT OF THOUGHT INTO MY CALCULATIONS.
256 X 256 PATTERNS!
BA (BAM)
IN OTHER WORDS, THERE ARE 65,536 LOSING PATTERNS MACRO-RECORDED INTO THIS GRIMOIRE, "ARCHYTAS REPLICATOR"!!

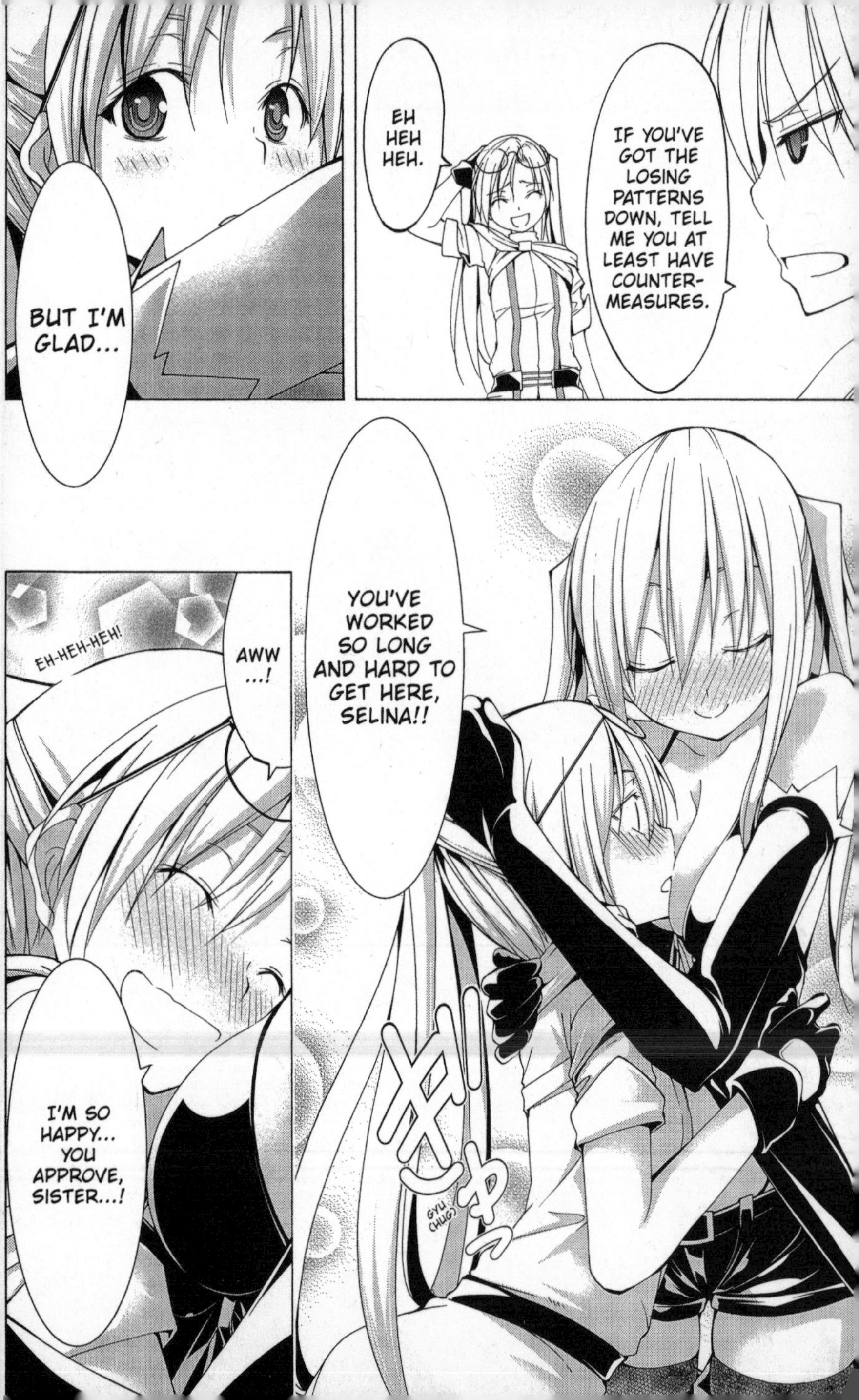
IF YOU'VE GOT THE LOSING PATTERNS DOWN, TELL ME YOU AT LEAST HAVE COUNTER-MEASURES.
EH HEH HEH.
BUT I'M GLAD...
YOU'VE WORKED SO LONG AND HARD TO GET HERE, SELINA!!
GYU (HUG)
AWW ...!
EH-HEH-HEH!
I'M SO HAPPY... YOU APPROVE, SISTER...!

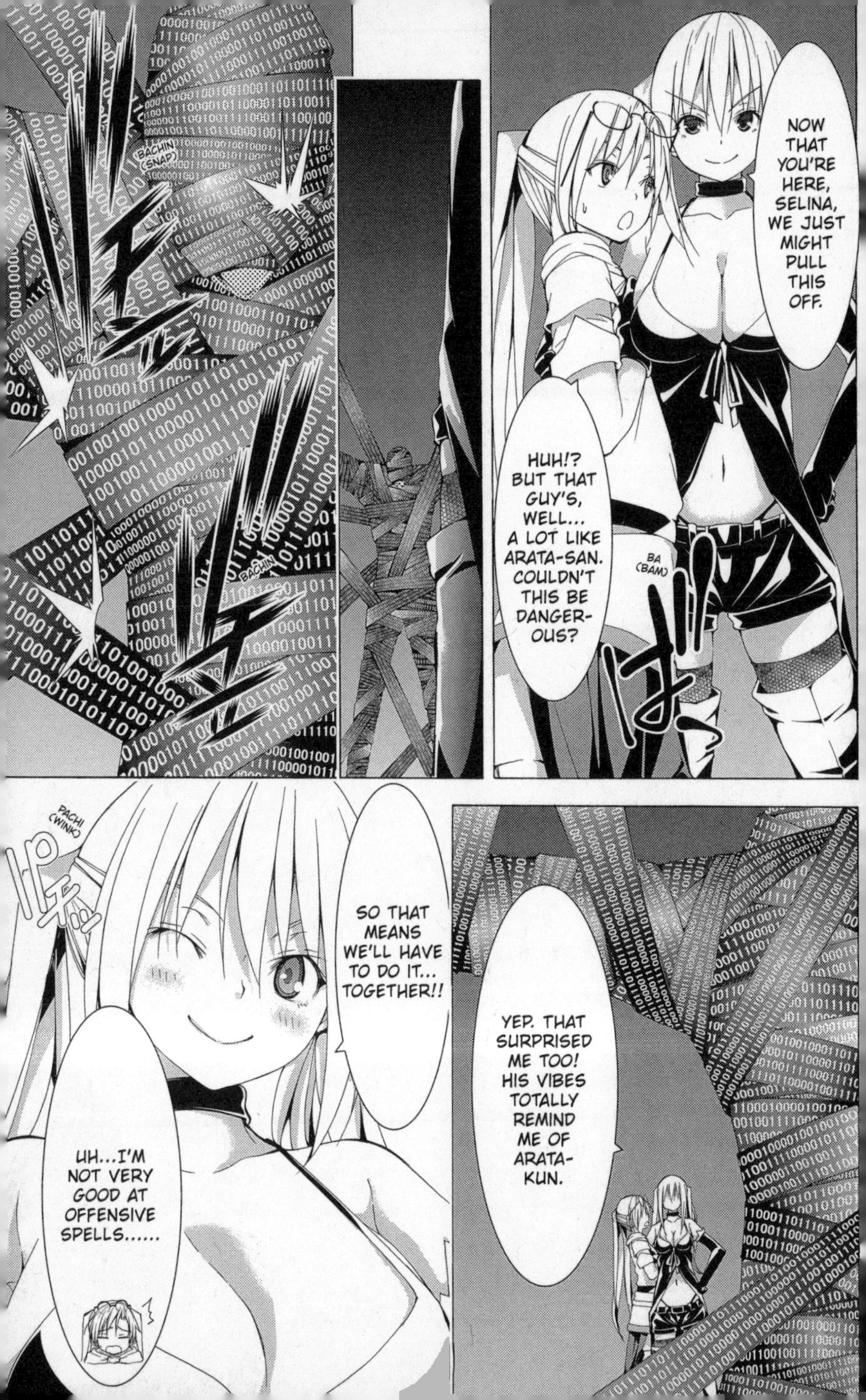
NOW THAT YOU'RE HERE, SELINA, WE JUST MIGHT PULL THIS OFF.
HUH!? BUT THAT GUY'S, WELL... A LOT LIKE ARATA-SAN. COULDN'T THIS BE DANGER-OUS?
BA (BAM)
BACHIN (SNAP)
BACHIN
YEP. THAT SURPRISED ME TOO! HIS VIBES TOTALLY REMIND ME OF ARATA-KUN.
SO THAT MEANS WE'LL HAVE TO DO IT... TOGETHER!!
PACHI (WINK)
UH...I'M NOT VERY GOOD AT OFFENSIVE SPELLS......

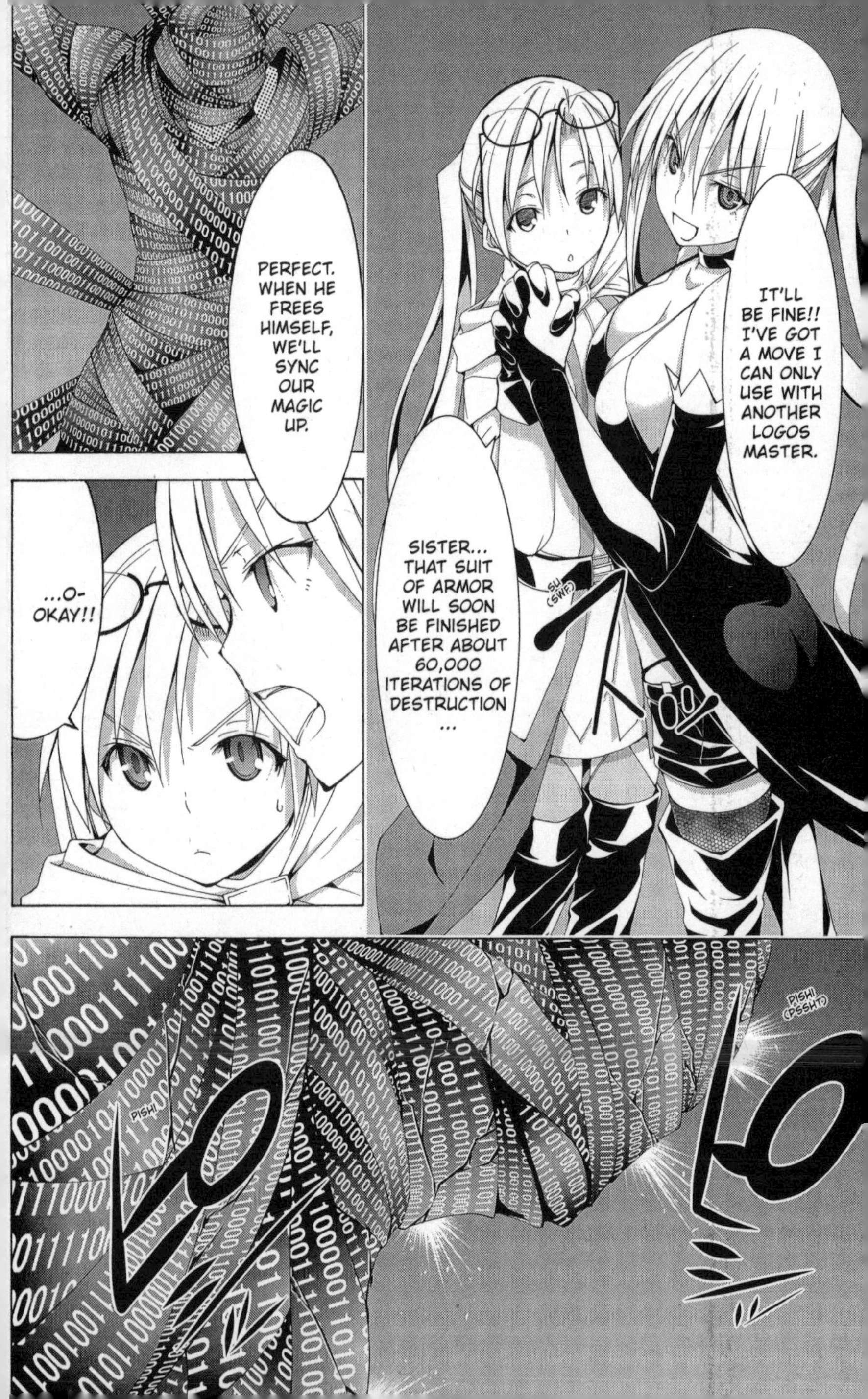
IT'LL BE FINE!! I'VE GOT A MOVE I CAN ONLY USE WITH ANOTHER LOGOS MASTER.
PERFECT. WHEN HE FREES HIMSELF, WE'LL SYNC OUR MAGIC UP.
SISTER... THAT SUIT OF ARMOR WILL SOON BE FINISHED AFTER ABOUT 60,000 ITERATIONS OF DESTRUCTION ...
SU (SWF)
...O-OKAY!!
PISHI (PSSHT)
PISHI

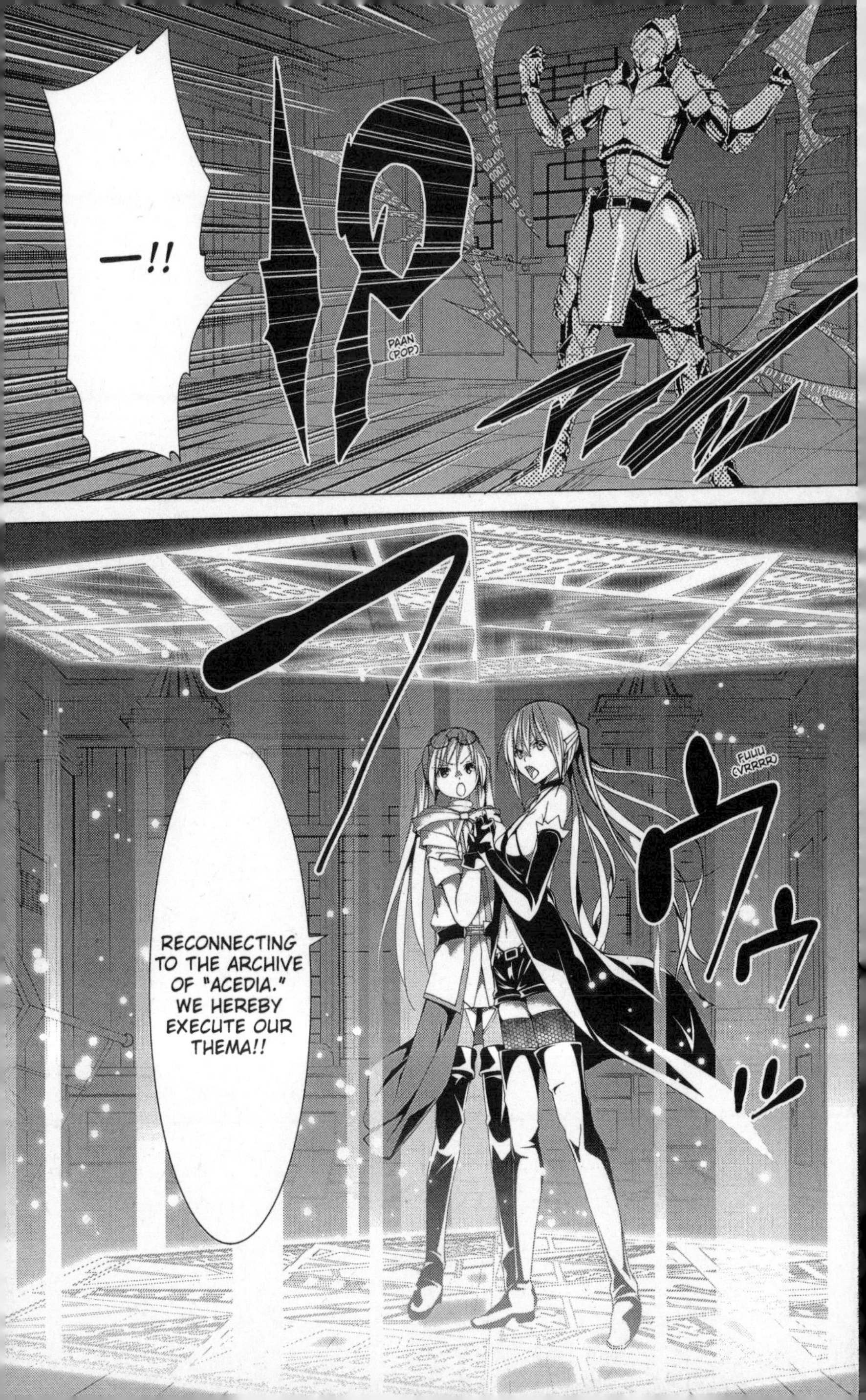
—!!
PAAN (POP)
FUUU (VRRRR)
RECONNECTING TO THE ARCHIVE OF "ACEDIA." WE HEREBY EXECUTE OUR THEMA!!

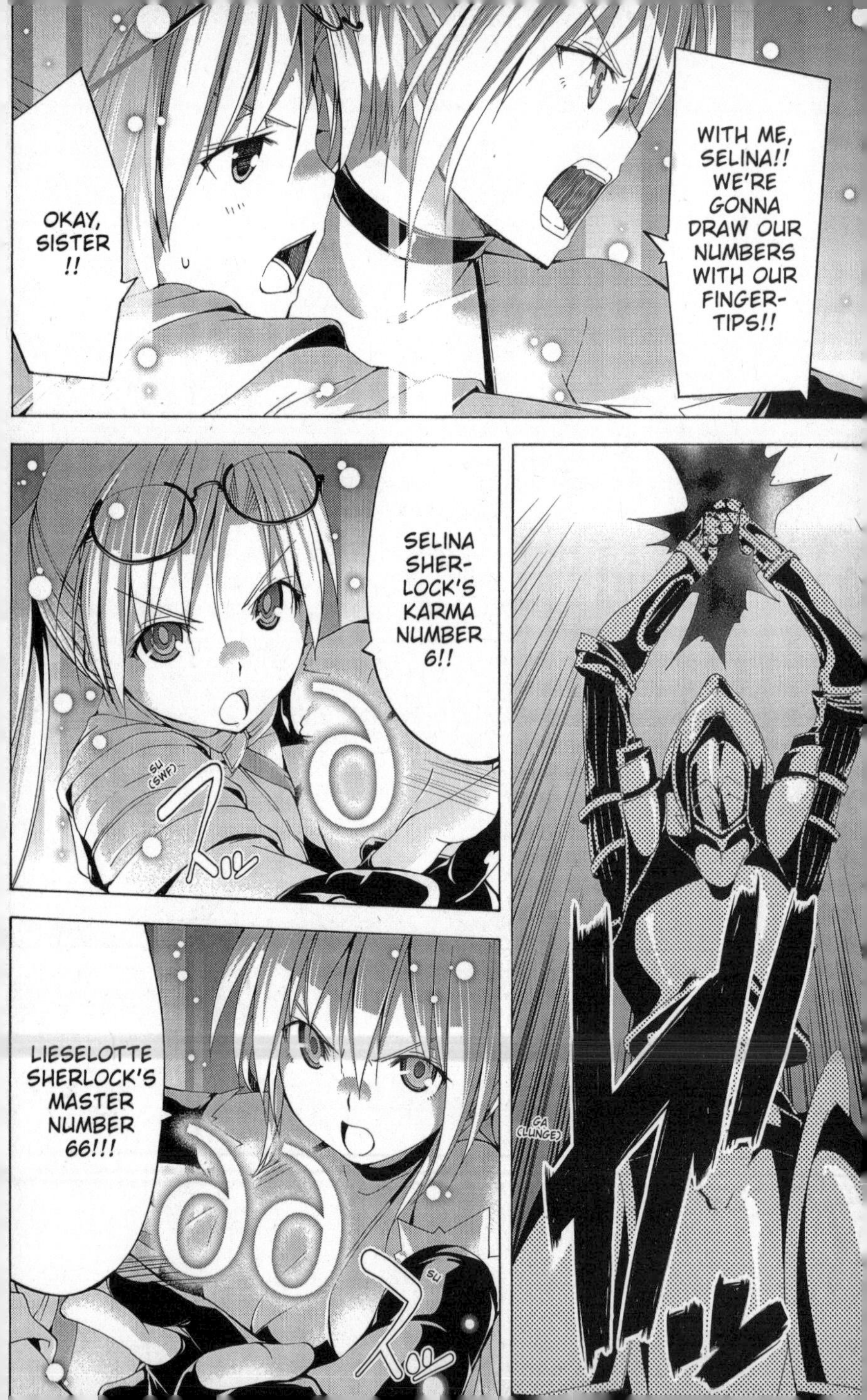
WITH ME, SELINA!! WE'RE GONNA DRAW OUR NUMBERS WITH OUR FINGER-TIPS!!
OKAY, SISTER !!
GA (LUNGE)
SELINA SHER-LOCK'S KARMA NUMBER 6!!
SU (SWF)
LIESELOTTE SHERLOCK'S MASTER NUMBER 66!!!
SU

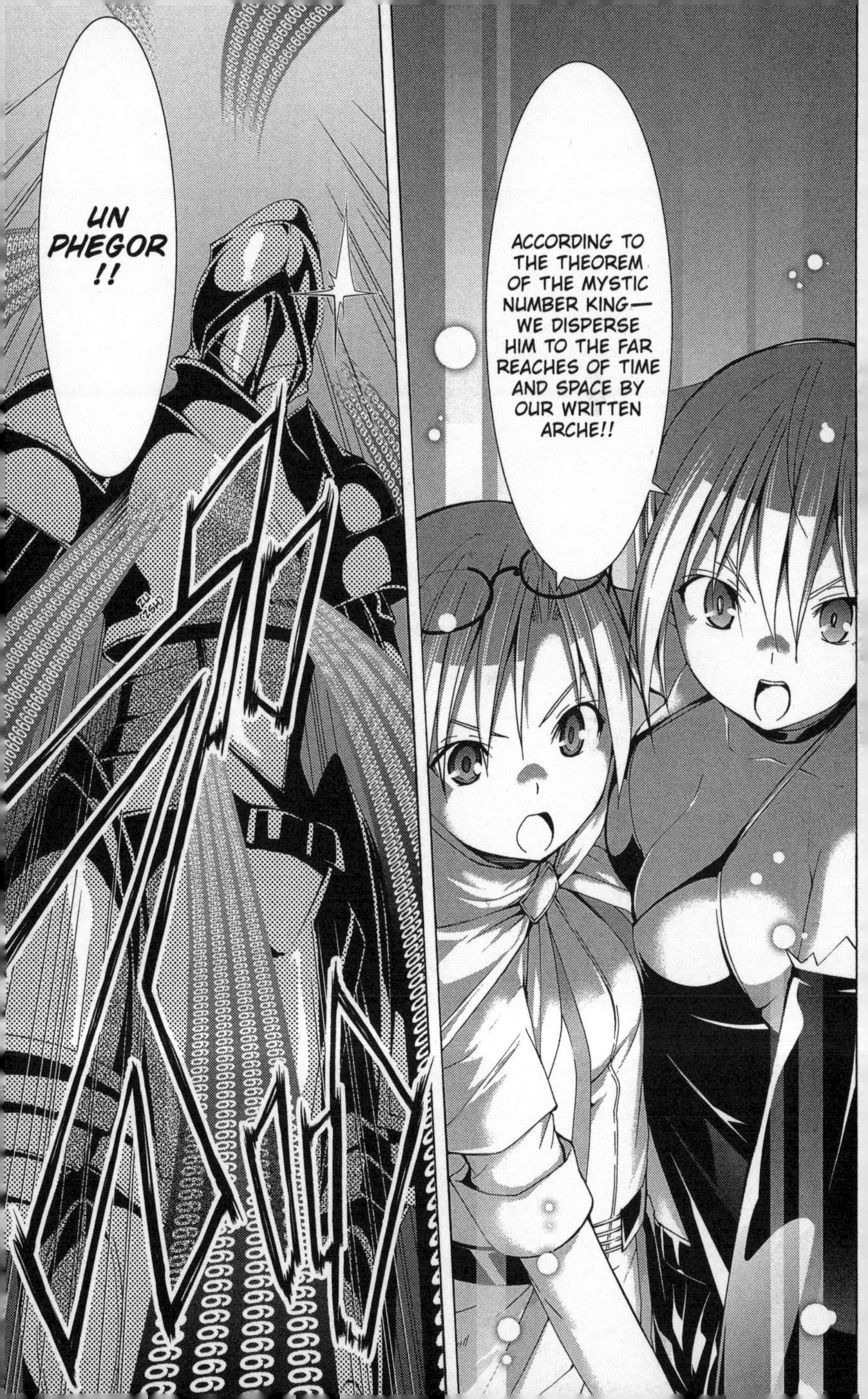
ACCORDING TO THE THEOREM OF THE MYSTIC NUMBER KING— WE DISPERSE HIM TO THE FAR REACHES OF TIME AND SPACE BY OUR WRITTEN ARCHE!!
UN PHEGOR !!

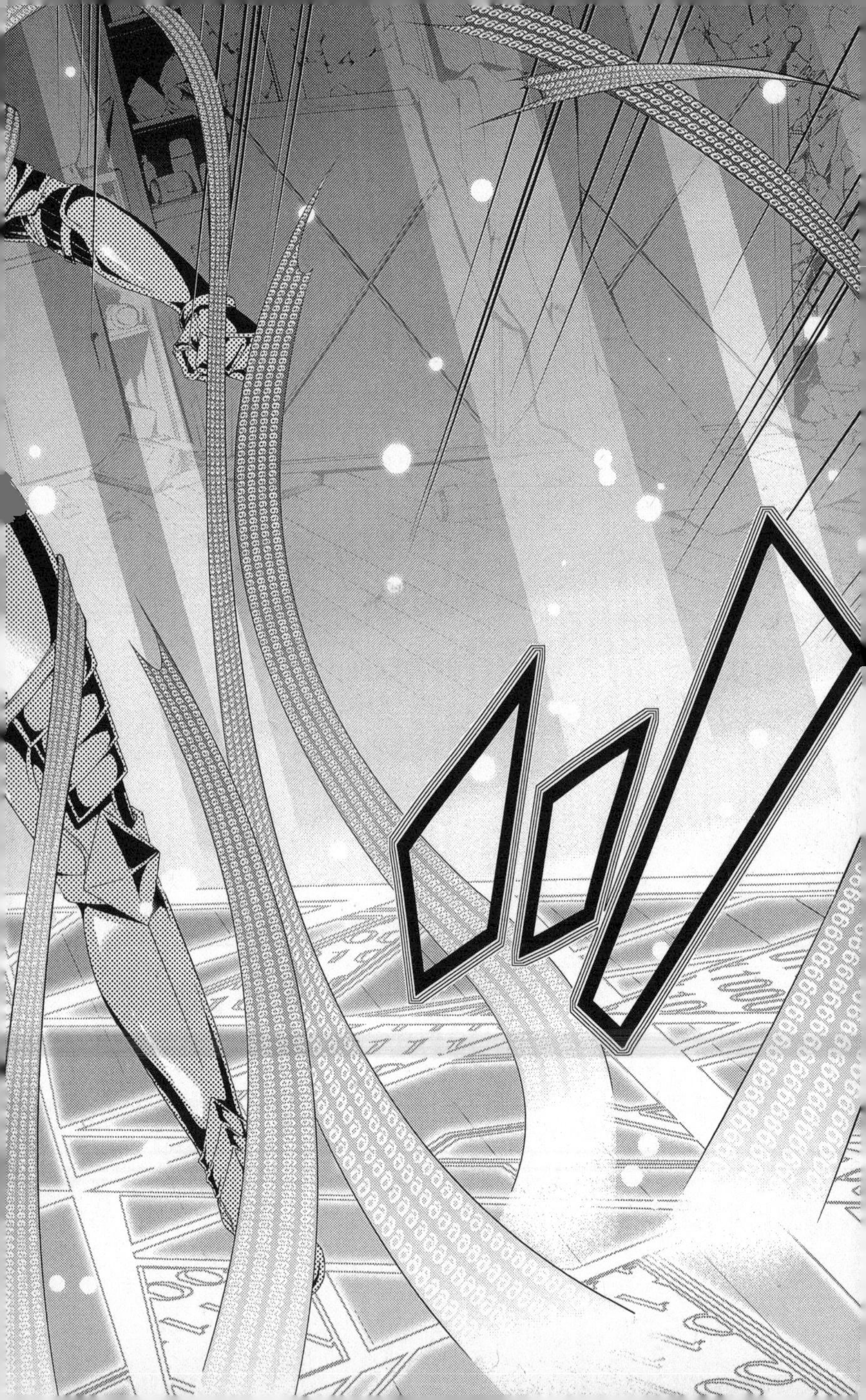

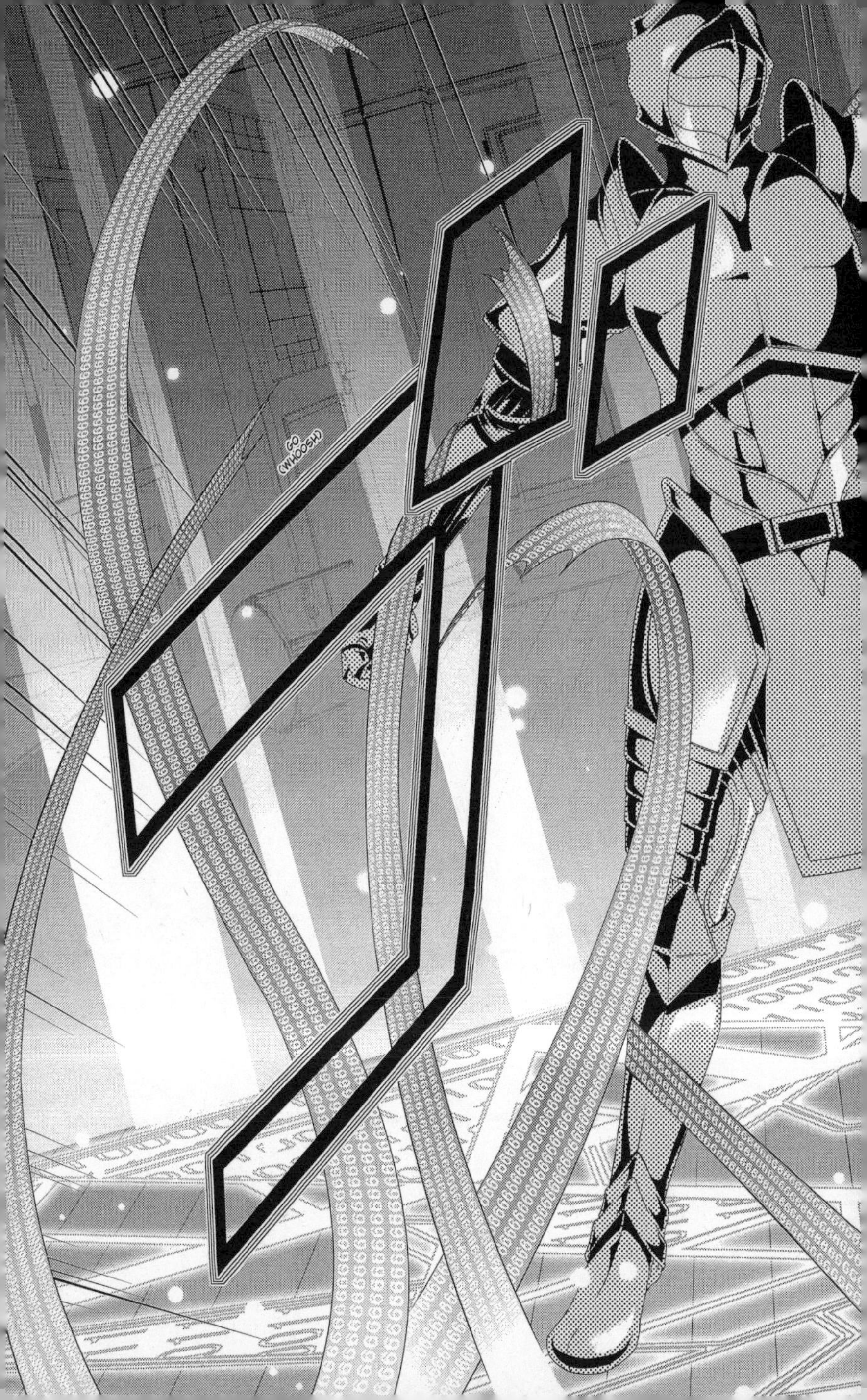
GO
(WHOOSH)

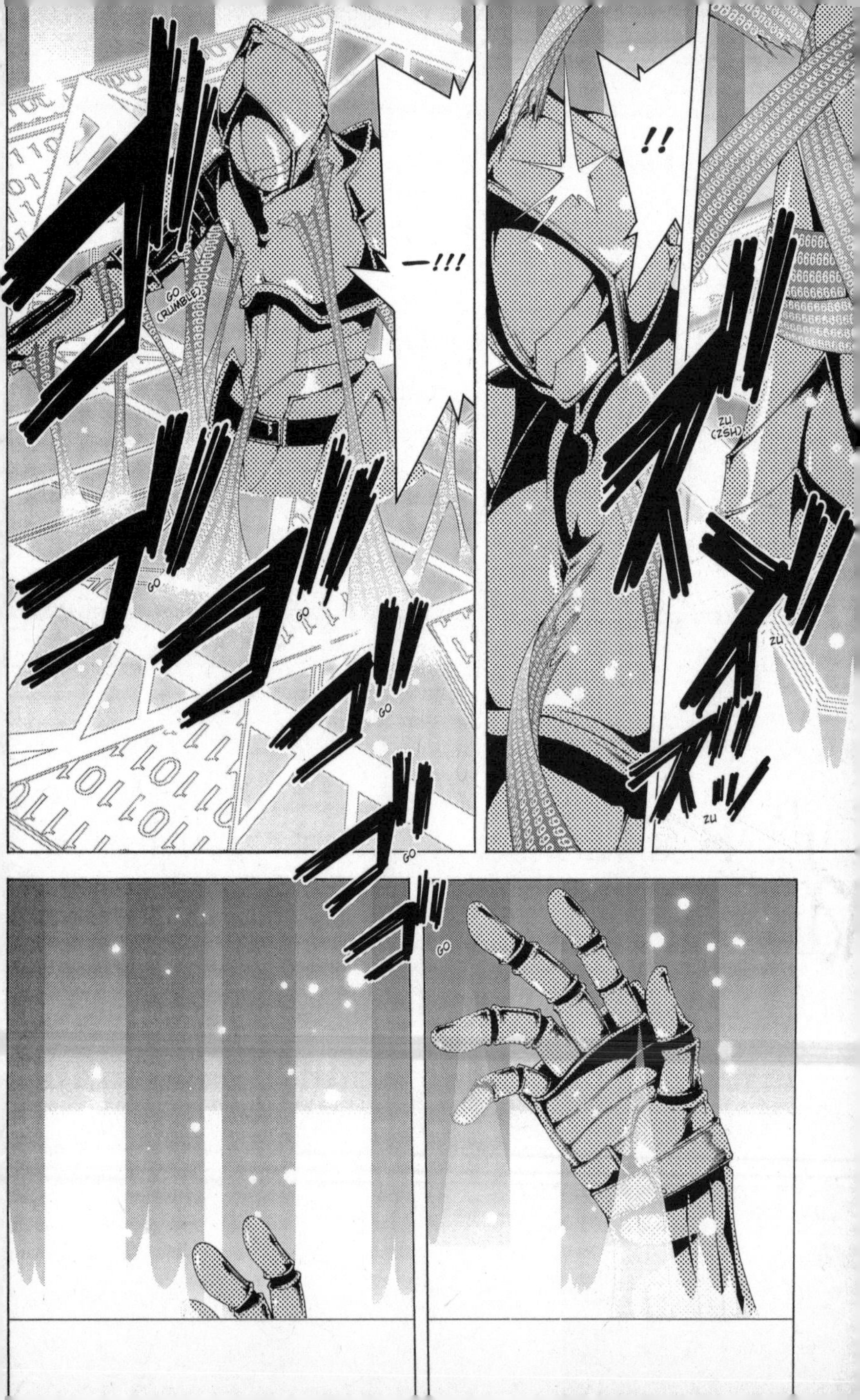
!!
ZU (ZSH)
ZU
ZU
—!!!
GO (RUMBLE)
GO
GO
GO
GO
GO

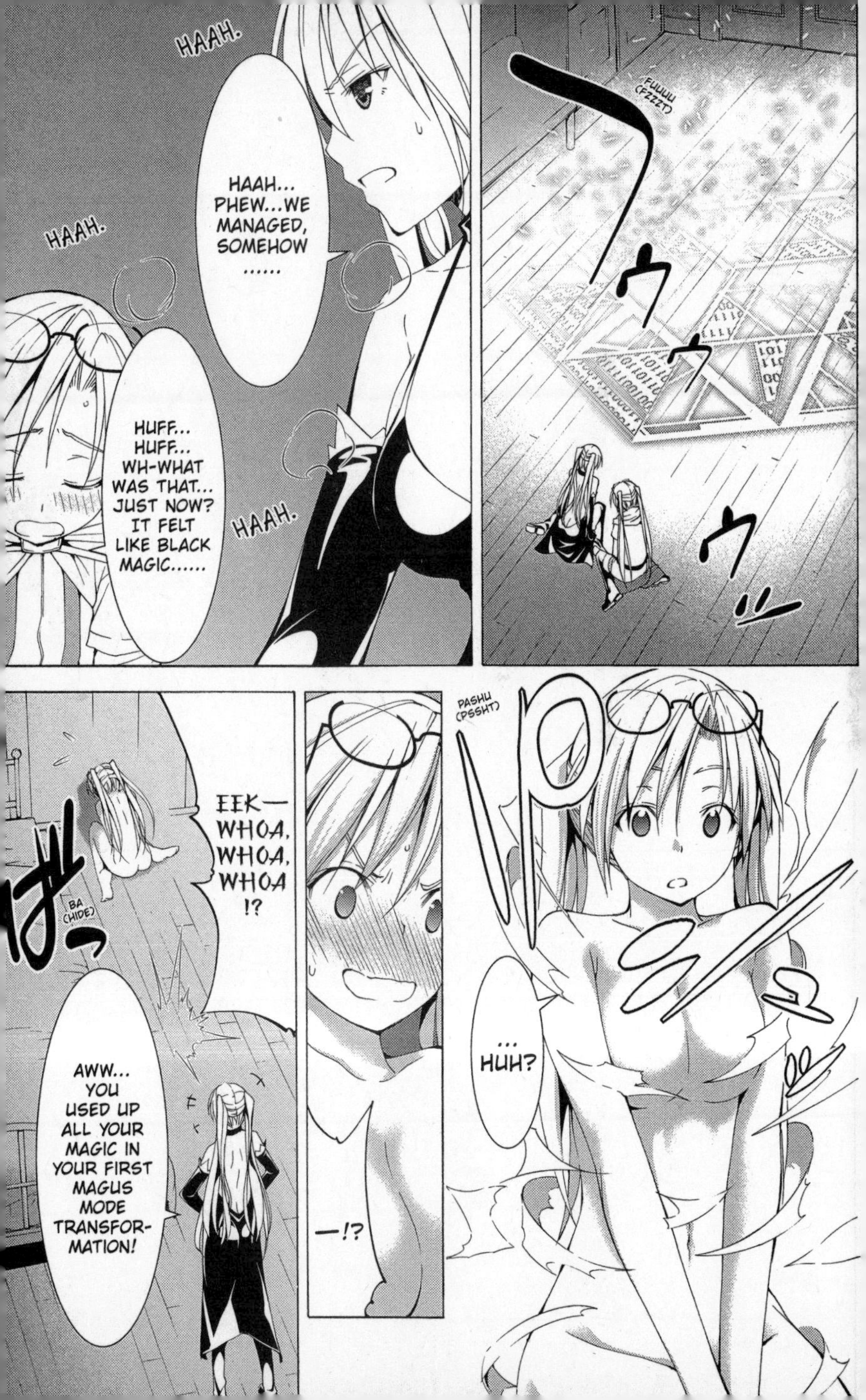
FUUUU (FZZZT)
HAAH.
HAAH... PHEW...WE MANAGED, SOMEHOW ......
HAAH.
HUFF... HUFF... WH-WHAT WAS THAT... JUST NOW? IT FELT LIKE BLACK MAGIC......
HAAH.
PASHU (PSSHT)
... HUH?
—!?
EEK— WHOA, WHOA, WHOA !?
BA (HIDE)
AWW... YOU USED UP ALL YOUR MAGIC IN YOUR FIRST MAGUS MODE TRANSFOR-MATION!

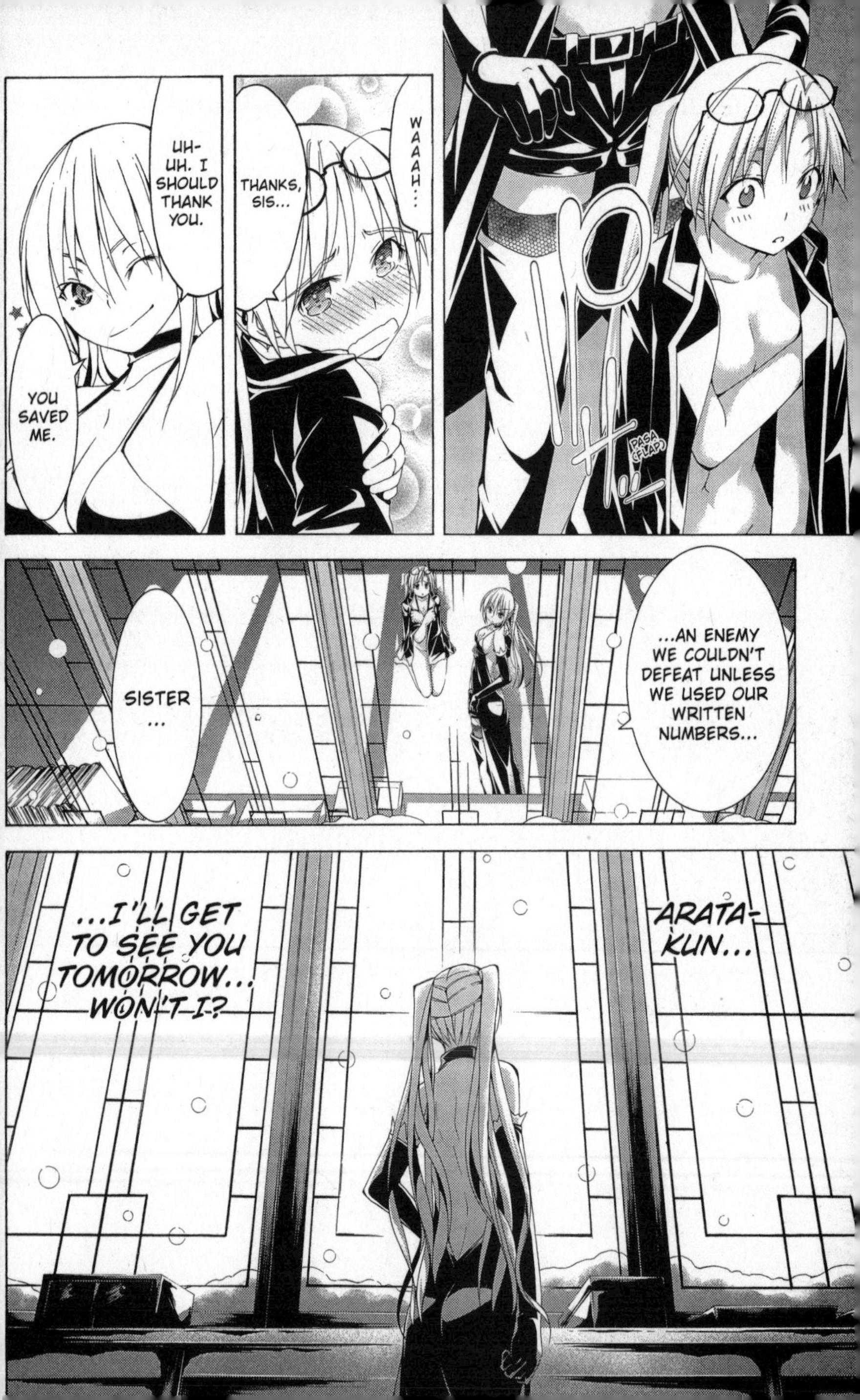
PASA (FLAP)
WAAAH...
THANKS, SIS...
UH-UH. I SHOULD THANK YOU.
YOU SAVED ME.
...AN ENEMY WE COULDN'T DEFEAT UNLESS WE USED OUR WRITTEN NUMBERS...
SISTER...
ARATA-KUN...
...I'LL GET TO SEE YOU TOMORROW... WON'T I?

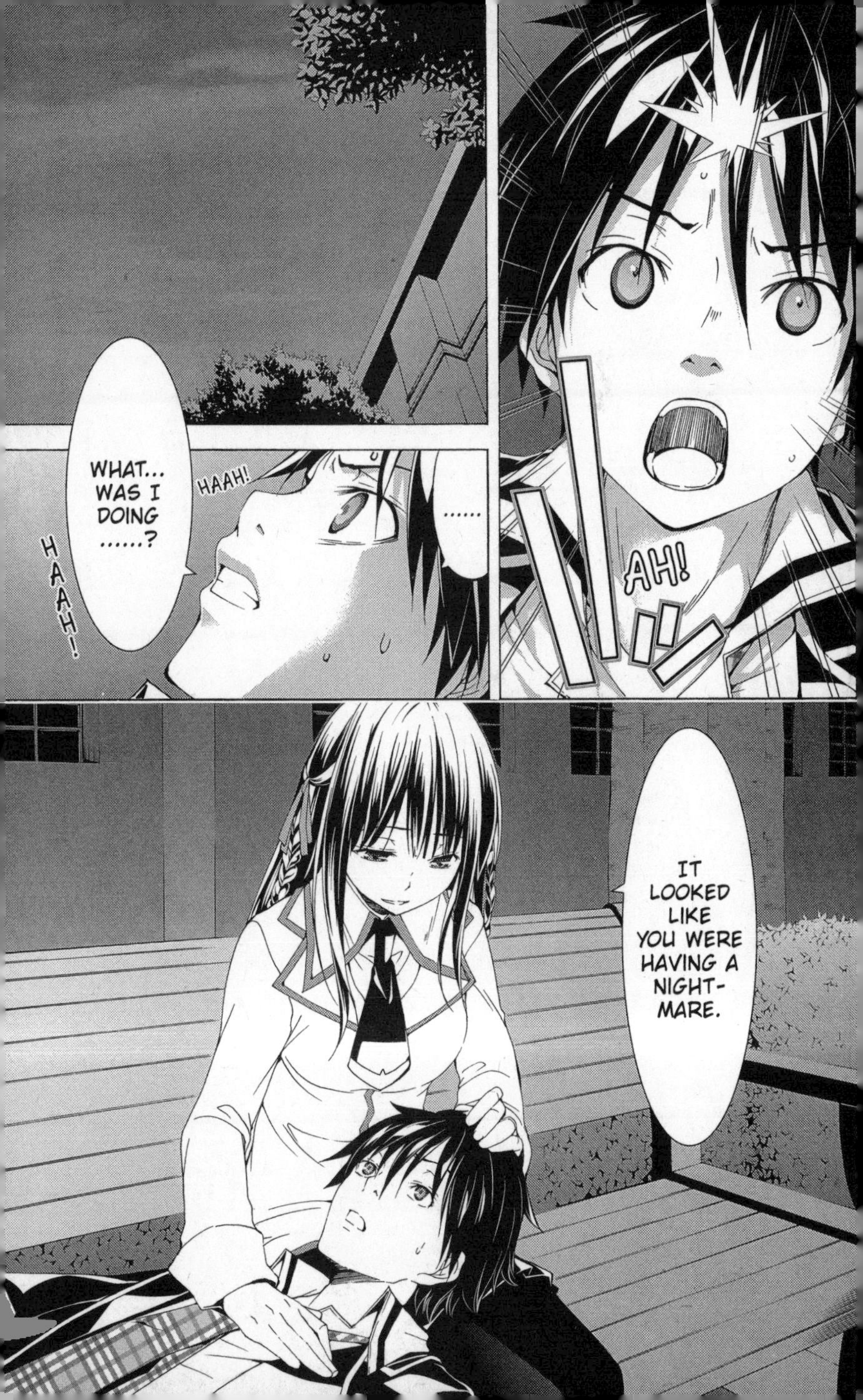
AH!
......
HAAH!
WHAT... WAS I DOING ......?
HAAH!
IT LOOKED LIKE YOU WERE HAVING A NIGHT-MARE.

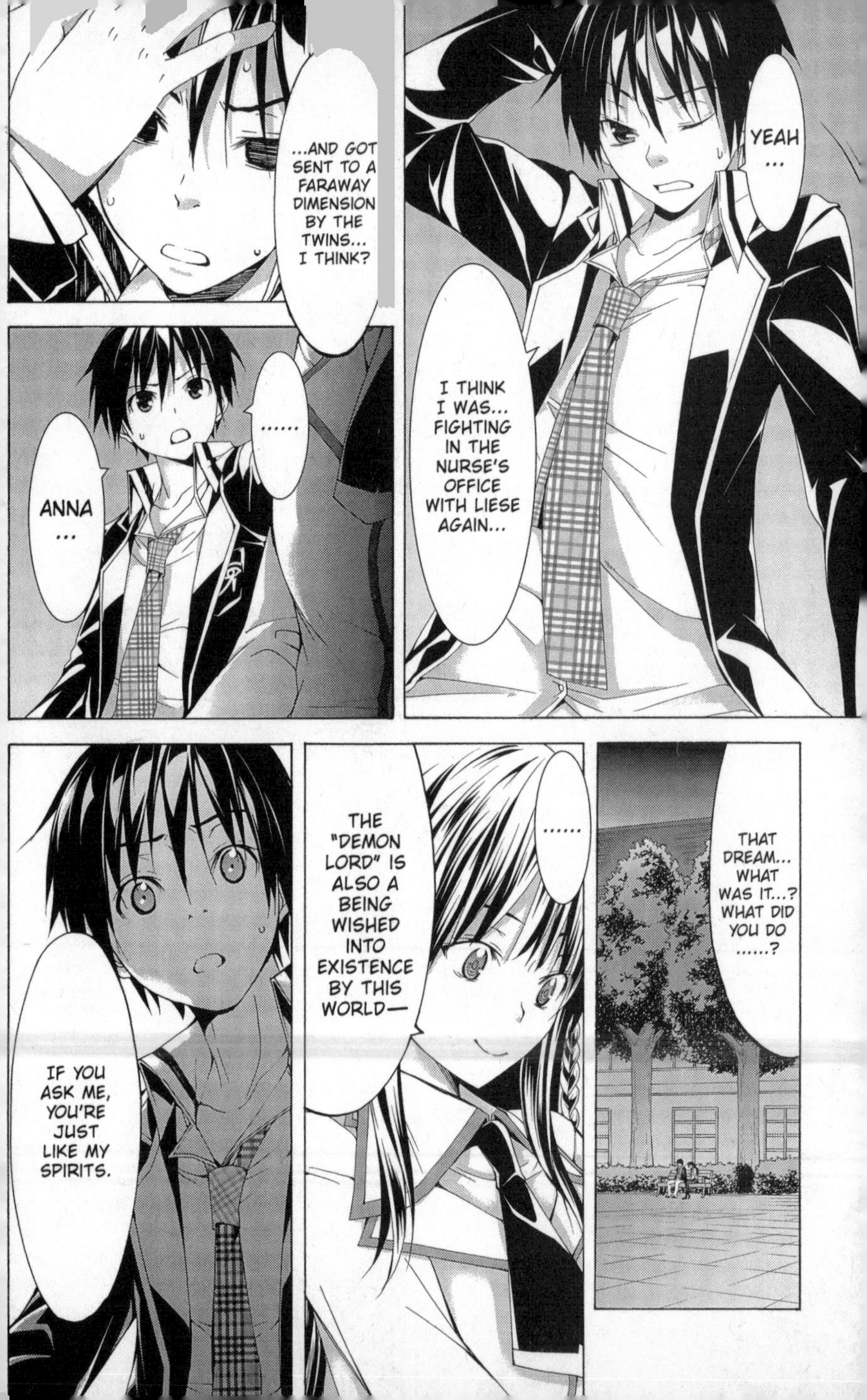
YEAH ...
I THINK I WAS... FIGHTING IN THE NURSE'S OFFICE WITH LIESE AGAIN...
...AND GOT SENT TO A FARAWAY DIMENSION BY THE TWINS... I THINK?
......
ANNA ...
THAT DREAM... WHAT WAS IT...? WHAT DID YOU DO ......?
......
THE "DEMON LORD" IS ALSO A BEING WISHED INTO EXISTENCE BY THIS WORLD—
IF YOU ASK ME, YOU'RE JUST LIKE MY SPIRITS.

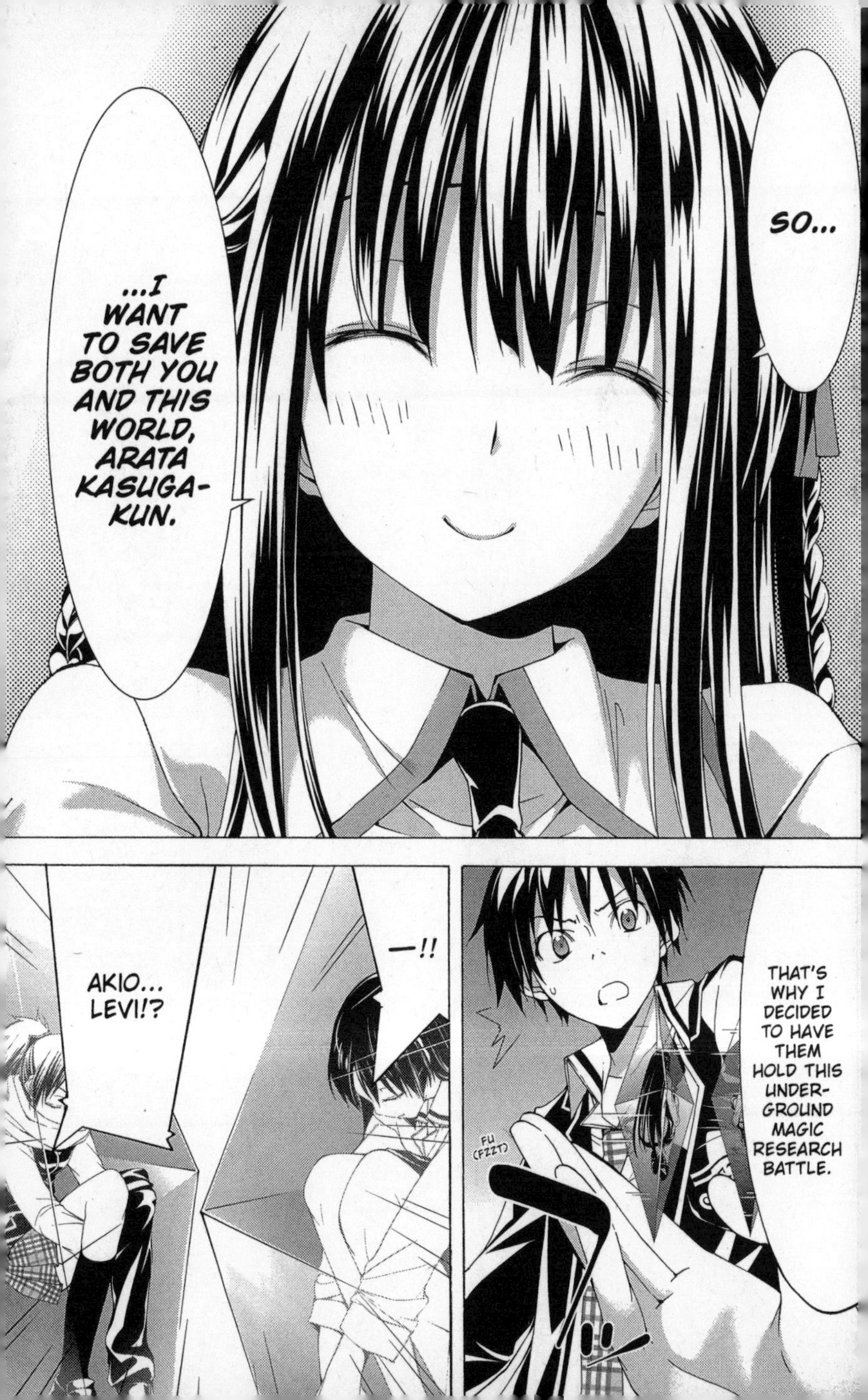
SO...
...I WANT TO SAVE BOTH YOU AND THIS WORLD, ARATA KASUGA-KUN.
THAT'S WHY I DECIDED TO HAVE THEM HOLD THIS UNDER-GROUND MAGIC RESEARCH BATTLE.
FU (FZZT)
—!!
AKIO... LEVI!?

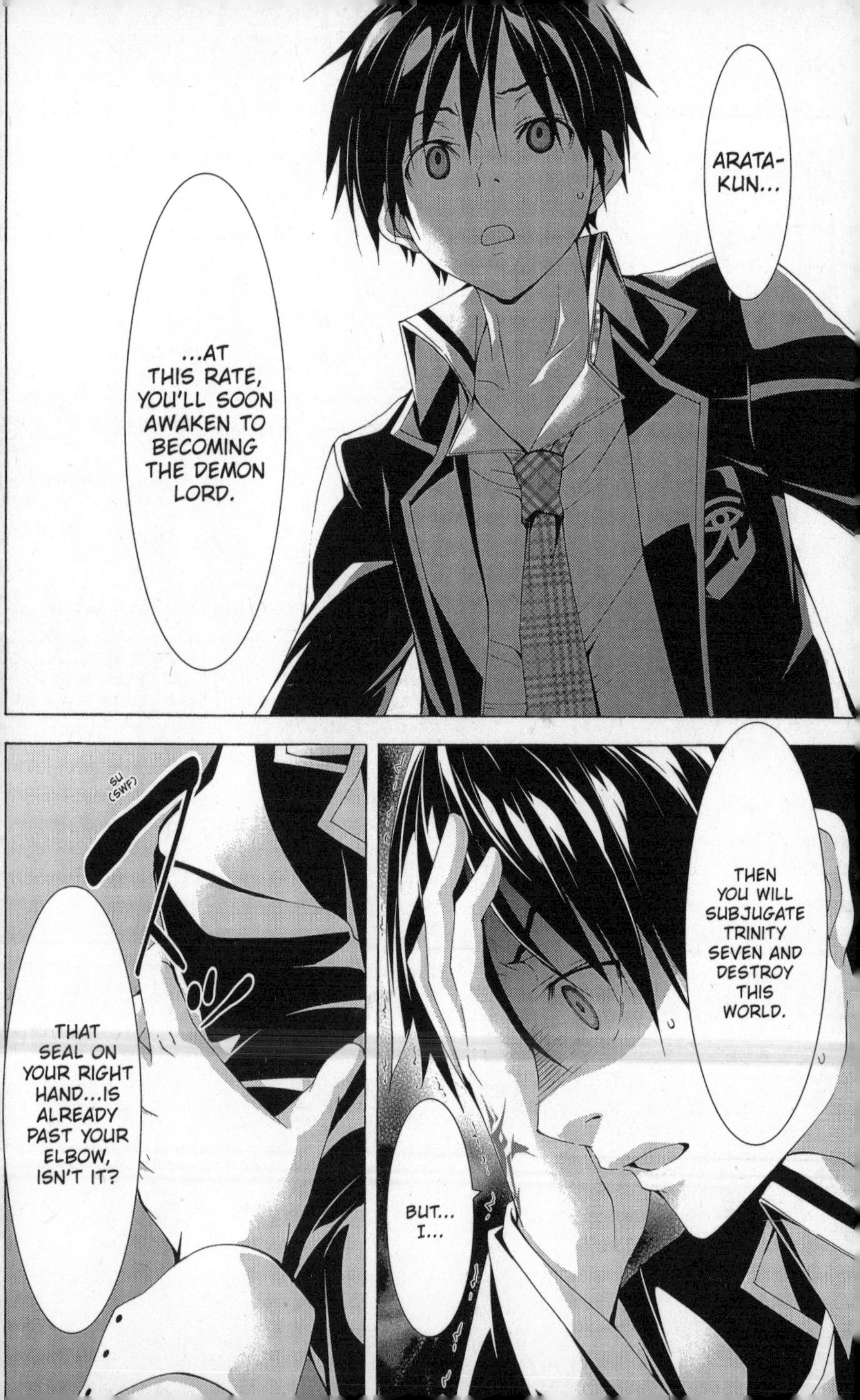
ARATA-KUN...
...AT THIS RATE, YOU'LL SOON AWAKEN TO BECOMING THE DEMON LORD.
THEN YOU WILL SUBJUGATE TRINITY SEVEN AND DESTROY THIS WORLD.
BUT... I...
SU (SWF)
THAT SEAL ON YOUR RIGHT HAND...IS ALREADY PAST YOUR ELBOW, ISN'T IT?

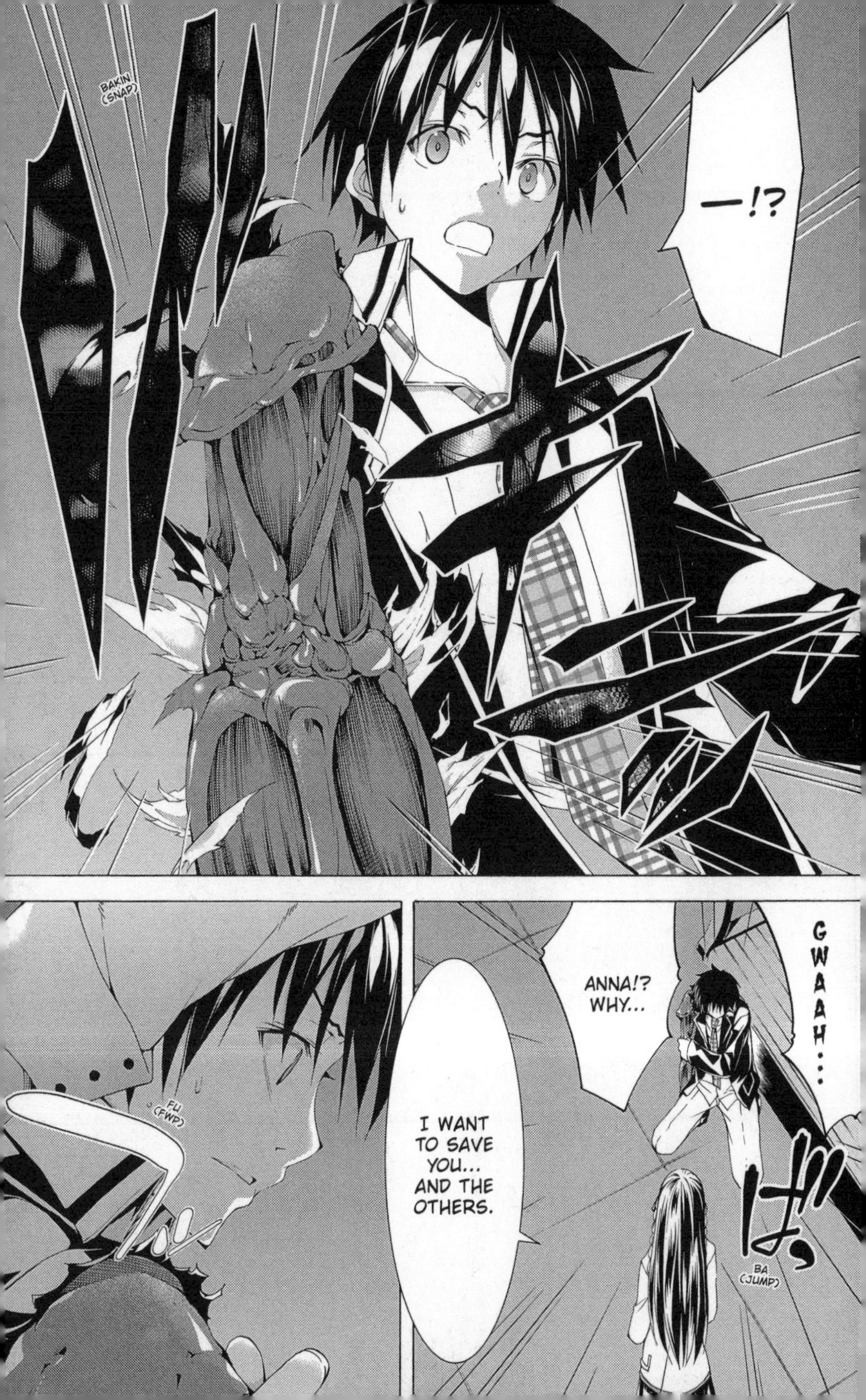
—!?
BAKIN (SNAP)
GWAAH...
ANNA!? WHY...
BA (JUMP)
I WANT TO SAVE YOU... AND THE OTHERS.
FU (FWP)

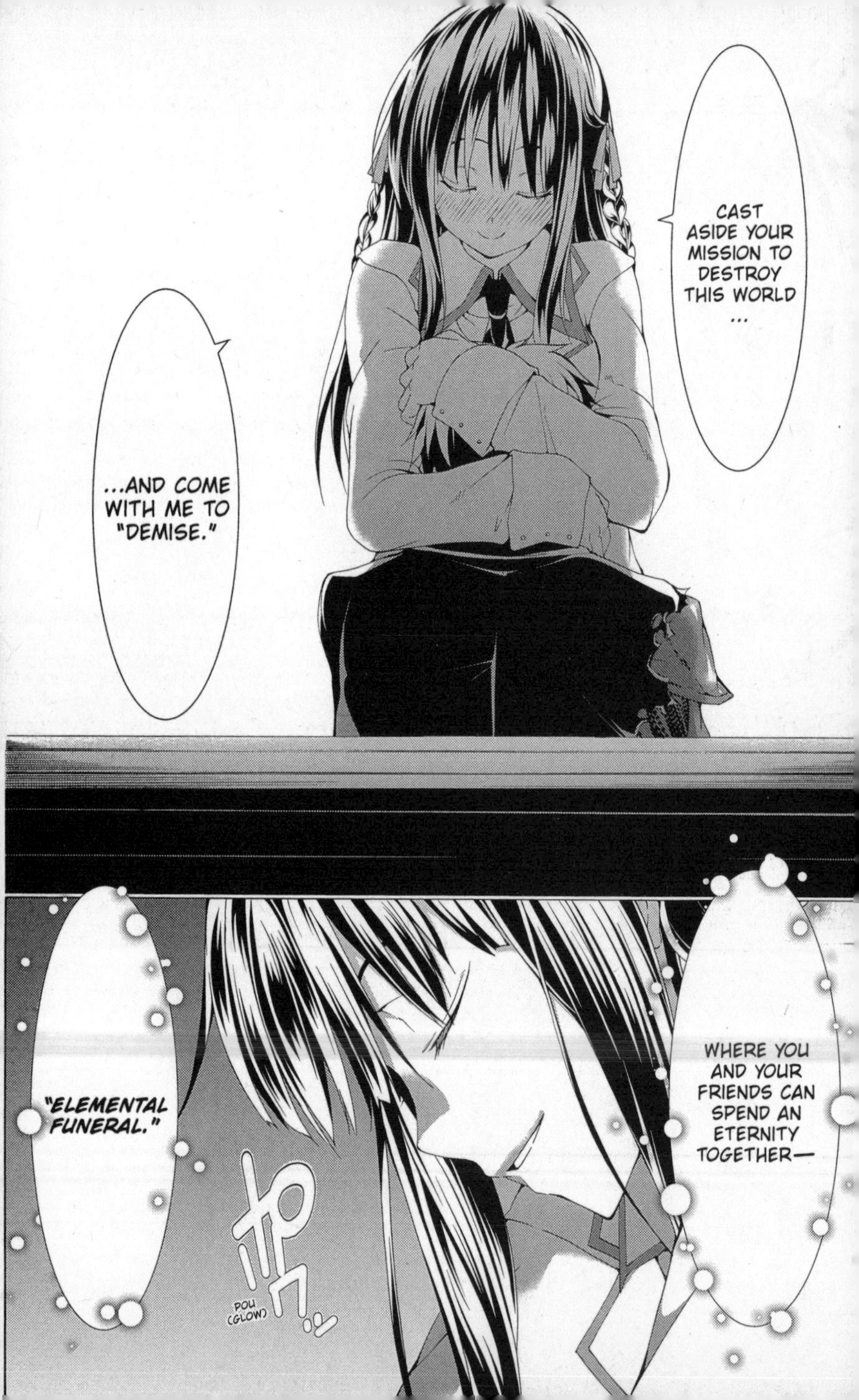
CAST ASIDE YOUR MISSION TO DESTROY THIS WORLD ...
...AND COME WITH ME TO "DEMISE."
WHERE YOU AND YOUR FRIENDS CAN SPEND AN ETERNITY TOGETHER—
"ELEMENTAL FUNERAL."
POU (GLOW)

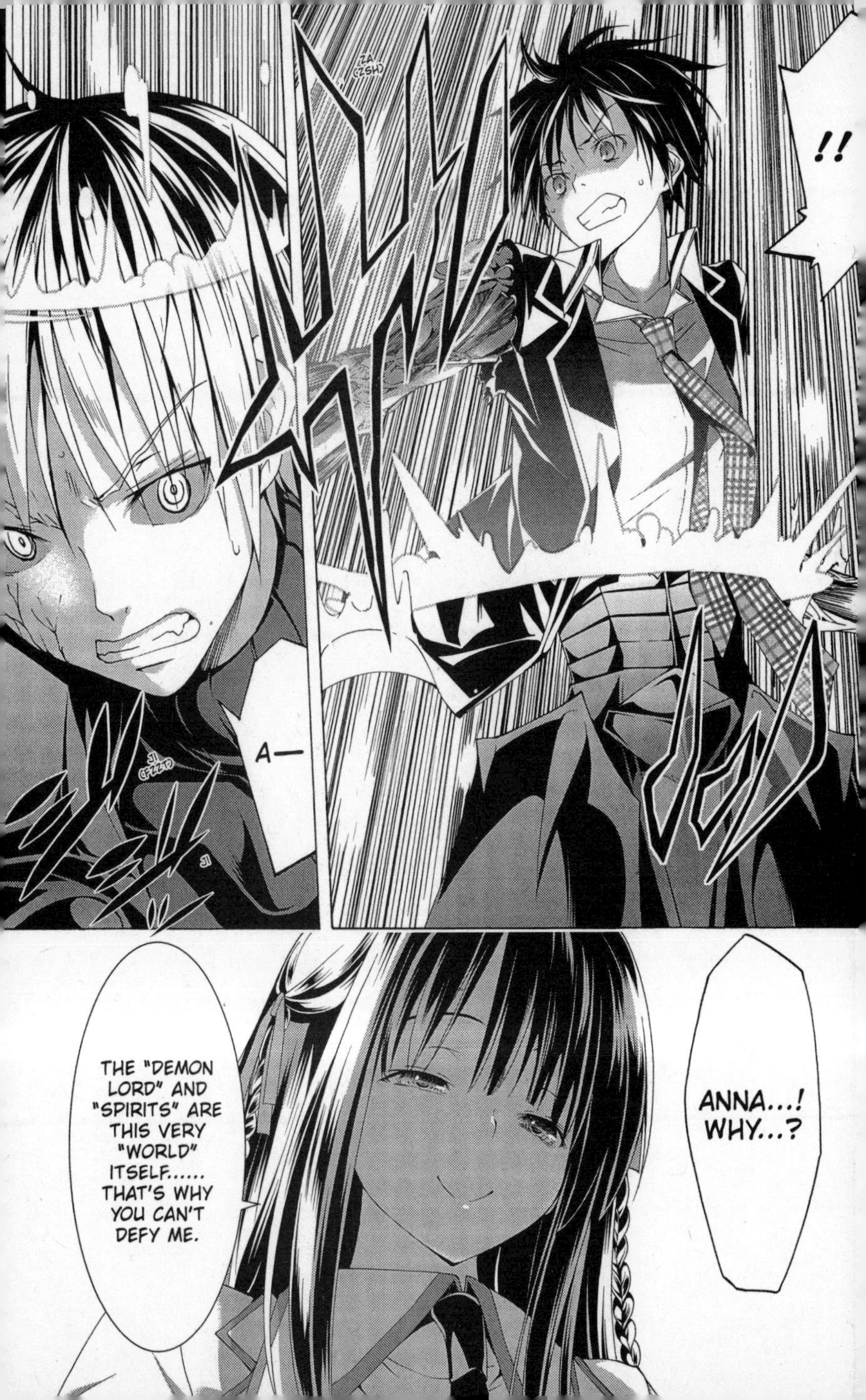
ZA (ZSH)
!!
A—
JI (FZZT)
ANNA...! WHY...?
THE "DEMON LORD" AND "SPIRITS" ARE THIS VERY "WORLD" ITSELF...... THAT'S WHY YOU CAN'T DEFY ME.

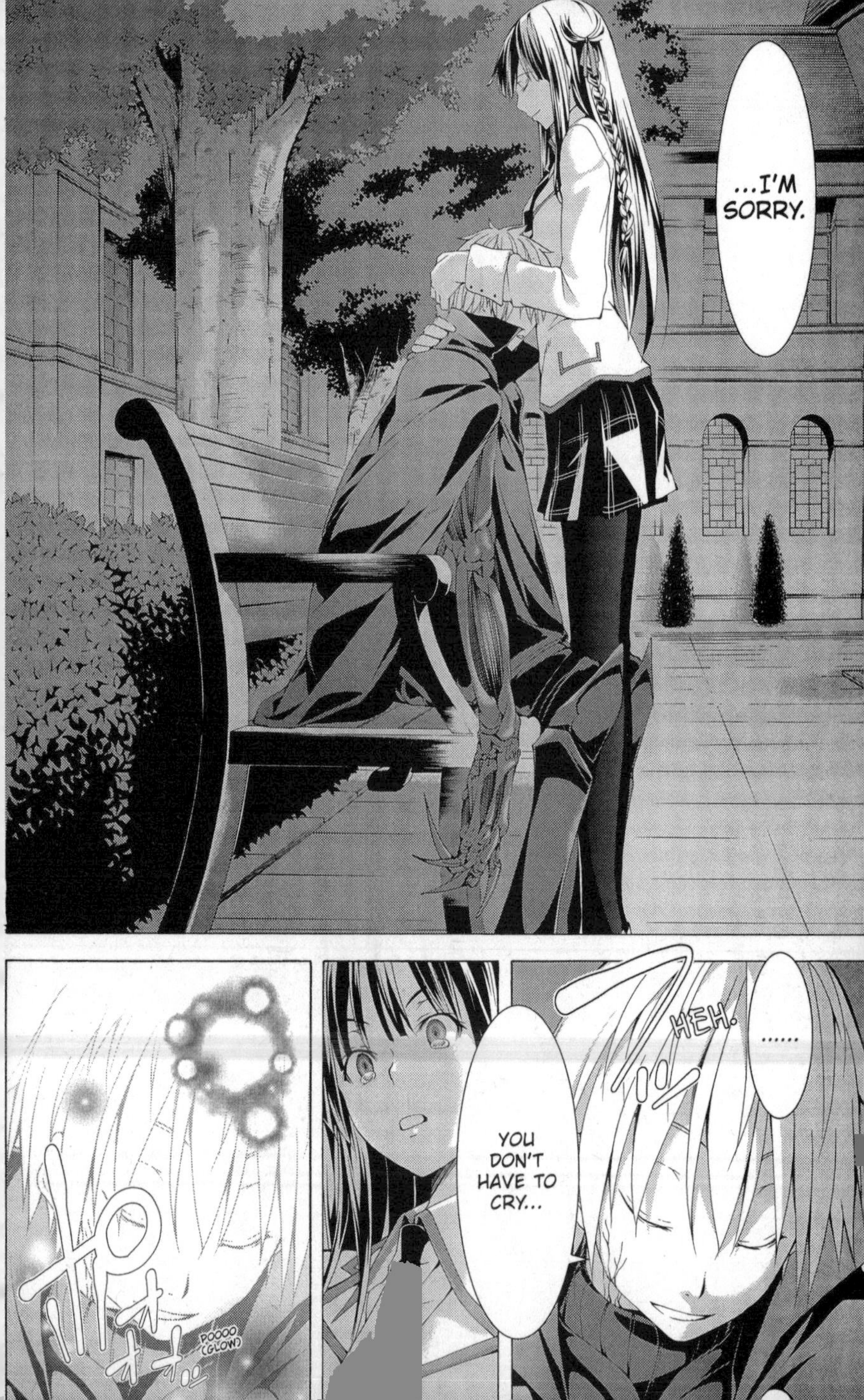
...I'M SORRY.
......
HEH.
YOU DON'T HAVE TO CRY...
POOOO (GLOW)

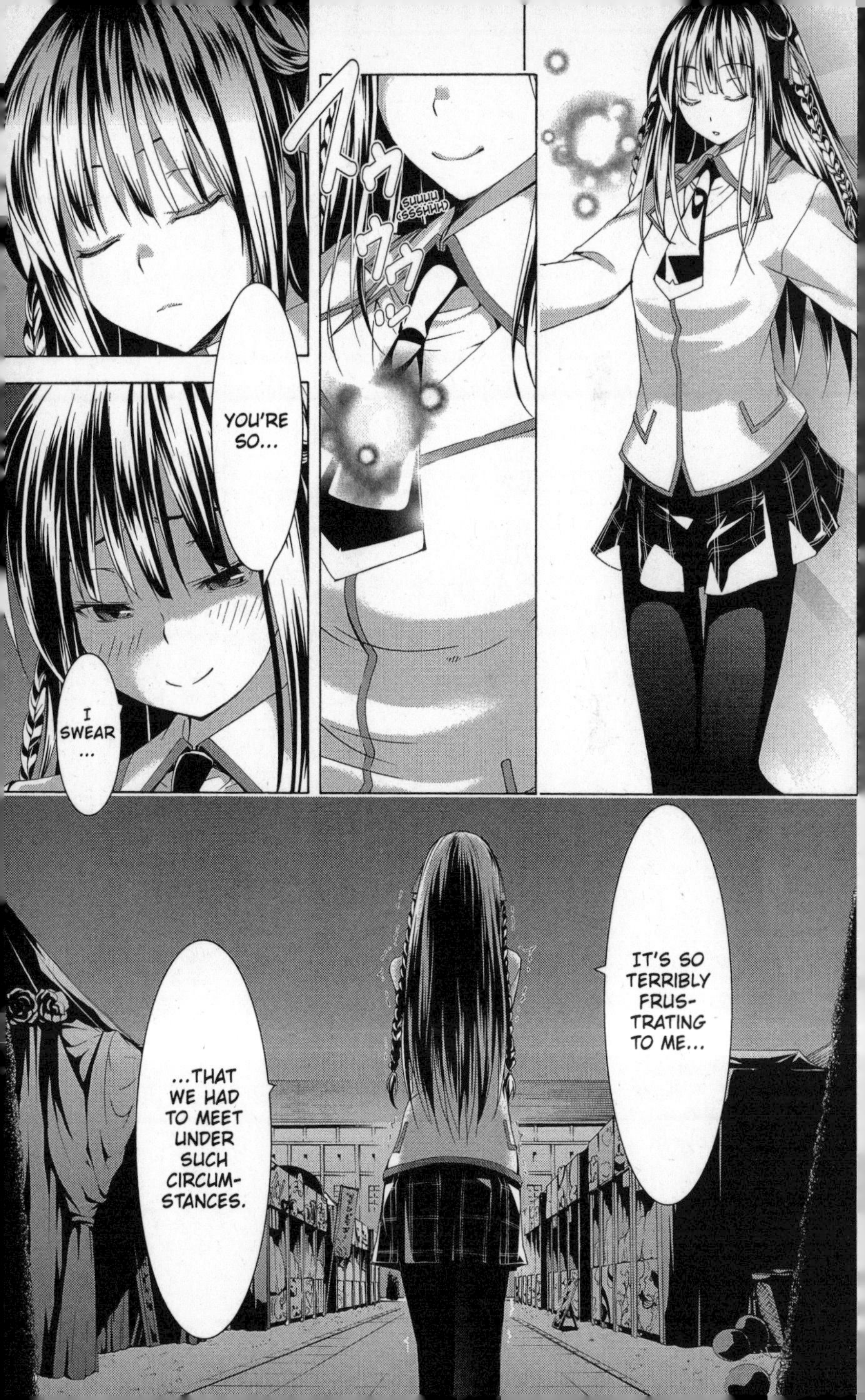
SUUUU (SSSSHHH)
YOU'RE SO...
I SWEAR...
IT'S SO TERRIBLY FRUS-TRATING TO ME...
...THAT WE HAD TO MEET UNDER SUCH CIRCUM-STANCES.

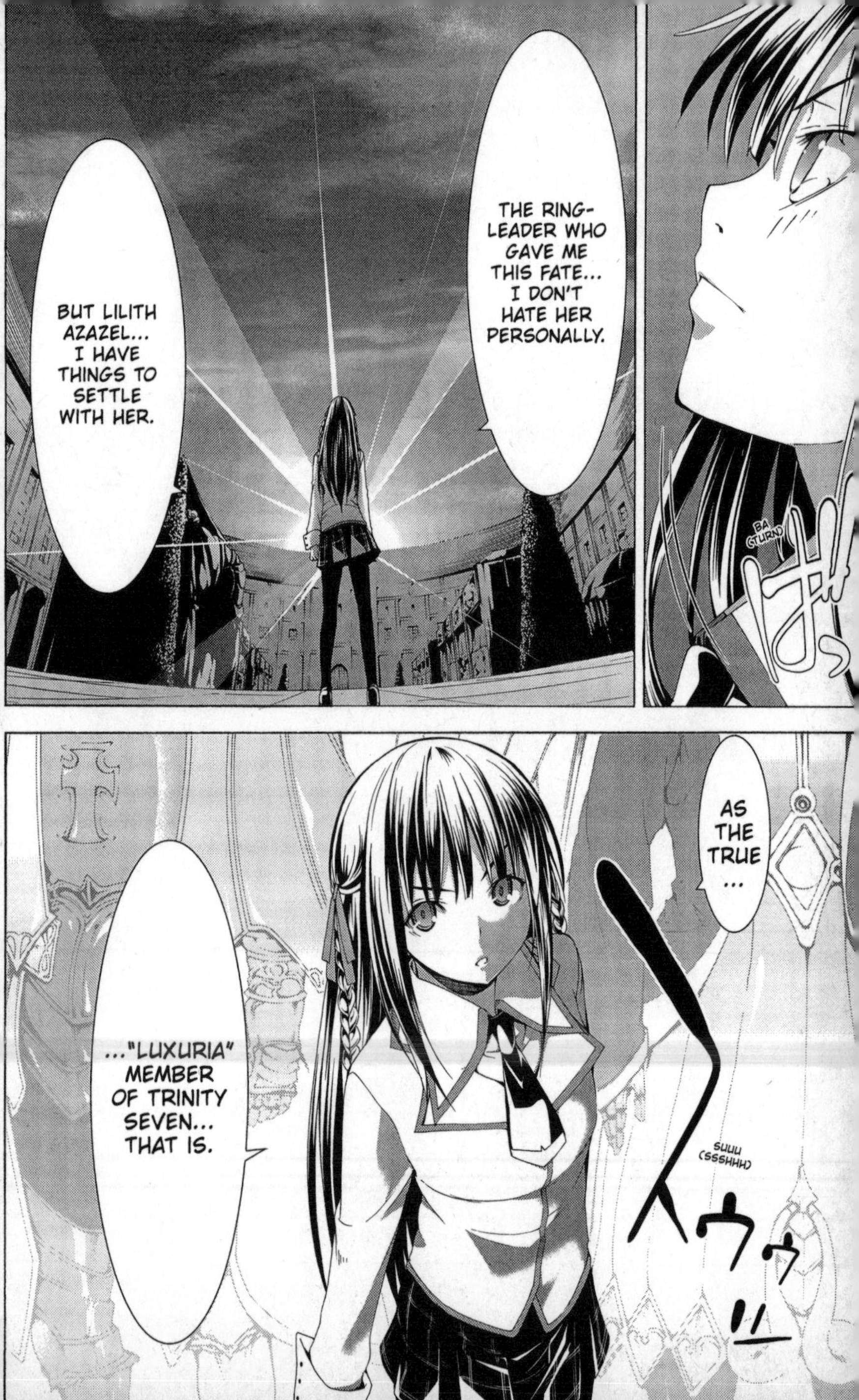
BA (TURN)
THE RING-LEADER WHO GAVE ME THIS FATE... I DON'T HATE HER PERSONALLY.
BUT LILITH AZAZEL... I HAVE THINGS TO SETTLE WITH HER.
AS THE TRUE...
SUUU (SSSHHH)
..."LUXURIA" MEMBER OF TRINITY SEVEN... THAT IS.

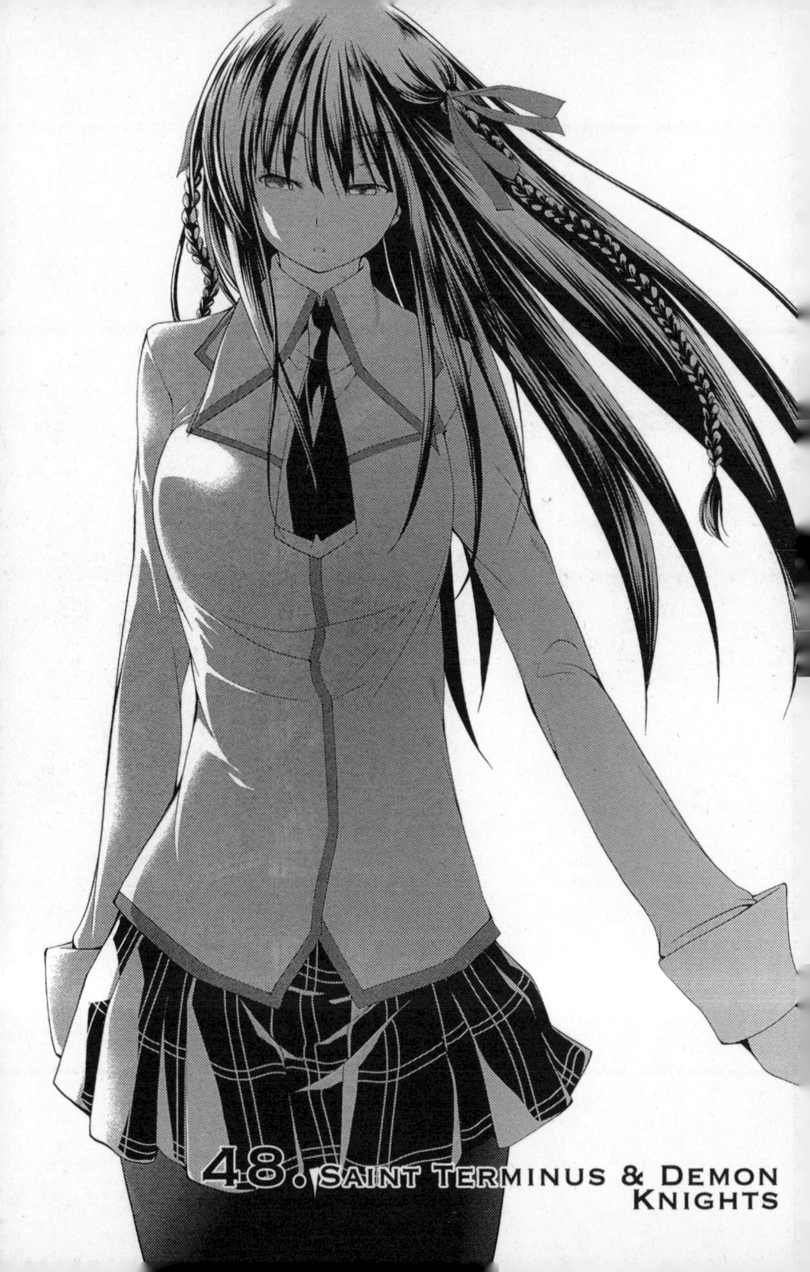

48. Saint Terminus & Demon Knights

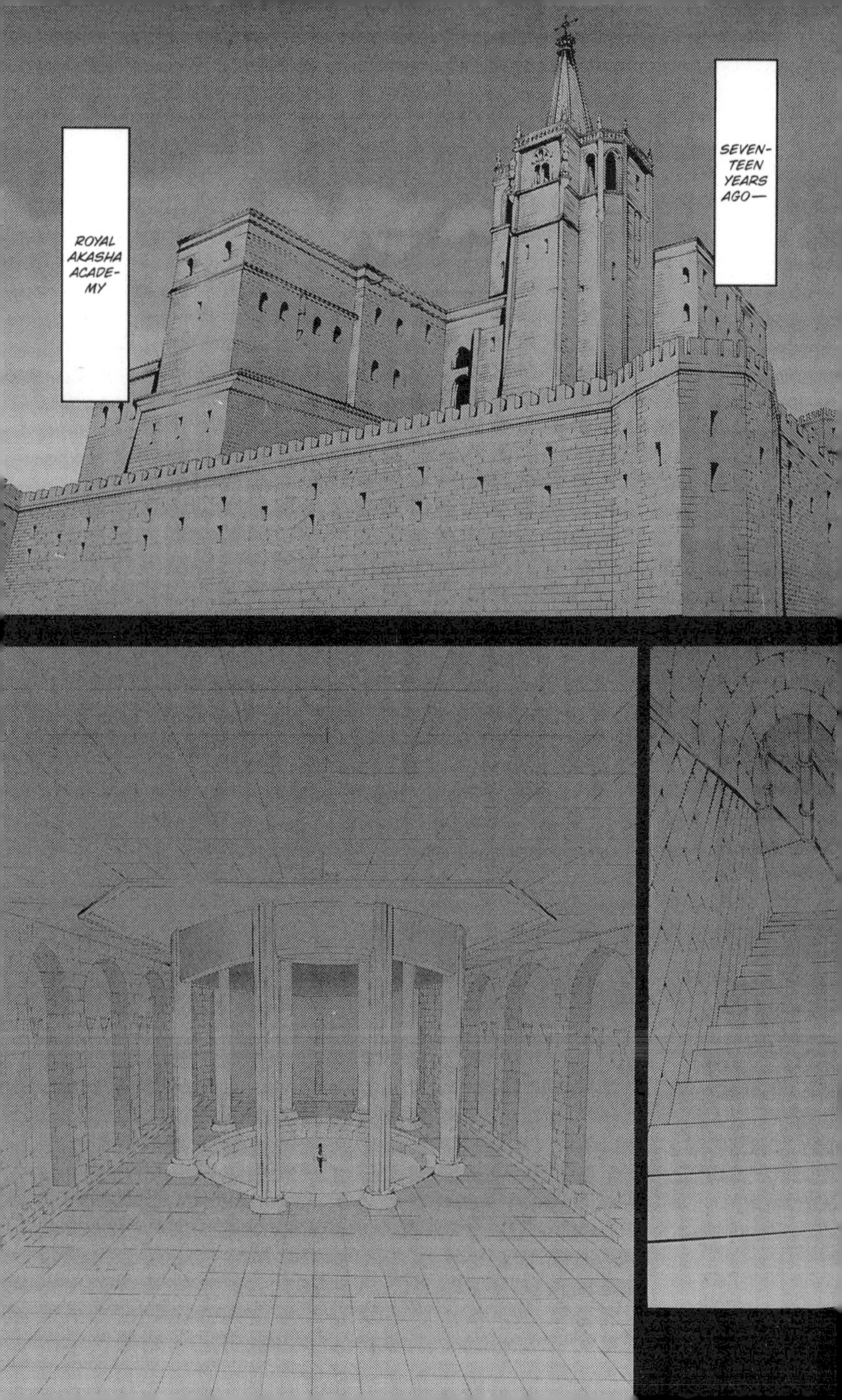
SEVENTEEN YEARS AGO—
ROYAL AKASHA ACADEMY

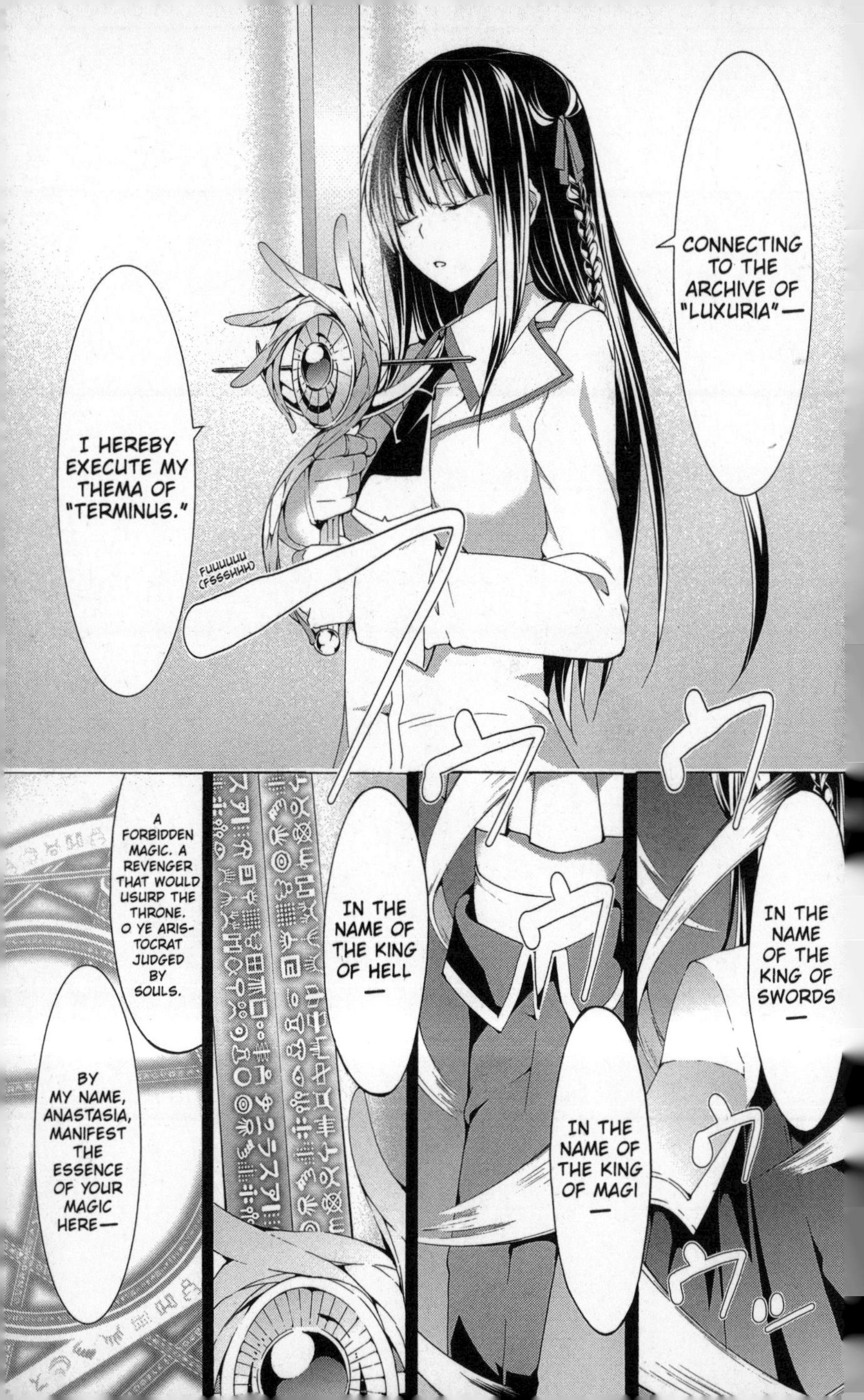
CONNECTING TO THE ARCHIVE OF "LUXURIA"—
I HEREBY EXECUTE MY THEMA OF "TERMINUS."
FUUUUUU (FSSSHHH)
IN THE NAME OF THE KING OF SWORDS—
IN THE NAME OF THE KING OF MAGI—
IN THE NAME OF THE KING OF HELL—
A FORBIDDEN MAGIC. A REVENGER THAT WOULD USURP THE THRONE. O YE ARISTOCRAT JUDGED BY SOULS.
BY MY NAME, ANASTASIA, MANIFEST THE ESSENCE OF YOUR MAGIC HERE—

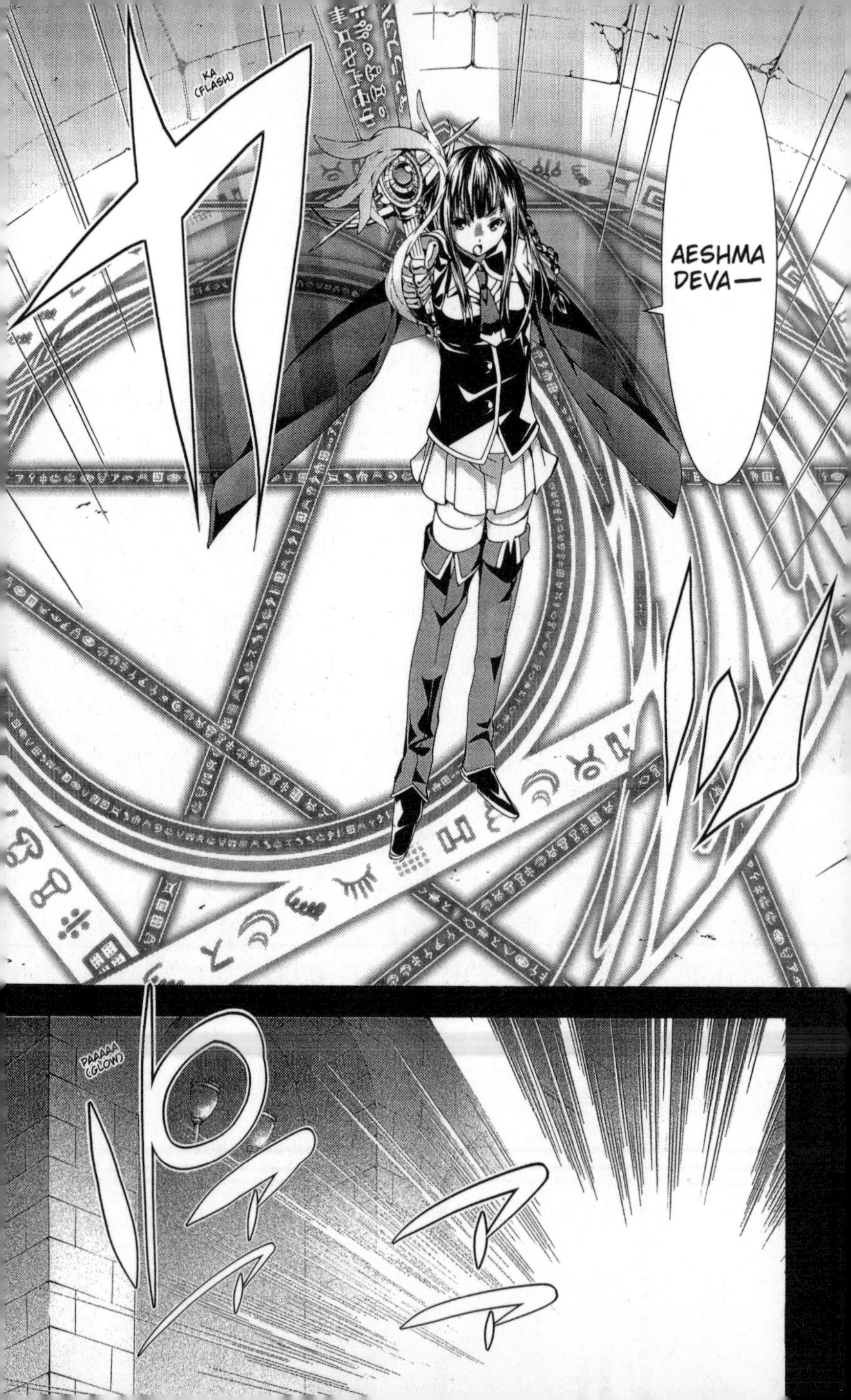
AESHMA DEVA—
KA (FLASH)
PAAAAA (GLOW)

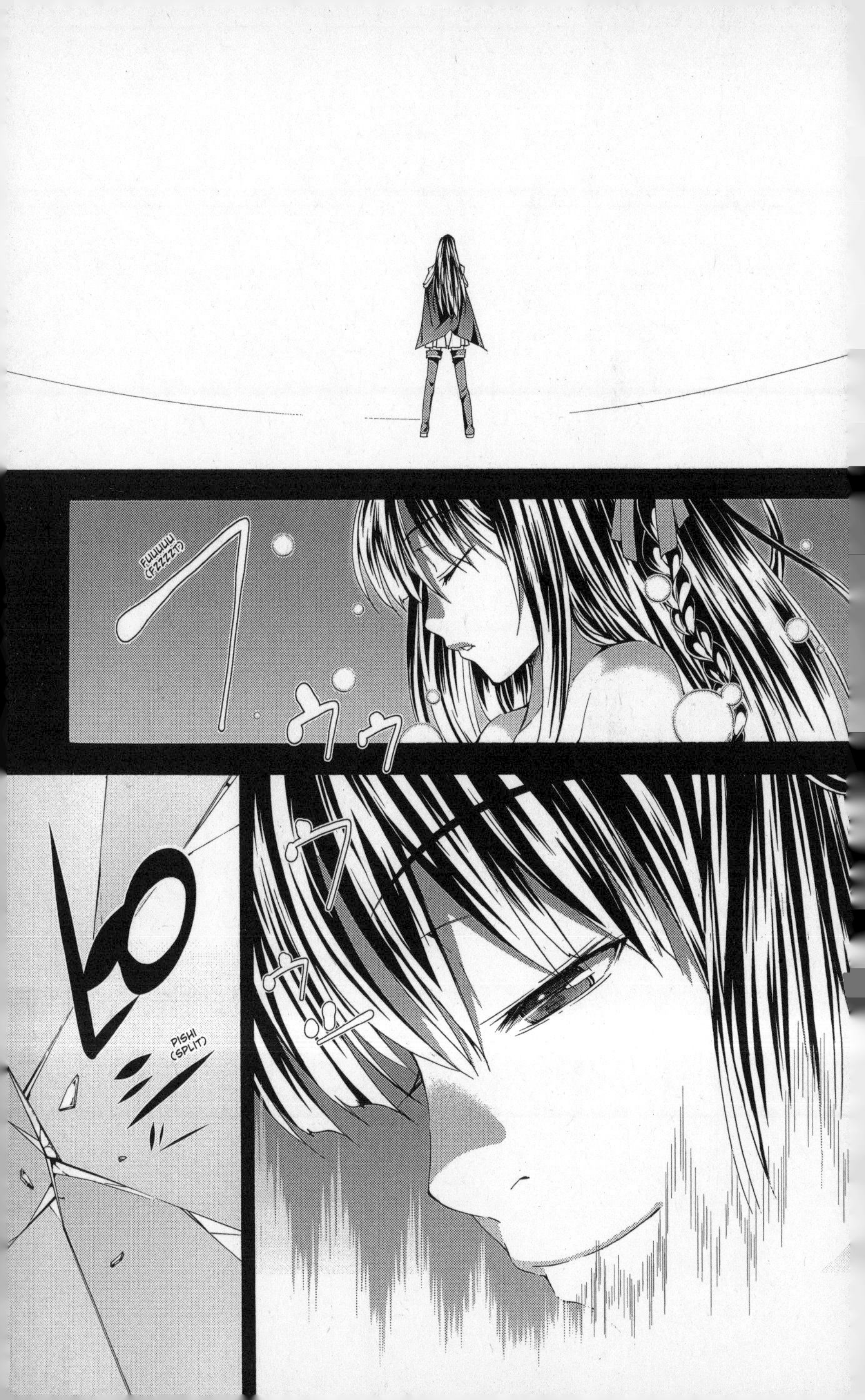
FUUUUU
(FZZZZZT)
PISHI
(SPLIT)

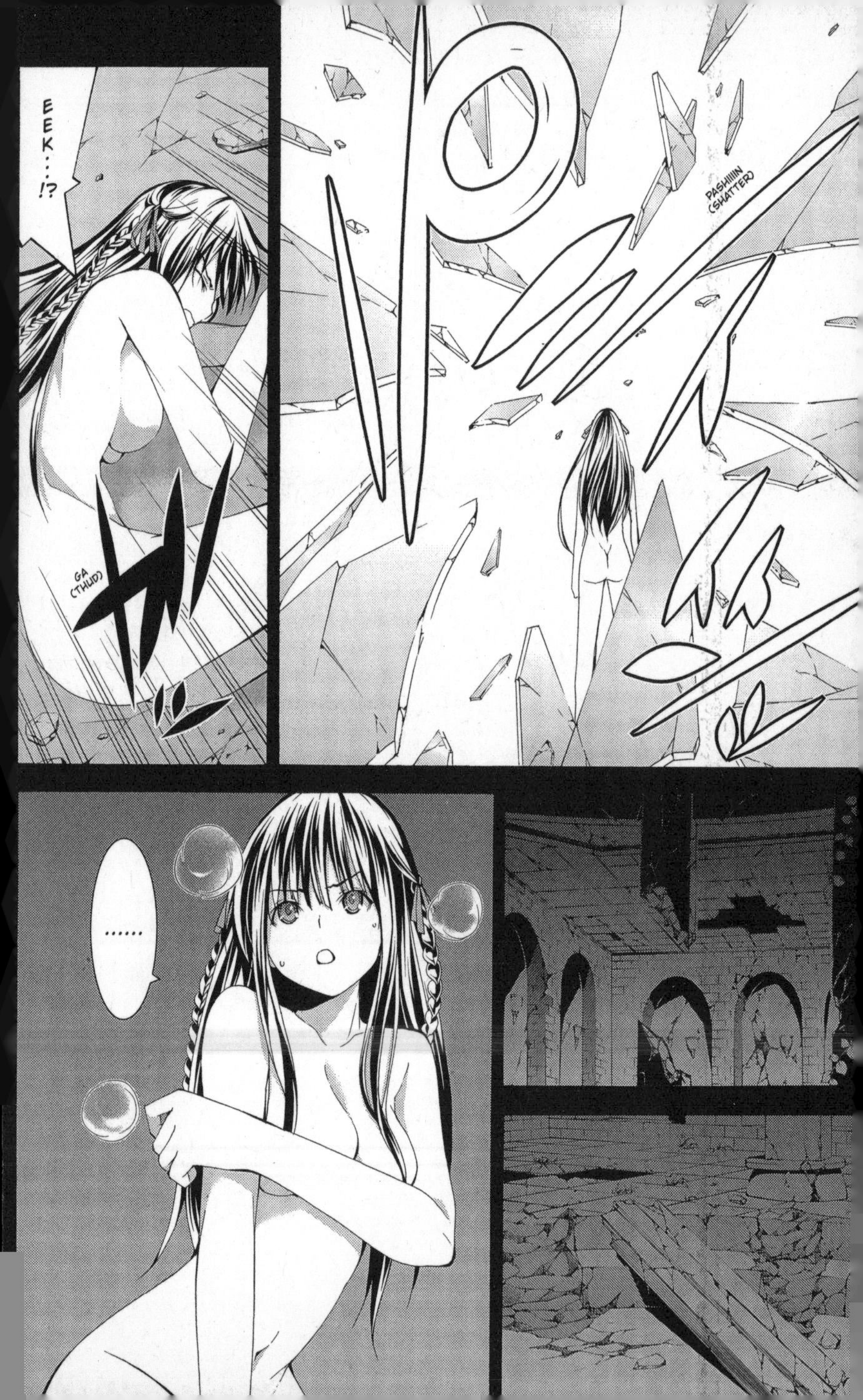
PASHIIIN (SHATTER)
EEK...!?
GA (THUD)
......

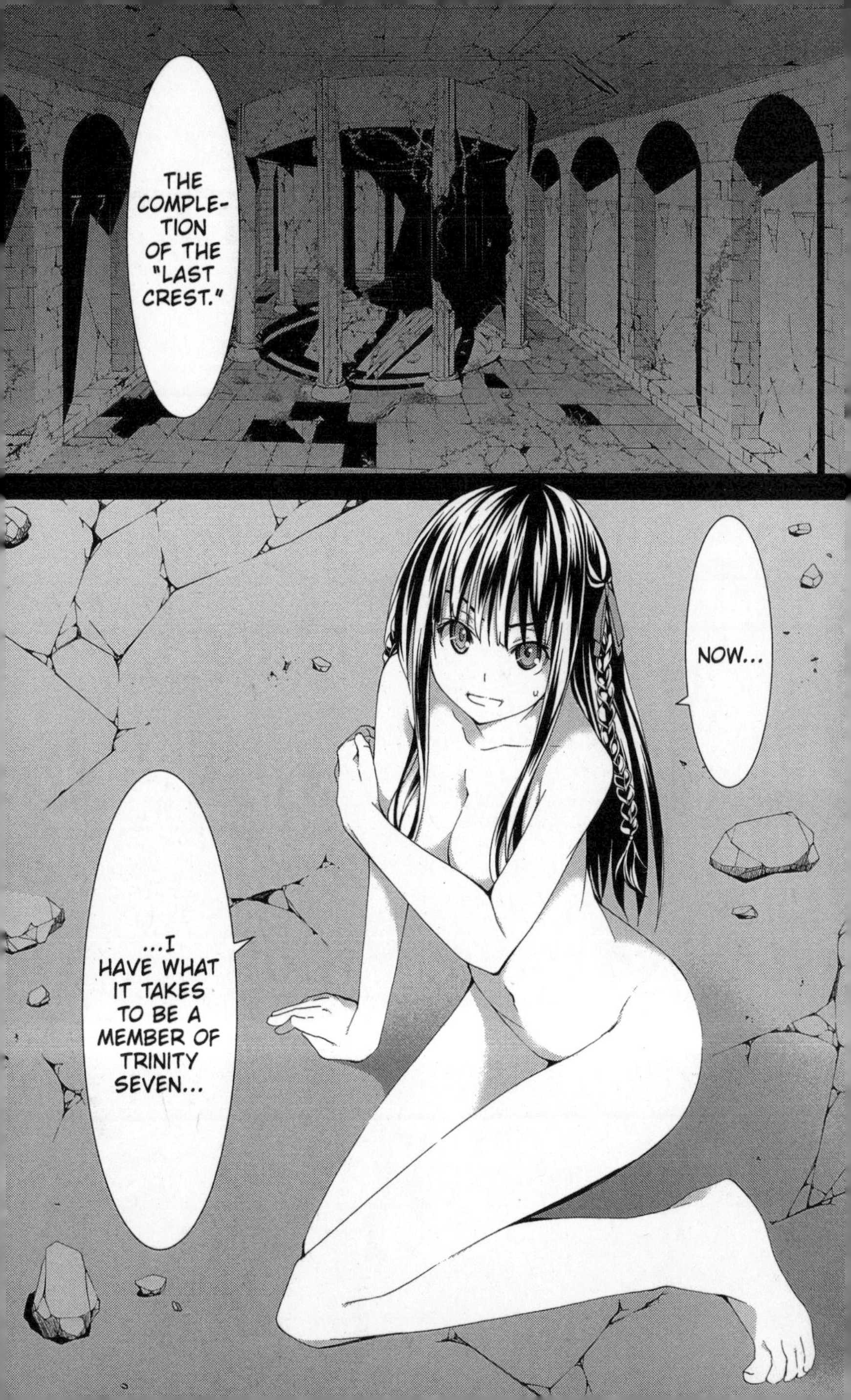
THE COMPLETION OF THE "LAST CREST."
NOW...
...I HAVE WHAT IT TAKES TO BE A MEMBER OF TRINITY SEVEN...

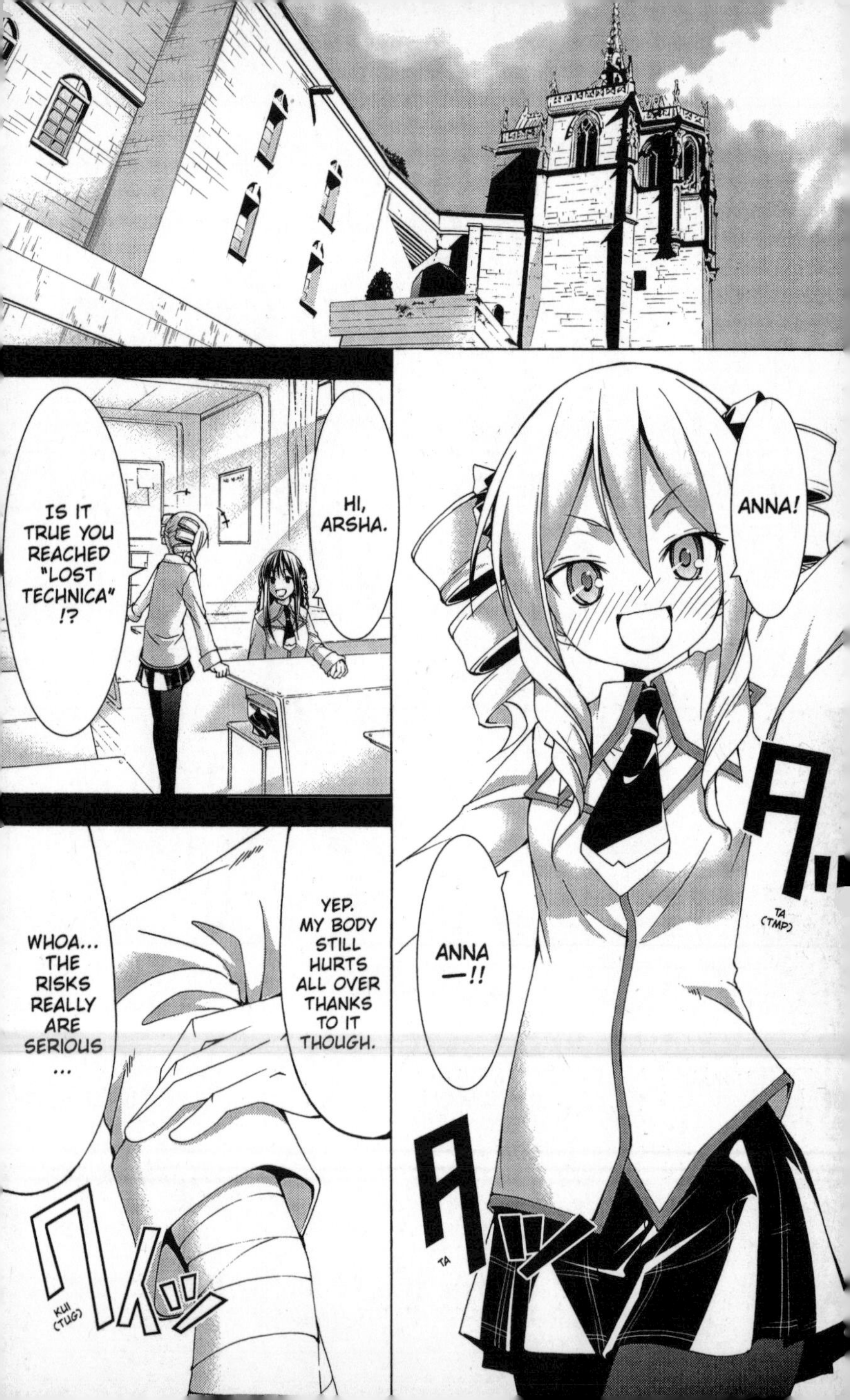
ANNA!
TA (TMP)
ANNA—!!
TA
HI, ARSHA.
IS IT TRUE YOU REACHED "LOST TECHNICA"!?
YEP. MY BODY STILL HURTS ALL OVER THANKS TO IT THOUGH.
WHOA... THE RISKS REALLY ARE SERIOUS...
KUI (TUG)

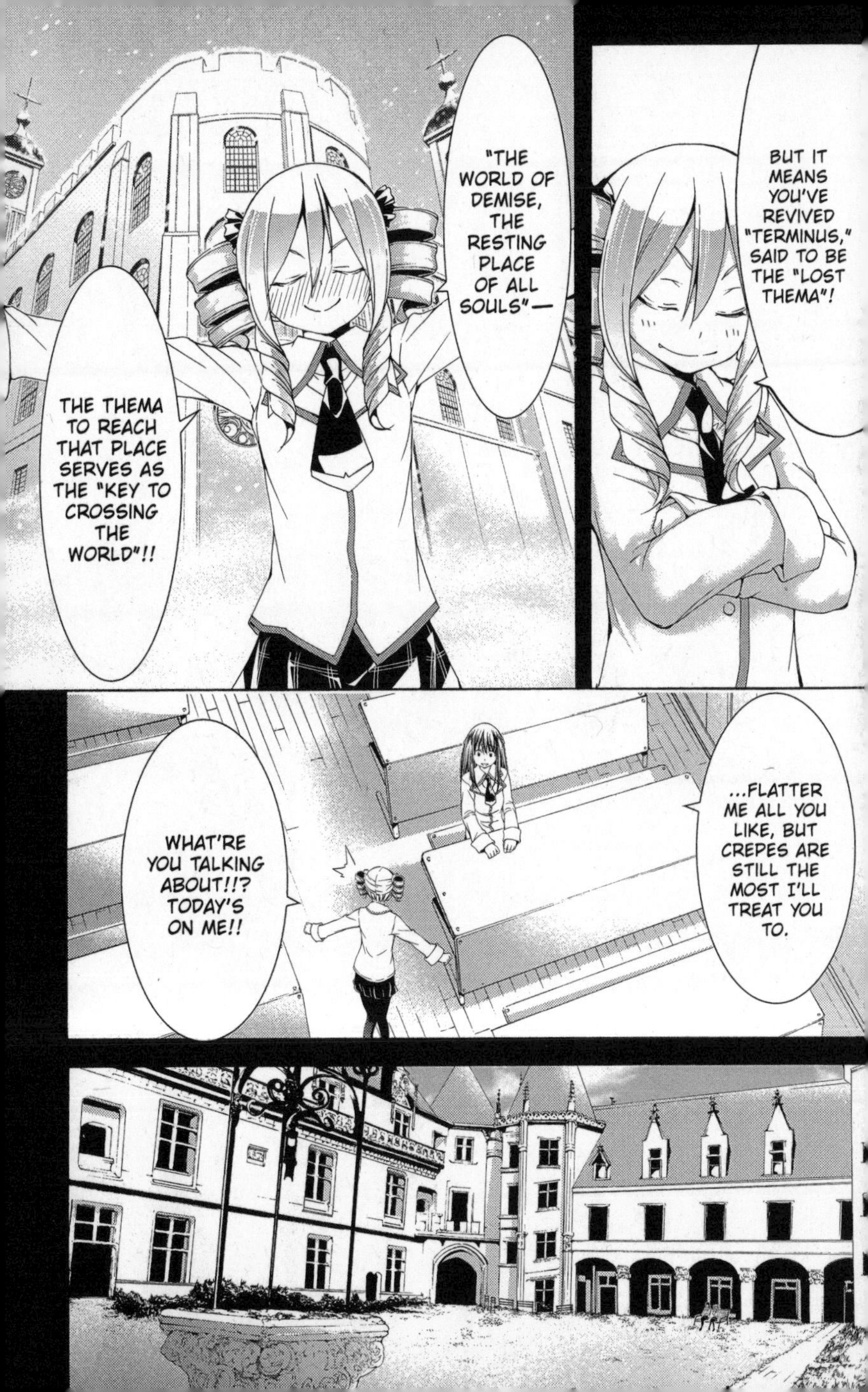
BUT IT MEANS YOU'VE REVIVED "TERMINUS," SAID TO BE THE "LOST THEMA"!
"THE WORLD OF DEMISE, THE RESTING PLACE OF ALL SOULS"—
THE THEMA TO REACH THAT PLACE SERVES AS THE "KEY TO CROSSING THE WORLD"!!
...FLATTER ME ALL YOU LIKE, BUT CREPES ARE STILL THE MOST I'LL TREAT YOU TO.
WHAT'RE YOU TALKING ABOUT!!? TODAY'S ON ME!!

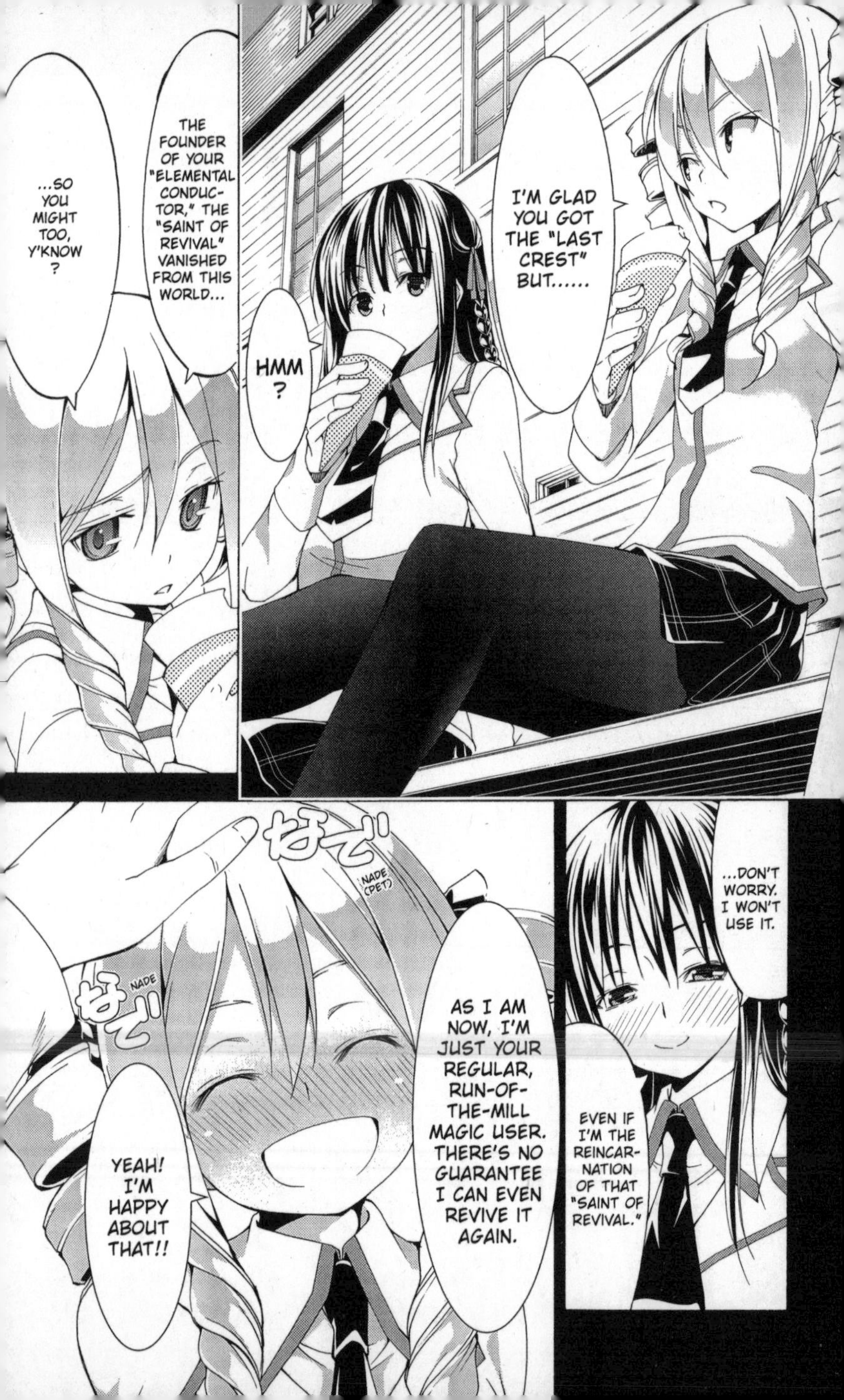
I'M GLAD YOU GOT THE "LAST CREST" BUT......
HMM?
THE FOUNDER OF YOUR "ELEMENTAL CONDUCTOR," THE "SAINT OF REVIVAL" VANISHED FROM THIS WORLD...
...SO YOU MIGHT TOO, Y'KNOW?
...DON'T WORRY. I WON'T USE IT.
EVEN IF I'M THE REINCARNATION OF THAT "SAINT OF REVIVAL."
NADE (PET)
AS I AM NOW, I'M JUST YOUR REGULAR, RUN-OF-THE-MILL MAGIC USER. THERE'S NO GUARANTEE I CAN EVEN REVIVE IT AGAIN.
NADE
YEAH! I'M HAPPY ABOUT THAT!!

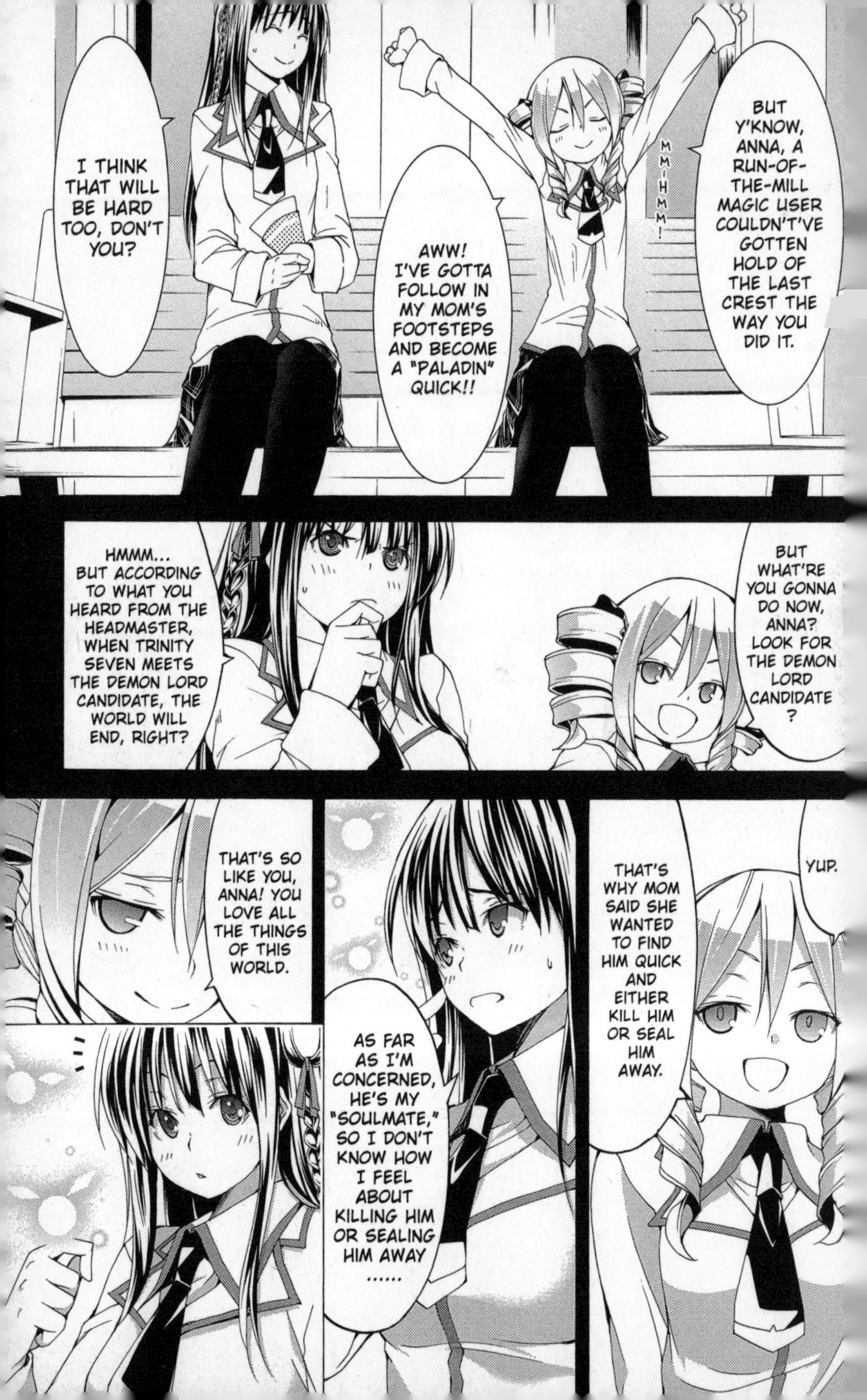
BUT Y'KNOW, ANNA, A RUN-OF-THE-MILL MAGIC USER COULDN'T'VE GOTTEN HOLD OF THE LAST CREST THE WAY YOU DID IT.
MM-HMM!
AWW! I'VE GOTTA FOLLOW IN MY MOM'S FOOTSTEPS AND BECOME A "PALADIN" QUICK!!
I THINK THAT WILL BE HARD TOO, DON'T YOU?
BUT WHAT'RE YOU GONNA DO NOW, ANNA? LOOK FOR THE DEMON LORD CANDIDATE?
HMMM... BUT ACCORDING TO WHAT YOU HEARD FROM THE HEADMASTER, WHEN TRINITY SEVEN MEETS THE DEMON LORD CANDIDATE, THE WORLD WILL END, RIGHT?
YUP.
THAT'S WHY MOM SAID SHE WANTED TO FIND HIM QUICK AND EITHER KILL HIM OR SEAL HIM AWAY.
AS FAR AS I'M CONCERNED, HE'S MY "SOULMATE," SO I DON'T KNOW HOW I FEEL ABOUT KILLING HIM OR SEALING HIM AWAY ......
THAT'S SO LIKE YOU, ANNA! YOU LOVE ALL THE THINGS OF THIS WORLD.

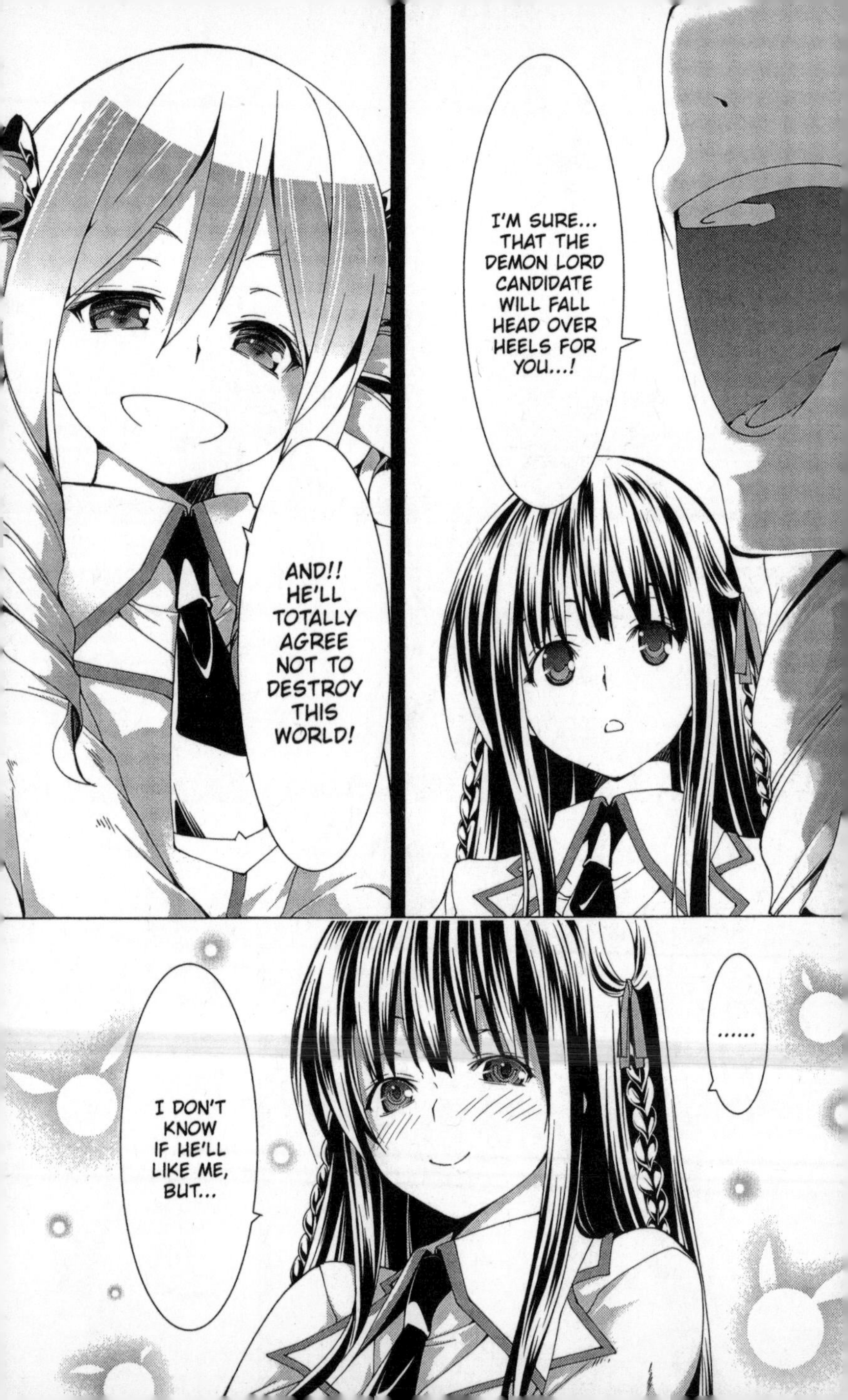
I'M SURE... THAT THE DEMON LORD CANDIDATE WILL FALL HEAD OVER HEELS FOR YOU...!
AND!! HE'LL TOTALLY AGREE NOT TO DESTROY THIS WORLD!
......
I DON'T KNOW IF HE'LL LIKE ME, BUT...

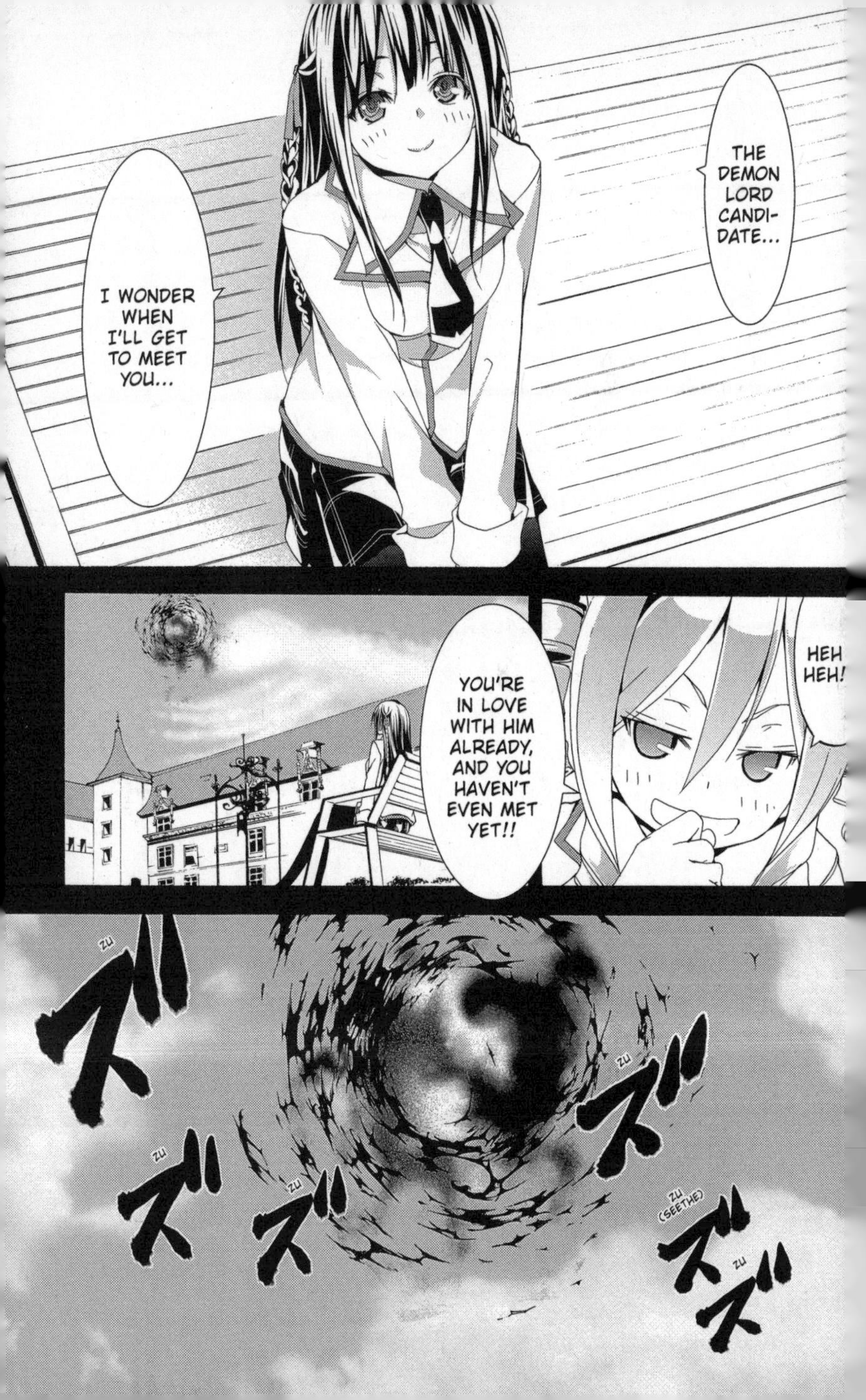
THE DEMON LORD CANDIDATE...
I WONDER WHEN I'LL GET TO MEET YOU...
HEH HEH!
YOU'RE IN LOVE WITH HIM ALREADY, AND YOU HAVEN'T EVEN MET YET!!
ZU (SEETHE)
ZU
ZU
ZU
ZU
ZU

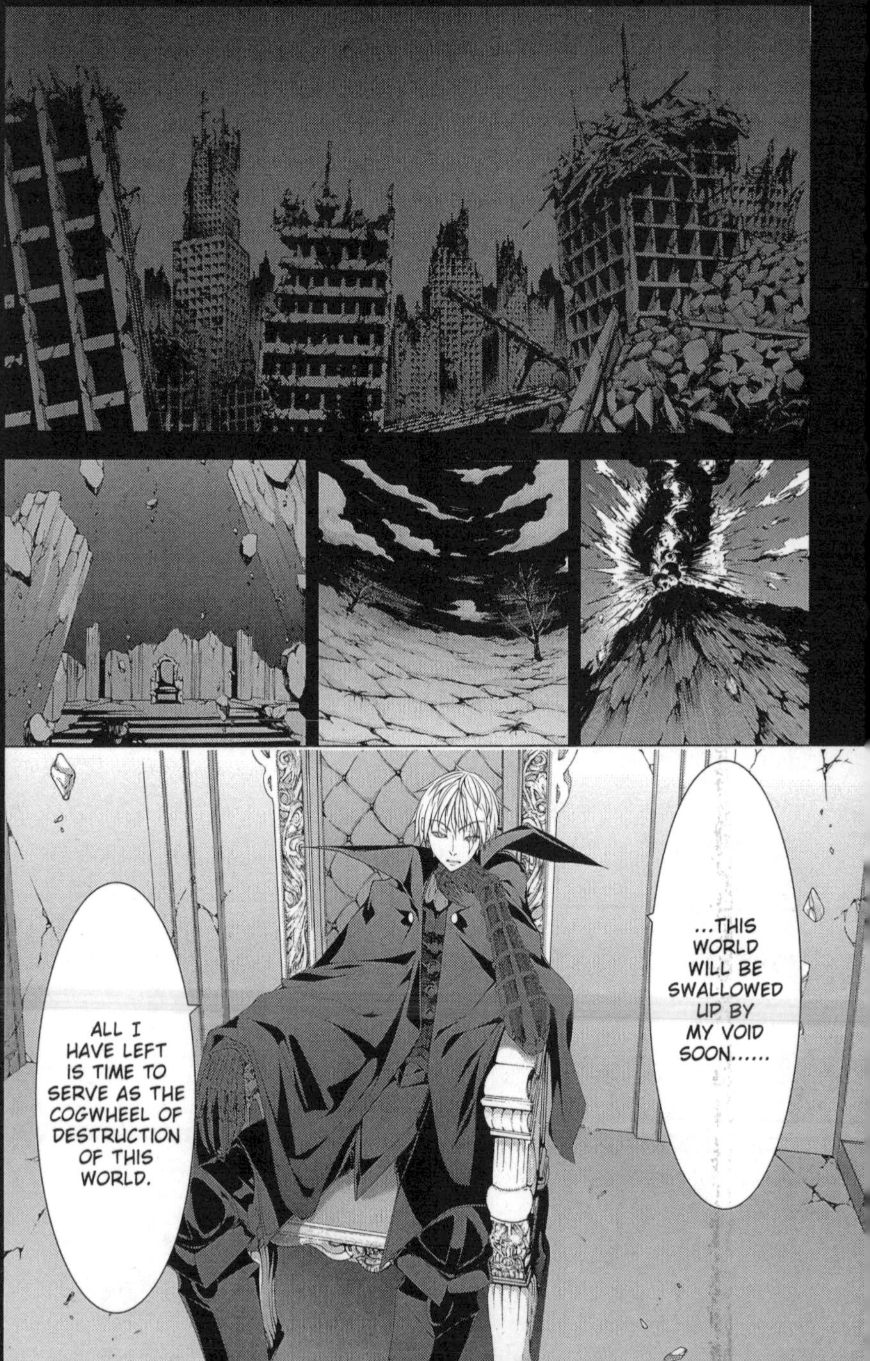
...THIS WORLD WILL BE SWALLOWED UP BY MY VOID SOON......
ALL I HAVE LEFT IS TIME TO SERVE AS THE COGWHEEL OF DESTRUCTION OF THIS WORLD.

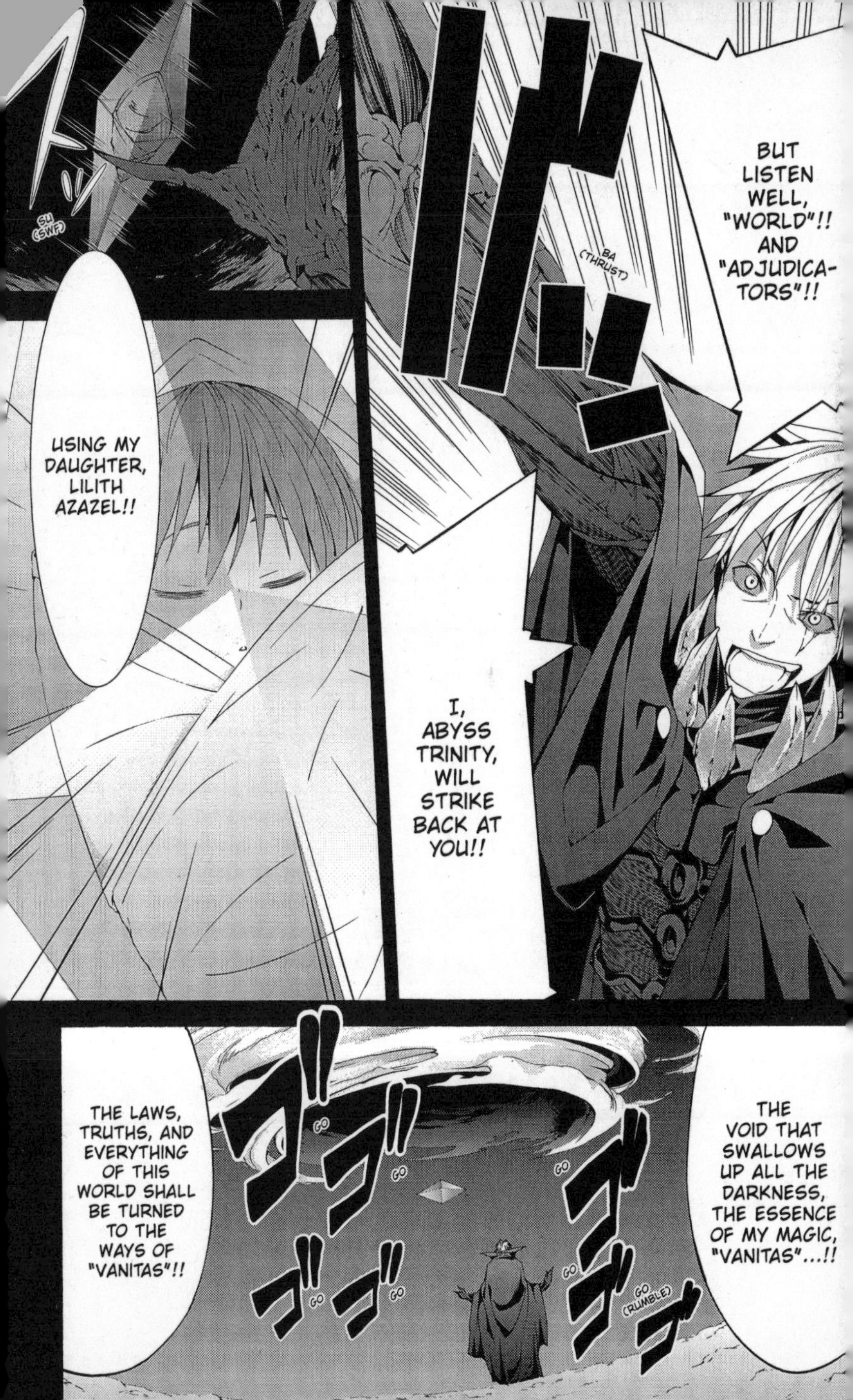
BUT LISTEN WELL, "WORLD"!! AND "ADJUDICATORS"!!
BA (THRUST)
I, ABYSS TRINITY, WILL STRIKE BACK AT YOU!!
SU (SWF)
USING MY DAUGHTER, LILITH AZAZEL!!
THE VOID THAT SWALLOWS UP ALL THE DARKNESS, THE ESSENCE OF MY MAGIC, "VANITAS"...!!
GO (RUMBLE)
GO GO GO GO GO GO GO
THE LAWS, TRUTHS, AND EVERYTHING OF THIS WORLD SHALL BE TURNED TO THE WAYS OF "VANITAS"!!

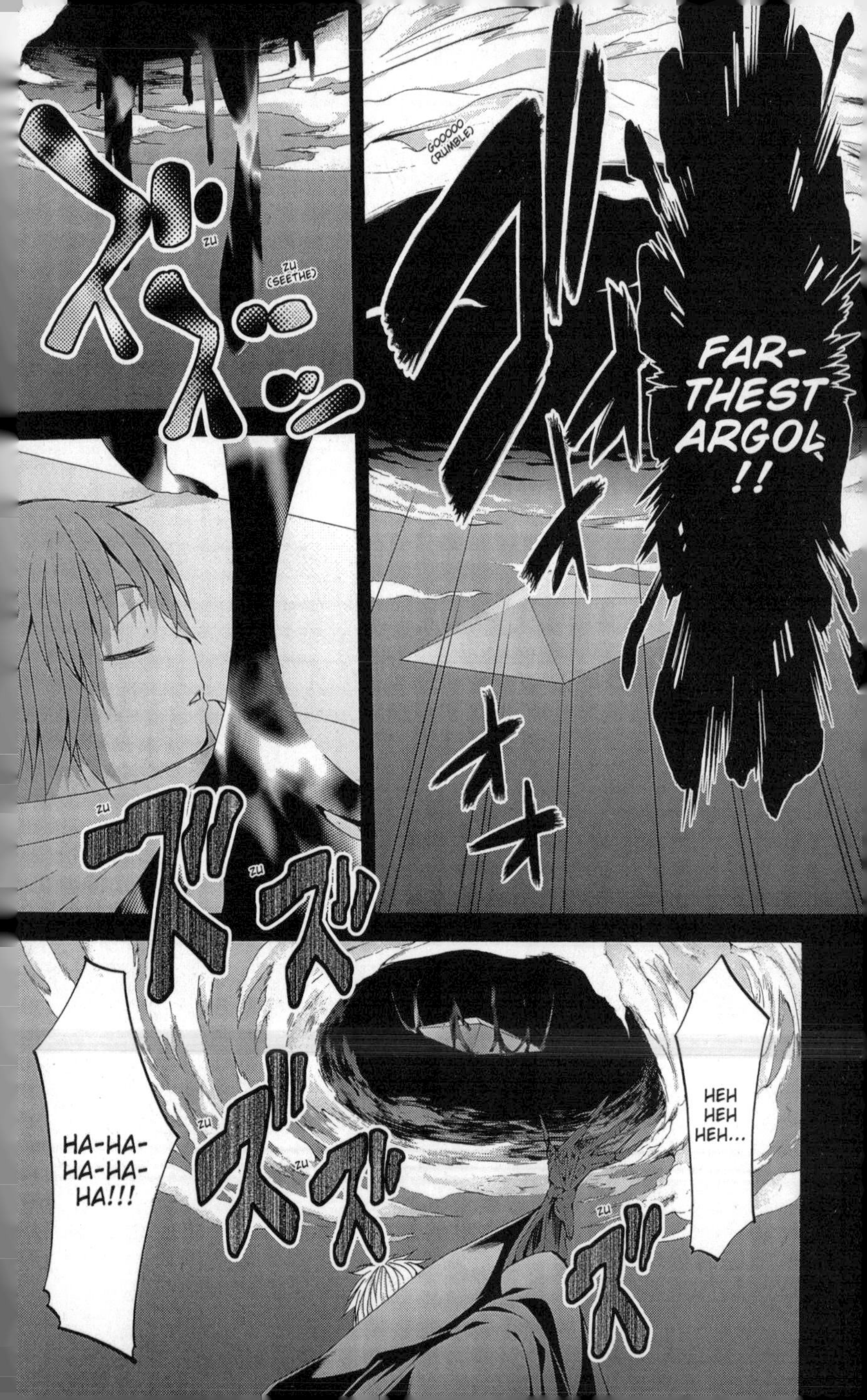
GOOOOO (RUMBLE)
FAR-THEST ARGOL!!
ZU
ZU (SEETHE)
ZU
ZU
HEH HEH HEH...
ZU
ZU
HA-HA-HA-HA-HA!!!
ZU

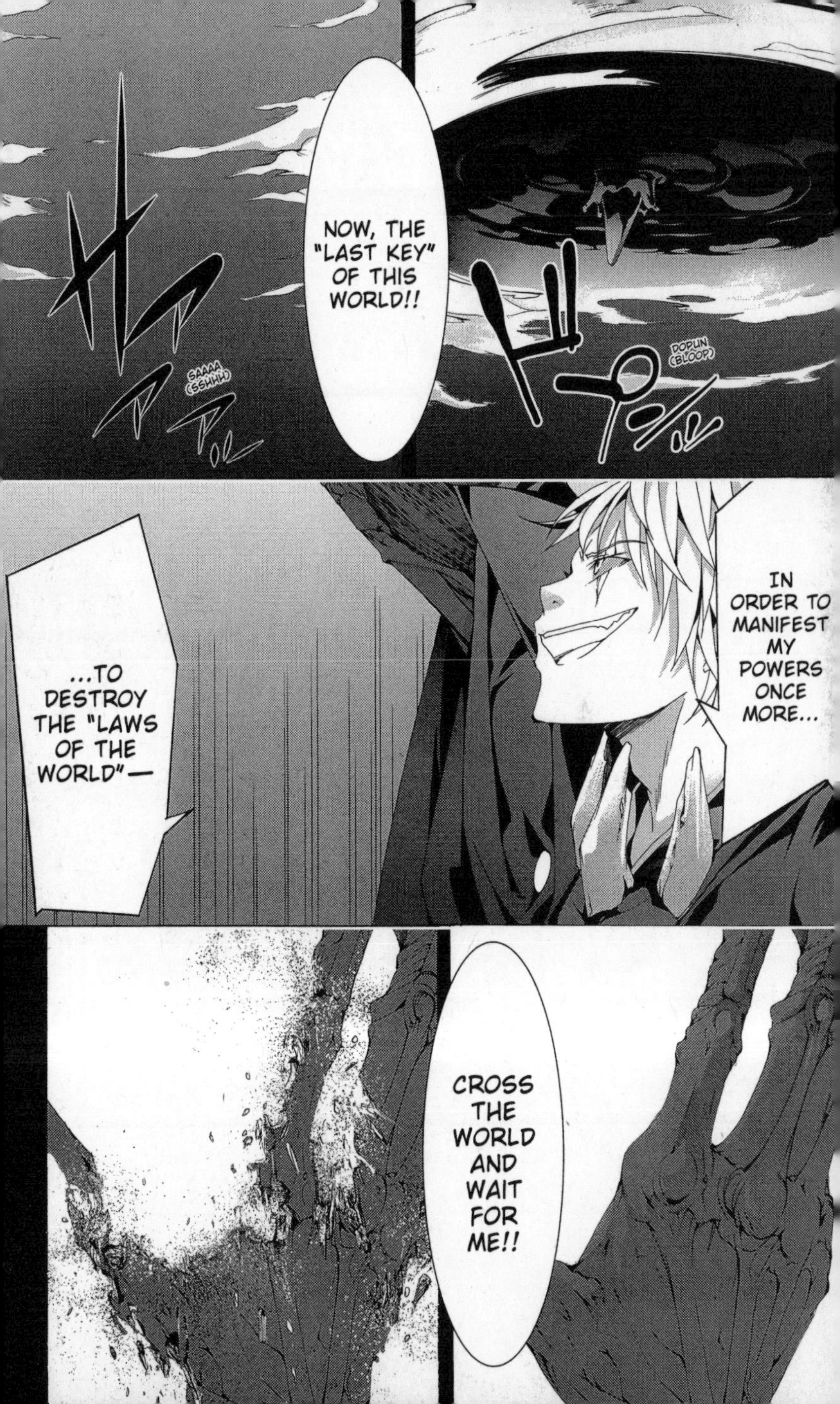
DOPUN (BLOOP)
NOW, THE "LAST KEY" OF THIS WORLD!!
SAAAA (SSHHH)
IN ORDER TO MANIFEST MY POWERS ONCE MORE...
...TO DESTROY THE "LAWS OF THE WORLD"—
CROSS THE WORLD AND WAIT FOR ME!!

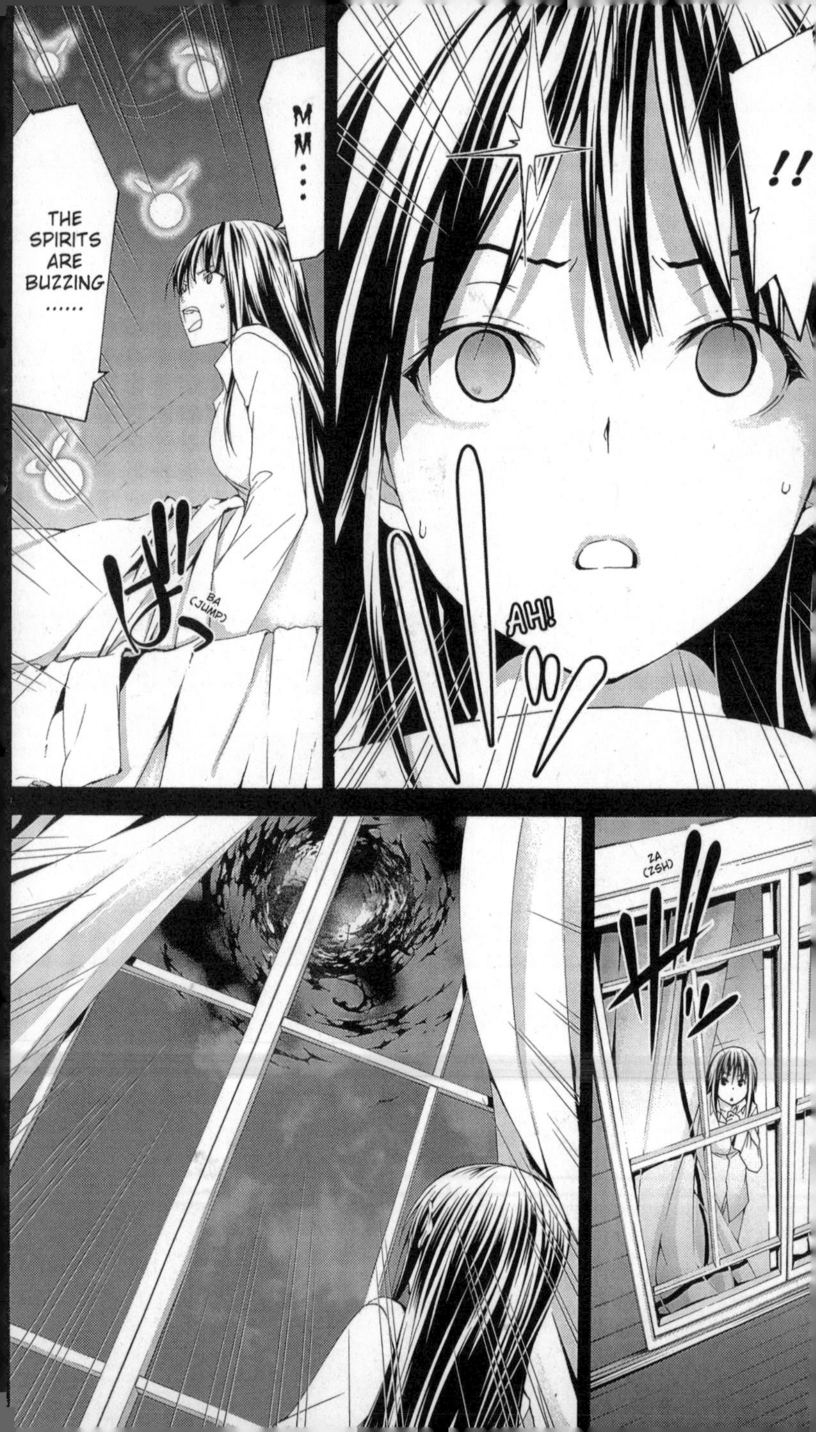
!!
AH!
MM...
THE SPIRITS ARE BUZZING ......
BA (JUMP)
ZA (ZSH)

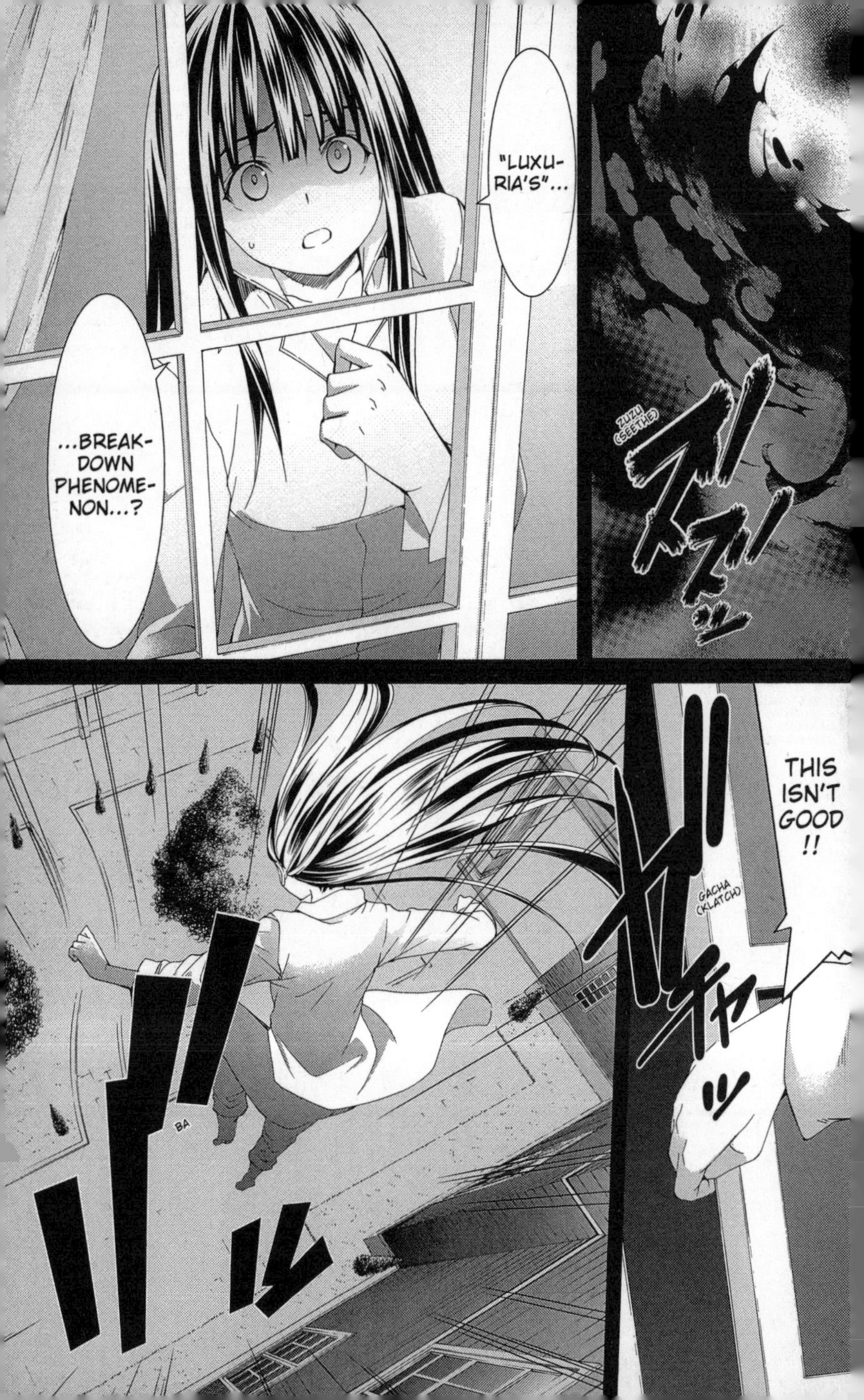
ZUZU (SEETHE)
"LUXU-RIA'S"...
...BREAK-DOWN PHENOME-NON...?
THIS ISN'T GOOD !!
GACHA (KLATCH)
BA

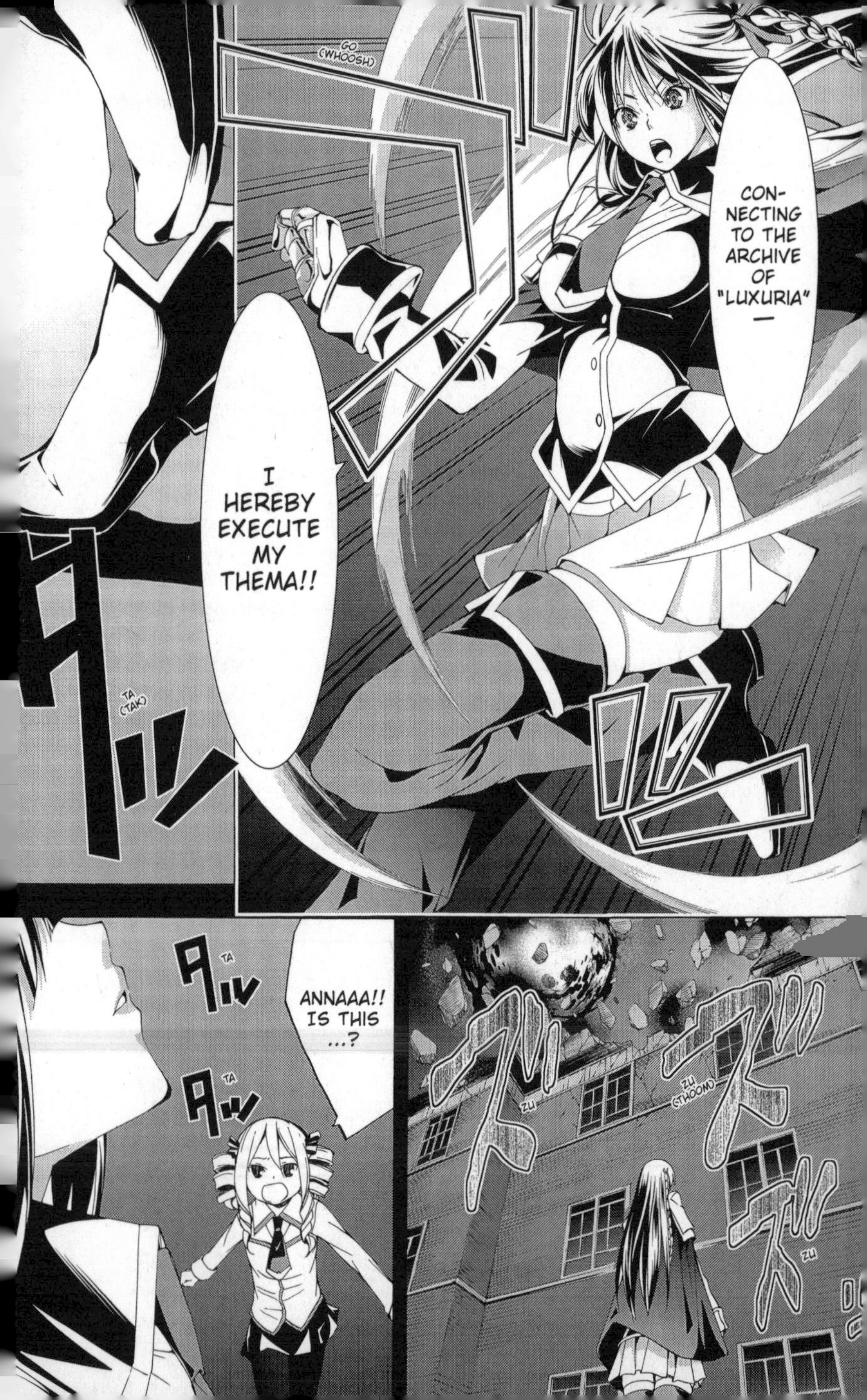
GO (WHOOSH)
CON-NECTING TO THE ARCHIVE OF "LUXURIA"—
I HEREBY EXECUTE MY THEMA!!
TA (TAK)
ZU (THOOM)
ZU
ZU
ANNAAA!! IS THIS ...?
TA
TA

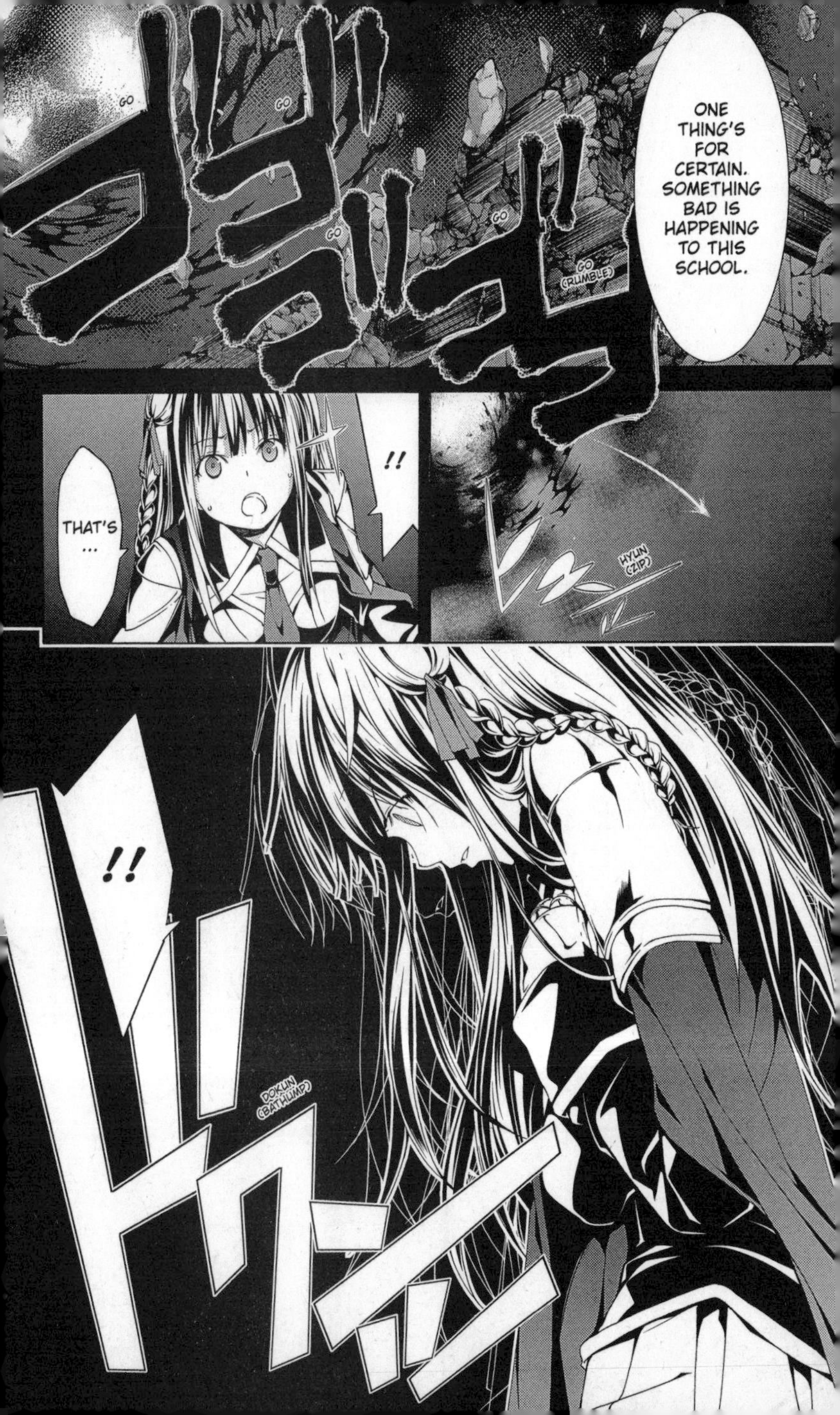
ONE THING'S FOR CERTAIN. SOMETHING BAD IS HAPPENING TO THIS SCHOOL.
GO (RUMBLE)
GO
GO
GO
GO
HYUN (ZIP)
!!
THAT'S ...
!!
DOKUN (BATHUMP)

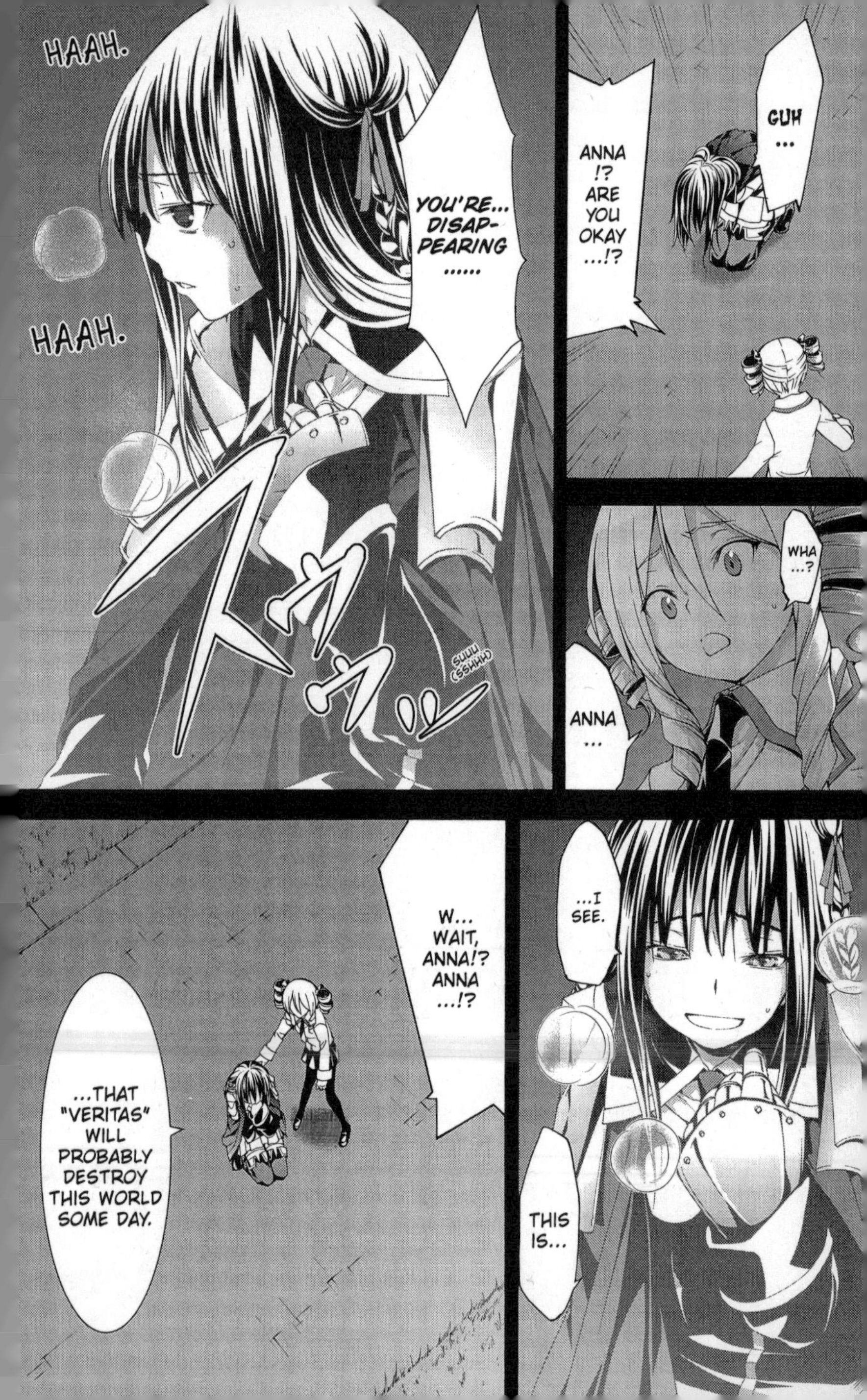
GUH...
ANNA!? ARE YOU OKAY...!?
WHA...?
ANNA...
YOU'RE... DISAP-PEARING......
HAAH.
HAAH.
Suuu (SSHHH)
...I SEE.
THIS IS...
W... WAIT, ANNA!? ANNA...!?
...THAT "VERITAS" WILL PROBABLY DESTROY THIS WORLD SOME DAY.

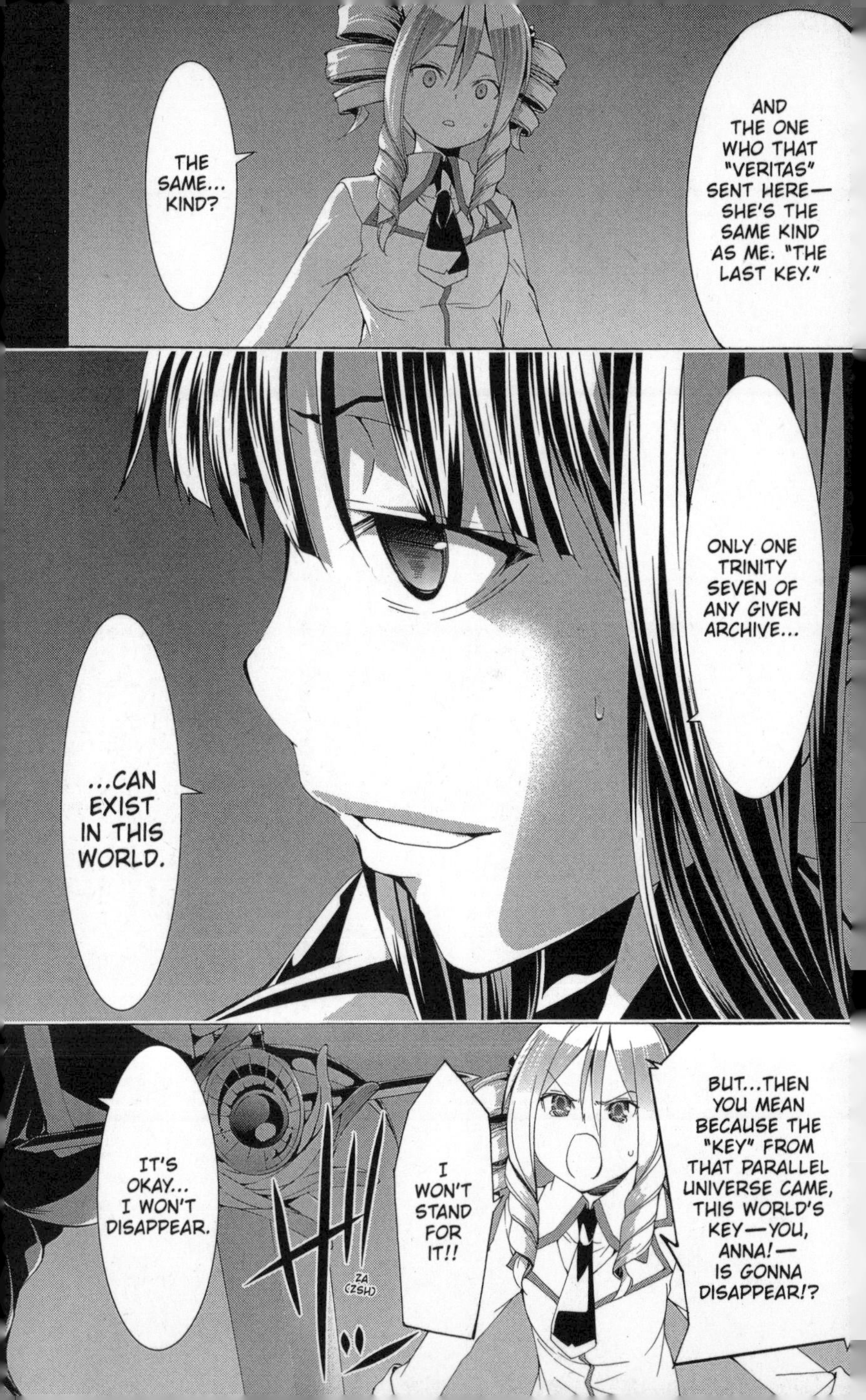
AND THE ONE WHO THAT "VERITAS" SENT HERE—SHE'S THE SAME KIND AS ME: "THE LAST KEY."
THE SAME... KIND?
ONLY ONE TRINITY SEVEN OF ANY GIVEN ARCHIVE...
...CAN EXIST IN THIS WORLD.
BUT...THEN YOU MEAN BECAUSE THE "KEY" FROM THAT PARALLEL UNIVERSE CAME, THIS WORLD'S KEY—YOU, ANNA!—IS GONNA DISAPPEAR!?
I WON'T STAND FOR IT!!
ZA (ZSH)
IT'S OKAY... I WON'T DISAPPEAR.

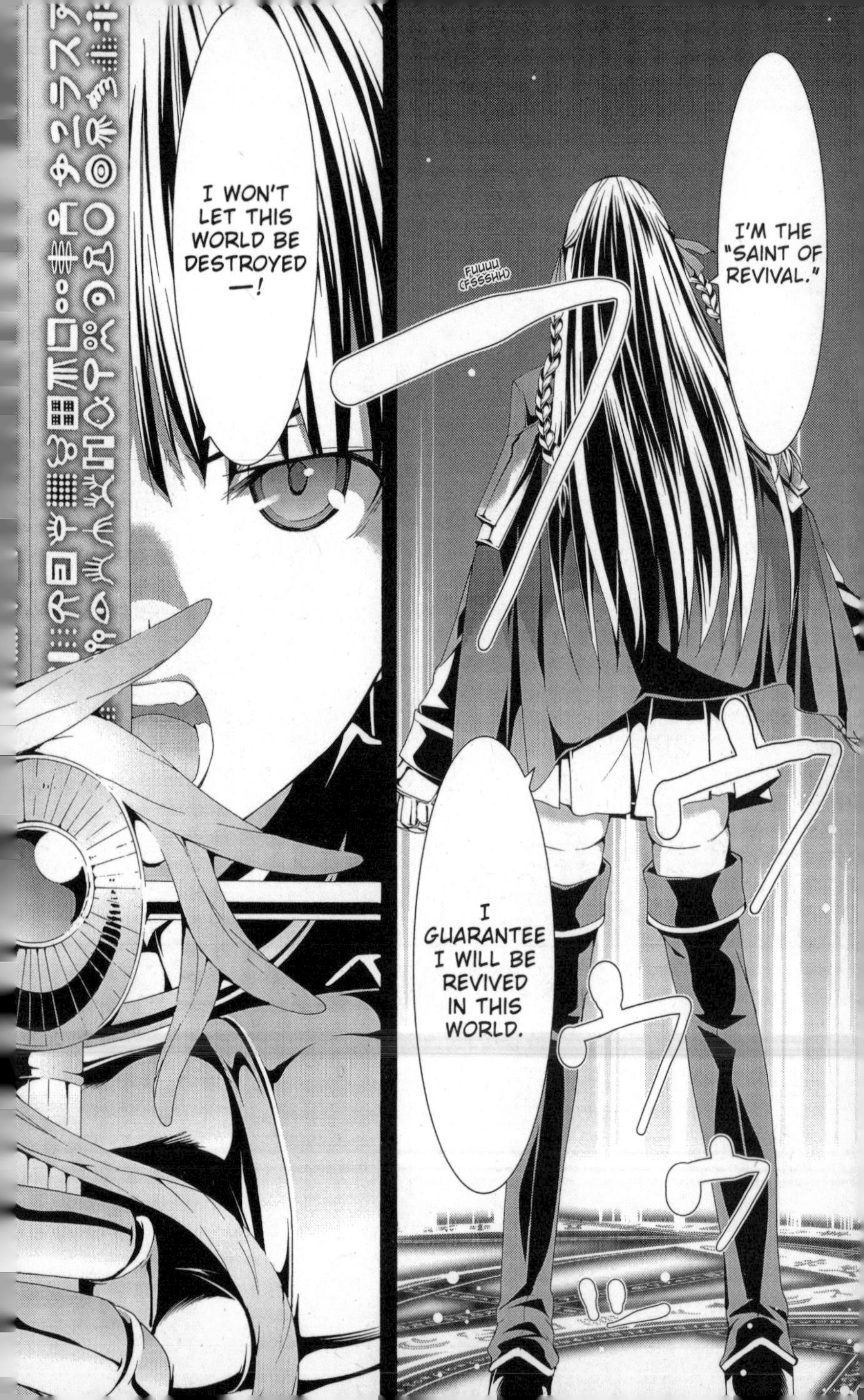
I'M THE "SAINT OF REVIVAL."
FUUUU (FSSSHH)
I GUARANTEE I WILL BE REVIVED IN THIS WORLD.
I WON'T LET THIS WORLD BE DESTROYED—!

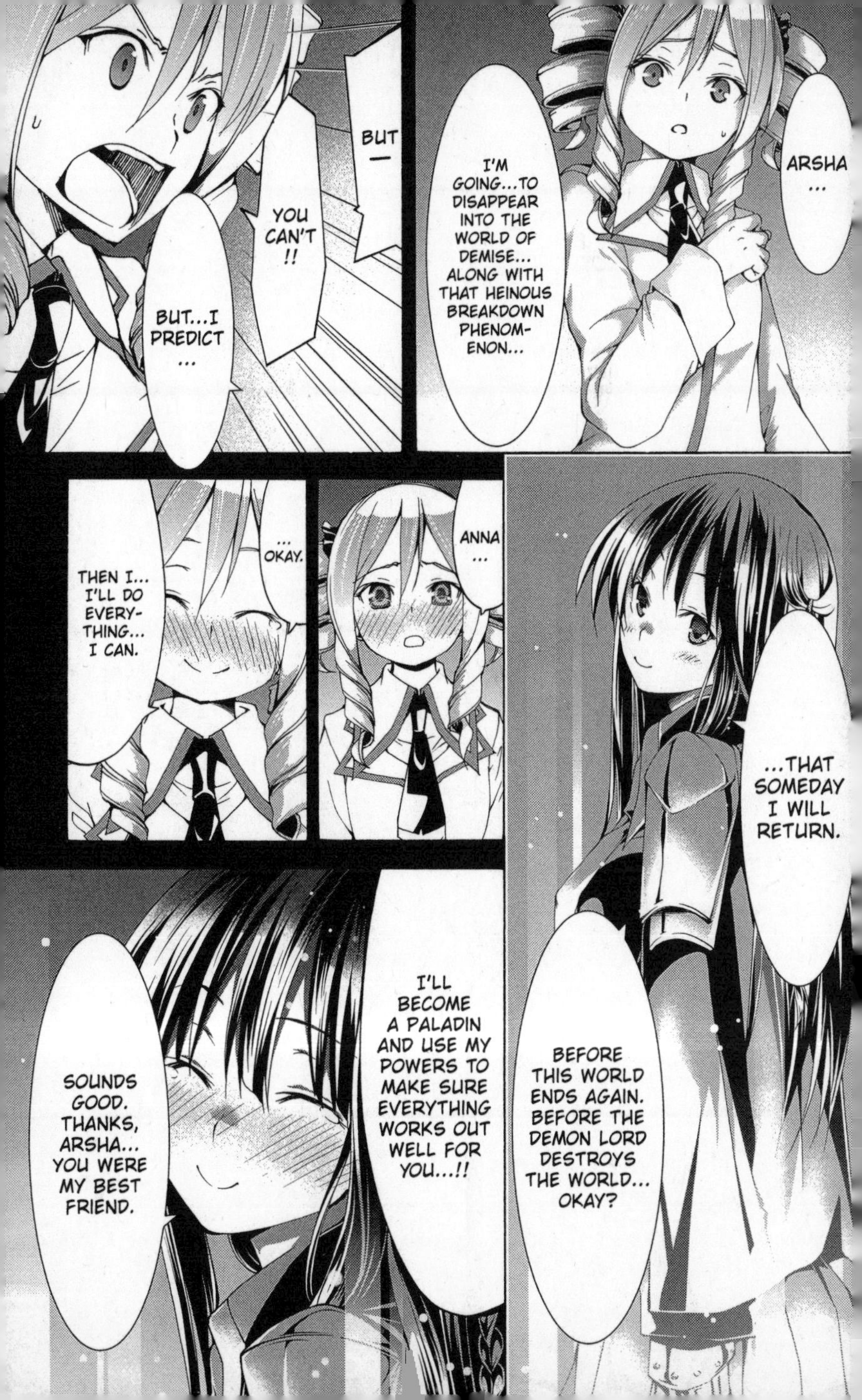
ARSHA ...
I'M GOING...TO DISAPPEAR INTO THE WORLD OF DEMISE... ALONG WITH THAT HEINOUS BREAKDOWN PHENOM-ENON...
BUT —
YOU CAN'T !!
BUT...I PREDICT ...
...THAT SOMEDAY I WILL RETURN.
BEFORE THIS WORLD ENDS AGAIN. BEFORE THE DEMON LORD DESTROYS THE WORLD... OKAY?
ANNA ...
... OKAY.
THEN I... I'LL DO EVERY-THING... I CAN.
I'LL BECOME A PALADIN AND USE MY POWERS TO MAKE SURE EVERYTHING WORKS OUT WELL FOR YOU...!!
SOUNDS GOOD. THANKS, ARSHA... YOU WERE MY BEST FRIEND.

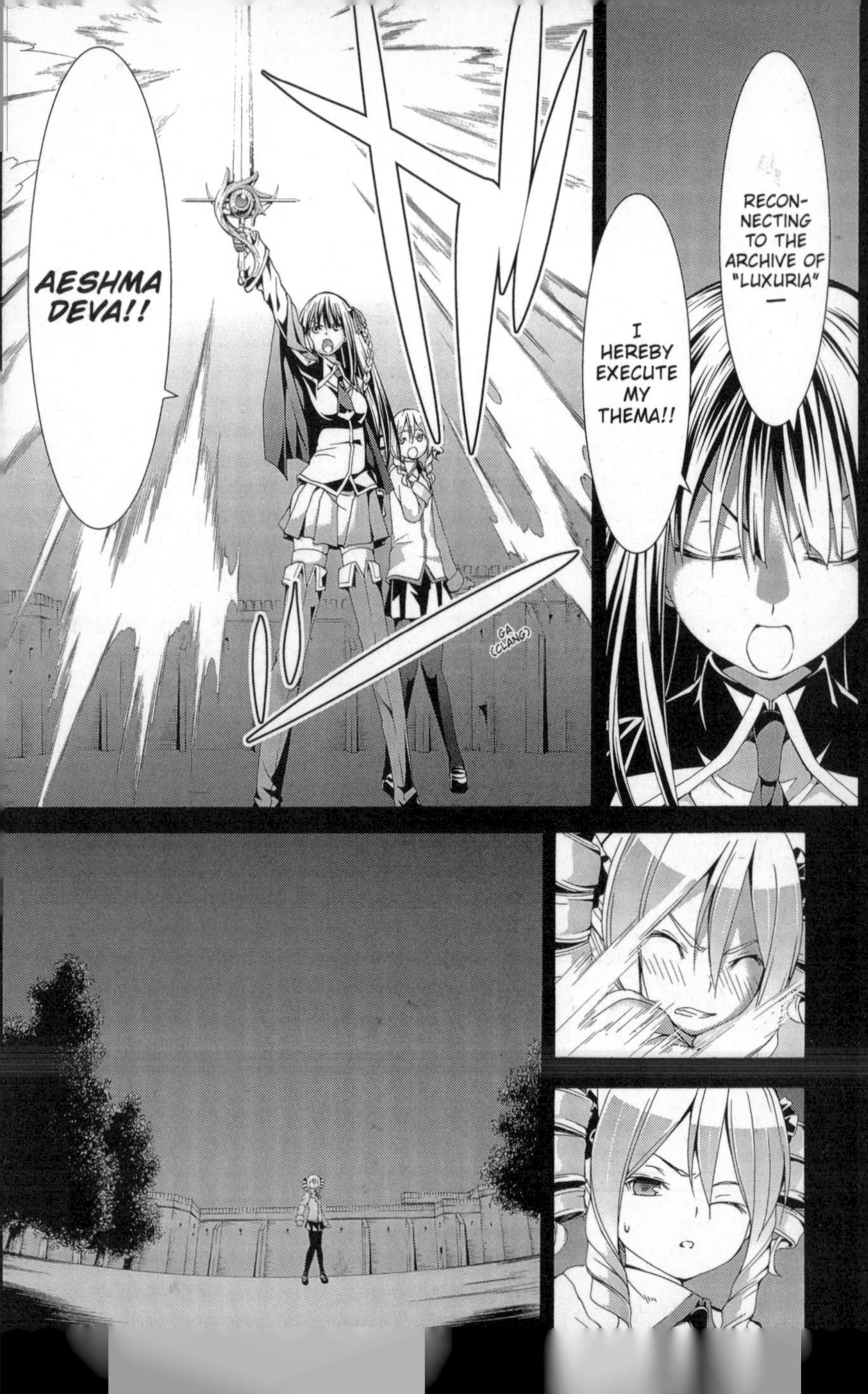
RECON-NECTING TO THE ARCHIVE OF "LUXURIA" —
I HEREBY EXECUTE MY THEMA!!
AESHMA DEVA!!
GA (CLANG)

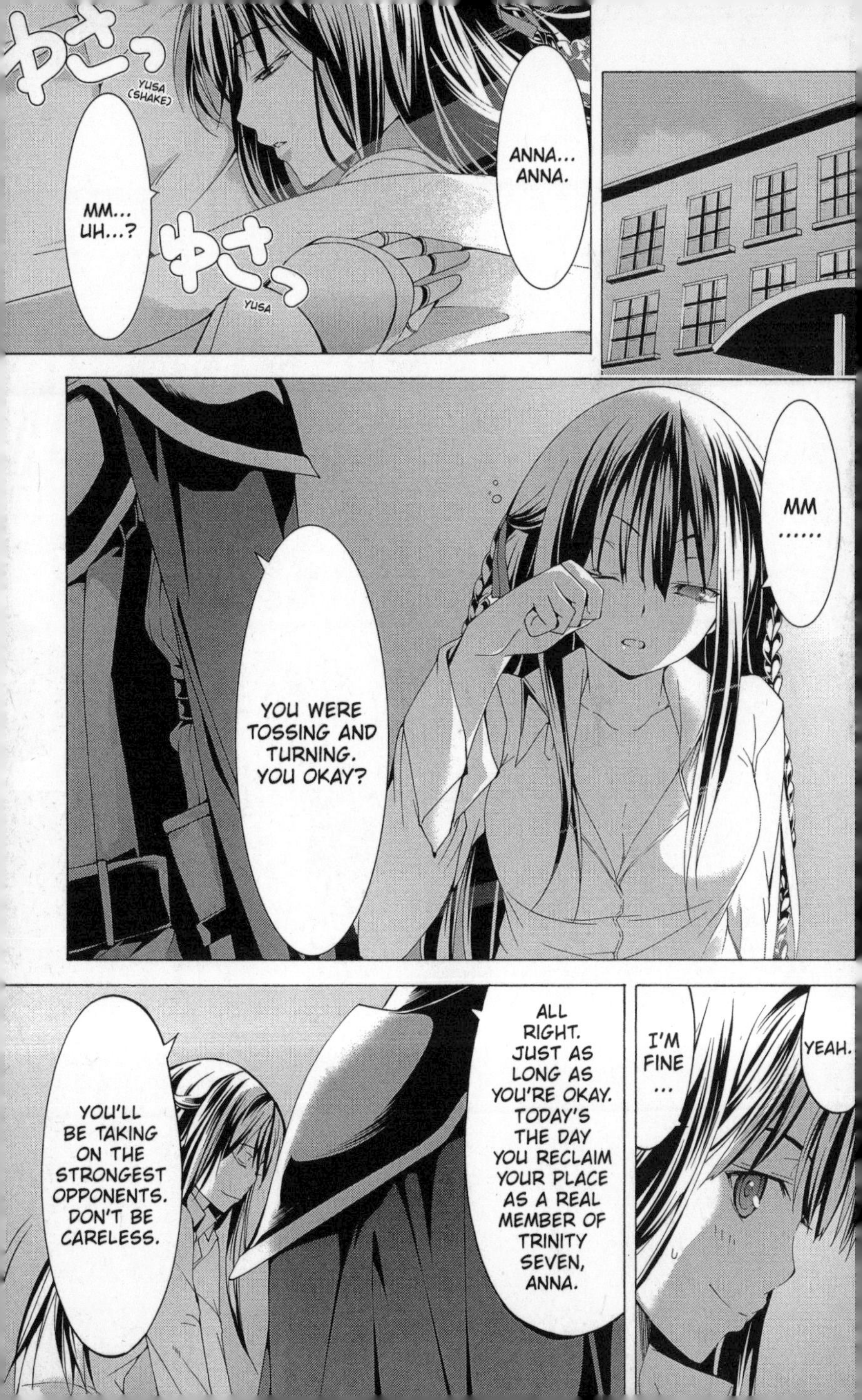
ANNA... ANNA.
ゆさっ
YUSA (SHAKE)
MM... UH...?
ゆさっ
YUSA
MM ......
YOU WERE TOSSING AND TURNING. YOU OKAY?
YEAH.
I'M FINE ...
ALL RIGHT. JUST AS LONG AS YOU'RE OKAY. TODAY'S THE DAY YOU RECLAIM YOUR PLACE AS A REAL MEMBER OF TRINITY SEVEN, ANNA.
YOU'LL BE TAKING ON THE STRONGEST OPPONENTS. DON'T BE CARELESS.

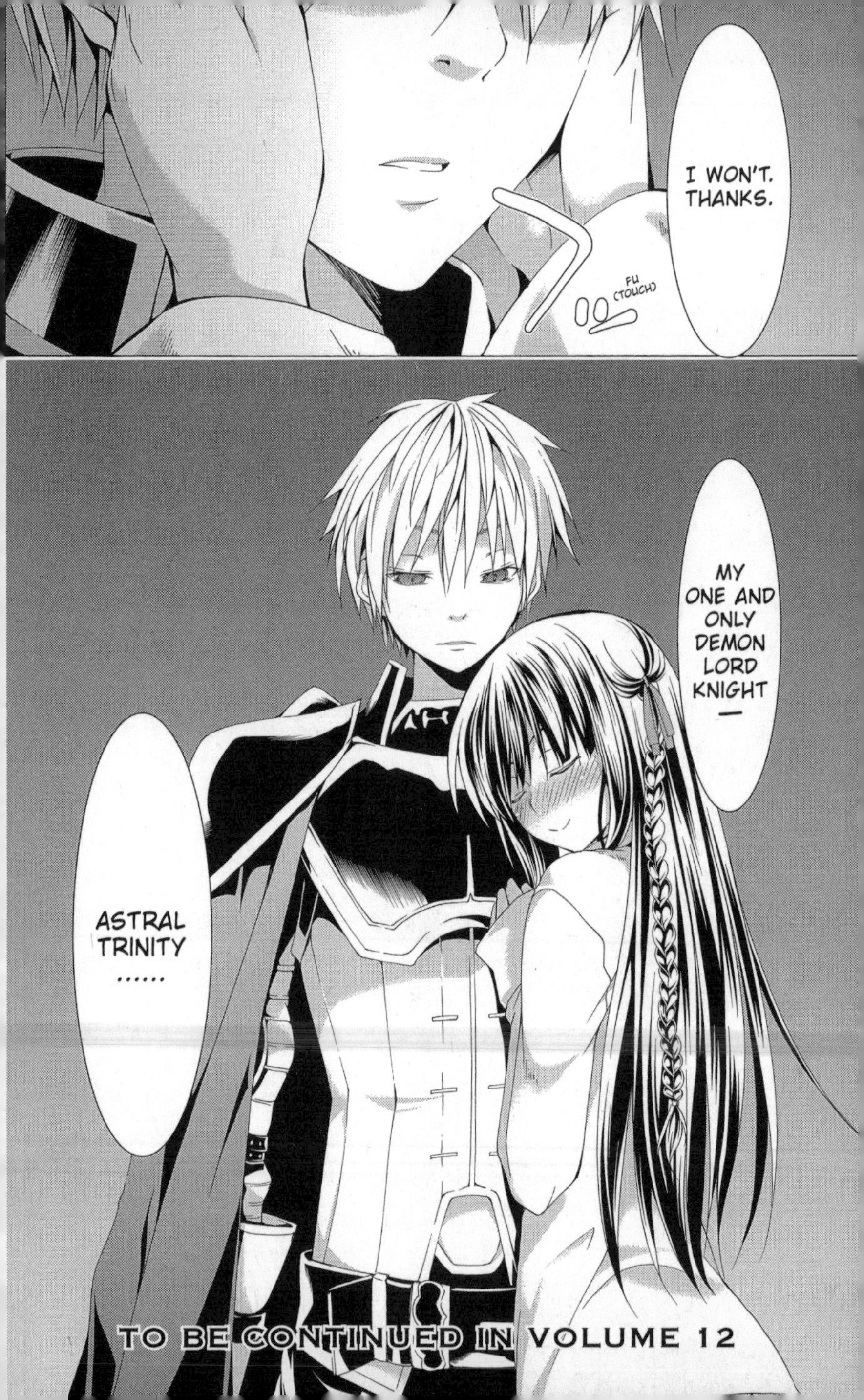
I WON'T. THANKS.
FU (TOUCH)
MY ONE AND ONLY DEMON LORD KNIGHT —
ASTRAL TRINITY ......
TO BE CONTINUED IN VOLUME 12

PREVIEW OF THE NEXT VOLUME

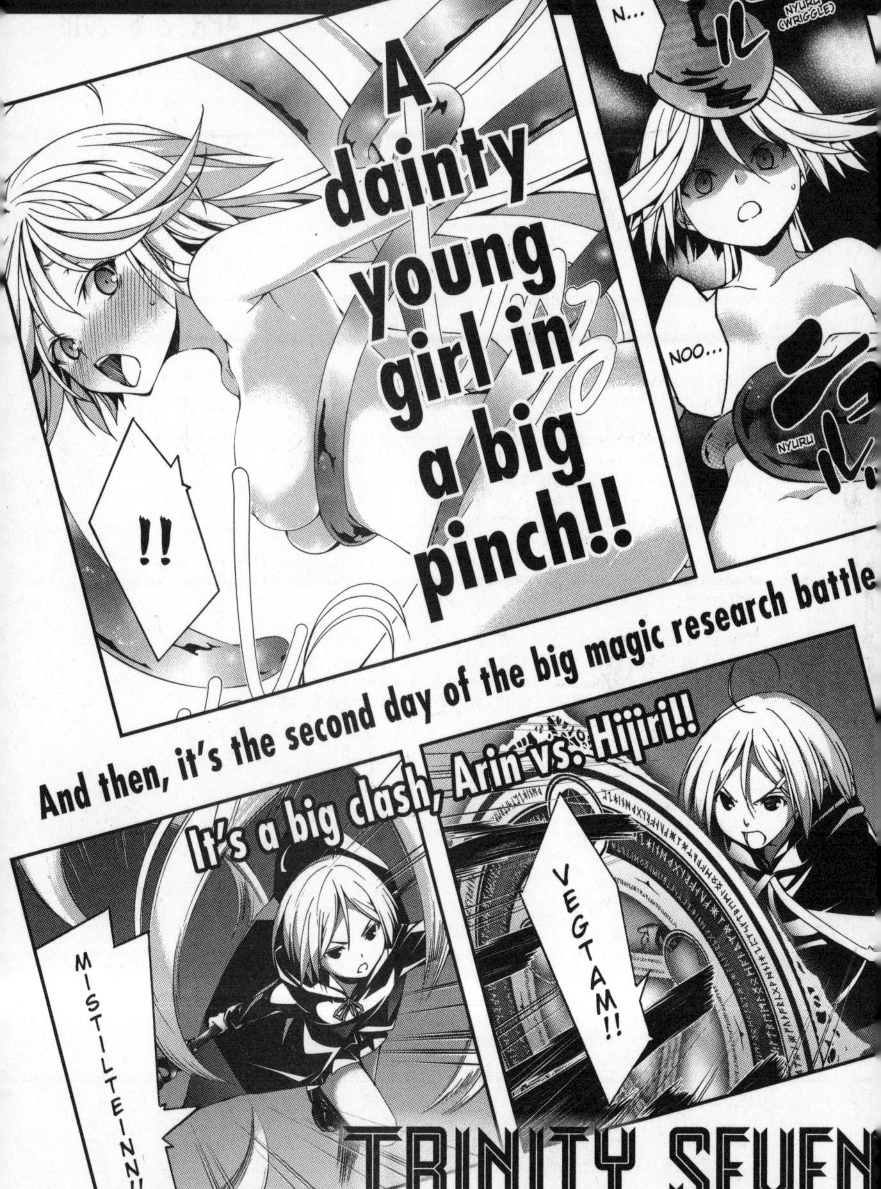
N...
NYURU (WRIGGLE)
NOO...
NYURU
A dainty young girl in a big pinch!!
!!
And then, it's the second day of the big magic research battle
It's a big clash, Arin vs. Hijiri!!
VEGTAM!!
MISTILTEINN!!

TRINITY SEVEN

THE SEVEN MAGICIANS

APR 2 6 2018

TRINITY SEVEN ⑪

KENJI SAITO
AKINARI NAO

Translation: Christine Dashiell

Lettering: Anthony Quintessenza

TRINITY SEVEN SHICHININ NO MASHO TUKAI Volume 11
© AKINARI NAO 2015
© KENJI SAITO 2015
First published in Japan in 2015 by KADOKAWA CORPORATION, Tokyo.
English translation rights arranged with KADOKAWA CORPORATION, Tokyo, through TUTTLE-MORI AGENCY, INC., Tokyo.

English translation © 2017 by Yen Press, LLC

Yen Press
1290 Avenue of the Americas
New York, NY 10104

Visit us at yenpress.com
facebook.com/yenpress
twitter.com/yenpress
yenpress.tumblr.com
instagram.com/yenpress

First Yen Press Edition: November 2017

Yen Press is an imprint of Yen Press, LLC.
The Yen Press name and logo are trademarks of Yen Press, LLC.

Library of Congress Control Number: 2015952616

ISBNs: 978-0-316-47079-7 (paperback)
       978-0-316-47085-8 (ebook)

10 9 8 7 6 5 4 3 2 1

BVG

Printed in the United States of America